Impure

Reinventing the Word

Impure

Reinventing the Word

*The theory, practice, and oral history
of spoken word in Montreal*

VICTORIA STANTON & VINCENT TINGUELY

English editor: Andy Brown
French editors: André Lemelin, Karine Picard, Karen Ricard
Translations: Susanne de Lotbinière-Harwood
Design: Andy Brown
All uncredited photographs by Victoria Stanton
Cover photo credits from top to bottom: Juan Guardado, Scott Inniss, courtesy of Ian Ferrier, André Lemelin

National Library of Canada Cataloguing in Publication Data

Stanton, Victoria, 1970-
    Impure : reinventing the word : the theory, practice, and history of spoken word in Montreal

Includes some text in French.
Includes bibliographical references.
ISBN 0-9689496-1-4

    1. Oral interpretation of poetry. 2. Sound poetry—Quebec (Province)—Montréal—History and criticism. 3. Performance art—Quebec (Province)—Montréal. 4. Poets, Canadian—Quebec (Province)—Montréal—Interviews. I. Tinguely, Vince
II. Lotbinière-Harwood, Susanne de III. Title.

NX513.M65S72 2001   C811'.5409'971428   C2001-902847-4

Dépot Legal, Bibliothèque nationale du Québec

conundrum press
266 Fairmount West,
Montreal, Quebec, Canada, H2V 2G3
conpress @ ican.net

This book was published with the financial assistance of the Canada Council for the Arts. Thanks also to André Lemelin and Planète rebelle.

The authors would like to graciously acknowledge the *Conseil des arts et des lettres du Québec* for their assistance.

The Canada Council | Le Conseil des Arts
for the Arts | du Canada

CONSEIL
DES ARTS ET DES LETTRES
DU QUÉBEC

CONTENTS

ACKNOWLEDGEMENTS

First, we'd like to thank all the artists who agreed to be interviewed as part of this project, many of whom went the distance in providing archival material, contacts, advice and constant encouragement. For your enthusiasm, your patience, and your faith in us, we salute you!

We want to thank *Broken Pencil* magazine for initially asking us to write an article about the Montreal spoken word scene, and thus acting as the catalyst for this book: 'Reinventing The Word: The Montreal Poetry Scene Speaks For Itself', *Broken Pencil* # 6, Winter 1998 [launched in Oct. 1997], Toronto.

Thanks especially to *Broken Pencil* editor Hilary Clark for the title of the initial article, 'Reinventing The Word', which has become our book's subtitle.

We must single out Ian Ferrier for suggesting that we continue our initial research into the Montreal spoken word scene, and turn it into a book. Mr. Ferrier's been like a combination Rock of Gibraltar and ÜberDad in his encouragement and support.

Thanks to Nancy Morelli at the Concordia University archives, Nathalie Derome for inspiring the title of our book, Sylvette Babin and Marie-France Garon for reviewing transcripts of the French-language interviews, and to Mitsiko Miller for helping to draft French letters to interviewees.

Corey Frost was a steady source of support and keen intellectual interest during the process of putting *Impure* together. He suggested that we have ourselves interviewed in order to be included in the book, and then agreed to act as our interviewer. We also want to thank him for looking over an initial, massive fourth draft of the book, and for his encouraging and useful advice.

Special thanks to André Lemelin, publisher of Éditions Planète rebelle, for shouldering the herculean task of shepherding *Impure* from its initially unwieldy, incoherent and chaotic state, to its final form.

Thanks to Emanuelle Tremblay for reading an early draft of *Impure* and making crucial suggestions that allowed us to visualize its shape and thematic structure.

Thanks to Karine Picard, Karen Ricard and André Lemelin for the painstaking work of editing the final French-language text.

Thanks to Susanne de Lotbinière-Harwood, for being so excited about our project and lending us her linguistic expertise — we are honoured to have had the chance to work with this highly acclaimed and award-winning translator.

We want to thank the following people who helped us give Ian Stephens a real presence in our book: Peter Brawley, Alex Espinosa and Endre Farkas for their wonderful archival material; and Gaëtan Charlebois, Matthew Hays, Philip Marchand, Kevin Press and Juliet Waters for permission to quote from their previously-published articles about Ian Stephens.

Thanks also to the authors who gave us permission to reproduce their previously published texts in order to reinforce or clarify various sections of our book: Andy Brown, Deborah Ann, Rob Labelle, Jean-Marc Massie, Marc Smith and Joel Yanofsky.

Thanks to the prescient and avant-garde Rob Allen of *Matrix* and Hal Niedzviecki of *Broken Pencil* for their support and interest.

Thanks to Miriam Sampaio and Jon Ascensio, who organized the *Impure* benefit, November 17, 2000. Thanks to Dominic Castelli for the use of Jailhouse Rock for the show, to all the wonderful performers who made the benefit such a success, and all the people who packed the joint when we really needed their help.

Thanks to Pat Dillon for invaluable background information on the Diasporic African Poets.

Thanks to Juan Guardado for contributing his live spoken word performance photographs to our project.

Thanks to Meg Sircom for her copyediting and support.

Thanks to Scott Duncan for permission to use his 1995 CKUT interview with Benoît Paiement of *Groupe de poésie moderne*. Thanks also for setting up the Toronto leg of the *Impure* book launch.

For setting up the Vancouver leg of the *Impure* book launch: thanks to Grunt Gallery, Vancouver poetry activist and slam organizer Steve Duncan, and T. Paul Ste. Marie, producer and host of THUNDERING WORD HEARD, a spoken word / music open-mic night at Café Montmartre.

And finally, we want to thank Andy Brown of conundrum press, for being there from the very beginning of this project. He's seen us through all the drafts, all the editorial meetings, all the emotional meltdowns and euphorias, tirelessly lending us his editorial, aesthetic and emotional support. Thanks also for his implicit faith that we could get the thing done.

Sections from *Impure: Reinventing the Word* have appeared in somewhat different form in the following publications:

'un écart immense entre l'ecrit et l'orale...', *Matrix* # 57: Summer / Fall 2000, Montreal.

'Readings: "Why does it have to be so boring?"', *Broken Pencil* # 17: Fall 2001, Toronto.

A NOTE ON THE TEXT

Some of the interviews in this book were conducted in French, some in English, and some in both languages. This book was originally intended to be an English edition and Éditions Planète rebelle was to publish a French edition. The French text was therefore translated into English. However, due to the unpredictable and cash-strapped world of small press publishing in Canada, the French edition will unfortunately not exist. Conundrum press has therefore elected to include the original French text in sidebars where the translation appears, out of respect for the bilingual culture of Montreal, but also to make the thoughts and opinions of the interviewees available to as many readers as possible. For consistency's sake all French words are italicized in the English text (the reverse is true in the French text) and many others are anglicized (such as Montreal instead of Montréal). For the same reason, quotation marks are used instead of chevrons throughout the French text, although this is not standard usage.

The biographies of the participants are included at the beginning of the book, as opposed to the more traditional format of including them at the end, because many readers will not be familiar with all the people interviewed and it is important to establish what their particular role was, or is, in the community in advance so that their comments throughout the book can be read in context.

Some of the francophone artists chose to conduct their interviews in English which may account for some irregularities in speech.

KEN NORRIS: bpNichol used to talk about how there is always a lot of amnesia in the avant-garde. I'm sure that most of the spoken word poets of the nineties have no idea of what the Four Horsemen or Owen Sound or the Vehicule Poets were doing back in the seventies and eighties. Most people don't really have a taste for literary history anyway. I do, so I always go back and look at the early stuff, whether it's Hugo Ball or Archibald Lampman. It's useful to know, but not absolutely necessary. That's maybe a strange sentiment coming from someone who is employed as a literature professor. But I think an active engagement with the project at hand, whatever form that active engagement takes, is what's really necessary. There is never a really deep written record, and so people wind up having to go back and reinvent everything from scratch, never aware that what they're doing was done in Zurich in 1916, or in their own city fifteen years earlier. That's OK. That's the way the avant-garde operates. As long as people eventually make their own advances, the whole project is justified.

PREFACE

I

This book came into being because we were curious. In the mid-nineties, we found ourselves part of an active community of artists engaged in a common practice which could loosely be described as performance poetry, but seemed to be more than that. We started wondering where this practice came from, and what it was about. We had heard of a few recording artists doing similar things, like Henry Rollins, Karen Finley and Ann Clark, dub poets like Linton Kweisi Johnson and Lillian Allen, and the recorded work of various poets and writers archived on the Giorno Poetry Systems albums. We'd heard in passing of Montreal's Vehicule Poets and Toronto's The Four Horsemen, and we saw veteran performance poets like bill bissett and John Giorno perform in Montreal. But our general impression at the time was that this activity had simply appeared in Montreal, practically overnight, like an answer to an urgent call.

By 1997 it was clear to us that there was a vibrant scene happening here. We wanted to document what was happening, so we interviewed as many artists as we could find for an article which was eventually published in *Broken Pencil* magazine. In the course of conducting these interviews we became more aware of the rich francophone and anglophone traditions in Montreal. Each interview opened up vistas we hadn't been aware of: the evolution of francophone performance poetry; the activities of the Vehicule Poets in the seventies; bilingual festivals organized in the mid-eighties; and a sense of the various small scenes that coalesced in the mid-nineties. The accumulation of all these movements, and many individual talents, contributed to what has now been labeled as the Montreal 'spoken word scene'.

Part of the joy of being part of the Montreal spoken word 'explosion' in the mid-nineties was the sense that traditional barriers were being breached. 'Spoken word' became not so much a coherently conceived performance as a space within which a wide array of artistic practices could meet: theatre, dance, poetry, storytelling, performance art, popular music, rap, and even stand-up comedy. Under the auspices of 'spoken word' one might hear slam poetry, which is generally memorized, and delivered energetically and rhythmically within a competitive framework; dub poetry, a musical and distinctly Jamaican form; simple readings of printed texts within a literary tradition; text-based performance art presented in an art gallery setting; activist messages; monologues or stories told in a theatrical setting; poetry springing from the urban hip-hop culture; experimental sound poetry; or work that draws its influences from all of these forms.

As the reader will discover, it's impossible for the artists we interviewed to even agree on what this practice should be called! However, in order to create a field of inquiry, we've defined 'spoken word' as being primarily about the artist presenting texts in a live setting. Generally, the people we've interviewed are writing and presenting their *own* texts, regardless of their backgrounds.

An important and exciting aspect of this project is its timeliness. We're discussing something that's happening *now*. The questions we asked were meant to gain an understanding of spoken word as a discipline, and as a growing, forming thing. We approached the book as participants in the spoken word scene, rather than as 'experts' — because we're not. In order to approach the task with some intellectual authenticity, the bulk of this book is constructed from the original interview transcripts. This allowed the practitioners of the discipline to describe it themselves, and ultimately determine what the shape of this book would be.

Having taken a subjective approach to this project, it reflects our own perspective so that inevitably there are gaps. Principally, the francophone performance scene is under-represented, given its rich tradition in oral-based literature, folk traditions of storytelling, and the performance poetry experiments of the sixties. Our coverage of Black and Queer spoken word artists in Montreal is also less than complete. We hope that this book at least serves to point out these areas for future research. Finally, in keeping with the spirit of our project, we've focused on Montreal, which we can claim some familiarity with, rather than spoken word as it is practiced in New York, Toronto, Vancouver or San Francisco. We wanted to work with the resources immediately at hand, but we think the book will be of great interest to spoken word artists and fans everywhere.

The interviewees are all people who are currently working, or who have worked within the Montreal spoken word performance scene. The only exception to this is John Giorno, a New York City poet. When we saw him perform in Montreal in 1996, we realized that Giorno was truly a pioneer of spoken word performance, with a career that started in the early sixties. He has performed consistently and frequently in Montreal since the early seventies, and his work profoundly influenced spoken word artists in Montreal. His Dial-a-Poem project inspired Fortner Anderson to start a similar one here in the early eighties, and his style and intensity galvanized the punk-influenced performers in Montreal in that decade. We think his comments add invaluable experience and insight to our book's theoretical discourse. Including John Giorno also acknowledges that although spoken word in Montreal is a strong ongoing practice, it in no way originated here. We can trace influences from the New York scene, from Chicago's slam poetry movement, from performance poetry practices in Toronto and Vancouver, from the *Québécois* folk tradition of storytelling and its contemporary urban expression, and from a variety of European avant-garde movements, beginning with Dada.

The book's structure opens with a general overview of spoken word, followed by a commentary on the theoretical foundations of the medium. Next, we've supplied a section which outlines various artists' practices, basically a 'How-To guide' for creating a spoken word performance. Finally, we've included a chronology of spoken word in Montreal, which runs from the sixties to the late nineties. Rather than a complete history, it is intended to give a sense of where the various interviewees fit into the picture — their particular contributions, their understanding of the importance of their work, and their sense of the time when they were active. We also think it's important for artists practicing spoken word today to understand that this is an art form that has deep roots in Montreal. There's a lot to be learned from our collective history.

Vincent Tinguely
Victoria Stanton

PARTICIPANTS

AKIN ALAGA

Akin Alaga is a Yoruba-Canadian poet. Although born in Toronto, his formative years were ingrained in the red soils of Nigerian philosophy. Accordingly, his art is heavily infused with Yoruba mythological characters who try to make sense of the Canadian presence. In 2000 Akin was designated one of three performance poets to look out for in the new millennium by the Noisemaker edition of *The Montreal Mirror*. Akin recently graduated from McGill University with a double major in English Literature and Political Science.

FORTNER ANDERSON

Fortner Anderson is a poet and a co-founder and producer of the audio publishing venture Wired on Words (wiredonwords.com). His work has been recorded on the Wired on Words compilation (WOW, 1993), *Millennium Cabaret* (Wired on Words, 1998) and *La Vache enragée* (Planète rebelle, 1998), and his own CD *Sometimes I Think* appeared in 1999 (Wired on Words). His poems have been published in the *Poetry Nation* anthology (Véhicule Press, 1998). He has performed his poems at the Cabaret (Montreal), the Rivoli (Toronto), the Banff Performing Arts Centre and St-Mark's Church (New York).

ANTHONY BANSFIELD

Anthony Bansfield, aka the nth digri, has been an influential force on the Montreal, Toronto, and Ottawa spoken word poetry scenes. He was a principal member of the Montreal poetry group the Diasporic Afrikan Poets as a performer, producer of events and editor and coordinator of the print anthology *The N'X Step* that showcased the group's works. Anthony's poem 'Rows of Photos' aired as a video on the MuchMusic series *Word Up* and was recorded for the accompanying CD of the same title. He has also appeared on the *WordLife* CD and was the CD's executive producer. He has performed in various cities across the US and Canada, including New York's famed Nuyorican Poets Café and the Brooklyn Moon Café.

ALEX BOUTROS & KAARLA SUNDSTRÖM

Telling tales with two tongues, Alex Boutros and Kaarla Sundström create transtextual pieces that move from individual voice to collaborative cacophony and back again. Their work is hybrid by nature — both literary and musical, spoken and rhythmed. Speaking to issues of social consciousness and identity, their work is a highly crafted blend of diverse oral traditions and genres. As active members of Montreal's spoken word scenes, they have produced numerous multidisiplinary performance events, including the wildly successful Legba Cabaret series. Along with their own CD *Mouthful*, they have appeared on *La Vache enragée* CD anthology and on *Ribsauce*, a text / CD compilation of women word artists, of which they are also co-editors.

PETER BRAWLEY

Born in Verdun Quebec — March 1947. Post-hippie: involved in the seventies Montreal art boom — St-Lawrence Main. Film co-op in the style of Cassavetes-Warhol / Worked: acting and writing with Lack, Moyle and Vitale on *Montreal Main* and the *Rubber Gun* show. Back to University in 1993 / Art education — degree in 1995. Writing, drawing, painting and sculpting. Peace.

ANDY BROWN

Due to performance anxiety Andy Brown remains behind the scenes as a writer, editor, designer, and publisher. He formed conundrum press in 1996, after cutting his teeth as an editor for the Montreal literary calendar *index*. Recently he co-edited *You & Your Bright Ideas*, an anthology of new Montreal writing for Véhicule Press.

JAKE BROWN

Jake Brown taught film and communications at McGill University and English literature at Concordia University until 1994. Then he started *YAWP!*, a spoken word / music cabaret which ran until 2000. *YAWP!* highlights included performances by Ray Manzarek, Michael McClure, Rufus Wainwright, John S. Hall, and many others. Today Jake performs "quasi-academic shaggy dog stories" on the Canadian spoken word circuit. He now lives simply and quietly in Westmount, Quebec, with his cat Ethel, who can count up to five.

JASMINE CHÂTELAIN

Jasmine Châtelain began seriously participating in Montreal's spoken word community in 1995 by co-producing *Vox Hunt*, an ongoing monthly performance / slam evening culminating in a trip for eight artists to the International Slam Championships in Michigan. She went on to produce several other literary events including, with Scott Duncan, *Tongue-tied / Langue-liee*, a bilingual spoken word festival. This led to actual paid work with QSPELL, the Governor-General's Awards and others, proving there is economic survival in the arts. She gathered all this experience and wisdom in order to sell her soul, move to Toronto, work in advertising, get married, have a kid, and is now currently a student training to be a midwife.

BUFFY CHILDERHOSE

Buffy Childerhose is a writer and perfomer currently labouring in the dank mines of print and broadcast journalism.

MARTA COOPER

Marta Cooper has played an active role in promoting oral literature and spoken word at McGill University and in Mile End since 1995. She has produced two reading and performance series, *Mainlines: Poetry Readings on the Main* and *FigureHead Productions*. She is a published poet, and her writing has won a number of awards, including the Lionel Shapiro Award for Creative Writing (McGill University, 1999).

IZ COX

Iz Cox has been writing and performing since she was fourteen. She has fronted numerous bands and co-hosted the series *The Devil's Voice* with Thoth Harris, as well as *Heartbreak Hotel / Heartattack Hotel* with Deborah Ann.

ANNA-LOUISE CRAGO

Anna-Louise Crago is a writer, storyteller and performer. Formerly a member of the all-girl circus troupe the Throw Ups she now rocks out with a blender in Women With Kitchen Appliances. She is permanently consumed with snapping the garterbelt of social justice and being a thorn in the asshole of the powers that be.

JULIE CRYSLER

Julie Crysler became involved in Montreal's burgeoning spoken word scene of the mid-1990s, both as a performer and an organizer of readings, including the *Other Muses* series and the *Coolest Girl in the World Cabaret*. She represented Montreal at the 1995 U.S. Slam Championship in Ann Arbor and has won slams in Boston and New York. Since her return to Toronto in 1996, she has organized a reading series at Buddies in Bad Times Theatre and has performed her work at a wide variety of Toronto events, including *The Scream in High Park*. Julie has produced two chapbooks and her work also appears in the Véhicule Press anthology *Poetry Nation* and on the Wired on Words CD *Millennium Cabaret*. She is now the editor of the legendary alternative politics and culture journal, *This Magazine*.

JEAN-PAUL DAOUST

Since 1976, Jean-Paul Daoust has published twenty books of poetry and a novel. He is one of the central figures in the Quebec poetry scene. He has participated in many literary reviews and magazines. He won the 1990 Governor-General's Award for Poetry (for *Les cendres bleues*). He is director of the poetry review, *ESTUAIRE*.

SIMON DARDICK

Simon Dardick, with Nancy Marrelli, are the publishers of Montreal's Véhicule Press which grew out of the artist-run gallery, Véhicule Art Inc. Since 1973 the press has been publishing poetry, fiction, and social history.

NATHALIE DEROME

Since 1983, the work of multidisciplinary artist and performer Nathalie Derome has imagined the expression *théâtre perfore* to characterize her singular integration of mediums (theatre, poetry, dance, music and visual arts) into shows with varied forms, from very long performances (*performance-fleuve*) to poetry 'on the hoof' (*poème sur pattes*). Her work has been seen in Quebec, English Canada, Europe, and the U.S. In 2000 she launched a CD containing her 'parodisiac' songs *Les 4 ronds sont allumés*. Her most recent interdisciplinary creation, *Du temps d'antennes*, a low-tech solo show produced by her company, Les productions Nathalie Derome, was presented in Montreal in the spring of 2001.

PASCAL DESJARDINS & PASCAL FIORAMORE

Together the two Pascals founded *Les Abdigradationnistes,* produced the *soirées Rodrigol* evenings, and the CD *Vierges, mais expérimentées.*

LOUISE DUBREUIL

Louise Dubreuil is an interdisciplinary feminist artist and cleaning 'lady'. Inter-Related Arts B.F.A. from Concordia U. in 1986. Nicaragua mural painting in 1985. Practical feminist education while teaching self-defense from 1988-1994. Intuition, intellect, humour, improvisation as well as organic and inorganic garbage are her consistent basic elements. Despite fears of both failure and success at receiving her first grant for the installation, video, performance project *Addictive Mind(s), Emotional Heart(s)* and being invited to perform in Quebec's Ilot Fleuri and Grunt Gallery's *Live — Performance Biennial* in Vancouver, she trusts she'll find a comfortable seat and enjoy the ride.

SCOTT DUNCAN

Scott Duncan is a writer, film maker and careerist family man, living in Toronto. A successful two-year stint (1994-1996) as member of Montreal's Fluffy Pagan Echoes overlapped the production of *Tongue-tied*, a word festival, and a brief and not very illustrious singing career. Since moving to Toronto in 1997, he has written and directed three short fiction films: *Caged* (1998), *Rainin' Threes / Trocar Lados* (2000) and *The Crooked Man, a Nursery Rhyme* (2001). He is currently writing a screenplay about a teenaged gangster unsure of his role in a violent crime.

RAN ELFASSY

Ran Elfassy is currently living in Toronto. She has not performed in a few years, but is generally regarded as being a performative individual. Her most recent books, those objects she makes just enough of to supply to her loved ones, are neither here nor there; *I Love You, Dirty Little Man*. Ran, like so many before and with her, simultaneously incites, propagates, feeds and cultivates the cult of her own beauty.

ENDRE FARKAS

Born in 1948, Endre Farkas escaped from Hungary in 1956. He was one of the original Vehicule Poets and has published eight books of poetry and had two plays produced. His writing has been translated into Hungarian,

French, Spanish and Slovenian. He has collaborated with poets, dancers and composers, created performance texts and toured extensively. He has edited anthologies, magazines and produced albums and videos. Currently he is working on a new play and a manuscript about the fur trade.

IAN FERRIER

Ian Ferrier has performed in Canada, the United States and Europe, and is slowly becoming one of the core poet / performers in the North American performance literature scene. His first CD / book *Exploding Head Man* was released by Planète rebelle. Rooted in the spellbound winters of his childhood, it has become the springboard for his current mixture of poetry and music, a show which features whispered vocals, electric guitar, Bryan Highbloom on saxophone, and lately a five woman a capella choir. Ferrier is a founder of the Wired on Words performance literature label, which records poets and writers on CD. At this writing he is working on a new CD / book.

GOLDA FRIED

Golda Fried spent seven years in Montreal like she would never leave, performing spoken word at various fun functions. Montreal is where she wrote most of her collection of stories, *darkness then a blown kiss*, published by Gutter Press in 1998. She then moved to Toronto where she developed an interest in rock photography and took photos of her favourite rock 'n rollers. She is currently married and living in Greensboro, North Carolina.

COREY FROST

Corey Frost, originally from P.E.I., moved to Montreal in 1992 to attend Concordia. In the next few years he edited *index* magazine, co-founded (with Colin Christie) the ambitious but short-lived ga press, and began to experiment with text-based performance. He then lived in Japan and travelled for two years, before returning to Montreal to focus on performances that mix deadpan humour with the creative syntax he learned while teaching English abroad. In 1999-2000 he self-published *Backwards Versions*, a trilogy documenting eight years of writing for performance, and in 2001 he recorded a solo CD-ROM, *Bits World: Exciting Version* (Wired on Words).

EDWARD FULLER

Edward Fuller has been apprenticing in the art and craft of performance, and writing, for many seasons. He lives in Montreal. He has some coals in the fire.

MICHEL GARNEAU

Michel Garneau was born in the year 1939 of our rascist era. He left college before the age of fifteen and went off to live life. Since then he has been working in all media(s) that use language — radio, television, cinema, documentary — as a writer and narrator. He has written about sixty plays, and has translated four Shakespeare plays as well as tons of poems and other plays. He has published approximately forty books. For the last six years, every Friday evening from 10 PM to 1 AM on Radio-Canada FM, he has hosted *Les Décrocheurs d'étoiles* — where the margin is in the centre and poetry still rules.

JOHN GIORNO

An originator of Performance Poetry, John Giorno elevated spoken word to a high art form. One of the most innovative and influential figures of 20th Century poetry, John Giorno's career spans forty years. His most recent book *You Got To Burn To Shine*, details his deeply personal memoirs, including the story of his relationship with Andy Warhol (Giorno was the star of Warhol's first film, *Sleep* in 1963). Founded in 1965, Giorno Poetry Systems innovated the use of technology in poetry, working with electronics and multi-media, and creating new venues, connecting poetry with new audiences. In 1968, John Giorno created Dial-A-Poem, innovating the use of the telephone for mass communications. Dial-A-Poem's enormous success, receiving millions of calls, gave rise to a Dial-A-something industry, from Dial-A-Joke, to phone sex, to 900 numbers. Giorno Poetry Systems has released over forty LPs and CDs of poets working with performance and music, numerous cassettes, videopaks, poetry videos and film. For over thirty years, John Giorno has been a Buddhist meditation practioner in the Nyingma tradition of Tibetan Buddhism. His teacher is His Holiness Dudjom Rinpoche. The AIDs Treatment Project was begun in 1984 as John Giorno's attempt to combat with compassion the castastrophe of the AIDS epidemic, helping people with AIDS by giving cash grants for emergency situations.

JONATHAN GOLDSTEIN

Jonathan Goldstein, a native of Montreal, is now living in Chicago where he is a producer at Public Radio's *This American Life*. His poetry and prose has appeared in numerous anthologies and magazines, among them *Open letters, Saturday Night,* and *Exile*. He is a regular commentator on CBC Radio and the host of the summer show Road Dot Trip. His first novel, *Lenny Bruce is Dead*, was published by Coach House Books in 2001.

DAVID GOSSAGE

David is one of Montreal's most respected and experienced musicians. He plays in virtually all styles of music but is probably best known for his jazz and celtic flute playing. David was musical director for District Six Productions in the mid-nineties, bringing jazz musicians and poets from all over North America together on stage. David is also a composer and has written music for dance, theatre and film as well as his own jazz, poetry and celtic recordings.

LEE GOTHAM

Lee Gotham is a poet, fiction-writer, performer and vintage motorcycle enthusiast. His novella, *L'Anormale* was published by Nonplus editions Nonplus in 1999. He is anthologized on the CD, *Millennium Cabaret* (Wired on Words, 1998) and in print, *Poetry Nation* (Véhicule Press, 1998) and *La Vache enragée 2* (Planète rebelle, 1998). In 1995, Gotham helped instigate a revival of spoken word performance in Montreal with his series, *Enough Said*.

THOTH HARRIS

Thoth Harris, born in 1972 in North Vancouver, B.C., has been published in the Véhicule Press anthology, *Poetry Nation* and in *Rider's Alley*. He self-published a short-story collection *BLANK*, and an anthology, *Poopdeck*. He is a spoken word performer and host, most notably in the ecclectic and manic-energy driven show, *The Devil's Voice* (co-piloted with Iz Cox). Thoth currently pursues film studies at Concordia.

HUGH HAZELTON

In search of poems with bite, Hugh Hazelton has long explored performance, and politicized, open-ended poetry in a variety of forms, from sonic to concrete. Travel, translation, and cross-cultural identification have resulted in his composing in English, Spanish, and French. He often reads with Latin American poets in Canada. He is the editor of White Dwarf Editions / Les Editions de la Naine Blanche / Las Ediciones de la Enana Blanca, which publishes experimental poetry and prose.

KAIE KELLOUGH

Kaie Kellough was born in Vancouver, grew up in Calgary, and currently resides in Montreal. He performed at the 1995 Jazz festival (Calgary), the 1997 African festival (Calgary), organized and performed at the 1997 Calgary Jazz festival's Word & Beat event, and performed with Decidedly Jazz Danceworks for their summer dance event. In Montreal he has produced events — *Fonics & Funk* — and has performed at numerous venues throughout the city. He writes fiction, essays, poetry, and has recently completed a manuscript titled, *Shadeshuffles*, as well as a chapbook called, *Musée d'oublie / Montreal melancholy*.

CATHERINE KIDD

Catherine Kidd is the author of the novel *Bestial Rooms* (Thomas Allen & Son), about a reluctant zoologist who attempts to describe the negative shape of her amnesia by filling in the stories peripheral to it. Her earlier work includes *everything I know about love I learned from taxidermy* (conundrum press, 1996), a collection of performance pieces with soundscape by collaborator DJ Jack Beets. Cat and Jack's performance work focuses on the relationship between the body and memory, and the beasts who prowl and tumble in the basement of ourselves.

D. KIMM

D. Kimm has published three books, including *Chevale* (1989) and *Tableaux* (1991) (both VLB Editeur) and has given several poetry-performance shows in collaboration with various musicians. Since 1994, she has worked as artistic director for events bringing together performing artists and writers. She staged several shows for l'UNEQ and for the *Festival de la littérature*. In September 1999 she presented her multidisciplinary show *La Suite mongole* at Tangente; she also produced a CD-ROM of *La Suite mongole* texts in collaboration with Joseph Lefebvre and the *Société des Arts technologiques*. This CD-ROM was the basis of an installation during the *Festival du Nouveau cinéma Nouveaux Médias*. *La Suite mongole*, CD-ROM and book, have been published by Planète rebelle (fall 2001).

TOM KONYVES

In 1978, Tom Konyves coined the term 'videopoetry' to describe his multimedia work. Based in Montreal until 1983, his poetry has evolved from his mid-seventies association with the Vehicle Poets — a period distinguished by Dadaist / experimental writings (*No Parking*, Véhicule Press, 1978), performance works and videopoems — to the reflective and almost delicate work created in the later Vancouver poems, notably *Ex Perimeter*, (Caitlin Press) and his selected poems *Sleepwalking Among The Camels* (The Muses' Co). In 1999, he was selected as People's Choice at the Edgewise Café's First Videopoetry Festival. Currently, Tom Konyves is a video producer and poet residing in Crescent Beach, BC, with his wife Marlene and their three children. Many of his poems can also be found on the website: http://amproductions.com/videopoetry/PoetryPerformance.html

NANCY LABONTÉ

Nancy Labonté was born in Montreal in June 1968 from the belly of a woman painter from Lithuania. She started writing when she started walking. For the second issue of *Gaz Moutarde* in 1990, she joined Jean-Sébastien Huot, Mario Cholette and David Hince to take part in a movement which used poetry, the 'I' and public readings as a support for expression. Her book *X-Fee* (Éditions du Jaspe, 1992) reflects the voice of this young woman. Unheard in Montreal's underground poetry scene since 1998, she still recites verse to the sun, the moon and her girl child, while waiting to see if she will one day be bold enough and vain enough to lie down naked in public poetry.

PATRICIA LAMONTAGNE

Patricia Lamontagne is the author of *Les Faits Saillants* (Paje Editeur, 1989), *Rush papier ciseau suivi de Allumette* (L'Hexagone, 1992), a nominee for the Emile-Nelligan Award, and *Somnolences* (Triptych, 2001).

ANDRÉ LEMELIN

André Lemelin defines himself as a cultural explorer. As an artist he has published short stories and oral stories in various literary reviews, then in book form including the book / record *Hold-up! Contes du Centre-Sud*, performed by Zéro de conduite. He has told his stories in numerous cultural cabarets, at the *Nouveau théâtre expérimental*, on Radio-Canada FM, and in festivals in Quebec and Europe. As a producer he started (in 1985), and headed (until 2000), *Stop*. In 1993 he co-founded and then edited (until 1995) *Lectures*, a free monthly about books. In 1996 he co-founded the poetry review *Exit*. In 1997 he set up Éditions Planète rebelle. In 1998 he co-founded *Les Dimanches du conte* with Jean-Marc Massie. In 2001 he founded *Les Productions si on rêvait encore*, whose main mandate is the annual production of the *Festival Voix d'Amérique*, devoted to orality.

GENEVIÈVE LETARTE

Geneviève Letarte is a Montreal writer, singer and performance artist. The author of three novels: *Les Vertiges Molino* (Lemeac, 1996), *Soleil Rauque* (La Pleine lune, 1988) and *Station Transit* (La Pleine lune, 1986), she also published many poetic pieces in various literary magazines and created two art books in collaboration with painter Louis-Pierre Bougie: *Flou comme la nuit* (Éditions Bonfort, 2000) and *Terminus Nord* (L'Atelier circulaire, 1990). She has produced two recordings on the Ambiances Magnetiques label: *Chansons d'un jour* (2000), and *Vous seriez un ange* (1990), and has created many performance works, including *Extraits d'un livre chante* (1987) and *Le Mystere du bois Blanc* (2000).

BILLY MAVREAS

Billy Mavreas, poster artist and co-founder of the *YAWP!* performance series, is a Montreal-born artist with comix, illustrations and visual poetics published worldwide. A book of comix, *The Overlords of Glee*, was published by conundrum press / Crunchy Comics in fall 2001. He draws inspiration from science fiction, dreams and the natural world. www.yesway.com is his small corner of the web.

DAYNA McLEOD

Dayna McLeod is a writer, video and performance artist living and working in Montreal. She has traveled extensively with her performance work and her videos have played in festivals internationally. In the summer of 2000, her ten minute, one-shot video, "How to Fake an Orgasm (whether you need to or not)" won first prize for Best Comedy in PlanetOut's First Annual Queer Short Movie Awards (www.PlanetOut.com) as well as the Audience Choice Award in the same category. In the fall of 2001, she released a CD with Stephen Lawson of her spoken word work, and toured *Dirty Beaver Tails*.

JUSTIN McGRAIL

Born in Toronto, educated in Montreal, moved to Vancouver, Justin McGrail is a poet and performer who has presented in bookstores, clubs, malls, galleries, cafés and festivals across Canada. He was a founding member of Montreal's performance troupe Fluffy Pagan Echoes and Van Slam Poetry along with being a member of the 1996 Vancouver team at the National Poetry Slam in Portland, Ore. He currently pursues a PhD in Victoria, B.C.

MITSIKO MILLER

Since the early nineties, Montrealer Mitsiko has been interested in the music of words and its relationship to various art disciplines. She can be heard reading heterogeneous texts in both official languages in her spoken word book *Back to Basics*; operating tos-and-fros with language levels in *Le Coeur en orbite*, the diary of a rebellious teen; launching herself into a multidisciplinary project dealing with the symbolism of anthropophagy in *Carnages*, where ficton meets another one of its loves, journalism, a profession she has practiced for three years. She also sings with DJ Ram on his first solo opus, *The East Infection*. Her hybrid style, and dynamic stage approach led to her involvement in the scene by hosting the event *La Vache enragée*.

HÉLÈNE MONETTE

A poet above all, Hélène Monette has published seven books of prose and poems, a collection of stories, two novels and several texts in literary periodicals. A few titles: *Montreal brule-t-elle?* (Ecrits des Forges, 1987), *Crimes et chatouillements* (XYZ editeur, 1992), *Kyrie eleison* (Les Herbes rouges, 1994), *Unless* (1995) and *Un jardin dans la nuit* (Boréal, 2001). Since 1980, Hélène has participated in public readings as part of happenings, festivals and tours. She produced some readings-shows with musician Bob Olivier. She took part in projects involving recorded poetry, radio, cinema and video, and worked at organizing literary and multidisciplinary events.

NAH EE LAH

nah ee lah has performed her work in Toronto, Montreal and New York. Her first solo CD project is *nah ee lah: poetry?* released in 2001 by yah ga yah productions. She also appears on two independent CDs — *When the love is not enough*, released in 2000 by Spirit of 3 and *Wordlife: tales of the underground griot* released in 1998 by Revword.

NORMAN NAWROCKI

Writer, actor, musician, Norman Nawrocki is a Montreal-based cabaret artist who tours the world solo and with his bands. He has four books and over forty recorded releases. He specializes in 'creative resistance', agit-prop, outrageous comedies and divorce music. More info: www.nothingness.org/music/rhythm

DAVID NEUDORFER

David Neudorfer, poet, brother, twin. In 5761 (2001) he released a book of poems entitled *Rough Earth*, a commentary on Jewish existence within Israel and outside the homeland. He is involved with the musical-poetry ensemble The Rhythmic Missionaries, and the Wooden Basement Haiku Group of Montreal.

JOSEPH NEUDORFER

Joseph Neudorfer is presently studying law at the *Université de Québec à Montréal*. He has self-published numerous chapbooks including: *The Beginning of Something* (1995), *Mountain Tasting* (1996), *And Poet I Hero Be* (1997) and *Alone by Lake Blue not Alone* (1998). While not in school, he has earned his grub treeplanting in the Canadian bush.

KEN NORRIS

Ken Norris was born in New York City in 1951 and came to Canada in the early seventies. He became a Canadian citizen in 1985. During the seventies he was one of Montreal's infamous Vehicle Poets and participated in a number of collaborative and mixed media poetry events. He is the author of over twenty books of poetry and poetics. Norris teaches Canadian literature at the University of Maine. He currently divides his time (almost equally) between Canada, Maine and the Caribbean.

ALEXIS O'HARA

Alexis O'Hara is a triligual artist who writes, performs and rocks hard. She performs regularly with her word-art-noise band Jimmy Brain. She has released a few chapbooks and some CDs. Her work has been featured in two anthologies — *Poetry Nation* (Véhicule Press) and *Slam: The Competitive Art of Performance Poetry* (Manic D Press). Alexis bends forms, channeling extraterrestrial spoken word and provoking scandalized tongue wagging in her wake.

HEATHER O'NEILL

Heather O'Neill lives in Montreal. She is the author of the poetry collection *two eyes are you sleeping* (1999) and the novel *Fourteen* (2002).

BENOÎT PAIEMENT

Benoît Paiement has been involved in a research project concerning poetic writing for the stage for over eight years. With the *Groupe de poésie moderne*, he has made regular appearances in Montreal as part of various events, and has produced four shows: *Imrajrinrezvrous* (fall 1993); *Le principe* (summer 1995 as part of the Fringe Festival); *Un inutilitaire*, at La Petite Licorne (January and April 1999); and *La centième fois du silence*, presented twenty-four times since March 2000.

TORREY PASS

Torrey Pass has been involved in the writing community of Montreal since arriving in 1992. He facilitated poetry workshops in the New School program of Dawson College and went on to attend Concordia University's Creative Writing program, from which he graduated in 2000. While the bulk of his work includes poetry and poetic prose, he is now playing with long fiction among the glaciers of northern British Columbia.

LOUIS RASTELLI

Louis Rastelli is a Montrealer who publishes *Fish Piss* magazine and his own little books of stories, plays music, resists gentrification and demolition of his hometown, is an amateur historian and a foremost expert on all things strudel. He has spent the last couple of years setting up a system of archiving and distributing local publications, the Montreal Archive. In 2001, he inaugurated Distroboto, a network of vending machines that sells zines and cassettes.

FÉLIXE ROSS

Félixe Ross graduated from the *Conservatoir d'art dramatique de Montreal* (1993), and loves absurdist and experimental theatre (*La Langue à terre*, at the Lion d'or). She appeared in the prime-time TV series *Virginie* for four years. She joined the *Groupe de poésie moderne* in September 1999. She also particied in the C.I.S.M.'s radio-theatre readings at La Licorne theatre for a few years. In June 2001 she played *Ceci n'est pas une pipe*, an incisive and disturbing text presented during the *Festival du Théâtre des Amériques*. She is currently working on the *Groupe de poésie moderne*'s next show.

TRISH SALAH

Trish Salah is a transsexual writer, critic, student, teacher and activist. She has performed on a number of diverse stages, including academic and literary journal launches, transsexual arts festivals, picket lines, LGBT Pride events, live web and radio broadcasts, and last but never least, spoken word cabarets. Her writing has appeared in a wide range of zines, journals and anthologies, and her poetry manuscript, *Wanting in Arabic*, is near completion. She is co-editor of the forthcoming collection of transsexual and transgender art and criticism, *Counting Past 2*.

JASON SELMAN

Jason Selman has been performing in his city of birth, Montreal, since 1996. The only child of Barbadian parents, his heritage and how it relates to his everyday existence is of primary importantance to him. Jason is a founding member of the 'Jazzoetry' collective The Rhythmic Missionaries, a group of poets and musicians who explore the boundaries of expression as well their outstanding brotherhood. Within the context of this group Jason also plays trumpet.

TETSURO SHIGEMATSU

Tetsuro Shigematsu is a Japanese-Canadian writer, performer and director. He uses humour as a subversive tool to express the horror of being a visible minority in a white society. He recently completed his first feature film, *Yellow Fellas*, and is working on a new one-man show. Tetsuro is available to perform at festivals, university concerts and bar mitzvahs. You can learn more about him at tetsuroonline.com.

ATIF SIDDIQI

Atif Siddiqi transforms his artistic practice every few years. Film / video is his current favourite and in this medium Atif is able to incorporate his love of writing, performance, fashion, creating beautiful images and telling stories. His study of the arts began in Karachi, continued in Dhaka, increased in Los Angeles and evolved in Montreal. An interdisciplinary artist, Atif has exhibited his paintings (1985-87), shown his fashion collections (1988-91), performed his poems and choreography (1994-98), released a compact disc and screened his short videos (1996-2000). He currently resides in Montreal, and is making documentary and feature films professionally in addition to pursuing his other artistic interests.

INOBE STANISLAUS

Head of a young production-promotion collective, Inobe is producer of the intimate poetic *soirée* known as Coco Café — currently Montreal's longest running spoken word series, and its francophone equivalent *Allongé*. An admistrative officer at the Royal Victoria Hospital, columnist and writer, and host of *Therapy*, a soulful club night of sweet garage sounds as well as *Soul Call*, Montreal's Carribean Lifestyle television show. A jack of all trades, master of a few, Inobe is slated to produce his first film *Dish!* for a 2002 release.

VICTORIA STANTON

Victoria Stanton is a text-based multidisciplinary artist who works both solo and collaboratively (Fluffy Pagan Echoes, 1994-1996; Officious Little Students, 1996-present; Play Group, 1999-present). Her creative work includes performance, public intervention, artist-books, zines and most recently, video. Her spoken word and visual performances have been presented in Quebec, Ontario, British Columbia, New York State, France and Italy. Her performance texts have been broadcast on regional and national radio as well as recorded for various spoken word and music CD compilations.

DEE SMITH

Dee Smith was a founding member of the Diasporic African Poets who appeared on Montreal stages frequently throughout the early- to mid-nineties and was recorded on the Wired on Words *Millennium Cabaret* CD. She lives and works in Toronto.

KAREN STEWART

Karen Stewart is a poet / performer who produced the wildly popular *Phenomenal Women* show, and currently produces *Soul Shack*.

ANNE STONE

Anne Stone's first novel, *jacks: a gothic gospel* (DC Books, 1998), is both formally and typographically experimental, conveying aspects of the story through the book's design. Her most recent novel, *Hush* (Insomniac Press, 1999), exists at the intersection of the body, language and identity. Informed by feminist novelistic innovation and criticism, Stone's writing straddles interstices, exploring oralities and the act of writing as sustained performance.

LYNN SUDERMAN

Five years ago, Lynn was abducted by aliens who forced her to leave Montreal. Cruel experiments with bad grammar ensued, and then, when they'd destroyed her ability to identify gerunds, they dumped her in Toronto. Today, she works at Conspiracy TV as the host of their daily news hour, The Grassy Knoll. She still has nightmares about split infinitives.

TODD SWIFT

Todd Swift — poet, screenwriter, editor, impresario — was born in Montreal in 1966. In the late eighties he began a series of reading events which helped to reintroduce bohemian poetry culture to Montreal's Plateau. As MC of *Vox Hunt* in the mid-nineties, he pioneered a unique mix of performance, poetry and vaudeville. He co-edited the widely inclusive survey of new poetries fusing stage and page, *Poetry Nation: The North American Anthology of Fusion Poetry* (Véhicule Press, 1998; second edition, 1999). In 1998 he moved to Hungary and began *Kacat Kabare*, the first English-Magyar spoken word series. His collection *Budavox: Poems 1990-1999* (DC Books, 1999) was launched in Panama City, New York and Montreal. He is half of the electronic performance duo Swifty Lazarus, with Tom Walsh. Their CD is out late 2001. His new book of poems is forthcoming in 2003 from the Irish press, Salmon. He is currently co-editing *Short Fuse: The Global Anthology of New Fusion Poetry* (Rattapallax Press, New York).

VINCENT TINGUELY

Vincent Tinguely is a self-taught writer. In 1992, he moved to Montreal, and in June 1994, he became a founding member of Fluffy Pagan Echoes, a performance poetry troupe which played an important role in the formative years of Montreal's spoken word scene. His poetry has appeared in the Montreal publications *index*, *Fish Piss*, *La revue des animaux*, and in both *La Vache enragée* anthologies. His critical texts have appeared in *Mix*, *Matrix* and *index*, and he currently writes spoken word news and reviews for the Montreal weekly, *Mirror*. Vincent Tinguely has collaborated with Victoria Stanton since 1995, when they began co-writing and co-publishing a zine, *Perfect Waste of Time*. In 1996 they formed Officious Little Students, a spoken word duo, and performed together in London, Ontario, Toronto, Vancouver and Montreal.

MAHALIA 'MISS THANG' VERNA

A graduate of sorts from Clement Grant's and Carol Flaubert's much-cherished Artkore / Isart gallery, in 1997, Mahalia 'Miss Thang' Verna joined a funky bunch called inobe productions. Along with the boys and girls of this multi-faceted cultural collective, Verna helped produce various fashion shows, art exhibits and cultural happenings, such as *Que es Diva*, *As Sweet as Chocolate* and *Coco Café*. Since 1999, Mahalia has stepped onto the stage of *Coco Café* and French sister show, *Allongé* to host the monthly spoken word *soirées*, all the while continuing to fulfill her tasks as producer and publicist at inobe productions. In the near future, 'Miss Thang' will be working alongside inobe to help him produce his much-anticipated first short film, *Dish!*

LEAH VINEBERG

Leah Vineberg is a writer / performer / director and has self-produced numerous plays including: *Flowers and Weeds*, *My Business is Words*, *The Women's Project*, *Definition*, and *Telegraph from Departure Bay*.

JEREMIAH WALL

Jeremiah Wall is an American-born poet folksinger with a long history of activism, iconoclasm, and resistance to established orders. He lives in exile from the guns and puns of American landscape, in the relative calm of rural Quebec where he is unco-operative with the anti-democratic Quebec regime, and equally alienated from anglo culture. He was the editor of *Dracaena* and ran a series at Hillel House called *Café Vilna*. He is a recent father and partner of an equally radical herbologist. He is hard to figure out or get along with, and likes it that way.

ZOË WHITTALL

Zoë Whittall is a writer, performer and promoter currently living in Toronto. She organized the women's open-mic event *Girlspit* in Montreal and Toronto from 1996-1998. Originally a zinester, at the time of this writing she is working on her first collection of poetry called *The Best Ten Minutes of Your Life*. Most recently, she won an honorable mention in the *Queen Street Quarterly* annual poetry contest and writes a music column for *Xtra!* gay and lesbian bi-weekly magazine.

DEBBIE YOUNG

Debbie Young is a nappy-headed, broad-nosed, thick-lipped, darkbrown-skinned, black, bushoomaan, Jamaican born and raised. She is a dub poet, actor, and playwright. There is no revolution without passion. http://www.debbieyoung.net

WHAT IS SPOKEN WORD?

"It's a very inbetween form"

Spoken word isn't new. However, the form it takes today draws on postmodern concepts of hybridity and fluidity that set it apart from traditional art practices. A characteristic of the form is its immediacy and accessibility to the audience.

PETER BRAWLEY: When you think about it, spoken word's the most ancient tradition in the world. In Western culture, to stand up and declaim was the whole test of philosophy in the ancient days.... It was one of the first arts. Despite all the folderol about postmodernism, I think that's one of its major things, going back to the *real* older things that modernism didn't want to know from. I mean what could be more direct than acting out a poem? And its such an involved semiotic.

THOTH HARRIS: Basically, spoken word is a living, breathing experience, unlike books, or movies, or anything that's mediated. It's unmediated. And I think we should make it as unmediated as possible. But at the same time, I think we should take the vibrancy and the life of it very seriously as a forum to communicate with people.

COREY FROST: I think spoken word has a relationship to writing that's similar to the relationship of publishing to writing. I think of spoken word as a means to convey writing to an audience, obviously. I don't mean that to sound belittling, because for me that's a very important activity. It's not just a medium. A spoken word performance is an artifact on its own, separate from the literary text. I think that spoken word

also produces a certain kind of writing that is maybe a subgenre of literature.

But there are two aspects to it. On the one hand it's a means of reinterpreting something that's been written, and on the other hand it's a style of writing, basically. Or it can produce a style of writing. For me, it's more the former. Although the stuff that I write for performance is different from stuff that I would write with a book in mind, I think that in both cases the writing happens, and then afterwards you let it go. It becomes text, something that can be shaped, performed again by yourself or by someone else, performed either in the shape of a book design or in the shape of a performance on stage.

KAIE KELLOUGH: I think spoken word is an art form on its own, but it's a very inbetween form. It's not necessarily literature, it's not necessarily theatre, it's not necessarily music, but those are the three closest art forms. They inform spoken word most.

VICTORIA STANTON: Spoken word works on various levels. Because it is a performance, there's the performance. Because it starts with a text, there's the text. Because it involves the audience, it's how the person deals with the audience. Because it happens in a space, it's how the person uses the space. And because it's a personality too, there's the personality that you're looking at and you're aware of.

ENDRE FARKAS: I started reading. Well, reading is one very simple form of performance. Fairly shortly after that... about 1974, I was interested in concrete poetry, I was interested in performances with other artists. When I first started I

III

'SPOKEN WORD' IS A GENERIC TERM APPLIED TO A WIDE RANGE OF TEXT-BASED PERFORMANCES. IN THIS CHAPTER, WE DESCRIBE SPOKEN WORD — WHAT IT IS, AND WHAT IT ISN'T — AND DISCUSS SOME OF ITS SOCIETAL FUNCTIONS AND THEORETICAL RAMIFICATIONS.

(Facing page) Poster from Impure benefit, November 2000
Photo by Charlie Gardner

(Previous page) Victoria Stanton from Split: one year later at Dare-Dare, April 2000
Photo by Patrick Mailloux

was interested in doing the readings and performances as a way of getting back to the oral tradition, because poetry did start out as an oral tradition. I liked the idea. In the oral tradition, the story teller or the bard talks to the community about the community, rather than just about me me me me. Their poetry or their art came out of the community.

"Very different from theatre"

Talking about the difference between spoken word performance and theatre helps bring out more characteristics of the former practice. While spoken word artists may sometimes create characters on stage, they generally write their own texts, and place an emphasis on speaking directly to the audience, rather than playing for an audience.

COREY FROST: One of the things that interests me most is the distinction drawn between spoken word being something that has some kind of directness, and theatre, which is acting. I wonder about calling a spoken word performance more 'direct' or 'honest', or 'sincere'.

VINCE TINGUELY: What I found in Fluffy Pagan Echoes' performance of *Resistance is Reasonable*[1] is that it felt constrained by the text, because it was a continuous text. We didn't have the opportunity to wander off, unless there was something going on where we weren't actually taking part. But that, to me, was the line that we crossed, from what you would call poetry performance, to something more performative or more 'theatrical'. When you're being a poet onstage, you're playing a role of "I am a poet, I'm onstage." Or being a spoken word artist. But the level of artifice is a lot more fluid there. You can be just some

guy with a piece of paper, reading. It can be dull as dirt, or it can be absolutely brilliant, but you feel that much closer to this *person*. And then it goes from there to something like Catherine Kidd performing in the bathtub, where there's more of a theatrical structure. But it's still a text that the performer created for the performance, as opposed to a text for a series of characters.

COREY FROST: I think it's important that generally, spoken word is always performed by the person who writes it. You're not writing for an actor, for another body.

ALEXIS O'HARA: I come from a theatre background, and yet I find that there are big constraints about contemporary theatre. I don't believe in the whole notion of the fourth wall, and the willing suspension of disbelief, and this is why for me spoken word is more interesting. Because you can have theatrical elements, you can have musical elements, and yet there is nothing that creates a sort of falseness — there is no myth surrounding the performance.... You are not Madame Pompadour from the seventeenth century who is talking to her courtesan. You are talking to your audience. And that is real, that is very real.

D. KIMM: The main thing for my show entitled *La Suite mongole*[2] was to succeed in saying the texts with feeling, without necessarily acting them. This is very important to me because otherwise you end up doing theatre, and becoming a character.

"An activist thing to do"

Part of the appeal of spoken word performance is its ability to carry a message to specific communities. It

D. KIMM: L'essentiel pour mon spectacle *La Suite mongole* était surtout de réussir à dire des textes avec émotion, sans nécessairement les jouer. Pour moi, cette différence est très importante sinon tu te retrouves à faire du théâtre et tu deviens un personnage.

[1] Montreal Fringe Festival, June 1995. Fluffy Pagan Echoes was a performance poetry troupe.

[2] *La Suite mongole*, Tangente, October 1999.

corrodes the rigidly codified stereo-types created by mass culture, and lends itself to both identity politics and radical countercultural currents of thought.

VINCE TINGUELY: Because we live in a mass culture, we're made to feel insignificant. You've got your favourite show on TV. It's the best show ever made, but it gets cancelled because not enough people are watching it, right? So you feel like, "Well, I just don't exist as a person. And according to this culture, I'm supposed to enjoy stuff with Arnold Schwarzenegger." But when you go into a little space, and there's forty people, and there's people on a stage giving you insight into their lives, it makes you want to say, "Yes, I experience things too. This is real."

VICTORIA STANTON: Identity politics is really common in spoken word performance — especially if you're younger and you're just learning about the world — because it is a really potent tool, when you're able to name your experience. That's when it crosses paths with activism. Even though it's not about demonstrating in the streets, it's about asserting your personhood amidst a mass culture. That, to me, is an activist thing to do.

JOSEPH NEUDORFER: I think spoken word can be either verbal or oral communication, not only verse. If you can broadcast political propaganda in such a fashion that's attractive to an audience, that can be spoken word.

NORMAN NAWROCKI: We've done shows for people who are illiterate, and so the spoken word tradition is the way to share ideas. There are many community cabarets we've done over the years

where we reach the people that organizers can't reach because the concepts are too complicated. What I love to do is to make concrete — understandable — complex things, so that people finally understand. "Ah! This is what that new law is all about. Ah! This is how the economy works." One good example is that for the *Cirque en Ca$h* at Centre-Sud a class of illiterate people came. The following day the teacher called us and said, "Thank you so much. My class was just talking about your show all day, I couldn't get them to stop." So for me, spoken word reaches people who can't read, and that's a really important part of the work that I do.

AKIN ALAGA: Oration is something that has propelled me since I was a child. I'm heavily interested in politics, so when I couldn't perform, I decided to discard performance because I'm very good at making speeches. When I'm making my political speeches with audiences, I have that relationship. When you get into speech-making and orating, a lot of body language is involved... and for me there's a connection. I want to be able to access that ability to bring things down to earth, from some other place.

"You have to talk to the community in their language"

Spoken word performance has popular appeal. 'Popular' in the sense of attracting a mixed audience. Such appeal has brought the work of serious artists such as Adeena Karasick, bill bissett and Gerry Shikatani to audiences beyond the sometimes insular artistic communities. This audience — informal, intelligent and sometimes vocally critical — helps define the shape that spoken word performance can take.

Norman Nawrocki at Concordia University September 1999

3

WHAT IS SPOKEN WORD?

ENDRE FARKAS: In the seventies, the written word had moved away from the community, became very exclusive, academic. You studied poetry, and most of the people didn't know what the hell you were studying, or the poems on the page became more and more esoteric, inaccessible for most people. When you come back to the idea, you have to talk to the community in their language.

ANNE STONE: I was sitting down reading some of the texts of performance theory, and thinking about women delivering papers about writing on the body two-dimensionally, with the paper in front of them and the table cutting them off at the waist. Where's the body, right? And so I get upset when I see people who are very into these theories... not coming out and seeing what happens at cabarets, and not seeing this generation of spoken word performers as actuating in some sense the very things that they are excited by!

Anne Stone performs at
Women We Love *at Le Lounge,*
July 29, 1997
Photo by André Lemelin

JUSTIN MCGRAIL: It is really hard to have a sense of artifice if you're doing spoken word poetry. Like with that joker with the mohawk writing those poems about how good he was in bed, Scott Duncan interrupted his poem with the cry of, "Fuck me!" He never showed up again. You can't survive because when people come to a spoken word reading, what they value about it is the idea that someone's up there, they're not trained as an actor, they're not trained as a musician, they can't sing, and they're not some creative writing grad, but shit, they've got something to say. And that's a commonality with the origins of slam poetry in the States. If you've got something to say, and you work on it, it's worth saying.

"Spoken word, it's anglophone"

While various artists in the francophone community perform their texts for audiences, for various reasons this practice is perceived as being different from what goes on in the anglophone spoken word scene.

NANCY LABONTÉ: On the francophone side, we have only a vague idea of what 'spoken word' is. It's mainly an American phenomenon from the start, and has little to do with how we 'do' poetry evenings here, even though there's a common thread. The francophone poet who gets up onstage to deliver his text doesn't do it with the same feeling as an anglophone. Which partly explains why francophone poets often have their texts with them or don't memorize them. On the anglo side, however, you have to know your text by heart, otherwise there's no reason for you to be onstage. The performance has to have rhythm, a beat, and be spoken from memory. That's one of the differences between oral literature and written literature.

D. KIMM: Sometimes I translate 'spoken word' as *littérature dite* [spoken literature], or *écrite-dite* [written-spoken], because I think anglophones and francophones often have different concepts of this poetic practice. For francophones, our tradition of *soirées de poésie* [poetry evenings] is closer to written literature than to spoken literature. In the shows I organize, there aren't only poets; I invite several novelists and short story writers who are also good performers. It was quite peculiar at first, they had never or only rarely been part of a show. However, onstage, it was harder to convey a passage from a novel than a poem, because the rhythms are different. Poetry has a more musical rhythm, and when a poet says her text well, it flows more easily — like a song.

SYLVAIN FORTIER: I discovered the French scene first. It all started when the people from the show *Zéro de conduite*[3] asked me for a text. Among other things, I discovered some documentaries about the *Nuits de la poésie* that were held and which are, in my view, linked to spoken word. I attended a *Nuit de la poésie* in 1991, but at that time I was only a spectator, I wasn't aware of the phenomenon. After that I got more interested, I met some performers, and by the time I did my first show, on April 1, 1995, I was really aware of the movement's vitality. So I didn't suddenly realize that there was a spoken word scene, it happened bit by bit, starting from the flash I had about poetry, about my artistic creation. Around 1994, 1995, it 'spoke' to me more, if I can put it like that, because I could connect the *Nuit de la poésie* directly to what I was doing.

D. KIMM: Nevertheless, francophone

soirées have existed for a long time. At the end of the nineteenth century, Émile Nelligan and *L'Ecole littéraire de Montréal* [Montreal Literary School] organized poetry evenings at the Château Ramezay. Except that since then, we've sort of always continued doing 'poetry' evenings. And so, in all of the francophone shows I've ever attended, I've never seen anyone deliver a text the way Victoria Stanton does, i.e. as a monologue. We do have an important tradition of French-language *monologuistes* here, but it's always been associated with comedy / humour. In fact, oral poetry — which is more spoken than read — came from artists who did 'real' performance, mostly women. First there was Marie Savard, who's now about sixty, who is one of the foremothers of performers, she did poetry-song shows; then she became a radical feminist and founded *La Pleine lune* publishing house. There was also Pauline Harvey, who did sound poetry. What these two women presented was really different from traditional poetry evenings. Today, performers like Nathalie Derome and Sylvie Laliberté are largely text-based but their shows use objects and accessories as well. Geneviève Letarte is also a special case because she came partly from theatre and partly from performance and she sings. But what she does is always very poetic, even though she tells stories. As for myself, I come from the *soirées de la poésie*, but I can also say I tried to contribute to their evolution when I started staging shows (because hardly anybody was doing it) that included a concept, musicians, stage directions, pacing, and lighting. At one point I felt like I'd explored all the possibilities and, in order to keep evolving, I chose to go the multidisciplinary route.

D. KIMM: Parfois je traduis "spoken word" par "littérature dite", ou "écrite-dite", parce que je pense que, souvent, les anglophones et les francophones ne conçoivent pas cette pratique poétique de la même façon. Du côté francophone, notre tradition des "soirées de poésie" fait qu'on tend à se rapprocher davantage de la littérature écrite que de la littérature dite. Dans les spectacles, que j'organise il n'y a pas que des poètes; j'ai invité plusieurs romanciers et nouvellistes qui étaient aussi de bons performeurs. Au début c'était assez particulier, car ils n'avaient peu ou jamais participé à des spectacles. Toutefois, sur scène il est plus difficile de rendre un extrait de roman qu'un poème, étant donné que leurs rythmes sont différents. Le rythme de la poésie est plus musical, et quand un poète dit bien son texte, ça coule plus facilement, c'est comme une chanson.

SYLVAIN FORTIER: Moi, c'est le milieu francophone que j'ai découvert en premier. Tout a commencé quand l'équipe de l'émission *Zéro de conduite* m'a demandé de lui fournir un texte. À partir de là, tout a déboulé. Entre autres, j'ai découvert des documentaires sur les *Nuits de la poésie* qu'il y a eu et qui sont, à mon sens, liés à ce qu'on appelle les "mots dits", le spoken word. En 1991, j'avais assisté à une *Nuit de la poésie*, mais comme à ce moment-là je n'étais ce spectateur, je n'avais pas pris conscience du phénomène. Par la suite, je m'y suis intéressé davantage, j'ai rencontré des performeurs, et lors de mon premier spectacle, le 1er avril 1995, j'étais vraiment conscient de la vitalité du mouvement. Donc je n'ai pas réalisé d'un seul coup qu'il existait une scène spoken word, ça s'est fait petit à petit, à partir du déclic que j'ai eu par rapport à la poésie, à ma création artistique. Vers 1994, 1995, ça m'interpellait plus parce que je pouvais rattacher les *Nuits de la poésie* directement à ce que je faisais.

D. KIMM: Les soirées francophones existent quand même depuis longtemps. À la fin du XIXe, Émile Nelligan et l'École littéraire de Montréal organisaient des soirées de poésie au Château Ramezay. Sauf

continued...

3 *Zéro de Conduite*, 1994-1998. Founders: Yves Lavoie and Daniel-Paul Bourdages; editorial committee: Yves Lavoie and Sonia Ritter.

5

qu'on dirait que depuis, on a presque toujours continué à faire des soirées "de poésie". Par exemple, à tous les spectacles francophones auxquels j'ai assistés, je n'ai jamais vu quelqu'un livrer un texte comme le fait Victoria Stanton, c'est-à-dire comme un monologue. Pourtant, on a une importante tradition de monologuistes au Québec, mais cela a toujours été associé à l'humour. En fait, la poésie orale, plus *dite* que *lue*, c'est plutôt venu des artistes qui faisaient de la "vraie" performance, des femmes surtout. D'abord il y a eu Marie Savard, maintenant âgée d'une soixantaine d'années, qui est l'une des ancêtres des performeuses avec ses spectacles de poésie-chansons; ensuite elle est devenue féministe radicale et a fondé la maison d'édition La Pleine Lune. Il y a eu aussi Pauline Harvey, qui a déjà fait des poèmes sonores. Ce que ces deux femmes-là présentaient était vraiment différent des soirées de poésie traditionnelles. Aujourd'hui, on peut voir Nathalie Derome et Sylvie Laliberté, des performeuses qui travaillent beaucoup le texte mais qui, dans leurs spectacles, emploient également des objets, des accessoires. Geneviève Letarte est aussi un cas particulier puisqu'elle vient un peu du milieu du théâtre et un peu de celui de la performance, et qu'elle chante. Mais ce qu'elle fait est toujours très poétique, même si elle raconte des histoires. Je suis pour ma part issue des soirées de poésie, mais je peux aussi dire que j'ai tenté de les faire évoluer quand j'ai commencé à faire de la mise en scène (parce qu'à peu près personne ne le faisait) avec un concept, des musiciens, une scénographie, un "pacing", des éclairages. À un moment donné, j'ai eu le sentiment d'avoir fait le tour, et pour continuer à évoluer, j'ai choisi d'aller vers le multidisciplinaire.

Nancy Labonté: Entre francophones, on peut se dire qu'on fait de la performance. Mais on ne peut pas dire ça à un anglophone, car le mot "performance" n'a pas le même sens du côté de la littérature québécoise que du côté du spoken word anglophone. Et c'est précisément là qu'il y a une nuance: on parle du spoken word anglophone, et on parle de la *littérature* québécoise.... Jean-Paul Daoust est un poète francophone qui fait de la performance, sauf qu'il ne dit jamais ses poèmes par cœur et a toujours ses feuilles avec lui. Mais c'est un des poètes qui s'attachent le plus à la tradition du spoken word, parce

Nancy Labonté: Among francophones, we can say that we do performance. But we can't say that to an anglophone, because the word 'performance' doesn't mean the same thing in the French-language literary scene as it does in the anglophone spoken word scene. And this is precisely where there's a nuance: in English it's about spoken *word*, whereas in French it's Quebec *literature*.... Jean-Paul Daoust is a francophone poet who does performance, except that he never says his poems by heart, he always has his sheets of paper with him. But he's one of the poets who's closest to the spoken word tradition because his texts have a strong beat, they're almost songs when he recites them. I'm sure that when he writes, the text is singing itself in his head.

Jean-Paul Daoust: I prefer the English-language term. 'Spoken words'. It does not have the same connotation as *les mots dits*. Because *les mots dits* [the words said], in French it's like a pun on *poètes maudits* [damned poets], on *les maudits*, [the damned]. It's OK... but the English-language expression has the advantage of being more technical. More realistic, too.

Geneviève Letarte: My first discovery of performance in Montreal goes back to when I was fifteen, when Robert Charlebois had his gang. Back then, it was probably also the Michel Garneau generation. All those people were doing shows that weren't really performances, but close. There were also poetry readings, as the *Québécois* tradition was very strong in this area. It wasn't spoken word at all, the approach was totally different. Poets didn't have to memorize their texts, nor do any staging — just read. Of course in events like these, phenomena always emerge.

Jean-Paul Daoust
Photo courtesy of the artist

Some people stood out because they were performers, like Claude Péloquin and the *Quatuor du jazz libre du Québec*, with poet Yves Préfontaine. And let's not forget the one and only Raoul Duguay, who in a way could be called a poet-performer. But I don't want to talk about that era too much because I didn't see everything....

FORTNER ANDERSON: One of the things I've noticed recently is that the series of storytelling evenings [*Les soirées de contes*] have a lot of similarities with the spoken word scene.... That seems to be something that has a very similar expression within the community, draws strong audiences, same kind of crowd, done in bars up and down St. Laurent Boulevard. They do musical interludes as well. It's interesting to speculate why Quebec culture has focused on that particular expression to gather people together. Within the literary community in Quebec there are actually very few poets who have

thrown themselves into the performance of their work. Most view the highest expression of their work to be on the printed page, the perfect-bound book published by a small publisher and sent off to languish in libraries across the province. I think there's been a refusal to accept and to acknowledge the artistry of poets who work primarily through performance, and whose work is primarily oral.

IAN FERRIER: I think it's still new. '*Mot dits*' or 'spoken word', those are the words that I hear. '*Poésie musique*' is another one. I think what Geneviève Letarte and Hélène Monette are doing, considering that they began at the turn of the eighties, was way ahead of a lot of the stuff that we were doing. It was just the fact that there wasn't that much surrounding them that it didn't happen on a larger scale. It didn't have a publisher but with André Lemelin [Éditions Planète rebelle] it probably will from now on.

que ses textes sont très rythmés, ce sont presque des chansons quand il les récite. Lorsqu'il écrit, c'est sûr que dans sa tête le texte se chante.

JEAN-PAUL DAOUST: Je crois que je préfère l'appellation anglaise. Les "spoken words", je trouve que ça n'a pas la même connotation que les "mots dits". Parce que les mots dits, en français, c'est comme un jeu de mots, sur les poètes maudits, sur les maudits. En fait, c'est correct... mais je trouve que l'expression anglaise a l'avantage d'être plus technique. Et plus réaliste, aussi.

GENEVIÈVE LETARTE: Ce que j'ai d'abord connu de la scène montréalaise par rapport à la performance remonte à quand j'avais 15 ans, à l'époque où il y avait la bande de Robert Charlebois. Dans ce temps, probablement que c'était également la génération de Michel Garneau. Tout ce monde montait des spectacles qui n'étaient pas réellement des performances, mais qui s'en approchaient. Par ailleurs, il y avait aussi les lectures de poésie puisque la tradition québécoise francophone était très forte dans ce domaine. Mais ce n'était pas du tout du spoken word car l'approche était totalement différente. Les poètes n'avaient pas à apprendre leur texte par cœur ni à faire de mise en scène – c'étaient simplement des lectures. Et, naturellement, dans ces événements, on rencontre toujours des phénomènes. Il y avait donc des gens qui se démarquaient parce qu'ils étaient des performeurs, comme Claude Péloquin et le Quatuor du jazz libre du Québec avec le poète Yves Préfontaine. Sans oublier le fameux Raoul Duguay, de qui on pourrait dire, d'une certaine façon, que c'est un poète-performeur. Mais je ne veux pas trop parler de cette période, car je n'ai pas vu tout....

WHY MONTREAL?

IV

"This is the bohemian sink"

WE WANTED TO FIND OUT WHAT IT WAS ABOUT THE CITY OF MONTREAL WHICH HAS MADE IT SUCH A GOOD ENVIRONMENT FOR A SPOKEN WORD SCENE. IS IT SOMETHING SPECIFIC TO THE CITY, THE AUDIENCES, THE MIX OF CULTURES WHICH GATHER HERE, OR IS IT JUST A COINCIDENCE? DID MONTREAL BRING A COMMUNITY OF ARTISTS TOGETHER, OR ARE THESE SIMPLY INDIVIDUALS WHO HAPPEN TO SHARE THE SAME SPACE? IS THERE EVEN A COMMUNITY?

> **GENEVIÈVE LETARTE:** *I think the reason is the lack of sovereignty. That would go with the history of culture. Durant les années 70, les Québécois étaient très souverainistes et désiraient ardemment l'indépendance du Québec. À un certain moment, l'art est devenu très engagé politiquement. Je pense que c'est étroitement lié à la situation politique du Québec, mais pas nécessairement d'une manière consciente et affirmée. Je crois que c'est vraiment dû à un besoin d'exister en tant que peuple. Pour moi, c'est évident! c'est un besoin identitaire... But it's also the co-habitation of the French and the English. I think that's a big part of it.*

4 Cabaret Music Hall, May 1998. Mitsiko Miller organized and hosted *La Vache enragée*, a bilingual spoken word series, from 1995-1998.

5 Daughter of Kate McGarrigle, of the Montreal duo Kate and Anna McGarrigle.

"East / west of St. Laurent"

Montreal's cultural milieu is characterized by the divide between the two linguistic groups, francophone and anglophone. Despite the mythos of 'the two solitudes', there is a certain amount of permeability, especially in the visual arts and the dance communities. What is striking about the spoken word scene, is that it has in some instances allowed a mingling of francophone and anglophone performers whose work is made up of the very stuff at the heart of current political debate in Quebec: language.

GENEVIÈVE LETARTE: I think the reason is the lack of sovereignty. That would go with the history of culture. During the seventies, the *Québécois* were ardent sovereignists, they wanted Quebec's independence very badly. At a certain point art became very political. I think it's very linked to Quebec politics, but not necessarily in a conscious and asserted way. I believe it's really due to a desire to exist as a people. To me this is obvious: it comes from a need at the level of identity. But it's also the cohabitation of the French and the English. That's a big part of it. Maybe the core of it.... It's a very powerful dynamic, a difficult but important one.... For example, concerning spoken word, it's clear that francophones are presently using anglophones as an example, because the tradition isn't as strong on our side. Francophones are trying to keep up with what's going on in the anglo scene, we want to make the most of this energy, but in our own way, to produce something different. And anglos probably do the same with francophones in other areas. So there's a dynamic created for sure.

VICTORIA STANTON: We've come to a point where we're having shows in which English-language writers / performers and French-language writers / performers can actually start seeing each other's work and feed off of each other. That it has actually lasted long enough to make some kind of impact on the French-language scene... is one of the really exciting aspects of it.

SIMON DARDICK: I think there's advantages to being English in Quebec... in that it is a much tighter scene. I think Montreal is in the margins in Canada anyway, in a certain way. We're a big city that is bisected or divided because of French and English, in terms of activity. Although they sometimes come together, it splits the scene and makes each one smaller. On the other hand I think that smallness makes it bigger in certain other ways. It makes it work together differently, there's just a different kind of dynamism here.... There is something very interesting about the English Montreal scene, sitting cheek to jowl with the French scene. Every once in a while it comes together. When Regie Cabico was in town from New York we went to the *La Vache enragée* benefit.4 He was performing, and Fortner performed, and you had a number of the French performers. It was blowing Regie's mind, to see some of these francophone performers.

JAKE BROWN: What I haven't seen is a large body of English fans going to French readings, and French fans going to English readings. There's almost none. Martha Wainwright5 told me this five years ago. She said, "It's been like this since my Mom started." The artists love each other, French and English.

8

The actual French audience loves an English artist when they see one, and vice-versa, but the English audience won't walk five blocks from St. Laurent to St. Denis, and the French audience will not walk five blocks from St. Denis to St. Laurent, for a reason that she thinks is not connected to the performances.

NANCY LABONTÉ: In Montreal there's always this pseudo-war between English and French. Francophones know very little about what goes on west of St. Laurent Boulevard, and anglos don't know much more about what's happening to the east of St. Laurent, our side. It's totally absurd — we hardly know each other and we live in the same city. Plus, we're bilingual! Probably half of the anglos speak French, maybe half of francophones speak English. But it's very rare that francophones and anglophones organize shows together. Shortly before *Gaz Moutarde* came into being something was attempted at Fokus Gallery on Duluth Street, where little poetry evenings were sometimes held. Across the street there was another gallery that occasionally presented small events in French. There was an attempt to break down the language barrier. But as I see it, anglo poets and franco poets don't have the same philosophy: there's two ways of thinking that are different, specific and incompatible.

NATHALIE DEROME: I think impure, impurity, it's a theme that's really important these days. Maybe it's a French-Canadian preoccupation, but I think it's more *mondial. L'impureté...* what's impure about talking to another culture; is it impure? Will I lose something if I speak English? Is it *l'impureté* to be close to somebody who is really different?... And that's the question — the core question.[6]

PATRICIA LAMONTAGNE: I started publishing poetry in 1983. In the eighties, poetry still had a strong tradition in Montreal. And yet, as far as I know, no anglophone poet was ever invited to take part in our poetry events. Never. Our poets were too into political discourse, militant, the good guys and the bad guys. There was an unbelievable dichotomy. A bit like the image of Montreal, east / west of St. Laurent Boulevard. Personally, I find this stupid. When I went to Banff, I was really surprised to see how much Canadians in general — other than *Québécois* — travel all over. They know poets from Edmonton, Victoria, Halifax. They know what's going on elsewhere, and I think we lack their open-mindedness. People at Banff told me that the anglos in Montreal are quite specific from the rest of Canada.

Nancy Labonté
Photo by Diane Dulude

Maybe it's the core of it... C'est une dynamique très puissante qui est difficile mais qui est importante... Par exemple, en ce qui a trait au spoken word, il est très clair qu'en ce moment les francophones prennent exemple sur les anglophones parce que la tradition est moins présente de notre côté. Les francophones essaient de suivre ce qui se passe sur la scène anglophone et veulent profiter de cette énergie, mais à leur manière, pour en faire quelque chose de différent. Et probablement que les anglophones font de même avec les francophones dans d'autres domaines. Alors, c'est sûr que cela crée une certaine dynamique.

NANCY LABONTÉ: À Montréal, il existe toujours une "pseudo-guerre" entre l'anglais et le français. Les francophones ne savent à peu près pas ce qui se passe à l'ouest du boulevard Saint-Laurent, et les anglophones n'ont qu'une mince idée de ce qui se passe de notre côté de Saint-Laurent, à l'est. C'est totalement absurde, on ne sait pratiquement rien des autres et on reste dans la même ville! En plus, on est bilingues! Probablement que la moitié des anglophones parlent français, comme peut-être la moitié des francophones parlent anglais. Mais il est très rare que des francophones et des anglophones organisent des spectacles ensemble. Un peu avant *Gaz Moutarde*, j'ai été témoin d'un essai qui avait été tenté: il y avait la Galerie Fokus, sur Duluth, qui organisait parfois des petites soirées de poésie anglophone. Et, en face, il y avait une autre galerie qui présentait à l'occasion des petites soirées francophones. À ce moment-là, on avait tenté de briser la barrière langagière. Mais, selon moi, les poètes anglophones et les poètes francophones n'ont pas la même philosophie; ce sont deux modes de pensée différents, spécifiques et incompatibles.

NATHALIE DEROME: *I think impure, impurity, it's a theme that's really important these days. Maybe it's a French Canadian preoccupation, but I think it's more mondial. L'impureté...*

continued...

[6] See Guy Scarpetta.

Nathalie Derome in
Retour du refoulé, *1990*
Photo by Danielle Hébert

what's impure about talking to another culture; is it impure? Will I lose something if I speak English? Is it l'impureté *to be close to somebody who is really different?... Et c'est ça la* question. C'est la première question.

PATRICIA LAMONTAGNE: J'ai commencé à publier de la poésie dans les revues en 1983. Dans les années 1980, la poésie était encore très forte de tradition à Montréal. Et pourtant, à ma connaissance, jamais un poète anglophone n'a été invité à participer à une soirée de poésie francophone. Jamais. Nos poètes donnaient trop dans le discours politique, le discours engagé, les méchants et les bons – il y avait une dichotomie incroyable. Un peu à l'image de Montréal, est/ouest du boulevard Saint-Laurent. Personnellement, je trouve ça stupide. Quand je suis allée à Banff, j'ai été vraiment surprise de voir comment les Canadiens en général – outre ceux du Québec – voyagent. Ils connaissent des poètes d'Edmonton, de Victoria et de Halifax. Ils savent ce qui se passe ailleurs, et je pense que leur ouverture d'esprit nous fait défaut... *People at Banff told me that the anglophones in Montreal are quite specific from the rest of Canada.*

7 Jake Brown hosted *YAWP!*, a spoken word series, from 1995-2000.

8 Spring 1996.

JEREMIAH WALL: English is a renegade language in Quebec. That's why the French people think the English have a pretty dynamic scene. Because we make more noise than French culture does. French culture is more the theatre, the bars, it's all set up now in Quebec. But English society has to make itself wherever it can, set up the tents and do the circus, it's like the circus is in town.

NATHALIE DEROME: I saw Geneviève Letarte once, and we were talking about how in this current there's something really 'anglophone'. Like a potluck, when you go to a brunch with English people, everybody brings something. And often these nights of spoken word performance or *La Vache enragée*, it's like that. Everybody makes ten or fifteen minutes and we share a melting pot.

"A lot more room to grow up"

It's generally acknowledged that Montreal has a culture unique in North America, engendered by the dynamism of the various communities that exist here. In addition, it is perhaps the lack of certain opportunities for the anglophone artists that helped create a need for spoken word.

HEATHER O'NEILL: New stuff always works well in Montreal, as far as the avant-garde goes. People from other cities, in the States, always hear about Montreal and the things they associate with Montreal are really new stuff, like the dancers they know about, and the *Cirque de Soleil*.... The name Montreal has a significance, especially in the States. What does manage to get out is of such high quality and so original. Because there's so few presses and it's such a challenge, the people who stick with it usually have a strong talent.

JEREMIAH WALL: One of the things that characterizes Montreal's scene is that you don't have a large commercial publication presence here. So this alternative publishing scene and / or promoting your work as a reader or performer, is gonna consume a lot more energy while you're here. Even if you're very serious and you want to publish in Toronto and New York, you need to exist in a community. There's so many people here who are good and vital, but they're not being published actively in this community, so they've got to go out and do a reading and enjoy each other's company. They're not meeting and saying, "I just published with the big publishing company," they're saying, "Oh, I went to this stage and I did that and we were in this magazine or we started this series."

JOHN GIORNO: I have a real great affection for Montreal. I've gone back for more than twenty-five years to perform.... It has a quality, because of the French thing there, one feels a certain looseness in Montreal that one doesn't find in Toronto.... Montreal is different. There is a whole scene that took place over the years that's not dependent on a single person, so that if that one person didn't exist, it doesn't exist.

IAN FERRIER: As far as performance poetry or oral poetry or spoken word goes, it's as strong here as anywhere I've ever seen. We get the same size audiences here as New York does and they've got ten times the population. And we get stronger audiences than in Toronto with twice as many people. So that breeds a lot more room to grow up in the scene and learn how to do it, and continue doing it. One good example is that Jake Brown's *YAWP!*7 show at the Rivoli in Toronto8 pretty well sold out. There was no other poetry thing in

Toronto that would sell out the Rivoli. A lot of that is because of the energy that he puts into promoting and getting posters out and doing all that stuff. There's also the people that fill the bills for those things. We kind of take it for granted here, somebody can do their show, and they can get four or five people to come and perform for them, without really sweating too much.

"Very American"

Francophone artists perceive Montreal's anglophone spoken word scene as originating in the United States; specifically, from the slam poetry scene, and the Beat poets.

JEAN-PAUL DAOUST: The way I see it, giving the text a beat, bringing it to life, presenting it live, comes from a very American mentality. It's part of our culture. And that's why, in my opinion, this movement appeared in Toronto, and especially in New York. Anyway, spoken word can be compared to jazz: both make it possible to improvise and, like jazz, spoken word has its roots here in North America. So I believe that some of our drive is local. And so I don't really see much difference between francophone and anglophone poets. On the other hand, anglo poets may be more realistic, more anecdotal. They can tell stories. This is something that strikes me, in relation to French poetry, which is more introspective. Often, on the francophone side, our poems are very short, while in English poetry they can be very long works with an epic quality throughout. This might even be what characterizes spoken word. But in Gaston Miron's *La Marche à l'amour*, there's a long lyrical flight that was magnificent when he recited it. Even though he was francophone, Miron can

be considered very spoken word. There's a reason why he was always reworking his texts; he read them so much that at some point, it couldn't help but impact his writing.

MITSIKO MILLER: It comes from North America, the slam thing. The style, the musicality, *le style rapide...* it's very inspired from the States. That, I find, is not very popular in the French community. Spoken word in the French community hails from the 'griot', the tradition of sitting around the fire. People who would cut wood in Quebec, and had no TV or radio, would actually tell stories. That's where spoken word comes from here in Quebec. I find that we have a tradition in the French community of beauty. Beautiful words. But you have to tell a story, it has to be more universal. That's why it's so hard for the French community to understand slam poetry, because for them it's just a show. But one of the biggest influences I find in the francophone spoken word community has been performance art in the seventies. Now, the new generation of spoken word artists is definitely French rap, which has been strong for the past six or seven years. It's really different, it's another style.

"It's cosmopolitan enough and vibrant enough and cheap enough"

It takes a large city to provide the kind of intellectual and aesthetic nurturing creative souls need. Of the three largest cities in Canada, Montreal has by far the lowest cost of living. In addition, the infrastructure of the inner city enables artists, musicians, dancers, writers and spoken word performers to form enclaves in specific neighbourhoods. Any disciple of urban studies theorist Jane Jacobs knows

JEAN-PAUL DAOUST: Pour moi, c'est une mentalité qui est très américaine que de faire *swinger* le texte, le rendre vivant, le rendre *live*. Ça fait partie de notre culture. Et c'est pour ça, à mon avis, qu'à Toronto, ou surtout à New York, que ce mouvement est apparu. D'ailleurs, on pourrait comparer la pratique du spoken word à celle du jazz: les deux permettent de faire des improvisations, et comme le jazz, le spoken word tient ses racines d'ici, de l'Amérique du Nord. Je crois donc que certaines de nos pulsions sont locales. Et, en cela, je ne vois pas vraiment de différence entre les poésies francophone et anglophone. Par contre, les poètes anglophones sont peut-être plus réalistes, plus anecdotiques. Ils peuvent raconter des histoires. C'est une chose qui me frappe, moi, par rapport à la poésie francophone, qui me paraît plus intérieure. Souvent, du côté francophone, on a des poèmes courts, tandis que dans la poésie anglaise, on retrouve de longs souffles très épiques. C'est peut-être même ça qui caractérise le spoken word. Mais dans *La Marche à l'amour* de Gaston Miron, il y a toute une envolée qui était magnifique quand il la récitait. Même s'il était francophone, on pourrait dire que Gaston Miron était très "spoken word". Ce n'est pas sans raison qu'il retravaillait toujours ses textes; il les lisait tellement qu'à un certain point, ça ne pouvait faire autrement que d'avoir un impact sur son écriture.

11

Todd Swift reads at the Casa del Popolo, December 2000
Photo by Juan Guardado from
www.madgenta.com

that neighbourhoods facilitate social interaction, and interaction among artists makes a 'scene'.

JEREMIAH WALL: Poetry is a minority culture, really. You don't think of people who are into literature or poetry as the ruling class of the society. They are the 'downwardly mobile' element. They start out maybe in the middle class and they go down to working at whatever job they can, or no job, so they can just struggle with their art and their craft. A lot of people come to Montreal to live this life. This is the bohemian sink. Literary arts tend to be the cheapest form.

COREY FROST: I think that the scene in Montreal wouldn't exist if there weren't so many unemployed people, or people who were willing to live on next to nothing, and involve themselves voluntarily, and just have that sensibility of being slightly counterculture because you're not participating in the production of capital.

KAREN STEWART: I think Montreal is unlike any other city in Canada because the cost of living is low enough so that you can live and do your art. Work in your art. And not die. As opposed to Toronto or Vancouver or anywhere else. In Toronto there's a survival thing that goes on where you work to survive, to pay the rent. But it's half the cost to live here, and we still have as much fun. It's a neat little place for artists, because it's cosmopolitan enough and vibrant enough and cheap enough.

ALEX BOUTROS: I think Montreal has something which Toronto doesn't have. It has the opportunity to put on shows for a lot less money. Because a) the performers don't demand as much, and b) the venues don't cost as much.... I think that anybody in Montreal can make a couple of contacts, and be given a helping hand to put on a show. And people do, constantly.

TODD SWIFT: Hosts of series just did not believe that you could actually make money from a poetry show — that you could bring in a large audience, and that's something that *Vox Hunt*[9] did. It has directly inspired Jake Brown, and he can not deny that. Now there is actually an incredible opportunity for people to perform. Poets don't feel isolated, they see it as being something that the community receives and they want to be a part of. And that's when you have something which is a 'scene'.

CATHERINE KIDD: Montreal is... sort of like a primordial ooze. It seems like a lot of people come here to steep in their own creative juices. I was pretty idealistic about it at first. I thought, "Wow, there's really a sense of community here and I really love this." And then over time, I realized, "Well, you know,

9 *Vox Hunt* slam poetry series, 1995-1997.

there's also the other side of it." Sometimes, people are very positive and very, very supportive, but there's the same sort of stupid, petty, political back-biting that you'd find anywhere. Which is too bad. Maybe it has something to do with lack of money.... I think that there's room for everybody to be doing it. In fact, it's better if everybody does, because if a certain art form, like spoken word, is going to be taken seriously, and going to ever get to the point where it's a — how about a viable means of making a living? — then there should be as many people as possible, as far as I'm concerned.

SIMON DARDICK: To me it's quite fascinating to see the generational crossover. Because you do have people who are not really *old*, but you have people like Fortner Anderson, and Ian Ferrier. And yet you have people who are barely out of their teens. You've got the whole gamut of ages involved in it.

ALEX BOUTROS: I find Montreal unique, but I don't want to pin myself down and say that there is a community of any sort. But I think there is a sense in Montreal, a very eclectic sense. And it's not just eclectic in the sense that you get poets and musicians and sometimes dancers coming together. As far as I can tell in a place like New York — yes you get the odd poet from the Nuyorican Café going somewhere else, but they have very set communities and very defined parameters. In Montreal there's been a lot of crossover. You'd get someone like Tanya Evanson playing *YAWP!* and playing *Unusual Suspects* and doing a *Girlspit*, and she could move. And I think that freedom to move from venue to venue is very unique to Montreal. And producers that I've talked to want-

ed that crossover. There's even been a crossover between the francophone and anglophone community, which is where you'd think the largest barriers would come up.

"**The community speaks to itself**"

Simon Dardick at work in his Véhicule Press offices
Photo by Andy Brown

The rise of spoken word culture in Montreal in the mid-nineties created a media storm. Although this has subsided, the media attention effectively established the practice in the minds of Montrealers, to the point where audiences consider spoken word performance as viable and interesting as more traditional forms of entertainment such as music, theatre or comedy. The initial success of spoken word has also created an ongoing evolution, one which constantly raises expectations and sets new standards for performance.

JAKE BROWN: People in the *Globe & Mail* wrote about the poetry scene here. *Cadillac Rose*, a [*Québécois*] TV show, interviewed me and Billy Mavreas, asking us about the anglos. "Are they really freaks, or no?" And Victoria was on the

CBC, explaining that she was running a political poetry show *Unusual Suspects*, which hadn't been done before. And so that's newsworthy, and of course if it's on the CBC people are going to hear about it, talk to other people, people who haven't seen a poetry show.

JASMINE CHÂTELAIN: A journalist from *La Presse* called me because he wanted to write an article on spoken word. He excitedly said, "Oh my God, what's going on in this city is so amazing. Did you know that francophone and anglophone artists were working together? Did you know that there was this festival, *Tongue Tied*? Did you know there's this thing, spoken word that's happening?" And I chuckled and said, "Well yeah, I was one of the people that did that."

LEAH VINEBERG: I think that there is a language in Montreal, and I think that actually it has an effect on the spoken word and performance art circuit. And you know that if you listen closely enough, when you're speaking onstage in the most codified manner, in a weird way you're speaking to your fellow codified friends (laughs). Montrealers speak in a codified language, and understand that language... and that's where I think that Montrealers are quite advanced, because Montrealers don't like to be bullshitted. We don't like to be faked out. We don't like to be spoken at and not listened to. I don't think that we like a gap between ourselves and our audience.

NORMAN NAWROCKI: The wonderful thing about Montreal audiences is that they tend to be more open. I can get away with more here than anywhere else. In many ways they tend to be the least repressed and the most responsive, the most open-minded and the

most willing to allow you to do your thing. The further west you go in this country, the more close-minded people tend to become. That's also because of lack of exposure. In Montreal, people are used to so much alternative culture. Like spoken word performances in English and French, and a mix of the two. Whereas, you go west, it's a much smaller scene, it's much more marginalized and the public in general just isn't used to this stuff. When I perform my sex education cabarets for violence against women or homophobia, a lot of people out there are, "(Gasp) He's talking about sex!" I can just feel the shudder and hear the gulps from the stage. They do appreciate it, but they're shocked that I'm actually saying things like this. Whereas in Montreal, I could take my clothes off on the stage and it wouldn't be a big deal.

PASCAL FIORAMORE: Compared to a lot of cities in the world, Montreal is very open-minded. I firmly believe this is due to the fact that we're in permanent culture shock here. A bit like in Amsterdam. That city is very eclectic, it too welcomes a lot of people from everywhere. There are lots of cafés where they give little performances, readings in German, in any language. I find their open-mindedness similar to ours. And this shows up in their artistic activities, in their creative spirit, like it does for us.

FORTNER ANDERSON: You would go to the Bistro 4[10] and there were poets who talked about real events in their lives that had actual meaning to the people that were listening. And people were affected by it. And that, fifteen years ago, was a very very rare occurrence. I mean, it didn't occur, poetry ceased to exist. Nobody read poetry books. Now,

PASCAL FIORAMORE: Comparativement à beaucoup de villes dans le monde, à Montréal, il y a vraiment une très grande ouverture d'esprit. Et je crois fortement que c'est dû au fait qu'ici, on vit en permanence un choc des cultures. Un peu comme à Amsterdam. Cette ville est très éclectique, elle accueille aussi énormément de gens de partout dans le monde. Là-bas, il y a beaucoup de cafés où il y a des petites performances, des lectures en allemand, en n'importe quelle langue. Je trouve que leur ouverture d'esprit est similaire à la nôtre. Et comme pour nous, ça se ressent dans leurs activités artistiques, dans leur élan créatif.

[10] A popular spoken word venue, home to *Enough Said*, *YAWP!*, *La Vache enragée*, *The Devil's Voice*, and other spoken word series. It closed in 1999.

there's a life. And I think that's due to the community working, everyone working towards that said need, that goal.... I think that in Montreal we're very fortunate, because this audience does not exist elsewhere. It doesn't exist in Los Angeles or New York or Vancouver or Toronto. Montreal has that opportunity where the community speaks to itself, through its poets.

DEBBIE YOUNG: I've lived in Toronto, and I've travelled parts of the States and parts of Canada, and I think Montreal, thus far, is a really good place to be for the artists. For the artist who wants to work on reaching a couple of people and developing self. Montreal is the only place that I've been able to do all the things that I just mentioned, and been able to *see* myself doing them. The nature of cities change, but I think in Montreal, you can manage to be experimental. Of course, when people really like your stuff they want you to produce more stuff like that. But if I choose to write five or six poems in the same way, it's either my own limited ability, or my own decision to do that, not because of pressures to continue producing in that way. And that's very very specific to Montreal. Because as an artist I don't feel that I'm being forced to be typecast.

TETSURO SHIGEMATSU: When I came back to Montreal, the spoken word scene seemed to be almost fully formed.... I'm actually here in this time and place and this is quite magical, because what's happening before me very few people know about. There's maybe even a historical sense that people might have had in Ferlinghetti's establishment. There's that excitement. But the price you pay for that excitement is that you have to wade through a lot of crap to get to those moments. I think it's probably one of the few authentic cultural phenomena that is occurring in the city, in the sense that it's very vital, it's very real. It's raw, it's unpolished sometimes, but that's part and parcel of both the medium as well as the accessibility of it. There's something very democratic about open mic night.

JAKE BROWN: It's been five-and-a-half years of joy for me. It's very hard work for no pay, and it's frustrating, but I never felt more alive in my life.... I think it's a rare thing to be able to participate in grassroots culture. It's a rare, valuable, precious thing. It's one of the last guarantees of democracy, just like Walt Whitman said. He said that real democracy only happens when you speak to the person next to you. Don't rely on others to speak for you.

Jake Brown backstage at Jailhouse, February 2000
Photo courtesy of Ian Ferrier

SPOKEN WORD THEORY

V

WE ARE UNAWARE OF ANY UNIVERSITY COURSES OR TEXTBOOKS ON THE THEORY AND PRACTICE OF SPOKEN WORD. THE EXPLANATION IS SIMPLE: BEFORE THE NINETIES, THE PERFORMANCE OF POETRY OR OTHER TEXTS WAS A CULTURALLY MARGINAL PRACTICE, ONE WHICH THE ESTABLISHED ARTS DISCOURSES PAID NO MIND. DIVIDED INTO STRICT CATEGORIES, IT IS LIKELY THAT THESE ARTS DISCOURSES DIDN'T REGARD SPOKEN WORD AS AN ART FORM IN ITSELF, BUT RATHER AS AN APPENDAGE OF THEATRE, LITERATURE, PERFORMANCE ART, OR POPULAR MUSIC.

When people began presenting their work in Montreal's spoken word scene in the nineties, it was largely without any sense of history. There was an implicit understanding that rules were to be broken, and risks were to be taken as a matter of course. The learning process took place in the clubs, cafés and halls, as performers studied each others' evolution. It was in these spaces that performance artists learned from poets, poets learned from actors trained in theatre, and actors learned from storytellers. The process of creating a hybrid art form was already well under way when a structure for it emerged: the 'poetry slam'. This is a competitive framework, with a time limit, and an emphasis on memorization, animation and audience engagement. Even at its height, the slam event only offered one outlet, an outlet not all spoken word artists in Montreal embraced. However, they did adopt memorization, animation and audience engagement as three criteria for the form.

1. Naming Spoken Word

'Spoken word' is a term that few of the artists we interviewed would accept for their own practices. We've taken the term as an umbrella under which their varying approaches to performance can be gathered. It's a recognizable term, and delineates the common element found in all their work: text which is spoken for an audience by the performer.

"I should not be afraid of 'spoken word'"

Naming one's practice has a lot to do with how one sees it, its origin and its intent. Performers often object to being called 'spoken word artists' because it generalizes their particular kind of work. They also worry that 'spoken word' already carries stereotypical associations which they'd rather avoid.

ALEXIS O'HARA: Well, I would like to be able to figure out what to call it. Because 'spoken word' is just not very evocative. I've talked about this with painter friends, all in a snit about how I just don't like the terminology that would normally apply to the work I do. And then they say, "Do you think that I want to be lumped in with every painter there is in the world?" I liken it to the whole feminism thing. There's a lot of women that'll shy away from being called feminists because they think that there's too much negative stuff attached to it. I've always considered myself to be a feminist, and so likewise I should not be afraid of 'spoken word'.

JEREMIAH WALL: I was always doing what is not only spoken word, but what I called 'beat coffee houses'. I would say whatever the dominant language pattern is, I'm going to use it in a pop song, but if I'm doing cultural criticism, I'll try to reinvent the language. 'Spoken word' is just like at some radio station; it's a big range of programming. Spoken word could be anything from poetry to doing theatre to even film, script writing that's eventually going to be done by actors in a film or onstage.

CATHERINE KIDD: I was avoiding using the phrase 'spoken word' for the longest time, just because you get sympathy on the one hand and suspicion on the other. It's preaching to the converted. People who are doing that, and call what they do spoken word are going to find identification there. But then you have no say over how reputation can run amok, or public perception can run amok. And lo and behold, you're earnestly doing your thing there, and run into some sense that, "Oh, wait a minute, a lot of people think of spoken word as being this thing that isn't very good."

JULIE CRYSLER: 'Spoken word artist' sounds bad. I usually say I'm a writer, but then it doesn't cover performance. They call it performance poetry, mostly, in Toronto. I think I change it based on what people are going to understand. Because it is so varied in terms of what people do. I find 'performance poet' sounds sort of tacky.

VINCE TINGUELY: I still call what I do 'performance poetry'. I insist on calling it poetry, because I've been writing poetry for so much longer than I've been performing it. I feel it's part of the same trajectory, that it's a literary form.

GENEVIÈVE LETARTE: I call myself a writer first, but I'm also a performance poet. In fact, I consider myself a multidisciplinary artist of writing. What I mean is that starting from writing, various things can come into being. I may make a video some day, who knows? But no matter what form my work takes, it always starts with writing.

VICTORIA STANTON: I think Fluffy Pagan Echoes called itself a performance poetry troupe.

VINCE TINGUELY: Scott Duncan called it 'rock and roll poetry'.

KAARLA SUNDSTRÖM: I think we're moving more towards music and having musical influences within our piece. Not just in terms of form, but actually singing. And as much as we don't want to be rendered into 'lyricists' — I mean, we want to be thought of as our words being more important than lyrics to a song — I think the word 'poetry', too, brings with it a lot of preconceived notions of what we would be all about without having heard us. The more we introduce music, the more our style is evolving, I'm finding that people are labeling us as 'rappers', oddly enough.

ANTHONY BANSFIELD: hip-hop and rap are fairly distinct.... Hip-hop is a larger cultural milieu, out of which rap comes and is one form of expression or one element of expression in that subculture. But as far as saying the difference between spoken word and rapping... I don't put too fine a point on it. I know you could say there might be conventions, and one might be a capella and one might not, or one might be more metered and one might be a little easier in the flow, having a little more space to

GENEVIÈVE LETARTE: Je me dis d'abord écrivain, mais je suis aussi poète-performeuse. En fait, je me considère comme une artiste multidisciplinaire de l'écriture. C'est-à-dire qu'à partir de l'écriture, il y a différentes choses qui peuvent exister. Je vais peut-être faire un vidéo un jour, qui sait? Mais peu importe la forme que prend mon travail, ça part toujours de l'écriture.

Alex Boutros and Kaarla Sundström at La Vache enragée, *March 1998*
Photo by André Lemelin

17

move. Even a capella within a beat. But those are formal considerations that don't really make a difference in the big picture. I might do one piece that's called a rap piece by some, spoken word by others. I was always the type of person that might do a spoken word piece at a rap show, do a rap piece at a spoken word poetry show.

"I am impure!"

'Performance art' presents another seemingly general term that might apply to what spoken word artists do, especially when their work goes beyond the voice. However, the term 'performance art' comes from the field of visual arts, and carries a lot of conceptual baggage.

COREY FROST: What I want to do is move more in the direction of performance art.... I mean, 'spoken word', even, is

Dayna McLeod
Photo by Juan Guardado
from www.madgenta.com

kind of a problematic label. Although it's a wide label. The first performances I did were material that really could've worked, more or less, at a poetry slam. The stuff that I want to do now would not work in that context. It wouldn't fit into those rules. But that means it has to find a venue that allows for a little broader definition of spoken word.

TETSURO SHIGEMATSU: We always try to present the best angle that we think will appeal the most to whomever we happen to be talking to. I guess that's one of the assets of being involved in something as ambiguous as spoken word.

DAYNA MCLEOD: I hate the term 'spoken word'. I hate being called a spoken word artist, I hate being called a 'slam poet'. I'd rather have the stereotype pouring-mud-over-myself-with-the-Bach-playing-in-the-background 'performance artist' term, than that. If I had to classify myself, I would say that I was a performance artist and a video artist.

ENDRE FARKAS: There were some people trying to come up with names [in the seventies], but the term that started it all was 'postmodern'. You know, postmodern dance, postmodern poetry, postmodern art... the visual arts had, I think, the most labels. It was a catch-all. And then multidiscipline, and interdiscipline. Some people had great debates about what's the difference. Out of that emerged the word 'performance'.

NATHALIE DEROME: When I started, Sylvie Laliberté and I said: "OK, we're doing performance." We were proud that it was *indéfinissable*, but in fact, it's not true. *Inter Art Actuel* magazine, in Quebec City, imposes what is performance art, and what is not. Sometimes they say, "No no no, this is theatre."

And they always say I am impure. I am impure! To say so is completely against the real *mouvement de performance*....

"I'm an artist, that I know for sure"

What could be more a general term than 'artist'? It serves as a place to start, and more significantly, for the many spoken word performers who also work in other media, it allows them to avoid being pigeonholed.

TOM KONYVES: When I first began writing, I would have called it poetry. The next stage was writing experimental poems. I also wrote and performed poems, which I called poetry performances. These performances were based on ideas or concepts I identified with the performance art I was seeing in the late seventies. When I did my poetry performances, I didn't bother to call myself a performance poet. If anything, I would have called it performance art-poetry and myself a performance artist-poet. But these terms really didn't sit well with me, way too elitist, like film-poet didn't sound right, either. After that I began to write and produce videopoems, which were poems meant to be experienced as videos. I called my videos 'videopoems' and myself a 'videopoet'. I had not heard these terms at the time. I guess naming ourselves was a means of defining the new work we were doing — we thought we were pioneers of poetry — but also the means whereby we succeeded in distancing ourselves from mainstream poets.

ENDRE FARKAS: I didn't call myself anything, I wrote poetry. Only when I started performing and people said, "What is it?" I had to think about it because just about everybody at that time, when they were asked what they were doing,

they were saying, 'Postmodern'.... I didn't call myself anything other than a maker of it. In fact, John McAuley had a newsletter he called *Maker*. It's the literal translation of 'artist' from Latin. We were 'makers'.

LEAH VINEBERG: Depending on who I'm speaking with, I have to call myself something else. I find it very difficult, and sometimes I find it very annoying as well, it causes a lot of undue stress. I'm an artist, that I know for sure.

ALEXIS O'HARA: For the longest time I never felt comfortable calling myself an artist, because I felt like I wasn't worthy of that somehow. It's like a mental thing I have to get over. I have to develop that *chutzpah* that so many men have about being able to use the terminology. I've met all these people saying, "I'm an artist," and they weren't even necessarily really producing anything. So I'm more comfortable with calling myself an artist now.

GENEVIÈVE LETARTE: I once took part in a show on CIBL hosted by Yvon Montoya and Pierre Thibeault, it was called *Frénétiques*. The year 2000 was approaching and they had asked questions about Quebec culture. They eventually produced a publication based on that broadcast. On the cover it said "Thirteen Quebec intellectuals address the question." But I'm not an *intellectual*! I'm an *artist*! Even though I'm a writer (laughs). To me, the difference is very clear.

"Everybody's expecting tit-and-ass jokes"

The line between some spoken word performances and stand-up comedy is blurry, especially when taking into consideration Lenny Bruce and Andy

Tom Konyves performs 'In A Station of the Metro'
Photo by Michel Dubreuil
from *Poetry in Performance*
(The Muses' Co. 1982)

GENEVIÈVE LETARTE: Un jour j'ai participé à une émission de radio à CIBL animée par Yvon Montoya et Pierre Thibeault, émission qui s'appelait *Frénétiques*. Ils avaient alors posé des questions concernant la culture au Québec à l'aube de l'an 2000. Finalement, ils ont réalisé une publication à partir de cette émission. Sur la couverture du livre, ils ont écrit "Treize intellectuels québécois répondent à la question". Mais je ne suis pas une *intellectuelle*! Je suis une *artiste*! Même si je suis écrivain (rires). Pour moi, la différence est très claire.

Kaufman, whose routines often veered off into regions not considered traditional material for humour.

JONATHAN GOLDSTEIN: I like making people laugh…. Sometimes I think if I really had the balls, I would do stand-up. Because the thing with spoken word is you can get off a couple of good laughs. And if they don't laugh, then that's OK because it's art. You have that safety net. But with stand-up, the barometer, the bottom line is you gotta get laughs. So there are a lot of comedians who start doing spoken word because it gives them greater room to do all kinds of other stuff.

DAYNA MCLEOD: I've been doing a lot of research on Eric Bogosian and Andy Kaufman. Just in terms of how they had a character, an asshole persona, in some of their stage performances, and just pushed it and let it ride. Andy Kaufman brings people up from the audience, and he basically *humiliates* this one guy, and you're at the edge of your seat…. A woman starts yelling at him from the back of the audience. He says, "What are you, some kinda feminist? The day you can come up here and knock me down is the day I respect you." This woman comes up onstage and they get in a fistfight and she knocks him down, and then OK, phew. It's all staged, but you're sucked in. Kaufman and Bogosian were introducing performance art into the comedy clubs. Which was what I wanted to get into, but it's such a slippery slope with that. Because everybody's expecting tit-and-ass jokes. It's very resistant to the formats.

JAKE BROWN: Just in the last eight months, what I'm trying to do is deliver a content that's similar to what I would be doing if I was a professor, but in a format that's comedic. So I was calling myself a 'dissident comedian'. People listen to me more when they're laughing, so I was using comedy as a tool…. If I could do what Mark Twain succeeded in doing, I'd be happy. He used [comedy] to make fun of the nabobs of American culture on a lecture tour. People would laugh their guts out, they'd pay money to see him. I guess he would call those 'lectures'. It was a real idiom. It's gone, almost.

"A living library of the stories"

'Storytelling' is a particular form of spoken word performance which has been practiced since time immemorial all over the world. It implies a narrative strategy, rather than poetic wordplay or nonlinear thought streams. Storytelling is especially strong in Quebec's francophone oral literature.

TETSURO SHIGEMATSU: If you say you're a storyteller, for some people that's OK, but it brings all this folksy kind of baggage with it. I remember telling one person — she was this very blue-blood aristocrat who was working for some government agency in Japan — "Well, I'm a storyteller. I tell stories." And she said, "Oh, you tell *stories*." And she gave it such an intonation that said, "Oh, you're a *liar*." And I realized that if you just invert the two words suddenly it has such a negative connotation…. Harking back to our university days, there was a lady in class who referred to me, just *en passant*, as the 'story keeper'. I liked the ring of that, I liked the way it sounded. She alluded to the fact that in some older societies, maybe tribal civilizations where there happened to be a strong oral tradition, there'd be a designated person within a tribe that was called 'the story keeper'. And it was their task not only to tell the stories, but also to be a kind of repository, a living library of the stories. So they would collect the stories and they would retell them. And they would choose an apprentice and these stories would be passed on.

"Anyone who wishes to can become a poet"

If spoken word performers come from a literary background, they might simply call themselves a poet or a writer. Again, this depends on how the individual relates to all that the term implies.

BUFFY CHILDERHOSE: I say I write poetry, but if I say I'm a poet, I feel like, "Oh, that's precious." It's also a weird authority. Someone else says that you're a poet.

Jean-Marc Massie
Photo courtesy of the artist

Excerpt: Jean-Marc Massie, *Petit manifeste à l'usage du conteur contemporain.* Montréal, *Planète rebelle*, 2001, p. 63-65. [excerpt translated by SLH]

The *conte-spectacle* [storytelling show] according to Jean-Marc Massie

Throughout literary history, the written tradition earned its credentials, its 'respect capital', to the detriment of the oral tradition. But then both had to yield to the rapid development and power of attraction of audiovisual techniques (cinema, television, video, interactive games...).

On the social level, villages became urbanized (in the best of cases) or simply vanished. The sense of the land became planetary, solidarity and community spirit gave way to individualism, everyone for themselves. In a context such as this one it would be unrealistic to believe that the form of the folk tale could remain intact.

Contrary to the traditional *veillée* [evening gathering] during which the storyteller told his stories spontaneously, in an intimate setting, in front of a familiar audience and very often using a method which was well-known by the community, today's storytelling events are becoming more and more programmed, and presented to an audience that may well have no ties with the storyteller. Like it or not, the oral story has now entered the realm of *entertainment*.

Therefore, the contemporary storyteller's (or 'neo-storyteller')[1] social and cultural ties with the audience are no longer as close and 'intimate' because they no longer necessarily share a common culture which he could no doubt tap into for his references. Today's storyteller must take great care in developing his repertoire at the same time as he must shape his own style.

Because the practice of the oral transmission of stories by elders has almost disappeared, the contemporary storyteller must draw on the repertoire of literary stories or into folk archives, or create his own stories. The ideal method might be a fusion of these two approaches.

In this era of the *conte-spectacle*, storytelling also means knowing how to choose from various narrative processes which borrow from literature as well as from theatre, cinema and song.[2] Certain techniques — such as the flashback, first-person narrative, pastiche, singing-storytelling and the combination of levels of discourse, to name just a few — supported by minimal staging and appropriate lighting, are all vehicles available to contemporary storytellers aiming to capture the attention of an increasingly diverse audience. Some people involved in the revival of storytelling in Quebec have taken this narrative experiment quite far. This has brought about a questioning of the genre....

1. I prefer the expression 'contemporary storyteller' to 'neo-storyteller' because the latter could suggest that today's storytellers are not as good as their predecessors.... As storyteller Michel Hindenoch so accurately observed during the international colloquium on the revival of storytelling in 1989, the particle 'neo' often has a pejorative meaning, and might suggest that today's storytellers could have arrived too late, that they are out of phase, maybe even inauthentic and subject to being disparaged (see Michel Hindenoch, '*Les nouveaux conteurs d'aujourd'hui et leur acculturation*', *Le renouveau du conte / The Revival of Storytelling, op. cit.*, p. 405-413.)

2. Where songs are concerned, 'Belzébuth' by the late Dédé Fortin, and 'The Yankees' by Richard Desjardins are, in my opinion, the work of songwriters who have marvelously married song and storytelling, as had La Bolduc, Félix Leclerc and Gilles Vigneault before them, to name only these few.

It's like somebody else has to say that you're beautiful. You can't really name yourself.

FORTNER ANDERSON: I'm involved with various names, 'spoken word' or 'performance poetry', 'performance art'. That's not really so much my concern. I have various thoughts on it, but for myself, my own personal practice, no. I'm first and foremost a poet.

NAH EE LAH: I didn't want to be called a poet because I knew that my writing was not like the poetry I had been exposed to in school.... School taught me that poetry was abstract, boring, and for the most part, irrelevant to my life experiences. The meanings seemed so deeply spun, they were weaved just beyond my reach. I have since realized that I do not need to redefine my work, nor do I need to label myself 'other'. I am not a spoken word artist, a poet, a dub poet, an MC or a writer. My work is for the ear, page, stage, but primarily for the spirit, because that's what compels me to write.

HÉLÈNE MONETTE: If I was pressed to come up with a definition I'd choose the term 'poet', because I don't consider myself a performer at all, I'm not very physical. True performers explore the body's possibilities, they're energetic, while I just stand behind the microphone. I've never considered what I do as performance, except once perhaps, after seeing myself on video. It was at the Lion d'Or, with Bob Olivier; I was gesturing a bit, but it became a parody of performance, to show that what I was doing wasn't that, precisely.... Writer, artist? I don't know who I am anymore, as a matter of fact. There was a point where I was really racking my brain about it, but now I think other people

name what I am. I'm living, just trying to live....

TODD SWIFT: I have consistently upheld the belief — system — that poetry is the highest cultural / intellectual art or pursuit currently an option, because it is both the most primal, open, elegant and transcendent. You can reach truth and beauty in a way not available through science or standard religion alone. I am a poet. This is the most important 'fact' about me. I believe I am a writer, then a poet, then a fusion poet, then a Canadian fusion poet, then an anglophone Canadian fusion poet. Sometimes I label other poets 'academic' or 'trad' and what my peers do 'fusion' or 'spoken word' or 'performance poetry'. In fact, anyone who wishes to be can become a poet. A poet, period. There is no hierarchy, ultimately. Just genres, styles and values. I choose to be considered a poet now. I've dropped 'performance' from the label. It is just an impediment to so many people receiving me. I had hoped 'fusion' would be a cross-pollinating label, but it hasn't seemed to catch on.

"It's a mixture of words and music and sound"

As the work takes on more complex elements than the simple performance of a 'poem', it becomes more difficult to define it simply as 'poetry'. These elements might be cultural, musical, or the way in which the text is conceived.

DEBBIE YOUNG: Since I've been in Montreal I've been calling myself a dub poet. Prior to Montreal, I was just identifying with poet... and now I'm even more specific.

JASON SELMAN: I'm starting to understand that what I'm doing is part of a jazz poetry tradition, whether I like it or not. But for me that's a goal, I don't want to isolate myself to that element.

IAN FERRIER: It's a mixture of words and music and sound. I used to call it poetry, but it's not quite that anymore, because I don't necessarily feel that it has to be something that you can read on the page. I call it 'performance lit', I guess, because I perform it. But that's about as exact as I can get. It does link to oral. It's all oral tradition as opposed to written.

CATHERINE KIDD: I used to say 'performance prose', because people would come up and say, "Oh, you're that poet." Again, that felt like an external label, because in my own mind, I'd never identified myself as a poet. I didn't think I was a poet, I thought I was a storyteller who made things rhyme because they were easier to memorize that way. Or because I liked the way it sounded, or because it was going to be spoken, I should be paying attention to the musicality. I never named myself a poet. I would say 'performance prose', because they're stories that are edited and tampered with to work on the stage. But I didn't like that phrase either, in trying to get away from the pretension of a phrase, you end up adding to it.... Jack Beets and I have been calling them 'word sound works'. What do we have? We have words, we have sounds, and it's work (laughs).

"I'm not a 'self-definer'"

Ultimately, finding a name for any practice sets limits on it. 'Spoken word' isn't a demographic, nor is it a definition; at best, it's a term that points to the common element among the

Jason Selman at Concordia University, September 1999

wide array of different practices we've encountered in this particular Montreal community. While performers might accept it, reject it, invent new ways of describing their work, or not name it at all, what is important is that the work gets done with as little concern about labels as possible.

ANNE STONE: I've tried different sorts of labels... with the novel *Hush*, I put on the back that I was a writer and a performance artist, because I was trying to avoid 'performance poet'. Because it's not really poetry. I did want to get at the voice and the sound, so when people looked at the book they could understand that there are portions of it that are really just written to be read aloud.... I'm leery of looking at things in a way that closes people off, and I find some people will close themselves off or offer excuses to push things away.

ALEXIS O'HARA: At one point I had this term I invented, late night after a lot of marijuana, that was 'trans-orationist'. I thought that was pretty cool, to go with using an oral form, to go beyond the

Massie, con't...

techniques (celles du *flashback*, de la narration au «je», du pastiche et du mélange des niveaux de discours, pour ne nommer que celles-là), soutenues par une mise en scène minimaliste et un éclairage approprié, représentent autant d'opportunités qui s'offrent au conteur contemporain pour capter l'attention d'un auditoire de plus en plus diversifié. Certains acteurs du renouveau du conte au Québec ont poussé très loin cette expérimentation narrative. Cela n'a pas été sans provoquer une réflexion sur le genre...»

HÉLÈNE MONETTE: À la limite, s'il fallait absolument se définir, je choisirais le terme "poète", parce que je ne me considère pas du tout comme une performeuse étant donné que je ne suis pas physique. Les vrais performeurs exploitent les possibilités de leur corps, ils sont énergiques, tandis que moi, je reste plantée devant le micro. Je n'ai jamais considéré ce que je faisais comme étant de la performance, sauf peut-être une fois, après que je me sois vue sur un vidéo. C'était au Lion d'Or, avec Bob Olivier; je gesticulais un peu, mais ça devenait une parodie de la performance pour montrer que, justement, je n'en faisais pas... Écrivain, artiste? En fait, je ne sais plus qui je suis. À un certain moment, je me cassais la tête à me questionner là-dessus, mais aujourd'hui, je pense que ce sont les autres qui me nomment. Moi, je vis, j'essaie de vivre...

SYLVAIN FORTIER: Je dirais que je suis un artiste étant donné que je fais de la musique, du théâtre et de la poésie. Je suis un artiste dans le sens large du terme, parce que ça inclut ces disciplines. Quant à me définir plus précisément, non. Je ne suis pas un "auto-définitionnel". Je n'aime pas avoir à dire: "Je suis un poète spoken word deuxième vague, blablabla..." Je ne m'amuse pas à ça. Ou si c'est le cas, c'est pour rigoler comme je viens de le faire. Je peux définir mon travail et affirmer que telle création est un poème, un roman-poème, une pièce rock, une pièce de musique actuelle, du jazz et ainsi de suite, mais je ne m'aventure pas plus loin.

PATRICIA LAMONTAGNE: Je n'arrive pas à me définir. Ma pratique artistique est trop large. J'écris, je compose de la musique, je fais de la mise en scène. Alors non, ça ne m'intéresse pas de me nommer. J'ai souvent dit en riant que j'étais une bâtarde, je trouve que ça me va très bien et je suis très heureuse avec ça. Le fait de ne pas me définir m'a laissé plus de liberté. Je ne peux pas dire que je suis une poète, comme je ne peux pas dire que je suis uniquement une musicienne. C'est un peu un *no woman's land.*

regular idea of just speaking. But it's a little wordy. It's good, it has a kind of snake-charmer appeal to it, but I'll have to find something a little more populist.

ALEX BOUTROS: We came up with the term 'mouth music', which is also not an original term. It's from a technique that a lot of drummers who are learning the tabla in India use, for example. Instead of practicing on the drum they learn how to say the rhythms orally. It seems to be working. At least it has 'music' in it.

NORMAN NAWROCKI: Pete Bailey said to me, "You know, your stuff, it's not really poetry. And it's not really storytelling, it's not really songs, it's not really theatre. It's really got rhythm to it, it's very rhythmic, and it's all about activist stuff, it's very activist, it's very rhythm activist, sort of rhythm activism." That's what I called it then. It's since evolved and now I consider it cabaret. I'm a cabaret artist, I do cabaret, and cabaret is broad enough to incorporate spoken word with music, with theatre, whatever, with 'poetry'.

SYLVAIN FORTIER: I'd say I'm an artist because I make music, do theatre and write poetry. I'm an artist in the broad sense of the word, because it includes these disciplines. As for defining myself more specifically, no. I'm not a 'self-definer'. I don't like to have to say: "I'm a second wave spoken word poet, blah blah blah..." I don't play at that. Or if I do, it's for laughs like I just did now. I'm able to define my work — I can state that this is a poem, a poem-novel, a rock piece, a contemporary music piece, jazz, and so on, but I don't venture any further.

PATRICIA LAMONTAGNE: I can't seem to define what I am. My art practice is too broad: I write, I compose music, I do stage direction. So no, I'm not interested in naming myself. I've often joked that I'm a bastard, I find this suits me very well, I'm happy with that. Not defining myself left me freer. I can't say I'm a poet, like I can't say I'm exclusively a musician. It's some kind of no woman's land.

Geneviève Letarte under a piano in the early eighties
Photo courtesy of the artist

2. IS SPOKEN WORD A TYPE OF LITERATURE?

Because of its emphasis on text, and because the artists produce the texts they perform, it can be argued that spoken word is closely related to literary forms of expression. We asked Montreal performers for their thoughts on the relationship of spoken word to literature. For many, 'literature' means the printed word, and the question revolved around the similarities and differences between texts written to be read, and texts written to be heard by an audience. For others, any kind of creative text is literary.

"A counterculture of the word"

There is a current of thought which links spoken word to a wider trend of popularization occurring in literature. Some features of this shift include an emphasis on a more accessible, unpolished vernacular language, autobiographical or confessional texts, pop cultural references, self-publishing of zines and chapbooks, and the acceptance of 'low' forms like comic book culture as legitimate forms of art.

IZ COX: If I read a literary magazine — as in the 'writers' literary, not all Canadian writers, but a lot of what I see today... I don't feel it. I get this blandness. Even though the words are great, and the sentences, and it's grammatically correct and the pictures are very clear, sometimes it doesn't make me want to *eat* it. It doesn't make me want to savour it, it doesn't make me want to take a bath in it or take it on as my self. What I see a lot is a style, when people get straight out of university and college they have this style to their poetry that's

very similar. Education is great, but get out there and see the world. I feel that there's this code of ethics of writing that really sometimes destroys a picture. It's like classical painting. I think that poetry is like Picasso sometimes, or like Van Gogh or Dali. It's mixed, it's cartoons, comic books. Actually, it makes me very angry that I don't see more of people who have this rawness to them.

JUSTIN McGRAIL: One thing I liked about what Fluffy Pagan Echoes did, and what I recognized later in the whole scene, was how in spoken word everyone's unique background had an easier way of coming out. In poetry on the page, there are concessions to poetry in general that you have to make in order to get it printed on the page. Whereas in spoken word there aren't as many constraints. I felt a lot more individuality could come out, so you learned a lot more about people. I've often said that I didn't know anybody in the group. I literally learned everything I knew about everybody through poetry.

GOLDA FRIED: As a writer, I like things to be real. I'm very aware of what people think. I never wanted it to be, "Oh, she's literary." (laughs) I wanted it to be, "Oh, she's a rock person," or, "She's unpretentious." Not that literary would necessarily be pretentious, but I think I was definitely scared of that.

TRISH SALAH: I'm very much interested in and working with a lot of the conventions of what is called poetic writing or literary writing. I certainly draw from the tool kit of high modernism in my writing, as well as a whack of other places. But my writing is also porno-graphic, and invested and obsessed with pop culture. So it suffers from the same disease a lot of literary writing suffers from, which is to say it's always sort of beside itself, or interested in something outside of itself and turning itself into that in one way or another. That's partly because the idea of literary writing, in its most classically-valued sense, isn't sustainable. It isn't desir-able in a certain way. It lends itself to not only canon-formation, but just a ranking of artistic forms, a ranking of cultural practices that I'm not that interested in supporting.

KAIE KELLOUGH: You do have a lot of peo-ple who will get up onstage and whose work isn't necessarily literature, but they can somehow make it entertaining. Or whose work isn't necessarily musi-cal, but they can still entertain with it. And even if they don't know how to bring the theatrical element they can put it in rhythm... so spoken word doesn't *have* to be literary.

Kaie Kellough
Photo courtesy of the artist

HUGH HAZELTON: I'm kind of losing patience with people who still write tra-ditional poetry. As far as my own stuff goes, I want to keep pushing the limits. That's how I see poetry: as always push-ing the limits. I'm not a performance poet, I'm basically a writer who has per-formance elements in his poetry. I was always very careful about that, the tim-ing and so on. The lines were getting longer and longer, I was reading more and more sound things — chanting, stuttering — into my poems. The last chapbook I did, a lot of it was printed sideways so that you could get the entire line in. I still play a lot with concrete poetry, with typography, so I have things that are set up centered, and then they look kind of like a human body.

VINCE TINGUELY: There's a real schism for some reason between creative writ-ing, which I think is an art, and the rest of the arts. They're very separate. One of the things that we found early on with Fluffy Pagan Echoes was that we could perform in a bar, we could do a reading series at Yellow Door, or we could be in a gallery. It worked every-where. I find myself more comfortable in a fine arts setting, in that headspace, in some ways, than I ever have in what you would call a literary scene. People seem more able to understand the idea of having a less structured approach to a text. I send a text to *Fiddlehead*, and it comes back, and the note — which I'm getting used to hearing — says, "Well, this isn't a short story. The characters aren't quite developed this way or that way." Very narrow parameters of what a story should be. In the art milieu it's much more open. They're not even sure what constitutes a painting or what constitutes performance art. It's all up in the air all the time.

RAN ELFASSY: A lot of the people that come into this kind of very text-based performance are coming at it in terms of writing, in terms of text.... I just think that most of the people who perform — there are definitely exceptions — tend to be coming from Canadian poetry, basically. That's something that kind of bothered me about the bad, the nega-tive humour performance of spoken word, it does tend to be confessional. There aren't really many people who are telling stories for the sake of stories and kind of leaping out of it. I was just as guilty of doing really confessional work. I don't think it's going to change.

ANNA-LOUISE CRAGO: Zoë Whittall be-came aware of both spoken word and the zine scene around the same time.

26

She really introduced me to so much in terms of spoken word and zines and whatnot. And to me, 'riot grrl'-type zines or anarchist zines were all about spilling your guts. You could totally rant your ass off and be nasty and use really cutting words and be a harsh teenaged girl. And so to me, the idea of doing spoken word was so much about reading what would be in the zine, which at that point was pretty much diary entries. I think zines are literary entities in and of their own. They're so portable and just there to be gobbled up in a very personal way.... I think spoken word has a literary source in that kind of zine world, and at the same time I think that zines are really sort of ambiguous, as to where they fit.

TRISH SALAH: In Montreal, there seems to be an ongoing and sustained energy around both performance and independent bookmaking of various sorts. I think of those things very much in tandem with spoken word, partly because that was my own entry point to it, and partly because the same networks which produced spoken word through organizing, and through an interest in spoken word's possible interruption of literature as a canonical practice, or as a canonical body of work, produced chapbooks and zines. They produced a counterculture of the word, whether it was coming out of a mouth or out of an offset press.

"We are changing our idea of what is literary"

Some spoken word artists see their work as a return to the Western oral traditions of past centuries. Any argument that it isn't literary is largely based on technical differences between spoken and written texts.

MICHEL GARNEAU: Language is an oral tradition. This is so obvious that we've come to forget it — especially literary people who, at one time, conceived that language meant writing. Which is terrible since, on the contrary, writing in a way means the death of language. True, writing remains, but it is merely our memory, it is there only to attest to language. Language, on the other hand, is in permanent evolution, it's alive. It's like a huge river and we've no control over what will end up in it.... Sometimes things of beauty, at other times, shit. When I was young, I had an older brother who learned poems by heart, and another who painted. An older brother who painted but who also would sit at the piano and improvise to seduce girls (laughs), basically. As the youngest I was always surrounded by poetry, I fell into this magic potion when I was little. As far as I knew, poetry had never been restricted to writing and later on, when I realized that most people mistook poetry for merely a written form, I found this awful. When I say about a poet that he is typographical (laughs), it's just about the worst insult. It means that his poems can only exist on the page — the poem has been written, has been read, is dead. For example, Mallarmé's *Le Coup de dé.* Seriously, I do have a certain respect for that history but at the same time, I find it utterly decadent. To me, poetry's great moments in typography feel like moments where something is ending. While the oral tradition, where there's always room for improvisation, allows the same text to be reborn in various ways when it's recited.

ZOË WHITTALL: I think that spoken word as a genre isn't ever taken as seriously as literature. It's seen as very youth, urban-oriented. There are also stereo-

Zoë Whittall, July 1997

MICHEL GARNEAU: Le langage est une tradition orale. C'est tellement évident qu'on en est venu à l'oublier. Et plus particulièrement les littéraires qui, à une certaine époque, ont conclu que le langage était l'écriture. Ce qui est terrible puisque, au contraire, l'écriture signifie en quelque sorte la mort du langage. L'écriture reste mais elle n'est que notre mémoire, elle n'est là que pour *témoigner* du langage. Le langage, lui, est en évolution permanente, il est vivant. C'est comme un immense fleuve et on n'a pas le contrôle sur ce qui se retrouvera dedans... Parfois ce sera de belles choses, d'autres fois ce sera de la merde. Quand j'étais petit, j'avais un grand frère qui apprenait des poèmes par coeur, et un autre qui était peintre. Un grand frère peintre, mais qui s'installait au piano et qui improvisait des choses pour séduire les filles (rires). Moi j'ai toujours été entouré de poésie, je suis tombé dedans quand j'étais petit. À ma connaissance, la poésie ne s'était jamais limitée à l'écrit, et lorsque plus tard j'ai réalisé que la plupart des gens prenaient la poésie uniquement pour une forme d'écriture, j'ai trouvé ça terrible. Moi, quand je dis d'un poète qu'il est typographique (rires), c'est à peu près la pire des insultes. C'est-à-dire que ses poèmes ne peuvent vivre que sur une page — le poème a été écrit, a été lu, puis il est mort. Par exemple, *Le Coup de dé* de Mallarmé. Sérieusement, j'ai un certain respect pour cette histoire mais en même

continued...

temps, je la trouve profondément décadente. Les grands moments typographiques de la poésie me donnent l'impression d'être des moments de fin. À l'inverse, la tradition orale, puisqu'elle permet toujours d'improviser, fait qu'un même texte peut renaître sous différentes variantes.

JEAN-PAUL DAOUST: Le lien que j'établirais entre la littérature et le spoken word est que, d'après moi, on renoue en ce moment avec quelque chose de très ancien qui remonte à une époque où la lecture n'était pas accessible à tous, lorsque l'imprimerie n'existait pas et que la majorité des gens étaient illettrés. Ceux qui lisaient se devaient de divertir leur entourage en leur faisant part de leurs lectures, et pour soutenir l'intérêt de leur public, il fallait qu'ils se montrent énergiques. Je pense que c'est ça, les racines profondes du spoken word. Et par rapport à la poésie écrite qui parfois peut devenir poussiéreuse ou, en tout cas, prisonnière d'elle-même, le spoken word aère le texte et permet au poète de garder contact avec la réalité, avec les gens qui l'entourent. Le spoken word va à l'encontre de l'image du poète dans sa tour d'ivoire, et je trouve que c'est bon. Il amène le poète à se déplacer et celui-ci doit arriver à faire ressentir quelque chose à son public. En ça, le spoken word rejoint sans doute notre culture parce que, maintenant, il y a la télé, le vidéo et le cinéma, et autrefois il y avait des conteurs. Je pense que ça fait partie de nous, d'ailleurs plus que des Européens qui ont peut-être davantage oublié leur tradition orale. Je crois que notre littérature est moins hiérarchisée à cause du côté historique; ça ne fait pas si longtemps qu'on a une littérature québécoise. Nous, on n'a pas eu Ronsard et compagnie. On était pris avec les moustiques et la découverte du pays, on n'avait pas le temps d'écrire. C'est peut-être tout ça qui fait que maintenant, on est plus libres qu'eux, parce qu'on n'est pas enchaînés par un lourd passé littéraire. Des lectures de poésie en Europe, c'est très tranquille. Quand des Américains – des Québécois, des gens de Moncton, de Toronto – arrivent là-bas, c'est évident qu'ils détonent... Le *Festival de poésie de Trois-Rivières* a beaucoup "décongestionné" les poètes européens. Tandis que les poètes de chez nous se lèvent, prennent le micro et se promènent, les autres poètes – souvent Français – sont là, figés derrière leur cravate avec leurs petites lunettes sur le bout du nez, à

types — sometimes based in truth (laughs). (In a sing-song cadence) if you talk like this, anybody can do spoken word. You can get up there and read the phone book. With slams and the whole contest and MuchMusic thing, sometimes it is like that. There's a pop music, top ten element to spoken word. But at the same time that I diss it, I also love it.

ALEX BOUTROS: The relationship between spoken word and literature I always categorize as 'uneasy' (laughs). I don't think that many of the people I talk to are comfortable with that relationship, because we're not comfortable with having to make a split between spoken word and literature.... It's difficult to say, "This piece is clearly literature and this piece is clearly spoken word." But there is a desire for some of us to be up onstage performing without a piece of paper in our hand.... Not simply to read your book on a book tour to promote it, but for the pure act. That is different from producing a book of poetry. It doesn't need to be written down, it can remain partly oral. There is a want for the interaction with the audience. Not that literary people don't have that desire, I think they do, but I think the way that the system works, you get a book published and you go on a book tour, and all the inbetween times, there isn't a lot of opportunity... I think for spoken word artists it's different. We frequently perform, any time, at the drop of a hat. Often for free (laughs).

KAARLA SUNDSTRÖM: It's very difficult, even in a classroom context, to talk about the orality of a text that is clearly there, without actually hearing it. Reading and listening — you can communicate in both, you can communicate the same thing, but there are differences

between the two. If I'm teaching in front of my class and I read a paragraph out of the textbook, students have a much harder time accessing what it is I'm saying. But if I just spoke it off the top of my head, somehow there's a different type of communication that is more immediate. Not to draw a clear division, but a text functions well when it's read privately. Speaking functions much better when there's actual human interaction possible.... You need to be talking *to* an audience if you're in front of them, which is why we can definitely say that we're not on the side of literature. Because it doesn't function as well to read our poetry, as it does to read somebody's book. It's a different type of appreciation.

JEAN-PAUL DAOUST: The link I'd make between literature and spoken word is that we're presently revisiting something ancient, that goes back to a time when reading wasn't accessible to all, when printing didn't exist and most people were illiterate. Those who knew how to read had to entertain the people around them by sharing their readings, and in order to keep their audience's interest, they had to be dynamic. I think that these are the deep roots of spoken word. And in relation to written poetry, which can sometimes get musty or, at least, a prisoner of itself, spoken word breathes into the text and allows the poet to keep contact with reality, with the people around him. Spoken word goes against the image of the poet in his ivory tower, and that's a good thing. It forces a shift on the poet's part and he has to make his audience feel something. In this way spoken word no doubt intersects our culture because, now there's TV, video and film, but before that there were storytellers. I think it's part of us, even more so than for Europeans, who have perhaps forgotten their oral tradition to a greater degree. Our literature is less hierarchical because of history — I mean there was no *Québécois* literature until fairly recently. We haven't had Ronsard and company. We were dealing with mosquitoes and discovering the land, we didn't have time to write. Maybe all of this explains why we're freer than they are now, we're not chained to a heavy literary past. In Europe, poetry readings are very quiet affairs. When North Americans — *Québécois*, or people from Moncton, or Toronto — get there, we obviously stand out…. The *Festival de Poésie de Trois-Rivières* has decongested European poets a whole lot. Our poets get up, grab the microphone, walk around, while the other poets — often French — are all stiff behind their ties, their little glasses on the tip of their nose, reading the text in such a way that we can barely hear it. For me, there's nothing exotic about spoken word. It's part of daily life. Besides, young poets are very close to this form of poetry, because the words that are written will often be spoken. Whereas before, we thought that the written word was not necessarily made to be spoken, or if so, exceptionally, on important occasions. Today, you go to a bar, there's music, atmosphere, people smoking, drinking, then, at a given moment, the poet appears. It's no coincidence that we launched a poetry festival here, I think it comes naturally to us. Otherwise, we wouldn't have done it. So spoken word may be a specialty of ours, making poetry accessible, emphasizing the oral aspect. I find this very important because in poetry, rhythm is of the essence. This may be how we're removing the cobwebs from poetic rhythm, updating it, making it contemporary.

KEN NORRIS: In editing *Word Up*[11], and in writing an afterword to it, I tried to make a case that spoken word is an intrinsic part of literature, always has been, always will be. It goes all the way back to the Irish bards, it goes back to Homer, it comes forward to Charles Olson, and now Sheri-D Wilson. Performance has always been an intrinsic part of poetry, and most poetry benefits from being read aloud. Even the conventional looking stuff that sits nicely on the page benefits from being read aloud. Robert Frost's poetry benefits greatly from being read aloud.

MARTA COOPER: Chaucer was not intended to be read on the page. It was read to the court. It was an oral literary tradition, in the Middle Ages. Most of the gentry were *orally* literate, which means these people had incredible powers of memory. Most people couldn't sit down and read a book, but the books were so expensive that you wouldn't do that anyway. A large part of Chaucer's job was to read to the court. There has been an extraordinarily short period of time that literature *has* been written and not spoken, and I think we're coming out of that now. Two people I think of off the top of my head who are probably on their way to becoming very successful writers, and will write their whole lives, and may well end up in the Can. Lit. canon, are Anne Stone and Catherine Kidd. I'd be very surprised if, when all is said and done, spoken word is not included in their bios in the *Oxford Anthology of Canadian Lit*. So I think we are changing canon, we are changing our idea of what is literary, and I think to a large extent it's a response to the audio-visual age.

DEBBIE YOUNG: If you read dub poetry, dub poets often write in quatrains, with couplets…. I studied the British way of

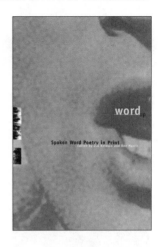

lire le texte pour qu'on l'entende à peine. Pour moi, le spoken word n'a rien d'exotique. Il fait partie de notre quotidien. Et d'ailleurs, les jeunes poètes sont très proches de cette forme poétique puisque souvent la parole qui est écrite va aussi être dite. Tandis qu'avant, on pensait que la parole écrite n'était pas nécessairement faite pour être dite, ou sinon, exceptionnellement, dans des grandes occasions. Aujourd'hui, on va dans des bars, il y a de la musique, il y a une ambiance, les gens fument, boivent, puis à un moment donné, le poète arrive. Ce n'est pas pour rien qu'on a lancé un festival de poésie ici, je pense que c'est vraiment naturel pour nous. Sinon, on ne l'aurait pas fait. Alors le spoken word, c'est peut-être une spécialité qu'on a de rendre la poésie accessible, en mettant l'emphase sur l'oralité. Et ça, je trouve que c'est très important car en poésie le rythme est primordial. C'est peut-être dans ce sens-là qu'on dépoussière le rythme poétique, qu'on l'actualise, qu'on le rend contemporain.

[11] Various authors. *Word Up – Spoken Word Poetry in Print.* Battson, Jill & Norris, Ken, ed., Toronto: Key Porter Books, 1995.

Jeremiah Wall, 1997

doing things, and there is a lot of overlapping. Well of course there would be! Jamaica was a British colony, we were educated in British school systems. So the iambic pentameter will jump out at you. If people know about these forms, then they will see how similar it is in some respects.

ATIF SIDDIQI: I think society in general has become much more orally-inclined than they were before.... With books being published on CD or on tape, that's encouraged the whole medium to become much more spoken and oral as well. With people being able to buy the CDs and tapes and drive to work — in a lot of American cities, for example — and being able to listen to a book instead of reading it, because of time constraints.

TRISH SALAH: I would say that in the recent wave of spoken word performance, articulated as spoken word performance, as I've encountered it in Canada, there is an investment in disrupting a notion of literature and literary value and of writing on the page as having a certain primacy or authority. I think that there are a whack of traditions, both non-Western — in terms of popular cultural forms — and Western; basically folk forms, whether those folk forms are rap or storytelling or narrative musical forms like ballads and such. Each of the whole array of twentieth-century performance art practices has their own agenda in relationship to literature, or doesn't give a flying fuck about it. I think there's certainly various types of cross-fertilization that take place, and various types of interruptions that spoken word effects within contemporary literary practice. I also think that it's a two-way street, and that popular forms as well as avant-garde

forms of spoken word draw upon literary tradition in myriad ways. There are certainly spoken word artists, as there are literary theorists and writers, who are interested in disavowing those connections, largely to make claims for their own practice.

"The orality of dub poetry"

While oral literature is considered 'new' in mainstream Western culture, it has always been a strong living tradition in the African diasporic culture. Both dub poetry and hip-hop forms of spoken word spring from this source.

JEREMIAH WALL: Black culture is avant-garde in this oral tradition or poetic application of the beat, and white people picked it up a few years later. Dub poetry was not considered at all part of the mainstream poetry scene in Canada, but Lillian Allen was the best-selling poet in her recordings and even in publication. People in the literary establishment went, "Well this is not poetry." But fucking right it was poetry.

DEBBIE YOUNG: What I've been taught, what I've learned, what I've seen, and experienced is that dub poetry is coming straight out of the oral tradition in West Africa. Brought straight over from the slaves. It's the type of poetry that says you don't need a lot of extra added things to talk to people. You can just talk to them straight, so that they understand what you're saying.... The conditions under which dub poetry came out forced it to be this way. It was about people not being able to go to university or high school. And people saying, "This is not the only way for you to deconstruct the society around you, to go to university or high school." Is the point of community to be able to talk to people openly? It's very different when you sit by yourself in a corner in your house and read a book. It's a very solitary act. I'm not disrespecting reading, because I read. We're talking about different ways that communities operate. The orality of dub poetry is necessary if it's going to stay true to itself. So in that respect, you need a performer / griot. You need somebody to talk to people. You need to use the body as an instrument. You need to use your voice. You need to use all of the abilities that you can, to engage people in that genre.

KAARLA SUNDSTRÖM: If you study Caribbean poetry and you've never heard *patois* from Jamaica, and you're reading a poem that is written in that type of language, it's a completely different experience than if you press 'play' and you hear the author or somebody who does speak *patois* perform it. Even if you don't understand *patois*, when somebody's performing it, you'll get it. It has a life of its own when it's spoken.

ALEX BOUTROS: I think that's the same for the way that a lot of spoken word artists in Montreal use English. There's something that happens there. I'm not saying it's a language of its own or a dialect of its own, but you don't get it when you read it on the page.

DEBBIE YOUNG: I think to read dub poetry, the rhythm of the language jumps out at you. The nature of dub poetry says — predominantly, not all of the time — that what you're saying must be clear. Dub poetry has been disrespected in the past, and probably continues to be disrespected, because it doesn't necessarily conform to the British way of writing.... Maybe it's not that different, maybe it's just a question of language

What is Dub Poetry?

DEBBIE YOUNG: Dub poetry, the phrase itself was coined in the late seventies, by Oku Onuora. He was not considered, prior to that, a poet as such, but when he was in jail — for supposedly being a Robin Hood of sorts — he was experimenting with the version side the record, where the instrumentals are. He was experimenting with that and was chanting to that. That's what the DJs were doing, but he was talking more than singing, so he coined the phrase 'dub poetry'. The genre was specific in that it was spoken in the Nation language of Jamaica which, because of slavery, is a *mélange* of West African languages with an English base. And what he was talking about was very specific to the working class and poor peoples of Jamaica. He was talking about the poverty levels, the degradation, and all the other socio-economic issues. And then people like Linton Kweisi Johnson were around at the same time. Linton had access to a whole different group of people, people living in England, and a lot of Jamaicans living in England, who migrated there. And so he had access to a lot more resources to do work with dub poetry, to put it on the map. In Jamaica there was Mutabaruka... Oku Onuora, Michael Smith — who is my favourite poet of all time. He was working with Linton too; he was stoned to death in the early eighties, I believe 1983. Miss Lou has to be credited first and foremost for all of this that I'm saying, because she, in the fifties and sixties, was brave enough to write in the Nation language and brave enough to write of some of the oral stories that have been passed along in the Nation language, at a time when, because of colonialism, the Jamaican language was looked down upon. Anybody who spoke it was considered to be a part of the underclass and not prestigious enough. And the academia reinforced all of this.

Debbie Young at her CD launch, April 6, 2000
Photo by Chris Kralik

and a question of choosing to not overindulge in metaphors and similes, and not overindulge in the density of the poem.

ALEX BOUTROS: I think there's a continuum.... Those readers at Harbourfront[12] can read with a great deal of feeling, but there's also oral work that can be very literary. There's a huge tradition of that, especially in African-influenced writing in Canada and in the States and the Caribbean. I think Kaarla's and my work is even moving away from the tradition of those oral literatures that are also literate, or 'lit/oratures'. I think we're moving more towards music and less towards a literary genre.

ANTHONY BANSFIELD: I did a study of Black Canadian writing, African Canadian writing. That was at university in Montreal, in the literature department, English Literature. I considered the spoken word stuff to be literature as much as novels. I was looking at novels written by Austin Clarke as well as dub poetry pieces by Lillian Allen, side by side. I don't make a big distinction in terms of whether it's literature or not. I do see it as literary.... I always saw spoken word pieces as part of a tradition in terms of culture. They're not something that I really segment off. For example, in my paper, I would quote some Calypsonians like Sparrow, or maybe somebody like George Lamming, who's considered a very literary type of writer. For my purposes they were equally significant, what they had to say on West Indian Caribbean culture, Afro-Caribbean culture, and political processes dealing with colonialism in mental terms and in material ways. I always looked at culture as a whole thing that could provide some insights as well as inspiration in whatever form, spiritually

Anthony Bansfield, September 1999

or socially. I don't really want to say that it's literary, it's not literary. To me they're points of reference in a culture.

"Splashy and flashy"

A common argument against spoken word's legitimacy as an art form, is that the live performance of text allows for a lack of 'literary' rigour and excellence.

MARTA COOPER: For people who tend to write poetry more traditionally, or who think of themselves as 'poets' as opposed to spoken word people, I think it takes them a lot longer to get up onstage. If you think of yourself as a poet the point is not to get onstage. Whereas the point in doing spoken word is to get onstage. This means everybody gets to see your work when you're very much in a developing stage, and perhaps your work isn't as interesting. Whereas when you think of yourself as writing, then that development is more private. Certainly a misconception which I held and which many people held and probably still hold, was that spoken word wasn't very good. For instance, there were a lot of people who used this fashionable voice, instead of developing their own voice.

SCOTT DUNCAN: A novel is more than the story itself. The interaction with the reader is to draw you into a universe through the narrative. In spoken word, I don't think you're so much drawn into a universe, you're presented one. A good spoken word piece deals in so many different aspects of language than simply words themselves. Because it's out loud, it comes with body language, performance artistry, acting abilities, and nuance. A writer has to rely so much more on just the words, and less on the rest of it.

12 An annual literary festival in Toronto.

And I think that's where the dangerous area is.

COREY FROST: What if someone said to you, "Spoken word is really about embellishing bad writing by making it splashy and flashy?"

VINCE TINGUELY: Well, it's quite possible to do that. But bad writers get published, too. Frequently.

PETER BRAWLEY: They say that about everything, self-indulgence, anything that's really available to anybody. Let's face it, that's one of its beautiful things, it's a real people's art. It does leave room to hear that naive brilliant thing in some younger person who's got something to say. In a way it's like existential psychotherapy, like R.D. Laing and all that jazz.

TODD SWIFT: I've been twice elected the Quebec representative of the League of Canadian Poets.... They weren't as interested in spoken word poetry, and they continued to adhere to the concept that really, poets are people that write books. They didn't see multi-media performances as equal to texts. In fact, I introduced the concept that people who wrote chapbooks or had CDs could also be members, which opened the way for a few performance poets to enter, but very few actually did.

VINCE TINGUELY: It's almost ideological, though. The people who bring up these criticisms of spoken word as no-talents parading their lack of talent on the stage, they set themselves up as an elite.... So of course they're going to attack anything that falls outside of their purview.... What struck me, before the spoken word scene happened, was that the young people who were trying to get things started were imitating older people. Showing up at their readings in suits and ties, just being very officious. They were career-building. My interest is in the work, not in the appearance of work, which is what I think is a career.

NAH EE LAH: Unfortunately, historically, the Western world's been dictating what happens around the *whole* world. That is the mentality that is infiltrating all aspects of everything, down to whether or not it's poetry if it's not on the page. So what happens to the cultures where they don't do poetry on the page, where they have griots whose whole tradition is to record orally the history, and to perform it? I am not interested in getting into the difference between poetry on the page or poetry on the stage, because to me, it's creation. It's not a short story, it's not a novel, it's creating.... That debate comes from a very arrogant stance. It comes from being bred in such a privileged way, where you believe that what you do is the essence and the norm. Instead of establishing a norm, and making everybody else find a name, let's just say we're all creating and leave it at that.

"Heavy Chevy shocking shit"

Many spoken word artists identify themselves first as poets or writers; performance is one of many means of conveying the poem. For these artists, there is no question that spoken word is a literary form; they're simply stretching it in new ways.

JOHN GIORNO: The thing I discovered in the early, middle sixties, was that the rock and roll club was a venue. The LP record was also a venue which one could take to the radio, and then

LP by John Giorno and William S. Burroughs
Cover design and photo by Les Levine

instead of being the three of us listening to an LP record there were ten thousand on the radio.... Performance is just another venue, plain and simple. It's just another venue for the poet. Now, previous to the last fifty years, the *only* venues were print: the book and the magazine. The written word, for me, is very important, because there'd be no poem if one didn't write it down. When something arises out of one's mind, the first place it goes is a piece of paper, whether it be on a computer or a typewriter. It's just, the book is no longer prime, nor is the magazine prime. But performance is more important in my case than the book. And then where you take it after that. The recording of the performance, and the CD and the video that gets made out of it, the broadcast of the video, the radio. Those are all extensions of performance. That's the subtlety, but it's all just another version, another venue, a facility of being that simple thing, a poet.

AKIN ALAGA: Well, I call it poetry, when it's a poem. Whether it's spoken word or not, for me it's still poetry (laughs). First of all, it's got to work on the page. It's literary, in the sense that I want to be able to publish it, and so then anybody else can take it and go and perform it, act it out.

JULIE CRYSLER: When I write stuff I try to make it work as both things. I think in a lot of cases I'm quite unsuccessful, but it was a great preoccupation of mine to figure out a way to display something on a piece of paper that would give people at least an idea of the cadence and what it might sound like.

SYLVAIN FORTIER: Yes, my texts are literary. But when I write, I pay a lot of attention to sound and rhythm. I often

read them out loud when I'm writing. And sometimes I change some words because out loud, they don't sound good. Usually, when I read my good poems, I notice things that won't be perceived when I recite them onstage. And vice versa: onstage, people will perceive things that would have less effect if they had only read the poem. So in this sense I'm playing on both fronts at the same time. In what I consider my better poems, I'm able to carry it off. When it happens I think all's well, my poems are well-balanced, they're strong in both areas... but when it's not so good, it's either more spoken word or more literary. Even when there's a good beat in the text, in the words themselves, it doesn't mean it'll necessarily sound good when I recite it. When you read it out loud, it's easy to hear if it works. And this shows up on the page too — it produces a better written text.... For me, poetry is a feast of language, a bit like theatre. And though rhythm is very important to me, images are too. I like to present my texts onstage because it adds a certain dimension, and I like seeing them on paper because then they take on another dimension. This is how I create. This is my concept of poetry. Let's say I don't consider myself specifically a spoken word poet or a literary poet; instead, the poetry I write belongs as much to spoken word as it does to books, to the literary realm.

ENDRE FARKAS: It's language. Since I work with words and language, literature is a body of work, of words, and that's certainly what I feel I do.... Words just carry meaning, there's no getting away from it. But I don't like being just "this kind of writer." I've experimented all my life, so far, and there were times when I wrote straight poems, there

SYLVAIN FORTIER: Oui, mes textes sont littéraires. Mais lorsque je les écris, je porte une très grande attention à la sonorité et au rythme. Souvent, je les lis à voix haute en écrivant. Et puis il m'arrive de changer des mots parce que, à voix haute, ça sonne mal. À mon sens, même quand tu as une bonne rythmique dans le texte, dans les mots mêmes, ça ne veut pas nécessairement dire qu'il va bien sonner quand tu vas le réciter. En le lisant à voix haute, c'est facile de vérifier s'il fonctionne. Et puis après, sur la feuille, ça paraît aussi. Ça fait un meilleur texte écrit... La poésie, pour moi, c'est une fête du langage, un peu comme le théâtre. Et si, pour moi, la rythmique est très importante, les images le sont aussi. J'aime rendre mes textes sur une scène parce que ça leur donne une certaine dimension, et j'aime les voir sur papier parce qu'ils en prennent alors une autre. C'est comme ça que je crée. C'est comme ça que je conçois la poésie. Disons que je ne me considère pas spécialement comme un poète de spoken word ou un poète littéraire; c'est plutôt que la poésie que j'écris appartient autant au spoken word qu'au livre, à la chose littéraire.

were times I did visual poems, other times performance. I'm not interested in just fitting into a niche. That can work for you. Most of the time it can work against you, because people do like to label.

PETER BRAWLEY: For an old fogie like me, people say heavy Chevy shocking shit onstage now. I can't even believe it sometimes. I guess everything's just going to go down, any kind of convention or taboo. But any reaction's gotta react against a thing. It is literature. You have to speak English, every word is just soaked with stuff.

HUGH HAZELTON: Spoken word is just literature that you're doing aloud. It's oral literature. But oral literature could be published in print form. I don't really see any contradiction between the two.... Aimé Césaire was doing this in the thirties, it's really declamatory, and it's inflammatory. I was glad to see all the spoken word stuff starting to happen, because sometimes I found the 'official' scene kind of stuffy. Sure, literary with a small 'l'. Anything's literary. Let's knock down the shibboleth of 'Literary', let's just take a hammer to the letters in stone in capitals that say LITERARY and use the word with the small 'l'.

COREY FROST: I prefer the term 'writing' to the term 'literature', really. It's like the difference between 'work' and 'text'. With 'literature', there's the sense of the perpetuation of the role of the author, I think. 'Literature' is something that is created by 'authors'. Those words go together. Whereas writing is a much more material everyday substance. I think of it as something that just exists. It's just lying around, you can find writing anywhere. It doesn't have that exclusive, canonical connotation.

Peter Brawley
Photo courtesy of the artist

TOM KONYVES: The focus of my experimental work was always the poem, the text, albeit in a visual context. I don't consider a memorized recital of a poem a poetry performance; there should be a visual context. If the poet recited the poem with his / her back to the audience, then I guess that would qualify. That said, I'd like to think that the relationship is one of evolution or modernization of literature: it's a new way of experiencing the poem. The visual context of the poem will colour the poem, rendering it ironic, comic or tragic; it will add a layer to the poem without which it would be incomplete.

MARTA COOPER: Half of the people who I think of as writers I also think of as spoken word artists. We just have a really vibrant arts community, and anybody I would include in the writing scene would be anybody who actually does write down their work, with a focus on language. Most of the young writers who I know, who do not consider themselves to be involved in spoken word, *do* think about the way their work sounds. And reading it is an important part of the work. I think you also see

35

ANDRÉ LEMELIN: Certains de mes textes sont littéraires. J'ose le croire... Mais les textes que j'écris maintenant, puisqu'ils sont destinés à être performés oralement, sont à moitié littéraires, et à moitié oraux. Je ne considère pas que ce sont des textes littéraires avec un "L" majuscule, qui relèvent, par exemple, de la tradition française, bourgeoise et institutionnelle de la littérature. Pas du tout. Ce sont des textes du quotidien. Ainsi, mes *Contes du Centre-Sud* décrivent des personnages qui existent vraiment — c'est de la fiction-réalité, du documentaire-fiction. Pour moi, le but n'est pas de "faire" de la littérature; c'est avant tout de dire et de partager des choses. Et j'ai choisi de le rendre de façon orale, sur une scène, en performance. Mais je les écris quand même, ces textes.

HÉLÈNE MONETTE: Moi, je viens de l'oralité. Au départ, je faisais des lectures publiques, ça n'était pas dans le but de publier tout de suite. Certains de mes textes sont très proches de l'oralité, du langage de la rue, de ce qui est ordinaire, courant. Mais j'ai parfois commis l'erreur de prendre des textes trop écrits – qui avaient plus été écrits pour être publiés – pour les lire. Je me suis alors aperçu qu'en les lisant en public, ils ne passaient pas, parce qu'ils étaient trop littéraires.

13 Various authors. *Poetry Nation*. Cabico, Regie and Swift, Todd, ed., Montreal: Véhicule Press, 1998.

that in a lot of the more established writers. Somebody like Robert Majzels, he *is* reading, but he's also performing while he's reading, because of what he does with his voice. He engages the audience. I think that any time you engage the audience, to a certain extent you are performing.

ANDRÉ LEMELIN: Some of my texts are literary, at least I dare say so.... But the texts I'm writing now, because they're intended to be performed orally, are half-literary, half-oral. I don't see them as being literary with a capital 'L', in the institutional *bourgeois* French tradition. Not at all. They're everyday texts. My *Contes du Centre-Sud*, for example, describe real people — it's reality-fiction, documentary fiction. For me, the goal is not to 'make' literature, it's to say and share things. I've chosen to do this orally, onstage, in performance. But I do write these texts.

ALEXIS O'HARA: I've been told by promoters in Montreal that I'm a performer and not a writer, and that annoys me. I write the fucking work, what is it that makes me not a writer? I'm a big fan of metaphors and meter and rhyme and rhythm and all that.... I read and I absorb things and I let that filter through in the work. I tend to write pieces that are specific to the time of the event. I tend to tailor-make performances, for instance, *Take Back The Night*.... So maybe there's not a permanence to it, but it's still writing, it's still literary.

DEE SMITH: I record on paper; it's a piece of literature; it has its own form and definitely its own STYLE. I do consider my work to be literary. It is just a revived form of literature. Whatever I've performed, I have a written copy

which can be read by others who might not get a chance to hear me perform it live. However they *might* get a sense of what I am trying to transmit from reading a piece in a book or in any other print form.

TODD SWIFT: I am actually an academic formalist by nature — my work only ventured into the vernacular 'street' stuff when I discovered how fun it was. But poetry is always literary. It's the critics who need to catch up with this — Dante was vulgar, remember. I also publish my poems in magazines and books, thus assigning them textual value.

HÉLÈNE MONETTE: I come from orality. At the beginning I gave public readings, with no intention of publishing right away. Some of my texts are very close to orality, to street language, to what is ordinary, current. But sometimes I made the mistake of reading texts that were too written — that had been written more to be published. I realized that when I read them in public, they didn't get across because they were too literary.

"Can I read this again and again?"

On the other side of the coin, some spoken word artists entered the scene from areas decidedly non-literary: from the theatrical or performance art milieus. Their texts are adapted to live performance, and don't necessarily translate well to the page. This leads to two questions: should spoken word texts be published? and, in what ways do spoken word texts differ from traditional poetic texts?

TODD SWIFT: The idea of fusion poetry suggested by the anthology *Poetry Nation*[13] raises the question, "What's the relationship between printed and otherwise mediated poetry to the idea of canonicity?" Critics prefer to return to the text, rather than to refer to the performative instances for poetry, something they cannot always do with, say, music. This bias is shifting, and artists like Fortner Anderson who choose to transcribe their words via the technology of CDs will be studied as listened-to artists as opposed to visual / textual artists. But experiment can occur visually / textually, as well as in performance. Adeena Karasick, postmodern spoken word poet par excellence, is a supreme example of this merging — this fusion — of worlds. The best 'spoken word' easily ranks alongside the best traditional verse, and sometimes surpasses it, for power of influence. When both spheres of creation come together, the result can be majestic.

VINCE TINGUELY: I think that the so-called spoken word scene has reinvigorated literature and writing in Montreal, as much as it has created this forum for people who are really more interested in performance than in being published. For one thing, it creates a social space that didn't exist. I'm not an academic, I didn't go to creative writing school, and therefore I've never had the social milieu which is so essential not only to learning the craft, but also getting published. So when the scene started, it served the same purpose.

NAH EE LAH: I think it's particularly important for me as a Black person to insure that my work is in a hard copy form. For centuries, other people have written their versions of our history and passed it off as truth.

VICTORIA STANTON: My goal isn't to publish my work. I've submitted texts for publication, but it's not really what I'm working towards, not at this point. I have an idea that I'd like to publish a book based on *Split*, the series of performances that I've done, but I don't even see that as a literary endeavour. I see that more as an artist's book, which is about documenting the performance. It'll be its own project, but it's still about the performance.

NATHALIE DEROME: I was published for the first time last year with *L'Oie de cravan*. It's a small press, and they do *La Revue des animaux*. I did not consider that I was writing, really. I just play with words and use them in a theatrical structure. I was always afraid of literature; maybe spoken word is better for me, because it's closer to theatre. It's really the separation of literature and theatre.

PATRICIA LAMONTAGNE: I've often refused to publish my texts, I felt they'd be uninteresting in print. Because when a text is spoken, the energy, the phrasing, the tone, all these levels can't be transcribed. This reminds me of something that happened in 1985. Hélène Monette got a grant to stage a poetry show, and I was the director. Our venue was Foufounes Électriques, and later on in Belgium. It was pure hell. We argued all the time because we didn't have the same vision of things. I was studying theatre at the time and I was trying to do a *mise en place* [placing] of the texts. And, as there were costumes and a narrative concern, it was closer to theatre than to poetry. So the show was located somewhere between performance and something else. And I realized at that moment that there's a huge gap between written and spoken; that when we write, we have to be aware of what we want to present onstage afterwards.

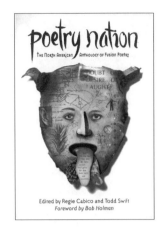

poetry nation

THE NORTH AMERICAN ANTHOLOGY OF FUSION POETRY

Edited by Regie Cabico and Todd Swift
Foreword by Bob Holman

PATRICIA LAMONTAGNE: J'ai souvent refusé que certains de mes textes soient publiés car je trouvais qu'ils auraient été inintéressants à l'écrit. Parce que lorsqu'un texte est dit, l'énergie, le débit, la tonalité, tous ces registres ne peuvent pas être transcrits. Ça me rappelle quelque chose que j'ai vécu, en 1985. Hélène Monette avait eu une subvention pour faire un spectacle de poésie et j'avais été la metteure en scène de cette expérience. On s'était produites aux Foufounes Électriques, et en Belgique par la suite. Cela a vraiment été l'enfer. On se disputait tout le temps parce qu'on n'avait pas la même vision des choses. Moi, à ce moment, j'étudiais en théâtre et j'essayais de faire une mise en place des textes. Et comme il y avait des costumes et un souci narratif, c'était plus près du théâtre que de la poésie. Alors le spectacle se situait entre la performance et quelque chose d'autre. Et j'ai compris à ce moment qu'il y a un écart immense entre l'écrit et l'oral et que, lorsqu'on écrit, il faut être conscient de ce qu'on veut présenter par la suite sur scène. J'en étais même arrivée à me dire que la poésie n'avait souvent pas intérêt à être dite. Qu'elle avait plutôt avantage à être relue, qu'elle devait demeurer dans un univers plus intime, plus personnel, pour laisser le temps au lecteur d'investir émotivement le texte. C'est pour ça que pendant quelques années, je n'ai pas été très productive. Ce n'est que plus tard que je me suis dit: "Il y a

37

continued...

l'oralité, il y a l'écrit, et ce que je veux faire sur scène n'a pas intérêt à être publié, la plupart du temps." Par exemple, cela explique pourquoi, sur le disque *La Vache enragée*, ce que j'ai fait oralement n'est pas ce qui est écrit dans le livret qui l'accompagne; c'est un autre texte. Pour moi, l'oral et l'écrit sont très différents.

BENOÎT PAIEMENT: Possiblement que la poésie est un genre littéraire qui demande à être lu, dit et entendu à cause du rythme – nécessairement à cause du rythme. Mais je pense aussi que toute forme littéraire, *short stories*, nouvelles, romans, est intéressante à être entendue, en entier ou en partie. Ce n'est peut-être pas la meilleure façon de définir la poésie. Par ailleurs, je crois qu'il y a une poésie qui est d'abord écrite pour être lue, mais qui pourrait être intéressante à être entendue, comme je crois également qu'il y a une poésie qui est essentiellement écrite pour être dite, performée et entendue. Moi, quand j'écris une nouvelle, j'ai évidemment en tête qu'elle va être lue, mais aussi qu'il serait intéressant, éventuellement, de l'entendre lire. Par contre, quand j'écris un texte pour le Groupe de poésie moderne, c'est clair que c'est quelque chose qui est fait pour être entendu, qui doit directement être dit. Et j'ai même en tête la voix de la personne qui va dire la ligne en question. C'est un réel facteur de stimulation, d'inspiration, que d'avoir des acteurs – c'est un peu comme des instruments de musique. *That's poetry. But very often,* aussi bien dans le milieu anglophone que francophone, on est venu nous dire après une performance: "Ah, c'est ça la poésie! Mais c'est bien!" *Because people think that poetry is* hermétique, *something that is not understandable. But I don't think so. To me, even the great poets from the nineteenth century,* Baudelaire, Verlaine, Rimbaud, *are very accessible. You have to take some time, though.*

Torrey Pass
August 1999

14 Various authors. *La Vache enragée – anthologie 2* CD / book. Miller, Mitsiko, ed., Montreal: Planète rebelle, 1998.

I'd even come to the conclusion that poetry was often not made to be spoken. That it gained from being read and re-read, that it must remain in a more intimate, more personal sphere, to give the reader time to get emotionally involved with the text. That's why I wasn't very productive for a while. It was only later that I thought: "There's orality, there's writing, and what I want to do onstage has no business being published, most of the time." This explains why on the record *La Vache enragée*,14 what I did orally is not what's in the booklet that comes with it, it's a different text. As I see it, oral and written are two different things.

TORREY PASS: I think spoken word often can play the line between being performance art and literature. It can play both sides. For example the *La Vache enragée* anthology that came out, there were poems that actually weren't on the CD, and on the CD that also weren't in the book. In a sense, all those pieces are literature. And yet a lot of pieces performed, if written down they wouldn't be sensical.

38

KAIE KELLOUGH: I guess the thing that would make a good literary piece is something that you can read again and again and rediscover each time you read. I would have to say that a lot of spoken word pieces that I've seen — I always think about that. Would I read this? Can I read this? Can I read this again and again? And a lot of the time the answer is no. I can't and I really wouldn't. I'd like to hear it and I would love to see it again, but I wouldn't necessarily want to read it.

"Spoken word is its own dog"

Here, spoken word artists discuss the similarities and the differences between their texts and other literary texts. Every form has its own limitations. A spoken word piece, delivered in real time to an audience, can never have the depth or detail of a novel. Is spoken word writing a practice distinct from other literary forms, as poetry is distinct from playwriting, or as playwriting is distinct from prose fiction?

BENOÎT PAIEMENT: Maybe poetry is a literary genre that needs to be read, spoken, heard because of the rhythm — necessarily because of the rhythm. But I also believe that all literary forms, short stories, novels, are interesting to hear, in whole or in part. So this may not be the best way to define poetry. On the other hand, there is a kind of poetry written to be read, but could be interesting to hear, the same way I believe there's poetry written essentially to be spoken, performed and heard. When I write a short story, I'm obviously thinking it's going to be read, but also that it would be interesting, eventually, to hear it read out loud. On the other hand, when I write a text for the *Groupe* *de poésie moderne*, it's clearly intended to be heard, to be spoken directly. I can even hear the voice of the person who's going to say that line. Having actors is really stimulating and inspiring — they're a little like musical instruments. That's poetry. But very often, after a performance, in the anglophone scene as well as the francophone one, people have said to us: "Now that's poetry! Very good!" People think that language is hermetic, something that's not understandable. I disagree. To me, even the great nineteenth century poets, Baudelaire, Verlaine, Rimbaud, are very accessible. You have to take some time, though.

ALEX BOUTROS: Kaarla and I write to perform. That's why we write, we write for performance. A lot of the poems that we have now, even though they started in written form, we've changed them so much that the form in which we generally perform them isn't even written down anywhere. We use the text almost as a memory guide. "Okay, let's write this line down because we're going to forget it." But we're going to say it *this way*. We're not going to say it just like how you read it on the page, we're going to say it with a particular rhythm or a particular melody or a particular emphasis or inflection. That's always a part of the process of writing, for us, especially when we write collaboratively. The text is secondary, even in the process. It really is a mnemonic device.

PASCAL FIORAMORE: *Les Abdigradationnistes'* texts are not literary. They're ideological, meaning that they can represent, contain images or critiques. In our texts — the ones I've written so far — in the language I'm working on, I use more musical expressions. As for puns, or for 'when it's spoken', speech, I focus more on playing with sounds than on developing the beauty of language. Paradoxically, and parallel to this, I write other texts to put in books. The book I'm working on has nothing to do with *Les Abdigradationnistes*. They're not texts I'd ever turn into songs. Although you never know... sometimes I write a text and then six months later I turn it into a song — even though at first I'd think, "No, I want this one to be literary."

BUFFY CHILDERHOSE: Some days I think that spoken word is its own dog. Spoken word is spoken word, there is stuff that just exists as that, and that's all that it needs to exist. There are pieces I've written that I never want to see in print, because they were written specifically for performance.... There's some work that is perfectly content on the page. But I also don't feel that it's a failure to have something just exist as performance. I respect the space that it occupies there, and I don't think that it necessarily needs to be able to exist in a different world. Because to a certain degree, you are crossing media.

ANNA-LOUISE CRAGO: Performing was a very secure thing, because I was writing stuff that would fit into a time-slot, and so I never had to go past a certain point.... Longer pieces can't be performed as easily, I mean, reading a novel takes a much more devoted audience, really (laughs). A less drunk audience perhaps. Just because, having performed in a lot of bars in Montreal, the attention span is quite obviously arrested. That's not a critique of audiences, you have to have short pieces at a certain point, right? So I think that more and more now I'm focusing on writing for writing. But I like to try to maintain the sort of spontaneity as if I were speaking it, in my writing, and that's the real challenge.

PASCAL FIORAMORE: Les textes des Abdigradationnistes ne sont pas littéraires. Ils sont idéologiques, c'est-à-dire qu'ils peuvent représenter, ils peuvent contenir des images ou des critiques. Puis dans nos textes – ceux que j'ai écrits jusqu'à présent –, dans le langage que j'essaie de travailler, j'utilise les expressions plus musicales. Au niveau du jeu de mots ou au niveau du "quand c'est dit", du parler, j'axe plus mon travail sur la recherche d'un jeu musical que sur le développement de la beauté de la langue. Mais paradoxalement et parallèlement à ça, je travaille d'autres textes pour les mettre dans un recueil. Le recueil que je suis en train de faire n'a rien à voir avec les Abdigradationnistes. Ce ne sont pas des textes que je mettrais en chansons. Quoiqu'on ne sait jamais. Parfois, j'écris un texte et six mois après j'en fais une chanson. Alors qu'au début je me disais: "Non, ce texte-là, c'est un texte que je veux littéraire."

VICTORIA STANTON: Recently, through working on *Split*, I started working on writing that is more prose-oriented, and that actually has some kind of narrative structure, although not necessarily very linear. And then I thought, "Oh, I'm *writing* now. I've started to write." But it's not something that I've taken up as my job right now and that I'm pursuing. I have ideas for stories that I would like to write, but when I start working on them, they might end up being performance pieces.

COREY FROST: I think of writing for publication and writing for performance as a continuum. They're not explicitly separate entities for me, but I do prepare things in a different fashion. If I have a story that I wrote, intending to publish it, and I want to perform that, I'll probably take it and do a pretty serious edit and change things for performance. My chapbook, *Tonight you'll have a filthy Dream*,[15] is all performances. I'm trying to find a way to design it in such a way

that it comes across that they're performed pieces, because I didn't intend them to be published pieces. So there's a difference, but it's a difference of degree. Some of my 'page' pieces work as performance and some don't, and vice versa.... I want to find a hybrid, where it's not about the sound, exactly, but it's not about the narrative or the ideas either. Which are, to me, the main elements, respectively, of performance and 'page' literature. But what I want it to be about is the syntax, something about the syntax and grammar that is immediately, intuitively remarkable for an aural audience, that I want to reproduce on the page.

"The reality of performance"

It becomes difficult to draw a line between spoken word and other forms of literature based solely upon textual differences. Some performers choose work that seems to function well in a public performance, but others draw from texts which were originally written for the page. The uniqueness of spoken word might lie more in that it is performed, and in all the ramifications which arise from this simple fact.

FORTNER ANDERSON: For me, these works exist when read aloud, when my voice or another gives them life. So it's onstage, before an audience, when I have the best opportunity to do that. That's why I take that opportunity to bring work forward and then to make the text vibrantly alive in that dark space.

DEBBIE YOUNG: I just can't get over how singular literature is. As an individual, you choose to read a poem, you choose to read a book. Then you have the ability to absorb the material. You have the

*Corey Frost
Concordia University
September 1999*
Photo by Owen Egan

[15] Frost, Corey. *Tonight you'll have a filthy dream — Backward Versions 2*. Montreal: self-published, 1999.

ability, on your own and with the help of the writer, to go places and see beautiful things and learn and expand your mind. Literature does all of these things, poetry on the page does all of these things. I respect literature, and I think one of the beautiful things about literature is that you can have it to mull over. But at the end of the day spoken word performances maintain that very immediate human contact, where you can talk and touch and see that people are real, and that the poet is real. And with literature, from my objective it's just a bit more difficult to do. Everybody asks me why I haven't published a book yet. And it's for that reason.

LEAH VINEBERG: There is a difference, I think, between spoken word and literature, because I think it is about turning a certain dial on the text by applying voice. It's not just voice, it's intention, and commitment, and listening, and presenting yourself. Being available for these words, hopefully. Dayna McLeod's done certain things that really have had me ask this kind of question. The language is — there's no question — it's spoken word, and what she's doing is spoken word, but she's created these characters. Heather O'Neill is a writer, but her presence and her voice, that creates something.

PATRICIA LAMONTAGNE: When I do stage-work, literature serves a higher purpose. Something called *la réalité scénique* [the reality of the stage]. In that situation, literature becomes simply an instrument, as I see it. I can't say my poetry is above, and that everything serves it. No. That happens when it's in a book. But when I do performance, everything serves the stage, and I try to figure out which means of expression is going to best convey this. It can be dance, a

scream, anything. So I don't know if there's a *link* as much as a *complementarity* between literature and the stage. In the end, it may be the same thing.

TETSURO SHIGEMATSU: If a spoken word piece happens to make good literature, I think that's more of a happy coincidence than a result of conscious intention.... However, I might suspect that in my own case, should I try to achieve both objectives simultaneously, one might always be at the expense of the other.... Something that you always have to be aware of when you're onstage, is that the audience never has the chance to stop and rewind or to go back a page. So comprehension always has to be in real time. As such, the writing or the prose or the spoken word that you're creating has to have almost an industrial proletariat clarity in the moment. Should you become tempted to err in the direction of your writerly love of words words words, then as a performer, you do so at your peril, and you'll pay the price.

GENEVIÈVE LETARTE: I once put together a performance titled *Extraits d'un livre chanté* [Excerpts of a book, sung]. In it I presented excerpts from a novel I'd written. Long passages of *prose*. In that case my performance was truly literary. Initially my book had a purpose of its own, and the goal of my show was to make it into a different art object, which eventually became *Extraits d'un livre chanté*. Personally, I've always loved the idea of singing or speaking texts that would not normally be spoken or sung onstage because they're not really songs, they're much too complex or they contain sentences that are too long, etc. My first performances were really with *texts*. That's where I found my pleasure, my challenge.

PATRICIA LAMONTAGNE: Lorsque je fais de la scène, la littérature est au service de quelque chose de plus grand. Quelque chose qui s'appelle la réalité scénique. Alors, pour moi, la littérature ne devient qu'un instrument. Je ne peux pas prétendre que ma poésie est en haut, et que tout est à son service. Non. Ça, c'est quand elle est dans un livre. Mais lorsque je donne une performance, tout est au service de la scène, et j'essaie de voir quels sont les modes d'expression qui vont le mieux l'exprimer. Cela peut être par la danse, ou au moyen d'un cri, n'importe quoi. Alors je ne sais pas s'il y a un *lien* autant qu'une *complémentarité* entre la littérature et la scène. Au fond, c'est peut-être la même chose.

GENEVIÈVE LETARTE: J'ai monté une performance qui s'appelait *Extraits d'un livre chanté*. Dans ce spectacle, je présentais des extraits d'un roman que j'avais écrit. C'étaient des grands bouts de texte, de la *prose*. Là, ma performance était vraiment littéraire. Au départ, mon livre avait une fonction qui lui était propre et le but de mon spectacle était de le prendre pour en faire un autre objet d'art, qui est finalement devenu *Extraits d'un livre chanté*. Moi, j'ai toujours aimé l'idée de chanter ou de dire des textes qu'on ne dirait pas ou qu'on ne chanterait pas sur scène parce que ce n'est pas réellement de la chanson, de ces textes beaucoup trop compliqués ou qui contiennent des phrases trop longues, etc. Les premières performances que j'ai données, c'était avec de ces *textes*. C'était ça mon plaisir, mon défi.

41

HÉLÈNE MONETTE: Par leur présence, par leur façon de dire leur texte, il arrive que des performeurs soient capables de rendre un texte très littéraire aussi facilement qu'ils le feraient avec un poème. Une fois, j'ai vu Nicole Brossard à *La Vache enragée* et elle m'avait énormément impressionnée. Le texte qu'elle avait choisi de lire était loin d'être évident. Et cela avait été tout à fait réussi.... Geneviève Letarte est proche de cela aussi. Je pense qu'elle est vraiment capable de livrer en performance un texte très littéraire.

HÉLÈNE MONETTE: C'est sûr que si j'écris un roman, je n'en lirai pas d'extraits. Je trouve que ça ne sert pas le roman. Mais peut-être que je me trompe. Ça dépend des motivations. Et ça dépend de l'audace qu'on a. Mais il arrive qu'on se retrouve avec un texte qu'on veut absolument essayer de présenter sur scène, et on ne sait pas s'il est trop littéraire pour le faire. Parfois le niveau de langue se situe dans une zone nébuleuse entre l'oralité courante et le littéraire. Est-ce que ça va toucher? Est-ce que ça va trouver une résonance chez les gens? Quand on se pose ces questions, il faut soit modifier son texte, soit le tester directement sur scène. Moi, c'est sûr que j'ai des textes qui sont carrément verbaux, qui sont davantage comme des conversations. Pas de mots recherchés, pas de structure trop compliquée. Et ce sont ces textes-là, probablement, qui gagneraient le plus à être entendus.

HÉLÈNE MONETTE: By their presence and their way of speaking their texts, sometimes performers are able to render a very literary text as easily as they would a poem. I once saw Nicole Brossard at *La Vache enragée* and she impressed me enormously. The text she'd chosen to read was no piece of cake. And it was beautifully done.... Geneviève Letarte is close to that too. She has the ability to deliver a very literary text in performance.

RAN ELFASSY: If I'm writing for performance then I'm very conscious of the reception. Is it going to be through the ear, and through the eyes? I think classic 'literature', which is written, tends to be very visual, unless it's taped. Its whole basis is visual. What I mean by visual is just that the way it gets into your head is through your eyes, as opposed to through your ears. Unless

you're blind. In terms of the creation of performance texts, I think the person who writes and who says, "Oh, I just write freely without thinking about its reception," is being kind of ideal and naive. I think you're constantly aware there's going to be an audience there.

GOLDA FRIED: I do notice it myself, when I'm doing a reading and it's poetry, I definitely give myself more freedom to make jokes. If it was just on the page, I wouldn't be so colloquial, I don't think. I definitely like the performance aspect. I always try to think about people I like, which is usually rock people like Patti Smith, Tom Waits. Or Courtney Love, who always says, "I consider myself a poet. I write all the lyrics. I'm not the best musician, but I'm into it for the poetry too."

HÉLÈNE MONETTE: One thing I know is that if I write a novel, I won't read passages from it. I don't find this enhances the novel. Maybe I'm wrong. It depends on motivation. On how bold you feel. But it happens that you have this text you absolutely want to try out onstage, and you're not sure if it isn't too literary. Sometimes the level of language is in some nebulous zone between everyday speech and literature. Will this touch people? Will the public respond? When these questions come up, you either have to modify the text, or test it directly onstage. I've got texts that are straightforwardly verbal, more like conversations. No fancy words, no complicated structure. These texts would probably benefit from being heard.

Golda Fried
Photo courtesy of the artist

We asked spoken word artists about their philosophy. What was it that motivated them to do what they do? Underlying this question was an interest in why spoken word has become such an accepted art form in the nineties, with performers appearing alongside rock bands in cabarets, as solo monologuists in theatres, with traditional poets and writers in literary readings and in the gallery-based performance art milieu.

"Is it my reason to live?"

At its most basic, the desire to create is a mysterious force, even for the artists themselves. On a personal level, spoken word artists often create in order to gain an insight into themselves, their thought processes and the world they inhabit.

ENDRE FARKAS: I feel I have no choice. To me, it's as relevant and important as breathing. Actually, it's interesting that the word 'inspiration' means to take breath in, and 'expiration' is to die (laughs). So right now, I'm working on inspiration most of the time.

PATRICIA LAMONTAGNE: I think there are two kinds of creators. There's the majority who create to serve their ego, so that their art will make them greater, more famous, more self-confident, etc. And there are others who serve their art; people who act as catalysts. That's what I try to do. I can't live without art, that's for sure. For me, art is a way of going to a higher level, of transcending myself, by calling upon my imagination. And I find that right now, imagination is very atrophied in our society, even among creators. The power of imagination is something greater than we are. I like being overwhelmed by that greatness. As an artist, my quest is to reach those states where I feel that I'm going beyond the concrete reality of "I'm eating watermelon."

DAYNA MCLEOD: An idea comes, and it needs to happen, and I need to do it. I'm not going to rest until it's done, or until it's developed, or until it's worked out. It needs to be full, it needs to be well-rounded, for me to be able to present it, or for me to be satisfied with the presentation. And it needs to be important to me, to be able to produce, because if it's not, it won't happen.

BENOÎT PAIEMENT: One way or another, I'm going to continue writing and performing, that's for sure. I can't stop.... Is creating my reason to live? It fills a very precious place in my life. My personal relationships, my friends, my loves, my family, are obviously very important. But that's something else.... Sometimes I tell myself that creating is what I do best. The rest of what I do doesn't interest me — it's negligible. My job, for example, is strictly to pay the rent....

MITSIKO MILLER: I just express myself, I've never had the impulse or the necessity to shock. I find that art is often a reflection of social values.... In the seventies, or in the sixties, you really needed to shock, because *les valeurs sociales* were very square. You needed some nudity, you needed to shake people a bit. But now, in our society, everything is possible. You can really be

PATRICIA LAMONTAGNE: Je pense qu'il y a deux sortes de créateurs. Selon moi, il y a la majorité qui font de la création pour servir leur ego, pour que leur art les rende plus grands, plus connus, plus confiants, etc. Et il y en a d'autres qui sont au service de leur art; des gens qui deviennent des catalyseurs. C'est ce que j'essaie de faire. Je ne peux pas vivre sans l'art. Pour moi, c'est une façon de m'élever, de me transcender, en faisant appel à mon imaginaire. Et je trouve qu'en ce moment, l'imaginaire est très atrophié dans notre société, même chez les créateurs. La force de l'imaginaire, c'est quelque chose qui nous dépasse. Et j'aime être dépassée par cette grandeur-là. Ma quête en tant qu'artiste est d'atteindre ces états où tu sens que tu dépasses une espèce de réalité concrète, du genre: "Je mange une pastèque."

BENOÎT PAIEMENT: D'une façon ou d'une autre, je vais continuer à écrire, et puis à performer. C'est sûr. Je ne peux pas arrêter de le faire.... Est-ce que la création est ma raison de vivre? Elle occupe une place très précieuse dans ma vie. Évidemment, mes relations personnelles, mes amis, mes amours, ma famille, sont très importants. Mais ça, c'est autre chose.... Parfois je me dis que la création est ce que je fais de mieux. Le reste, dans ce que je fais, ne m'intéresse pas. Pour moi, c'est négligeable. Mon travail, par exemple, est strictement alimentaire....

Geneviève Letarte: Je pense que ma pratique artistique a un rapport avec une quête existentielle. Elle est liée au fait que l'individualité, c'est aussi l'universalité. Moi, ce qui m'intéresse, c'est l'âme humaine. Quand j'écris, quand je donne des spectacles, je me dis que c'est par rapport à ça que je me mets à jour. Et peut-être que les autres, à travers ce que je fais, peuvent se mettre à jour aussi. Pour moi, l'art est donc une nécessité. Une nécessité philosophique. C'est sûr que je ne crée pas pour l'argent, et je le fais de moins en moins pour l'ego. C'est facile de vouloir être un artiste, parce que c'est très valorisant, évidemment. Écrire, faire des spectacles, c'est très narcissique. Mais même si ça reste toujours narcissique, on dirait qu'en vieillissant, on s'en distance, on le fait moins pour être aimé, et alors ça devient plus intéressant. On crée davantage parce qu'il faut le faire, tout simplement.

Jean-Paul Daoust: Denis Vanier a dit une phrase magnifique: "J'écris pour pas tuer." (rires) Je l'aime beaucoup, celle-là. Parce qu'évidemment, la réponse classique est: "J'écris pour être aimé". Lui, il dit: "J'écris pour pas tuer". Ça revient au même. Il y a une petite variante. En fait, je pense que lorsqu'on écrit, on est poussé par un besoin viscéral de communiquer ses émotions, mais en les organisant en mots pour essayer de les transmettre. Et je crois qu'en nommant ses émotions, en nommant les choses, en plus de se libérer, on s'approprie une forme de réalité qui, à ce moment, nous pousse plus loin. J'aime bien la phrase de Rimbaud "La vraie vie est ailleurs". Je pense que la poésie nous amène ailleurs. Et c'est peut-être là où on est le plus vrai. Alors en ce sens, pour moi, l'écriture est comme un laboratoire. Parfois il y a des expériences qui sont réussies, et d'autres qui le sont moins. Mais peu importe. Je me dis que si moi, ça me fait avancer, ça fait avancer les autres. Et j'ai comme l'impression que tous les écrivains écrivent le même livre, mais sous différentes variantes. Je crois que ce que je fais se greffe à ce que d'autres font et, finalement, on forme une immense mappemonde littéraire. Chacun découvre des choses et on élabore une fresque. Et je trouve que c'est dommage que quelqu'un qui peut écrire ne le fasse pas. Il faut se rendre non pas jusqu'à l'écriture, mais jusqu'à la publication. C'est-à-dire qu'il faut que l'écriture — qui est privée — devienne publique.

yourself, and of course you might not have a large audience, but you'll have an audience. It's a question of dynamics, it would be really boring if it was objective. Just doing something and people applauding, "Ah, this is fun! This is beautiful!" I'm not interested in beauty. I'm interested in interacting with people. That's why I like spoken word, and that's why I like the oral tradition, it's all about talking to people.

Anna-Louise Crago: One of the philosophies behind writing was understanding that art in whatever form — and we didn't even necessarily name it — could keep you somewhat sane. It could keep your feet on the ground, and could give you rushes that were parallel to other rushes that all the cool kids were peddling, that you didn't have to be a part of.

Debbie Young: I think for me, writing keeps me sane. Beginning and end. It keeps me sane. And to be able to reflect on a packaged thought — because often that's what the poem is, a packaged thought — legitimizes it for me.

Fortner Anderson: The project of the writer to apprehend their own thought, to make it real so as to recognize it on paper; I think that would be it. One of the things I've thought about recently is, if thought is formed in the act of speech or in the act of writing, and if that in fact is thought made real, what is the reality of feeling? How is sentiment made real in the world? I think that's part of what I try to do as well. These works are a making real of emotion, sentiment. That's not an aesthetic philosophy, but I think that's the impulse which guides the creation. To see it outside of itself, to see it made real. To make it apprehendable, if not understandable.

Geneviève Letarte: I think my art practice has to do with an existential quest. It's linked to the fact that individuality is also universality. I'm interested in the human soul. When I write, when I give shows, I tell myself that this is why I'm revealing myself. And maybe through what I do, others can reveal themselves as well. So art is a necessity for me. A philosophical necessity. I certainly don't create for the money, and less and less to feed my ego. It's easy to want to be an artist, because it can boost your ego. Writing, doing shows, is very narcissistic. But though it's always narcissistic, as you get older you get detached, you do it less to be loved and then it becomes more interesting. You create because you need to, quite simply.

Jean-Paul Daoust: Denis Vanier said something magnificent: "I write so I won't kill." (everyone laughs) I love that. Because obviously, the standard answer is: "I write to be loved." And he says: "I write so I won't kill." It comes to the same thing, with a bit of a slant. In fact, I believe that when we write, we're driven by a visceral need to communicate our feelings, which we try to transmit by organizing them into words. And by naming our feelings, by naming things, in addition to freeing ourselves, we appropriate a form of reality which, at that moment, pushes us further. I like Rimbaud's statement, "Real life is elsewhere." I think poetry takes us elsewhere. And maybe this is where we're the most genuine. So in this sense, I see writing as a laboratory. Some experiments succeed, others don't. But no matter. I tell myself that if it's making me go further, it'll make others go forward. My impression is that all writers write the same book, but under different guises. I believe that what I do grafts itself onto what others do and, in the end, it's like a huge literary world map. Each one of us discovers things and we work out a fresco. It's unfortunate when people who can write don't do it. You need to get to more than just writing, you need to go all the way to publishing. In other words, writing — which is private — must become public. This is where I find spoken word interesting, it allows writers to share their discoveries.

"Theory's good, but afterwards you have to get into practice"

Contrary to popular stereotypes, spoken word artists are neither necessarily anti-academic, nor ignorant of performance theory. However, their philosophies are more likely to be rooted in their practice than in something they read in a book.

ENDRE FARKAS: I'm a more intuitive person than analytical, and so a lot of the things that I've done, I've intuited. Then afterwards, somebody could say, "Oh, that's what you were trying to do, that's what you were doing." I guess I leave that to other people. Usually you get philosophical *after* the event. I'm suspicious of anybody who has a lot of philosophy before they do anything, because usually the work never gets done. They're good theoreticians. A lot of 'language' writers, on the West coast, I read their essays and I find it fascinating, then I read their stuff and I say, "Huh? What's that? No, that doesn't say anything about what you said here." Theory's good, but afterwards you have to get into practice.

JAKE BROWN: I think there are formal rules of unity in music, literature and the classic arts. You could prove it in music. (Hums "Pop Goes the Weasel"

and hits a wrong note). It's offensive to the ear; with the language we use, it doesn't 'go' with the preceding note. There's a theory of harmonics, of course, that gives to the formal relations of unity. It's really obvious when formal unity is broken in a melody line. I think that when you start talking about the formal relations of a painting, it's much more difficult and less concrete. It's not as obvious to the eye as to the ear when one doesn't make formal unity. And in literature, it's even harder to talk about formal unity — because you can have abstract literature that has formal unity. I think that *Jacob's Room* by Virginia Woolf, which is straight stream-of-consciousness, has a very tight formal unity, and I think that *Ulysses* by James Joyce does not. I'm not an expert on *Ulysses*, and you could have an army of *Ulysses* scholars come and demonstrate that I'm wrong, but I find *Ulysses* rambling and *Jacob's Room* not. Yet they have the same narrative device of stream-of-consciousness. I think also that in matters of taste, there are objective things. They're self-evident. If a person is educated to appreciate a certain set of criteria, they will recognize those sets of criteria when they see it in art. If you teach them a different set of criteria to value, they'll recognize those. But if you don't teach any set of criteria, I think you get the flabbiest recognition of art that there is possible, because really you're just going on the lowest common denominator. It seems to go that way. It's easier and faster to get into a pop melody hook in music than it is to get into a complex composition, but for those of us who have — through fortune and effort — had a chance to learn to appreciate more complicated stuff, it's night and day. One is much more powerful and resonant than the other. This

45

seems to be true across the board. There is such a thing as an education and a philosophy of looking at the world that is necessary to recognize art that is helpful to humans living on earth.... I think that art should always be trying to make something beautiful, and maybe even especially when it's something horrible that you have to say.... I think that the principles by which that is able to be done are objective, or have enough of an objective quality so that we can justifiably theorize on it, and say, "I think that this is the kind of philosophy that might lead to good art," or, "This is the kind of style of manipulation of form that might lead to good art."

SYLVAIN FORTIER: Je n'ai pas *une* philosophie, j'en ai plusieurs. Ça dépend des textes que j'écris. Parfois, quand il y a quelque chose qui me tracasse, je peux écrire pour vomir ma bile. D'autres fois, ça peux être pour rigoler, pour faire rire celui qui va me lire ou qui m'entendre, ou moi-même. D'autres fois encore, c'est parce que je veux faire quelque chose de beau. J'ai toutes sortes de buts. En fait, ça serait plus simple de dire les buts que je n'ai pas. Je ne veux pas fonder d'école, je ne veux pas être le pape d'un mouvement quelconque. Je ne veux pas apprendre quelque chose aux gens. Voilà. Pour moi, tout peut être prétexte à la création, sauf montrer la bonne voie à quelqu'un.

SYLVAIN FORTIER: I don't have just one philosophy, I have many. It depends on the text I'm writing. If something's bothering me, I can write just to vent my poison. Other times it can be for a laugh, to make the person who'll read me or hear me laugh, or myself. Other times it's because I want to make something beautiful. I have all sorts of goals. In fact it would be easier to state the goals I don't have. I don't want to start a school, I don't want to be the pope of some movement. I don't want to teach people anything. There. For me, everything can be a pretext for creating, except showing someone the way.

Sylvain Fortier at
La Vache enragée
Photo by André Lemelin

ALEXIS O'HARA: I think humility in spoken word is very important. For me there is far too much message-driven work that is coming from a false place. I guess my one philosophy is to try to be true at all times. What I mean is to find the honesty in expressing things the way that I see them, and understanding that I'm just one perspective.

"The art must be alive"

Spoken word is a way to create ideas and images in the minds of audience members, thereby revealing the world in a new light. This act sometimes verges on the spiritual.

RAN ELFASSY: I thought of this in the hospital, which is a bizarre place to come up with theories about art — but it was just that I was thinking art should be like a catheter. In some ways very serious, it does perform a function, a very real function, a total utility. But it's basically there to take the piss out of you. Ba-da-boom. That's why it's there, right? I don't think it should be *only* there to take the piss out of you... it should be something a little absurd. I'm trying to provoke with my work. Not necessarily a hostile provocation. I think it should be either good-natured or hostile, but it should be a sort of shock, so that all of a sudden for a moment you're standing in front of an idea. You're looking at it naked, just, "Ah! I never thought of it in that way before." That's really important. My philosophy is that creativity that does not step outside of rules — the rules of making, or the rules of what we have to talk about — if you don't step outside of that and imagine for a brief second something different... then you're basically an artisan, you make craft.

JONATHAN GOLDSTEIN: I love people who see the world in a different way, present the world in a different way. Not the way that you're force-fed, but a sort of vision. Whatever you want to call the magic of the mundane. The poetry in everyday life, when you isolate it like a haiku. Pablo Neruda has this line about those matches that you strike, and they don't light right away. They pause, they hesitate for a second. He describes that instant, it's like a match that forgets that it's a match, and then suddenly realizes and bursts into flame…. It brings out the poetry in just the little bullshit things that happen. I don't meditate so much, but it's kind of like that. It's like creating a meditative living, the semblance of that, through writing. Like slowing down time. Being able to take the moments and savour them, hold them in your hands for a while, and play around with them.

THOTH HARRIS: I'm really into the idea of communicating what reality actually is, and when you can find a language for that, I think you can actually transform it. I think one of our biggest problems is language which leads to people misunderstanding each other, misunderstanding themselves, and misunderstanding reality. I feel that people should actually try to examine how they see things and learn the art of concentration. Not just concentration, but awareness…. I think art is all about empathy, to actually see what someone else is seeing. Empathy is a real dying art. It's not just being able to make people see what you're seeing or hear what you're saying, but to be able to express what the next person is seeing or saying.

PETER BRAWLEY: That's what it's all about, you've got to really love the people. You're out there, you're talking to

Jonathan Goldstein, May 7, 1999

people. That's why I always tried to keep stuff in my work that was real simple, despite all the hip oblique shit that I tend to write. I'd always try to have simple little beauty things, and love, and all this stuff, because you can't be out of the human milieu. Nobody can do that. I guess that's why I'm so anti-nihilist. It's so easy to think that way, that there is a nihilism in the spoken word scene. I don't think there really is, it's so hyper-traditional.

ENDRE FARKAS: My philosophy's nothing new or shattering, it's basically against the dehumanization of systems, institutions, attitudes that too easily fall into habit. By doing weird things, you question habit. Performance is often about ritual. I think humans are ritualistic. We forget a lot of it by now, because ritual falls into habit, but the performance artist brings us back to the notion of the ritual, that you're doing something for a sacred reason. Not necessarily religious, but there's a sacredness to the performance, that it somehow connects you to other spirits and other organic processes. That's part of the community.

47

ANTHONY BANSFIELD: I had a piece on some of the connections between certain rituals, cultural nuances. Pouring a little rum from the top of the bottle onto the sidewalk before you take a drink, that kind of thing. I was looking at those in an African context, and a Pan African context.... I guess those things come from a philosophical context for me, some of my readings and observations and just talking to people on African culture, and how some of these forms find their way around the diaspora.... Maybe that can creep into somebody's dome and fortify an identity.

LEAH VINEBERG: I think art's very mystical, mysterious, it's very divine. Because art is really alive, and I believe that anything that is alive is really divine. It's like time, you can participate in it or not, but it's there for you. It should be new to you. If it's not, then it's not alive.

AKIN ALAGA: My philosophy is Ogun, the Yoruba deity. There are seven Ogun, seven personalities or faces of Ogun, which is stronger than saying functions. One of them is the god of creative instinct. But at the same time, what I really love about him is that he's also an outcast, loner god. That's why it's really significant to me that I started to write when I felt like an outcast. I channeled a lonely instinct into creativity. He's also a terrorist, but that's supposed to be (laughs) some kind of symbol for political activism. He's a whole bunch of things. So my philosophy usually has something to do with him.... Some poems are about something else, but then I put one small mark here at the side, so only if you're a careful Ogun reader, you say, "Ah, here's Ogun here." Even if I'm talking about my daughter, the voice in which I talk about it is heavily Ogun. The

eyes, the lens through which I'm looking at her is Ogun. That philosophy's very complex.... I'm trying to figure out now how Ogun translates himself here in Canada, without shouting, "Ogun!" I'm trying to let what I think is essentially Ogun translate itself, or be able to identify it as it translates itself here, in order to not come out onstage and say Ogun this and Ogun that. That's how I'm trying to make that relationship with the audience.

TODD SWIFT: I have several core beliefs. Poetry is the highest form of human communication and celebration. Poetry must engage with its historic and present communities. Poetry should attain to significant speech open to all or most or many. Poetry contains multitudes; all are welcome; no one way is the only way. Poets must be good to one another, recognize the shared struggle. Anyone who follows these tenets is likely to feel a lot better about themselves as an artist, even as a person, especially if others in their community are working within the same understanding. It has to be about a comprehensive vision — comprehending not simply the easy differences, but the vast, difficult differences we suggest to one another. My poetry is a secular religion, in other words. Or would you prefer, a politics?

"Being aware of language"

Spoken word artists, whether they come from literary, performance or visual arts backgrounds, have a fascination with language. How words connect, how they affect the listener.

ANNE STONE: I'm incredibly concerned with being aware of language as my medium, as a palpable, textured thing, just the way a visual artist who works in

Akin Alaga
Photo courtesy of the artist

acrylics (rubs hands together) *feels* that shit between their fingers and smells it and has this real sense of it. I want that. And also, I'm very concerned with the very old idea that the words that you think in, and the way that you place them, your particular language within another language, like within English, the way that you're forming the semantic clusters that you're using are going to change — regulate — your consciousness and what you can see and not see, and what's articulated can lead you in certain directions. So with writing, I'm very interested in that, and how that relates to power dimensions in the smallest everyday little things that you do, and how that affects interrelationships. How it's, in a sense, political. I'm also very concerned with issues of class and gender, and playing with those, and with possibilities. What does it mean to construct a narrative? What does it mean to let that go, to shatter it, to rupture it? What can you do with something that's unspeakable, how can you circulate it, what happens?

ZOË WHITTALL: I think when I started out writing, I had a big philosophy around writing for social change. And then for a while I had a big philosophy around writing to ding my ex-lovers, and more funny stuff. Now, I'm particularly interested in storytelling, and what kind of words, what kinds of sounds and rhythms translate into telling people stories. I used to sit down and think, "How can I write about this issue?" Now I sit down and it's, "How can I write?" I'm looking at the craft, and I'm looking at the words, and looking at how it fits together and how that sounds.

THOTH HARRIS: Just learning the language a bit, it's actually really complicated. It's even more of a complicated structure than music, because there's no pre-described form or formula, we have to learn it ourselves. I've always liked the idea of reinventing the wheel, I don't know why it's considered so heretical to reinvent the wheel. I think we should all reinvent the wheel, that way we'd figure out how things work and see things. I mean, a wheel is actually quite complicated.

CATHERINE KIDD: I think I'm trying to mend some kind of Cartesian split. Spoken word isn't acting, you're not putting anybody on, and it's not philosophy or religion, despite all the pre-show rituals (laughs). It's not philosophy or religion unless in some broader sense of a conversation or a communication.... That would be the philosophy, about how a body stores its stories. How if you change the story, you change the teller. Sometimes the same piece can be delivered more humourously or more somberly, dark and creepy or light and airy. You change that about the story and your whole constitution changes. Just like diet and exercise, the same thing, when you start to rewrite your own stories or look at them a different way, it affects everything. How you carry yourself, your voice. When you look at the same story from a number of different perspectives, it pushes out your own frontiers. I know from writing the book *Bestial Rooms* that that's the process of the protagonist. When she starts to take into consideration her mother's account, her father's account, their points of view, and work them into her own story, it makes her a bigger animal. I think that the metaphors and the images that you take in and that you absorb change you, so the body is a carrier of text, or the text is a carrier of the body (laughs).

Catherine Kidd
July 1997

"Food for people's spirit"

Part of the motivation for spoken word performance is the circulation of ideas: issues of gender, race and class, environmental issues, social justice issues, globalization, marginalization, and all points inbetween. The question is, can this circulation create real social change?

ALEX BOUTROS: Kaarla and I are concerned about circulating information. For us, it comes in the form of stories. But you could circulate it in the form of a newspaper article, or you could circulate it in the form of an academic essay. Because when you know, then you can do something with that knowledge. But when you don't even have that knowledge, you can't really do anything.

ANNA-LOUISE CRAGO: The overriding philosophy came out of little anarcho-punk circles. In the whole do-it-yourself get-it-out-there. Just make what you can out of what you've got, and that's valid for what it is. DIY is not discouraging you from honing it, but you don't need to have a whole back-up or theoretical understanding of why you're doing it.

ANTHONY BANSFIELD: Some of the artists from the *Wordlife* CD[16] went down to the Nuyorican Poets Café... we did a little feature. I compared the stuff that the six of us from Canada were doing, to the stuff the New York poets were doing. They were both very good but the difference often lay in an earnestness in the stuff that we were doing. I think the New York poets had a bit of a jaded feel. Sometimes it's like, "How good a performer could I be? How much could I amaze you with wit and with style?" Whereas I think some of the pieces we

were doing were more, "There's an important thing I gotta say here. Hear me out." That's always the way I prefer to approach whatever I do.... If it's worth saying, then it should be said, and if it's purely for the sake of style and flash, too much of that after a while becomes like mind candy. I don't want to sound really profound, or like I'm dead serious about all this, because there's a pleasure factor too, if I just have fun with words. But I think that people respond to it, that you're up there doing a piece *because* it has something important to say.

HUGH HAZELTON: Lately, my poetry's been more politicized, which I see as interesting. When I've taken flack from that, well, you have to put your own culture into the context of other cultures. In Latin America, there's never been a problem with that at all. There's a whole school of Central American writers who integrated talking about the history as part of their poetry. Ernesto Cardenal, a Nicaraguan writer. Roque Dalton also. Art for art's sake and all that stuff never interested me. I like the integration of the two, and then bringing in other elements. I have a poem about death that was more or less triggered by the death of my stepmother several years ago. But I bring in political elements. She's dying in a cancer ward where there is a television on and on the television they're talking about, "Good evening, this is the news. Tonight artillery pounded enemy positions," without mentioning the country or anything.... Actually, she died with the television on.

NAH EE LAH: I don't think that as a Black person in North America I have the privilege of doing art for art's sake. It's a privilege to be able to write about the sky and not attach it to the fact that the

16 Various artists. *Word Life: Tales of the Underground Griots* CD. Bansfield, Anthony, producer. Toronto: Revword, 1998.

sun is giving us cancer because we're destroying our environment and the ozone layer is depleting. My personal experiences and how I view my environment does not permit me to view it in abstraction. Writing and performing for me is a tool to reach out to the communities. It's a way of saying we need to think a little more about what's happening. So my philosophy is really to provoke thought, and for me it's a release. When I'm walking I hear the comments, how people look at me, how they respond to me. That's my reality. How can that not come through in my writing? People asking me all the time where I'm from, like I can't be from here. And so for me it's a release, because if not, I would go on a rampage through the city, and I would just be trying to destroy every system.... Since I can't change the world myself, I want to put my thoughts out to maybe provoke other thoughts in other people's heads and to get wheels turning.... Art is an integral part of change, art is an integral part of evolution, and it's food, it's food for people's spirit.

JAKE BROWN: I want people to know concrete facts about the history of the planet, and the history of social relations on the planet that they might not otherwise know. I want them to know the ramifications that they might not know of facts that they might know.... There's kind of an ur-issue that takes precedence over all of my activities, including art and teaching and having a life, which is this: David Suzuki's last edition of *The Nature of Things*, the season closer [for the 1999-2000 season]. Much of what I've been saying onstage, he said in a very calm, effective way to a national television audience, which is that the planet is about to die, unless there's a significant shift in the

nah ee lah
Photo by Chris Kralik

way we think about things.... I'm thinking while I'm still alive, I must broadcast this message in any form that I can, to as many people as I can, and that'll be my moral obligation.... I'm able to read quickly and with a big intertext in my head, so I'm recognizing things over and over again, old wine in new bottles. Then I open the connections, so that's where my skill is. That's what I'm trained to do, so I'm going to put those skills in the service of broadcasting this message.

ANDRÉ LEMELIN: A philosophy?... I'd say I have a utopia. Creative work should have critical content. Content that reflects on the political, on the social. I demand this type of content of myself, especially as opposed to entertainment. We live in a leisure society which is void of any critical content. Sports, for example, are just pure form, there's no political content there. Certainly there is one in the 'meta-sports' sense, two countries competing, the game is played at the ideological level. But in spectator sports, people watching two hockey teams moving around on the ice, there's no critical content in that. In opposition to these

ANDRÉ LEMELIN: Une philosophie?... Je dirais plutôt que j'ai une utopie: la création devrait posséder un contenu critique. Un contenu de réflexion de l'ordre du politique, du social. Ce type de contenu, je l'exige pour moi, et surtout par opposition au divertissement. Aujourd'hui, on vit dans une société de loisirs qui est dépossédée de tout contenu critique. Le sport, par exemple, est uniquement de la forme pure, sans contenu politique. Certes, il y en a un au niveau "métasportif", quand deux pays se rencontrent, ça se joue au niveau idéologique. Mais si on reste au niveau du spectateur, des gens qui vont regarder deux équipes de hockey se déplacer sur la glace, on n'y retrouve aucun contenu critique. Moi, par opposition à ces formes culturelles dépossédées de contenu, je veux que l'acte de création ait sa spécificité, justement en tant que discours critique.

Cette réflexion, je l'ai aussi dans le milieu du conte. Évidemment, tous ne partagent pas mon avis. Il y en a qui disent: "Moi, je veux faire oublier leur réalité au monde. Pendant que je raconte une histoire, ils ne pensent plus à leur travail." De mon côté, je dirais plutôt: "Non, justement, il faut leur y faire penser, il faut leur faire prendre conscience que travailler 40 heures par semaine à heures fixes est aberrant."

empty cultural forms, I want the creative act to have its specificity, precisely as critical discourse. And I've had these same thoughts concerning people in the storytelling milieu. Obviously, not everybody agrees with me. Some say: "I want to make them forget their reality. When I'm telling a story, people forget about their job." I say: "No, on the contrary, you have to make them think about it. Make them aware that working forty hours a week on a fixed schedule is sheer nonsense."

KAARLA SUNDSTRÖM: Anybody who is idealistic or has any sort of political activism in their blood sees the stage as a forum upon which one can evoke dialogue about certain issues. As much as we don't want to be up there saying, "You should do this! Why is everybody acting in this way? You're all wrong!" It's not just that. It's also about appreciating culture, participating in culture, it's entertaining, it's a lot of things. But simultaneously it's also about representing realities that are perhaps sometimes poorly represented, or invisible. Which is to say we talk about being queer, often, but we also talk about all of the other types of issues that intersect with anything that anyone could encounter within Western society.

JOHN GIORNO: I wrote 'Pornographic Poem,'[17] a found poem, really gay, in-your-face, which in 1965, 1966, was incredibly radical. Nobody used pornography. Between the end of 1965 to 1969, you have no idea of the change. In 1969 there was a nude person on the cover of *Life* magazine, because of *Hair*. It happened really quickly. 1965 was still the fifties. Nobody used sexually-explicit images, no artist ever did.... The fact that Bob Rauschenberg, Jasper Johns

and Andy Warhol were gay — even *more* reason to not allow themselves to be seen as gay artists, because it would have killed their careers. To them, their careers were most important. So when I did it, I thought to myself, "I'm a poet. Fuck *their* careers. I'll do what I damn please and do what I want to do. I'm a gay man." It seems simple when I say that, but we're talking walking blindfolded in traffic. You had no idea whether it was a gigantic mistake or whatever. But I didn't care, I was going to do whatever was in my heart.

VINCE TINGUELY: My work's politicized because I'm politicized, for better or worse. It's just become part of what I am. I can't — short of a lobotomy — get rid of a certain perspective on the world once it's there, because the political understanding that I have of the world came via an emotional impact. Intellectually, I knew something was wrong a long time ago. When I was a teenager, I could intellectually understand that ozone depletion was going to be a problem down the line. But it impacted on me emotionally at a certain point, and that was when I changed. That was when I became politically conscious. So because it's part of my consciousness now, it comes out in my work.

TETSURO SHIGEMATSU: If I share some anecdote from childhood, and it's been told and re-told many times and I think it's nearing the point where I'm going to 'freeze the design', so to speak, people will point out that even though it's a simple story on the surface, it's rife with political questions, issues about gender, sexuality, religion, all these really big themes. And I think, "Wow!" because if I ever began with tackling those themes in mind, I probably could never get

[17] Various authors. *The New York School of Poets*. New York: Random House, 1967.

started. I'm telling autobiographical stories, but over the years I've become at least more aware sociologically that some of the stories that I'm telling, and part of their interest and their relevance, is that I happen to be Japanese-Canadian. And it just so happens that in this particular time in history, there's not a big Asian-Canadian literature or other Asian-Canadian performers who are working in the same tradition as I am. So by virtue of the fact that I was born at this time in history, I happen to be breaking ground, or doing things that have not been done before.

VICTORIA STANTON: A motivation for me to write, is to get a sense of why the world works the way it does. And then what role I play in the world, and how it came to be that I am who I am and that I do what I do.... It's always a set of relationships, and that's what I am writing about. Often it is political, but not exclusively.... Sometimes I think just the act of *doing* the kind of work that we're doing is political in itself.

ANNA-LOUISE CRAGO: I think I get frustrated, because I'm so politically keen and involved that sometimes I'm conscious that my writing becomes a vehicle for messages, as opposed to being its own integral force. And so I think political awareness will always, and should always, be omnipresent in my life, but that said, I also don't want to just make the most flowery manifesto I can.

"There must always be some fun"

An important element, and an often overlooked motivation for spoken word performance is the sense of joy and exhilaration that arises from interacting with the audience.

Victoria Stanton at La Centrale, December 1998
Photo by Guy L'Heureux

VICTORIA STANTON: The Talking Heads have had such a big impact on me because they're really *playful*. Sometimes that playfulness is also political, because as an adult, you're not supposed to be absurd and silly. I don't mean childish, but childlike. That's kind of taboo for adults. That's what artists do, real people in the working world aren't supposed to have fun. So having fun in itself is a political thing.

COREY FROST: Incorporating humour into art is in itself kind of a taboo.

RAN ELFASSY: I think the art should be very serious, but the artists shouldn't be serious about themselves. And I think that's part of the problem with the performance thing, that the really good people aren't telling you that they're good. Whereas the people who aren't that good are so eager to convince you that they're the genius that is unrecognized, that they are screaming just so they become famous and remembered.

LOUISE DUBREUIL: There are a lot of hard things about being an artist, I think, so just try to add in some fun. It's my

PASCAL DESJARDINS: Ce qu'on fait avec Les Abdigradationnistes, ça n'a jamais été sérieux. Ça a toujours été improvisé. On n'a pas de philosophie. On commence à peine, en fait, à en réaliser le potentiel.

PASCAL FIORAMORE: Oui, maintenant on se rend plus compte du pouvoir d'action que nous avons.

motto. It doesn't mean there's no stress involved, or no anxiety, but that there must always be some fun. When I had a hard time justifying myself as an artist, it was because I was having a good time... but that's a whole psychological *saga.* I do not have a dental plan, and I don't have a car, and I don't have a retirement plan, but I have some enjoyment (laughs)!

PASCAL DESJARDINS: What *Les Abdigradationnistes* do has never been serious and it's always been improvised. We have no philosophy. We just thought it up without really giving it any direction. In fact we're just starting to realize our potential.

PASCAL FIORAMORE: Yes, we're becoming more aware of the possibilities behind what we're doing.

NATHALIE DEROME: I have no philosophy. The only one is pleasure. Because it's really hard, and it's really a strange *métier,* profession. It's a nice philosophy, to give something very small to a lot of people, and to have energy to respond and answer questions. I'm closer to nature when I'm doing shows. It's like with nature, when you go to the real nature, you are not the master. Doing shows, it's the same.... You have no protection, but you're not in danger, you're nude. How do you deal with this? In a way it's really self-conscious, "I'm nude!" and in a way it's really generous, "I'm nude with you!" It's like, to believe that intimacy, it could be *politique.* And it's *écologique.* After, there's nothing. That's why I like theatre better than publication. Afterwards you have no books, nothing! It was a meeting, and that's all. But, it's *utopique.* That's why I think I stay in the profession... and that's why it's so beautiful that there are these currents like spoken word. It's like something subterranean is trying to exist....

Pascal Fioramore and Pascal Desjardins:
Les Abdigradationnistes *CD cover*
Vierges, mais expérimentées

Fluffy Pagan Echoes
(from left) Justin McGrail, Victoria Stanton, Vince
Tinguely, Scott Duncan, Ran Elfassy
January 1995
Photo by Susan Coolen

GROUP PIECE FOR FLUFFY PAGAN ECHOES

VICTORIA

I	need	a	sound	check
I	need	a	sound	check
An	nish	in	nah	beh
A	week	in	the	sun
Whispering	winds	in	the	willows
		incest		
		incept		
		insane		
		innate		
		in	god	we
trust	the	man	with	the
star	bright	star	light	first
star	I	see	to	night
star	clusters			
star		fields		
star			dust	
star				mania
star	walker	is	a	friend
of				mine
is	a	friend	of	mine

(all)   is a friend of mine

Text by Vince Tinguely

55

voice #5	voice #6	voice #7
quebec	separate	ici
quebec	separat	ici
quebec	separa	ici
quebec	separ	ici
quebec	sepa	ici
quebec	sep	ici
quebec	se	ici
quebec	s	ici
quebe		ici
ueb		ici
e* elongated	long with pauses "e"	
Oh Canada	Oh Canada	
vendu	vendu	
vendu	vendu	
vendu	vendu	
vendu	vendu	

Allez-y, repartez à zéro!
Allez-y. Allez magasiner chez
Steinberg, Eaton, ou Cooprix
Derrier vos carosses en
aluminium Alcan.

Approchez! Montez-vous un stock
de nos 'nouveaux-oeuillets-a
boutonnière-fabriqués au Canada
pour les canadiens et faites
du ski en robe de noce.

14

Handwritten notes at right margin:

cut 2

C₂ long on S 2-6
switch back & forth
2 "here/ici"

finish on C₂

dances
them profile

④ CU S-5/CUT   profile #7

C₁/1 3 5/
C₂ 2/4/6

cut to black
C₁ CU S-5 profile
C₂ field of depth profile CUT #10

① CU S-7 fade to 1

Face-Off / Mise au Jeu
text by Endre Farkas
Photo by Christian Knudsen

SPOKEN WORD PRACTICE

VI

1. Writing For Performance — Conception

There are two general approaches spoken word artists use to create their work. For those who come from a more-or-less literary background, the germ of an idea is quickly put into text, and the text in turn becomes a performance. However, for those who focus mainly on presenting work to an audience in a live setting, the approach to composition is more immediately in the body and mind.

i. Writing from the Body

Some spoken word artists begin composing texts in relation to the body, and the movement of the body through space. Although the text is eventually committed to paper, this often only happens at the end of the process of composition.

TRISH SALAH: How I get started sometimes is by talking in my head. I either get drunk enough or introverted enough, and I wander the streets and I think out loud. Usually first in my head, and then out loud, and start playing with how I hear the sounds and the language I'm composing — or that's composing me at that particular moment. Then I run for a notebook (laughs) and start jotting it down.

D. KIMM: Walking or biking or doing the dishes, I'm often saying my texts to myself, at times very loudly with a lot of intensity. That's how I learn them and work on them.

DEBBIE YOUNG: I walk down the street and a rhythm, a beat will come into my head, and then I will put words to that beat. As opposed to words, and then a beat.... So the work is oral, at first. That's how my mind processes it. And *then* it gets written down on paper where I'll do the nit-picking, making sure it fits into a type of stanza, this type of thing. So first of all it comes to me musically; poetry and music are intrinsically linked in my head. I think it's the whole reggae dub thing.

ANNA-LOUISE CRAGO: I think it's fabulous, because I've learned to continue playing pretend even though I'm no longer a kid. I'll just get into some sort of imaginative frenzy, and then out of that, or out of some horrible emotional episode — sometimes I'll have very happy events, other times nasty sludge in the way of life — it'll just push it all out. It just *has* to come out or my head'll explode.

To me, for so long writing was just a must-do. If I don't do it, I'm not going to sleep for three days. If I don't do it, I'm not going to be able to go on with my day. It was such a necessity and at the same time I was very passionate about it, so it wasn't a begrudged necessity. And I think I write for a lot of those same reasons, but I think my life's rhythm has calmed down a certain amount.... It's not like I feel like I'm discovering some divine truths, I think it's like my imagination is working overtime. If I don't go home to write about what it felt like to pretend I was a statue, I'll be out there

IN THIS SECTION, WE FOLLOW THE PROCESS OF BRINGING A SPOKEN WORD PERFORMANCE TO THE STAGE. THE PROCESS BEGINS WITH THE CONCEPTION OF A TEXT, AND THE PREPARATION OF A TEXT FOR LIVE PERFORMANCE. EVEN THE SIMPLEST KIND OF SPOKEN WORD PERFORMANCE, THE LITERARY READING, REQUIRES A CERTAIN AMOUNT OF PREPAREDNESS. AS THE PERFORMANCE BECOMES MORE COMPLEX — IN DURATION, THE SIZE OF THE VENUE, THE USE OF VOICE, MUSICAL OR OTHER KINDS OF COLLABORATION — SO DOES THE PREPARATION. CENTRAL TO ACHIEVING A HIGH LEVEL OF AUDIENCE ENGAGEMENT ARE THE MEMORIZATION OF TEXTS, MOVEMENT AND OTHER THEATRIC SKILLS.

D. KIMM: En marchant ou en faisant du vélo, ou en lavant la vaisselle, je suis souvent en train de dire mes textes, parfois même très fort, avec beaucoup d'intensité. Je les apprends et je les travaille comme ça.

for another three hours pretending, so I should go home and write (laughs).

NATHALIE DEROME: There were no words in my performances at the beginning, or only a few words. And suddenly I started to talk, so I started to write more. But I'm not writing. I'm walking in a space and eating cherries and I put on music and dance and sometimes I talk alone, and when the show arrives I write it. In the end, I put it on paper because it helps *mémoire*.... I think I'm not writing, I'm stealing ideas.... I think the work is to make the path of all the cultures I know and try to find the culture I don't know.

PATRICIA LAMONTAGNE: Well, I certainly don't sit at a table to write. I'm almost always standing, I need space. The question I ask myself, when I do stage work, is which is the best medium to get people to feel what I want them to feel. My focus is always what I want people to feel — not what I want to say. And also, what I want them to feel the most. Once I've found the emotion, I have my focus, and from that 'centre' I really have a 360° way of working. For example, I can think: "I imagine sharp sounds," and with this in mind I put my 'tools' in place. I've never written in a linear way for the stage, I prefer working vertically. It's not chronological either, there's no beginning, middle and end. It's a bit like patchwork. In 1985, 1987, at *Espace GO* — in those days it was the *Théâtre expérimental des femmes* — I wrote something very vertical, not unlike polyphony. Like an orchestra conductor, I always have to be standing up to feel the emotion in my body. For me, a word is nothing, and even less so onstage. I firmly believe this. You may have the most gorgeous sentences in the world, the cleverest

ideas, but the fact is that the stage embodies a physical energy. That's where something happens here and now. And the goal is emotion. Emotion — not necessarily joy or sorrow, but something that happens in the body. A physical sensation.

CATHERINE KIDD: Jack Beets and I worked out that it takes about a month from beginning to end, to put together a performance piece. First I write the thing, so it's externalized and re-absorbed, and then edited towards the performance medium.... I do find — and this is one of the attractions of performance to me — that words come very fluidly through my *hands* when I'm typing. They bypass cerebrality altogether. That's when I like it best. There's only so much you can keep in your head, and head wisdom doesn't take into account slower wisdoms like time, the passage of time, and process. I trust the text that tends to come from that kind of process.

ii. Sound / Visualization

As important as movement, sound or images often trigger the creative process, or else they figure in the composition of a text.

IAN FERRIER: I'm looking for voices that you might hear on the edge of sleep, when you're just falling asleep and everything becomes chaotic for a minute. At that point, in my own imagination, I'll hear a voice talking, or a fragment of a sound. I'm looking for the authenticity of that inner voice, and also for the soundscape to give a texture to that, and a context to it.

ANTHONY BANSFIELD: The pieces usually have a sound, first. Sometimes the sound takes the form of words, and

PATRICIA LAMONTAGNE: Ce qui est sûr, c'est que je ne m'assois pas à une table de travail pour écrire. Je suis presque toujours debout, j'ai besoin d'espace. La question que je me pose, quand je fais de la scène, c'est quel est le médium qui va servir le mieux ce que je veux faire ressentir. Alors mon "centre", si on veut, c'est ça: ce que je veux faire ressentir. Non pas ce que je veux dire. Quand j'ai trouvé l'émotion, j'ai comme mon "centre" et, à partir de là, je travaille vraiment à 360 degrés. Par exemple, je peux dire: "Ah oui, j'imagine des sons dans les aigus", alors là je mets mes médiums en place. Mais je n'écris jamais de façon linéaire quand je fais de la scène, j'aime plutôt travailler avec la verticalité. Et ce n'est pas chronologique non plus. Il n'y a pas de début, milieu, fin. C'est un peu comme du *patchwork*. En 1985, 1987, à l'Espace GO, avec le Théâtre expérimental des femmes à l'époque, j'avais écrit quelque chose de très vertical, un peu comme de la polyphonie. Et comme un chef d'orchestre, il faut toujours que je sois debout pour ressentir l'émotion dans mon corps. Un mot, pour moi, ce n'est rien et encore moins sur la scène. Je le crois profondément. Tu peux avoir les plus belles phrases au monde, les meilleures idées, mais il reste que la scène, c'est l'incarnation d'une énergie corporelle. C'est le lieu où il y a quelque chose qui se passe, *here and now*. Puis, le but, c'est l'émotion. Émotion — pas nécessairement joie ou peine. Quelque chose qui se passe dans le corps. Une sensation.

58

sometimes it's just a little chant. Normally I write it down later. I might go back to orally shape it, and write a little more down. I think more and more they've come as sounds, little patterns, little riffs, little drumbeats (laughs). But I'm a lazy artist, very honestly. I sometimes might sit down and force myself to write something, or to create something, but normally I just do that as it comes to me, for the fun of it.

KAARLA SUNDSTRÖM: Occasionally Alex and I have called each other and said, "Okay, write this down!" More and more, I think we start with something that sounds good. A good line or a good melody. We remember that — we'll record it on a tape too, just in case — and we'll start structuring things around that. It usually turns into a chorus, something that we've written first, but it changes all the time. We're very particular about what it sounds like in the end. We have to agree on things, so there needs to be conversation about order and thematic material. But we don't follow a route.

ALEX BOUTROS: And it doesn't happen that the text comes first, and then the sound. It's simultaneous. In terms of content, we always have lists of pieces. We want to write about this topic, we want to write about that topic. But that tends to go by the wayside because we find these lines that we like and then build the piece around that.

NAH EE LAH: Right now, I write when I'm inspired. I don't visualize it. I hear the sentences in my head. Sometimes I'll have an idea, and I'll start off writing two or three lines, and then the piece will start. So often, after I write the piece, I take out the first two or three lines. Because it's getting me started,

and then I'll write the entire piece. Or I'll hear a song in my head, and I know that if I don't have pen and paper, then I'll get one line, but the line will be gone. If I think it, and don't actualize it, it'll be gone. I can't retrieve it. If I'm in that mode where it's just coming — write write write write, finished. Then I'll go back and edit it.

SYLVAIN FORTIER: I often read my texts while I'm writing, to make sure there's a good beat, or the sound is OK. This is important to me. I also use randomness — that is, I write letters of the alphabet, sequences of letters, and then I check with the computer dictionary and it suggests words: "This word does not exist, but there's this word, this word, this word," then, oops, suddenly there's a word that interests me because of its sound, because it evokes an image. So I write it down. This is how I start a poem. Except that I find it very important to keep some meaning, to not be only rhythmic or attached to an image. There has to be a thread, one I'm able to follow. And I go on from there. When I write I'm not thinking that my audience is going to read me or hear me. I'm wondering if I'm comfortable with the images, with the beat, the sounds, etc. So sometimes I get a bit lost, but there's always that thread connecting me to my original idea.

JULIE CRYSLER: I would have a series of images. Usually it was a sentence, a particular image, a series of sounds that seemed to be expanding. I would have to sit and write it down, and as I would type, it would grow very very quickly. Speaking and writing at the same time, driving my room-mate crazy. Then as I'd read it through I'd start to realize what the next line was. The stuff that I like the best that I've written has come

SYLVAIN FORTIER: Souvent, je lis mes textes pendant que je les écris, pour m'assurer que la rythmique est correcte, de même que la sonorité. C'est important pour moi. Aussi, je me sers de l'aléatoire, c'est-à-dire que j'écris des lettres, des suites de lettres, et ensuite je les vérifie avec le dictionnaire de l'ordinateur et ça me suggère des mots. "Ce mot-là n'existe pas, mais il y a tel mot, tel mot, tel mot"; puis, oups, il y a un mot qui m'intéresse par sa sonorité, parce qu'il évoque une image. Alors je l'écris, et ainsi de suite. Et c'est comme ça que je débute un poème. Sauf que, pour moi, c'est très important de garder un certain sens, qui ne soit pas que rythmique ou uniquement rattaché à une image. Il faut qu'il y ait un fil. Un fil que, moi, je suis capable de suivre. À partir de là, je continue. Quand j'écris, je n'ai pas en tête que mon public va me lire, ou m'entendre. Ce que j'ai en tête à ce moment-là, c'est si moi je suis à l'aise avec les images, avec le rythme, les sonorités, etc. Certes, parfois je peux me perdre un peu, mais il y a toujours un fil qui me rattache à mon idée de départ.

Julie Crysler
October 5, 1999 in Toronto

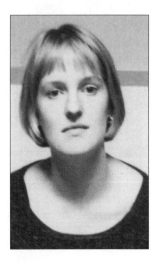

out very quickly. It's not laboured and slow, but comes out of speaking... so the sound of the voice, the music of the language and the rhythm of the language is part of it from the very beginning.

ANDRÉ LEMELIN: Some stories I build in my head, mentally. Actually, I visualize them. For example, '*Le Bloc de ciment*' [in *Hold-up! Contes du Centre-Sud*, CD / book], I remember it clearly, I was sitting in the *Carré St-Louis*, and by visualizing it, seeing it, telling it to myself, it literally ambushed me, overcame me, came alive inside me. I headed to the *Saint-Sulpice* bar and wrote down my story in one go, right there on the *terrasse*....

LEAH VINEBERG: After writing 'Narcissus vs. Machiavelli', there were certain pieces that I would be writing, but it was coming so quickly that I started speaking them into a little dictaphone. This started becoming quite different, and in a weird way... I don't know how literary they were. Bits of them were extremely complex writing, and bits of them were extremely simplistic. The voices were changing. When I took the work off the page, the voice started changing. It made more room. I think at that point I went from doing spoken word — as reciting poetry — to performance.

TETSURO SHIGEMATSU: One story I wrote, I dictated it entirely into a microphone. And good or bad, it was hard to edit down, because there was just a lot of fat that didn't need to be there. I find sometimes if I'm just typing, and maybe because my fingers don't go as fast as my mouth, subconsciously I'll begin to edit. If I go back and re-polish it so it has the peculiar rhythms of speech, that's probably a better process for me.

But I don't read it out loud any more. Although mentally, in my mind, I do try to hear a voice.

JOHN GIORNO: I used to be very fussy, pruning, and I had to have a live microphone. I wanted to hear the sound of the word from the beginning, while I'm working on it, so that if there's some awkwardness in the words, I know what the problem is. I used to have a live mic just to hear it over speakers. You hear the quality of the word and the quality of the phrasing. I wanted to hear what it really sounded like as I was writing it down longhand. If there was any problem with it, I would get rid of the problem at the beginning, before it got onto the computer, or before it got onto the page in the typewriter. Because when you hear it amplified, it's apparent.

SCOTT DUNCAN: My stories often came from a visual image I'd have in my head. For instance, the last 'Loon Story' I told came the weekend my grandmother sold the cottage where I'd spent every summer growing up. I was at the lake practicing strokes in the old cedar canoe and my grandmother was on her veranda yelling for me to come in to eat lunch. I was crying at the time. Two loons would dive and resurface around me. This led me to think about the canoe sinking and me joining the loons so that I wouldn't have to leave the lake. The nice thing about stories is that you can meld something real — which I think a lot of people can relate to — with something magical. That can be entertaining for the audience — and for me — and may also shed light on whatever it is you are discussing. I played a game with myself with my stories as well. I always tried to stick a television set somewhere in the story.

ANDRÉ LEMELIN: Certaines de mes histoires, sont construites mentalement. En fait, je ne les construis pas, je les visualise. Par exemple, "Le Bloc de ciment" (*Hold-up! Contes du Centre-Sud* , CD/livre), je me le rappelle très bien, j'étais assis au carré St-Louis et à force de la visualiser, de la voir, de me la raconter, elle m'a littéralement assailli, envahi, habité. Je me suis aussitôt dirigé au bar Le Saint-Sulpice et puis là, sur la terrasse, dans un jet, j'ai écrit mon conte.

*Scott Duncan
October 1999 in Toronto*

COREY FROST: I'm a really slow writer, so I do a lot of pre-editing before I start. Everyone always tells me I shouldn't do that, but that's the way it is. I tend to think about things quite a bit. If I'm writing a piece specifically for performance, I don't really have to say it out loud. I have a grasp of how it's going to sound. So I tend to finish at least a draft of it completely, on paper or on the computer screen rather, and then when I feel like it's got a rough shape, I print it out. Then I start memorizing it, and after I memorize it, it evolves quite a bit. You write some things and you think it's going to sound good, but you start repeating it and you realize it's just awkward.

iii. Collage

A text is a distillation of interrelated concepts through the artist. Several of the people we interviewed described their writing process as a collaging of ideas.

GENEVIÈVE LETARTE: My creative process, it's really like (sounds of explosions), it goes every which way. It's hard to explain.... Everything connected to performance is more like collage. It can start on the street and end on the computer. Or the other way around. It can start off as a song and end up spoken.

ANDRÉ LEMELIN: Due to my background, I draw on a kind of undefined mixture: visual arts, literature and philosophy. Out of this came a working 'method' that evolved through an analogy with the visual arts: a very intuitive, very free stage of research before outlining the work. Then the work and the outline take shape simultaneously. Linearity is broken apart, the work emerges out of a certain chaos.

JAKE BROWN: My pieces all come the same way. When I'm alone, which is as many as six or eight hours a day, I'm reading. When I'm reading, I'm reading history, cultural history, aesthetics, history of aesthetics, novels, and I'm reading incessantly. When what I've read makes a web in my head, that's the piece. The web will connect everything that I've been reading. It has to come as an epiphany, if it doesn't come I don't have a piece. Really, to show how the machine is operating, because normally you don't see the parts operating. If human social relations are a machine, there's lots that we don't normally acknowledge as operating, but they power it. Things like self-interest and shortsightedness and the fact that humans are like animals and not like animals. People don't usually put all of this together, but I try to get them to think of all of it in one moment.

TRISH SALAH: I sit with a blank page in front of me, or a blank screen in front of me, sometimes, and crib lines from other people. Go through any number of books and put quote after quote after quote on the screen, and then start messing the words around, and start wondering what poem might emerge between two lines of two different people's text. Maybe not even keeping those lines of text, more often than not, although perhaps keeping a word from each of them or something like that. This is more writing that I imagine in relation to my own voice, and that arises in relation to my own voice somehow. Even if it's other people's language and other people's quotes, it's like, "OK, where is my voice between these two lines from two different people's text?" That's how things get started.

GENEVIÈVE LETARTE: Mon processus de création, *it's really like (sounds of explosions)*, ça va dans tous les sens. C'est vraiment difficile à expliquer... Tout ce qui a rapport avec la performance, c'est comme du collage. Ça peut commencer quand je me promène dans la rue, et ça finit avec l'ordinateur. Ou ça commence avec l'ordinateur et ça finit dans la rue. Ça commence chanté, puis ça finit parlé.

ANDRÉ LEMELIN: Avec ma formation, je puise dans une espèce de mélange très flou: arts visuels, littérature et philosophie. Ce qui en est sorti, c'est une "méthode" de travail qui s'est construite par analogie aux arts visuels. Une étape de recherche très intuitive, très libre, avant le plan, l'esquisse de l'œuvre. Puis l'œuvre et l'esquisse se construisent en même temps. La linéarité éclate. L'oeuvre prend naissance dans une sorte de chaos.

LOUISE DUBREUIL: The only name I can really stick to my art work as a whole, is that I'm a collage artist.... Whether it be in performance, or in my visual art as well. Or when I do video.... I like to take things that normally wouldn't go together, and make them speak together, either because they kind of fit well together, or because they clash. But, to say that to people — usually they think you just do little collages.

2. Writing For Performance — Execution

Having started a text either mentally or on paper, the spoken word artist shapes it specifically in the direction of live performance. If the text was originally written for the page, it must be re-worked for the stage.

i. The Text in Performance

Here, spoken word artists discuss some of the particular differences in quality between text written for the page, and the text in performance.

CATHERINE KIDD: I thought that the performance work was kind of an extension of my other writing, it was like another medium for it. Rather than the page being the medium, body and voice were the medium. But now it seems to be another thing altogether. Even the process of writing a piece that I'm going to perform onstage is nothing like writing a short story or trying to write that damn novel. Often words on the page posit themselves as absolutes. "It's on the page, it exists for immortality, it must be true." Whereas performance, the words just go off into space, it's a temporal medium. They're only there while they're there. And when it's fin-

ished they're gone. It became its own thing, the performance writing and doing performance. And now it has a big influence on my other writing because I became more and more interested in the idea of text inhabiting body and now just about everything I write has something to do with body parts.

BUFFY CHILDERHOSE: I remember when I started writing performances. I showed a friend of mine some poems, and she really liked them, except she said they were so different from the way that I spoke and the way that I told stories, and why was it that I never wrote in what was my normal voice. I started thinking about it a lot, and then tried to write stuff in the way that I would just tell a story.

TRISH SALAH: I don't know if I've ever read fiction aloud. There are two lines of demarcation. One is fiction, it's not something I've ever read, let alone performed. It's hard for me to imagine how I would perform anything that satisfied anything like the classical structure of a short story, say. Postcard fiction's another animal, and is likely — coming from my hand — to be more prose poetry than anything, anyway. So once you're on the poetry side of the line, the question is, "Am I writing poetry that I'm going to perform, or am I writing poetry that I'm going to read?" Because I feel utterly comfortable reading almost anything that falls on that poetry side of the line. But which pieces ask something more than that? I don't know how I make that discrimination, actually. It's pretty intuitive. I think if I want to be rhetorical and polemical, that's an easy enough way to select something for a more performance-conscious mode.

JEAN-PAUL DAOUST: I enjoy showing the ambiguity that I am a writer, a poet, and that I can also produce texts that are more fragmented and more open, which allow verbal flights that would be unsuitable in other texts. I have lots of texts I never do in public because I believe they need to be read quietly at home. And others I know must be read onstage. I'm very aware of this.

ii. Editing For Performance

When editing a text for performance, the author pays close attention to the qualities which will set the text apart from one written for a reader. This process may be carried out mentally, by sounding out the text, with an 'outside eye', or by reviewing audio and video recordings. By their nature, performance texts remain more fluid and changeable than texts written for publication.

KAIE KELLOUGH: As I write poetry, I always sound it out. I scan it. Sometimes I go to the extent of doing it with a metronome to make sure the music is there, on the page. Sometimes I even sing it to make sure it works.

HÉLÈNE MONETTE: When the text is finished, I read it out loud over and over again. It's very important to rehearse. I time myself, I experiment with sounds. I try to see where I'm stumbling on a word, if some words are hard to pronounce. I try to put in voice inflections at the beginning, the middle and the end, so I won't stumble. At times it has become like a partition. I used to code my texts with slashes or little circles or little "shhh-s," which are meant to lower my voice. I sometimes try to give myself a musical code....

CATHERINE KIDD: When I've written something and I start to read it out loud, and I catch my stutter or falter or there's a glitch somewhere, that would be the place where I go in and sand it down. Make it simpler, because it's to be spoken. Make it more musical.

KAARLA SUNDSTRÖM: We don't always write rhythmically. We don't always write exactly rhymed as we want it to be. Often it comes out that way, and you're hearing something and you write it down. Other times you're not getting that, so you have to slog out the ideas and try to find the good rhymes. After that, when you like it, you try performing it and then you have to cut and splice and work with what you have.... Sometimes we're shoe-horning a lot of words into beats. It's not really strict, and it's not like we have four beats per bar. For us, there has to be a rhythm.

ANNE STONE: I'm more about reading the text afterwards and having it open up to me, and finding out what it does. I love to take it and move it away, and then become deliberate after I have something. Like with the novel,[17] when I did it out loud, I found by the time I had done it a few times, I had re-done the text on the page. So certain things would get broken, cut, reformed, all these things. I could look at the page and the phrases would invert quite regularly, so that it felt good for the voice. So there was this other text. And people would ask to follow along in the book and be utterly confused! (laughs) I thought to myself, "No, don't follow along!"

ANNA-LOUISE CRAGO: I sort of feel like I'm sewing a quilt, and sometimes it will feel like I've sewed it up tight so it's not going to fall apart. But I constantly re-write passages. I think sometimes the

JEAN-PAUL DAOUST: J'aime bien montrer l'ambiguïté: je suis écrivain et poète, et, en même temps, je peux faire des textes plus éclatés, c'est-à-dire qui permettent des envolées orales qui n'auraient pas leur place avec certains autres textes. Il y a des poèmes que j'écris que je ne lis jamais, parce que je me dis qu'ils sont faits pour être lus tranquillement à la maison. Et il y a des textes que je sais qu'ils sont faits pour être lus sur une scène. Ça, j'en suis très conscient.

HÉLÈNE MONETTE: Quand le texte est fini, je le pratique à voix haute, encore et encore. Pour moi, c'est très important de pratiquer. Je me chronomètre, j'expérimente des sonorités. J'essaie de voir si ça bute sur tel mot, s'il y a des mots difficiles à prononcer, j'essaie de mettre l'inflexion de la voix au début, dans le milieu ou à la fin, pour ne pas buter. Ou c'est déjà devenu comme des partitions. Je codais mes textes avec des barres obliques, ou des petits cercles, ou des petits "chut", qui voulaient dire: on baisse le ton. Parfois je tente de me faire un code musical...

Anne Stone
May 1999

17 Stone, Anne. *Hush*. Toronto: Insomniac Press, 1999.

first version is just as correct as the fifth version, it's just quite different. And there were times when I was so neurotic that I would refuse to read without having a pen in my hand so I could make the corrections or the revisions as I was reading. Which isn't to me a sign of being completely dissatisfied with a piece. It's just a sign that a piece changes.

ALEXIS O'HARA: I'm always going back and changing things that I've written before. Which is funny about chapbooks because it seals them, but then when I go to perform them again maybe it'll be different. And you can sample your own work. You can take a line that you really liked out of a piece that didn't work and move it into an entirely new piece. There's too much emphasis placed on structure, I think, and sealing things and making them permanent. There are no rules to what we're doing at all, there shouldn't have to be.

BUFFY CHILDERHOSE: With writing, I'll sit down at my computer, take the scrap of paper, and start trying to order it in a 'literary' way. When I see something that I think lends itself more to performance, I'll take the scrap and memorize it. I end up playing a game of 'Broken Telephone'. I'll write something, and then I'll memorize it — the first draft — and then I'll record it. As I deliver it I'm making changes. Sometimes I make mistakes in the delivery of the memorized piece, and when I play it back I realize, "Oh no, that's what it's meant to be." Or I'll drop lines and realize they should have been dropped. A lot of the changes are on the spot, as I do it. Then I take that tape, and I transcribe that, and then I memorize that version. Then I record that and whittle things down, so I may go through six cycles, and it's very very very different from what I had to begin with.

TETSURO SHIGEMATSU: In regards to my process for pre-performance, I tend to work with a video camera. I do a performance, then I watch, and I take mental notes and I do it again. And just by a process of elimination, improving and noticing things, I analyze myself through video tape.

Michel Choquette is one person who I really clicked with as a director. Our collaboration evolved to the point where today he works with me as a co-writer. And so, I perform, he directs, and we both write it together. His background was as an entertainer – he worked for *National Lampoon*, and as a comedian — whereas I came from a performance art background. And so there's always this creative tension between being entertaining and accessible and funny and fast-paced and providing good value for the money, and on my side, always wanting to push the

Tetsuro Shigematsu
Photo from his web site

envelope, being more culturally or artistically ambitious, and concerned about content and relevance. So together with those two criteria being met, we tend to create material which I hope will be perceived as having the best of both. Even as I write things on my own, I feel that I have internalized this way of working, this check and balance. It's actually very good working with someone who is perhaps more pragmatically-minded, for me as an artist.... By working with Michel, I always know that he's going to put the brakes on. It's kind of like running with your eyes closed along the beach. Running as fast as you can, you know that someone's going to be there to pull you back. So in a sense it liberated parts of my imagination to collaborate with someone who provides that critical voice.

NORMAN NAWROCKI: For a lot of the shows I have consultative committees. Friends, colleagues, peers, people from eighteen to eighty. I put together focus groups and I have them come over to my apartment and I workshop pieces. Not just a poem or a song, but an entire show. These are people from the neighbourhood who come, and they're unemployed, they're pensioners, they're on welfare, they're high school students, whoever they might be. I present my script with the songs, the words. "Well, what do you think?" And then we have discussions on it. I go and rework the material and come back and present it to them again. I love to work like that. So, I've done that for the last two solo shows, and we've done that with our community cabarets as well.

iii. Integrating Elements of Performance

Composing the performance piece in written form doesn't mean it's finished. In order to reach completion, a piece must work on the stage. To carry out the difficult task of polishing the piece, performers must visualize themselves in performance. The text must be integrated with the musical qualities of spoken word, and with complimentary performative elements, such as sound accompaniment, props and movement onstage.

DEBBIE YOUNG: When I'm writing, I see myself performing it. So I don't see the poetry on paper, I see it onstage. In my head I see myself doing, *doing* the poem. It's very clear to me, clear as day. When the words are not there I can still see myself doing the poem, doing the idea of the poem.

CATHERINE KIDD: I read the piece into a little hand-held tape recorder, which I play for days and days and days until it becomes this mindless mantra backdrop. When I'm in the bathroom, when I'm going to sleep. It really does feel like I have to turn off conscious censors and editorial boards, to absorb it.... It's not like I read a line, close my eyes, say it to myself. It's osmotic, memorization is osmotic, which again I trust, because it's not just my head that's going to be up there onstage (laughs). I trust the way a story will inhabit my feet and my hands, and how it will make them move too. All I really have to do up there is be as transparent as possible, or as responsive to the words as possible.

JOHN GIORNO: When I finish a poem, that's that. But then I rehearse it for months. Because even though intellec-

JEAN-PAUL DAOUST: Souvent, il arrive que je vais écrire des textes en sachant qu'ils vont être lus. Si j'ai une commande pour le *Festival de poésie de Trois-Rivières* ou pour une lecture, si je sais que je vais lire à minuit à telle place, à tel moment, je prépare le texte différemment d'une publication. Il y a des textes qui tombent dans le spoken word, ils s'en vont vers ça. Il sont déjà orientés en fonction de l'endroit où je vais les lire. Par exemple, en mai 1999, dans le cadre du *Festival de l'Union des écrivains*, on m'a demandé d'écrire un texte érotique pour l'émission *C'est bien meilleur le matin*, diffusée à Radio-Canada. Pour le faire, j'avais une page, 30 lignes maximum. Je savais que ce texte-là allait être lu à la radio. Alors, évidemment, je l'ai rendu très spoken word, dans le sens que c'était une poésie qui se voulait la plus familière possible. C'était très important pour moi que ça *passe* dans le micro. Que ça ne soit pas un texte qui soit difficile à dire ou à comprendre... Qu'il soit fluide. Ça m'empêchera peut-être de le reprendre pour la publication; ou j'aurai à le changer, à enlever des choses qui sont de trop, qui relèvent plus de la langue orale que de l'écrit. Quoique c'est rare que je modifie un texte tant que ça. Quand je sais que le texte est là, d'habitude, il continue tout seul après. Même s'il finit momifié sur une page.

D. KIMM: Je n'écris pas de textes spécialement pour la performance. Moi, j'écris, puis à un moment donné, il y a un spectacle, et là je me dis: "Tiens, je vais faire ce texte, je vais le retravailler." Quand je retravaille un texte pour la scène, je le change souvent, puis la version finale devient souvent celle de la scène. C'est-à-dire que tout ce que je dis sur scène, il faut que j'aime le dire. Lorsque je répète seule, je peux le dire 50 fois avec toujours autant d'émotion. S'il y a un bout de phrase qui passe mal, je l'enlève. Ça épure le texte d'une façon incroyable. Quand je travaille sur un texte qui va être lu sur scène, ensuite je ne pourrai plus revenir en arrière.

tually you've finished, all the concepts are there, all the words and images are there, inside of those words are musical melodies that one has no idea are there. The only way you can bring them out is by performing it. What I mean by melodies is, you put four or five words together, and just by saying them, there are qualities in those words that are different from the way I'm talking now. Because now I'm talking in discursive words and they're about intellectual thought, and they're not about the sound of the words. So by rehearsing, things come out. Melodies come out. And once it comes out, you don't ever have to think about it again. It comes every time you say it.

JEAN-PAUL DAOUST: I often write texts knowing they'll be read. If I'm commissioned by the *Festival de poésie de Trois-Rivières* or invited to do a reading, if I know I'm reading somewhere at midnight, then I'll set up the text very differently than if it's for publication. Some texts fall into spoken word, they just go in that direction. They're already geared to the place where I'm going to read them. For example, in May 1999, for the *Festival de l'Union des écrivains*, I was asked to write an erotic text for the morning show *C'est bien meilleur le matin* on Radio-Canada. I was allowed one page, thirty lines maximum. I knew this text would be read on the radio, so obviously I made it very spoken word, in the sense that it's a kind of poetry that tries to be as informal as possible while still providing images. It was very important to me that the text come through well over the air, that it not be difficult to say or to understand.... That it be fluid. When it's a commission, I know where the text is going. This may prevent me from publishing it later on;

or I may have to change it, remove a few prepositions, things that are superfluous, that are more spoken word than written, although it's rare that I change a text much. Once I've got the text down, it usually continues on its own afterwards. Even if it ends up mummified on a sheet of paper.

D. KIMM: I don't write specially for performance. I just write, and then at some point for a show and I decide: "OK, I'm going to do that text, I'll rework it." When I rework a piece for the stage, I change it often, and often the stage version becomes the final version. Meaning that I have to love saying everything I say onstage. When I rehearse by myself, I have to be able to say it over fifty times with as much emotion every time. If there's a part of a sentence that doesn't work or doesn't turn me on, I remove it. This cleans up a text in an incredible way. When I work on a text for the stage, after that I can't come back to the older, more written, version.

VICTORIA STANTON: When I work on my own, I start to play with the text while moving with the text. The writing evolves somewhat with moving through the space, working in the studio. But when I write, actually write, I'm always reading aloud. I'm always saying it over and over again. So sometimes this process of memorizing happens while I'm writing, because I say it so many times. Sometimes I even continue writing it after I've learned it. Even though I might be memorizing an earlier version of it, it's important for me. I can't write otherwise. Because the reading it over and over while I'm working on it keeps me very aware of the rhythm of the flow of the piece.

ATIF SIDDIQI: In the past... I always started from the texts and built movement and music and soundtrack and costume and everything else on that, layered over the text. Most often I tried not to be literal, and not to enact or mime anything from the text, but to use much more abstract movement to emphasize something and punctuate the text in some way.... A lot of times I've found, by preparing and rehearsing a piece, with whoever was being an outside eye, that the words were so much to intake and digest that the movement was being lost. Or the movement was so nice to look at, but you couldn't focus on the words. So then I had to pare things down a lot, and perhaps punctuate things differently. Like do a movement, and then say a line of text. Finding different ways of saying it. But the general theme of the text, where it was situated, determined a lot of the movement and the style of how it was going to be delivered.

ALEX BOUTROS: We used to script it all out and put things that we said together in italics, and try to find different fonts to articulate what was going on (laughs), but it became too cumbersome. It became too difficult to script. It tends to remain mostly in our heads. If I say a big chunk by myself, or Kaarla says a big chunk by herself, that's written down, and that's memorized, for the most part. But the rhythm that we say it in, or the melodic material that we say it in is obviously not written down, because it can't be.

DAYNA MCLEOD: I've tried from the beginning to memorize the work.... I write for the ear. Some of the stuff that I've written is like a run-on sentence, it goes for a page. It's all in the delivery. When you read a performance text

sometimes, and if you don't have a sense of their rhythm or their style, and it's not obvious in how it's laid out, or how the punctuation is, or just because of the restrictions of the language, you don't feel that you're getting the full gist of it. But if I can pace it, how I'm saying it to you, then it works.

JUSTIN MCGRAIL: Writing for performance totally freed up where the words ended up on the page, and again it got me more interested in rhythm and using internal rhymes. When I started writing those poems on the page, everything I wrote ended up looking like arrowheads or S's or zig-zags. When I look back I realize that was an attempt to create some sort of direction or pattern or speed. It informed itself right into my hand, literally. I remember when I started doing that more and more, and I freed myself up, then I was conscious of the fact that I was just writing to be heard. It wasn't for the page. Realizing 'spoken word', in a sense, was what freed my poetry up. That's how I found my voice, by literally saying the poems aloud.

iv. Visualizing the Audience

In their preparations, spoken word artists acknowledge the audience to a greater or lesser degree. For some, the audience is everything; for others, it is a minor consideration. In all cases, it is an inescapable fact that the ultimate goal of their work is to perform it in front of the public.

JOHN GIORNO: Sometimes if I'm working on a poem for weeks or months, and if I have a part with a few lines that are not quite working right... week after week I still can't figure it out, it doesn't sound right to me but I don't know how to

Atif Siddiqi
Photo by Norman Cardella

make it right, then I just stand up and do it into the microphone. I visualize an audience and *say it to the audience*. And whatever was wrong would become apparent, because when you're talking to someone, you know what you're talking about. Now I don't need a live mic any more, if I'm working I just say it, and can hear what it sounds like.

TETSURO SHIGEMATSU: Sometimes it'll get a big laugh, and sometimes it'll get a small laugh. When I get a small laugh, I'll analyze it: "Oh yeah, I inserted this extra word into the punch line." Something innocuous to the layperson, but as a writer, if you affect the rhythm you affect everything. And I realize where I'm writing from now is that I'm always conscious of the fact that people are listening.

BUFFY CHILDERHOSE: I know I've written pieces for particular shows, and been aware of the audience as I wrote it, and I really would prefer not to do that. If I'm going to impose external limitations and constraints, that's not the kind of constraint I want to put on my work

(laughs). I could say it's positive experimentation, but I don't think so. This relates back to journalism. I have to be so acutely aware of my audience in so much of the writing that I do, it's nice to be able to abandon that relationship in which I always have an audience or an editor standing over my shoulder. I'm very seldom thinking of an ideal audience, or a particular group of people. I would like it to be able to go beyond the boundaries of a certain community. If you're too aware of your audience, it seems kind of manipulative.

JULIE CRYSLER: I think that there is this thing in journalism where you're trying to provide service — in the jargon of the biz — service to your readers. And I'm not trying to provide my audience with a service. When I first started writing, I started having success with a couple of particular pieces. They were fun to do and fun to perform, and fun for the audience. I tried to write more pieces like that, and as soon as you try to recreate the effect of a particular piece, it starts to lose its power. I had to move away from that notion of trying to recreate the successful poem again and again. But you must be aware of the audience, because when you're crafting it, you're trying to create a piece that's going to be effective, and is going to communicate something.

BENOÎT PAIEMENT: When I write I'm aware that the text is going to be spoken. I'd have no reason to write if I knew it wasn't going to be read or performed in front of an audience. This would produce a kind of weakening of my creative abilities. Writing wouldn't interest me anymore, I would think about it differently.

BENOÎT PAIEMENT: J'écris en ayant à l'esprit que ça va être dit. Pour moi, il n'y aurait vraiment plus aucune raison d'écrire si je savais que ça n'allait pas être lu et joué. Je pense que ça entraînerait un affaiblissement dans mon processus créatif. L'écriture ne m'intéresserait plus, je n'y penserais plus de la même façon.

Julie Crysler and
Buffy Childerhose
October 5, 1999 in Toronto

v. Readings: "Why does it have to be so boring?"

Literary readings represent the simplest kind of spoken word performance. They are generally conceived as a means for literary authors, who normally work in solitude, to share their work with the public. Spoken word artists argue that even a literary reading is a form of performance, and that writers unfamiliar with the world of the stage ought to take that into account, or spare their audiences the pain of a dull reading.

KAARLA SUNDSTRÖM: In terms of audience response, whenever we're performing for a specifically literary event, I don't think we're quite as comfortable. Even if people like it, the response isn't what I want. I would prefer people to be moved, loud and raucous and interacting. It goes to show that our work is moving away from that type of response, and I think we're starting to stick out a bit like a sore thumb. We want to retain the storytelling aspect of our work, that's something that we want to explore, but that has also always been an oral tradition in itself. We can draw from both traditions and not necessarily be defined by a literary one.

FORTNER ANDERSON: The performances are becoming much more polished. And people are creating work specifically to be performed. For many years it was soft-spoken, timid poets reading their precious verse, and it was excruciating, it was awful... poetry was the mummied corpse kept alive by academia.

MICHEL GARNEAU: It's hugely presumptuous to put oneself in front of people and say: "What I'm about to say is interesting enough to make you stay seated, quiet, for half an hour, maybe hours." A personal morality of mine makes it necessary to try to supply some content. We must give our audience pleasure, something to remember in order to justify what we're offering. I prepare accordingly, and try to give the best performance possible. I just suffered too much, all through that era when it was understood that you were going to be bored. I saw poets stand stock-still behind a microphone with a bunch of papers and read for periods of time that were downright inhuman (laughs). In fact it wasn't really all that long. For example, I saw Margaret Atwood reading. Just standing there in front of the microphone, she had darkish glasses and a big hat, you couldn't see her. And she went through — with her horrible voice — an hour of bitchy bullshit...! (laughs)

JOHN GIORNO: I forget the year exactly, but it might have been 1963 that John Ashbery, who lived in Paris, moved back to New York. And Frank O'Hara gave a poetry reading at some gallery in the seventies on the East Side. I went with Andy Warhol. It was a hot, June night, really hot, and it was packed, because John was famous at that point, in his little quote 'world'. It was packed, a hundred some odd people at this gallery, and they had no sound system! Microphones, which we take for granted, didn't really exist before. There were such things as PA systems if you were a politician. It sounded like a foghorn to a large audience, but in a small situation like that, it was not even possible to rent a sound system, I think. Maybe in Saint Mark's, for the poetry, they had a little primitive PA system that was not much better. Two speakers on the side that echoed, the quality was horrible. So there were a hundred and twenty-five

MICHEL GARNEAU: C'est une présomption extraordinaire que de se mettre devant des gens et dire: "Ce que je vais vous dire est assez intéressant pour que vous restiez assis là, tranquilles, pendant des demi-heures, peut-être des heures." Et moi, j'ai une moralité qui fait qu'il faut essayer de fournir de la matière. Il faut donner du plaisir à notre public, il faut lui donner de quoi se souvenir pour justifier, tout simplement, ce qu'on propose. Je me prépare en conséquence et j'essaie de faire la meilleure performance possible. C'est très important et j'ai trop souffert de cette époque où c'était entendu qu'on allait s'ennuyer. J'ai vu des poètes se planter derrière un micro avec une liasse de papier puis lire ça pendant des temps qui étaient inhumains (rires). Mais ce n'était pas si long que ça, en fait. Par exemple, j'ai déjà vu un récital de Margaret Atwood. Plantée devant le micro, *she had darkish glasses and a big hat, you couldn't see her. And she went through — with her horrible voice — an hour of bitchy bullshit...!* (rires)

MICHEL GARNEAU: Dans les années 60, c'était des lectures. Ensuite, c'est devenu des récitals; je me disais, parce que j'ai toujours travaillé dans le milieu du théâtre: "Non, moi, je veux monter des spectacles. Je suis un *showman*. J'aime ça. Je ne vais pas avoir honte." Le spectacle, c'est quelque chose de fondamental dans l'être humain, c'est comme ça que le conte est né, lorsqu'il y a eu quelqu'un qui était un *showman* dans l'âme... Alors il ne faut pas le refuser. Et à partir du moment où quelqu'un accepte de faire du spectacle, ça peut être très, très libre. Par exemple, il y a eu Raoul Duguay avec *L'Infonie*, avec le globe terrestre à tête et puis des cornes et tout. Lui, il allait jusqu'au bout. Avec Raoul et juste un musicien, j'ai donné des spectacles qui étaient complètement éclatés. On avait des tas de textes, il y en avait qu'on savait par cœur, d'autres qu'on avait écrits la veille. On demandait aux gens de nous dire des phrases et on écrivait là-dessus. Ça, c'était dans les années 70. Mais nous, on ne parlait plus de récitals ou de lectures. On présentait des spectacles. Et cette notion est particulière et très importante. Ensuite ça mène à la performance, où il y a différentes façons de faire du spectacle ou de dire les choses. Et à partir du moment où on le fait, on travaille par cœur. C'est-à-dire qu'on travaille les poèmes pour les posséder assez pour pouvoir les bouger, les mettre sur du rythme, sur de la musique, les *rapper*, n'importe quoi.... Je trouve que les diverses influences font que, maintenant, quand les performeurs se mettent devant des gens pour dire des choses, ils s'occupent d'en retirer un certain plaisir et essaient d'en donner à leur public. Je pense que c'est un progrès moral qui s'est fait.... Et à partir de ce moment, le spectacle rejoint la tradition orale beaucoup plus, évidemment, que la lecture. Car lorsque tu fais une lecture, tu es pris avec ta feuille.

John Giorno performs
Photo courtesy of the artist

people, and John and Frank up at the front there, we couldn't hear a word. Andy kept saying over and over again, "It's so boring. It's so boring," (laughs) and, "Why does it have to be so boring?" And it was true. So I think that was one of those things that one remembered. Why does it have to be so boring?

MICHEL GARNEAU: In the sixties, there were readings. Then it was recitals, but because I've always worked around theatre I'd think: "No, I want to organize shows. I'm a showman. I love it and I refuse to be ashamed of it." 'Performing' is basic to human beings, that's how storytelling was born, there was a born showman somewhere.... We mustn't turn our backs on this. And the moment you say 'yes' to the 'performance', things can get very very free. For example, Raoul Duguay with *L'Infonie*, wearing a globe on his head, with horns and all. This guy went all the way. With Raoul and just one musician, I gave shows that were completely wild. We had tons of texts, some we knew by heart, others we'd written the night before. We'd ask people in the audience to give us a sentence and we'd write about that. That was during the seventies. But we weren't about readings and recitals anymore, we were presenting shows now. This notion is specific and very important. It leads to performance, where there are various ways to do shows and say things. The minute you do this, you start working from memory. Meaning that you work poems to know them enough to be able

to move, to give them a beat, music, you rap them, whatever.... I think that because of the various influences, when performers get in front of an audience nowadays, they're conscious of getting pleasure from that and aware of providing pleasure for their audience. I think this is moral progress.... From then on the show obviously connects with oral tradition, much more than with literature — because when you give a reading, you're stuck with the piece of paper.

HÉLÈNE MONETTE: I wonder if the screen created by the poet's piece of paper doesn't create a distance, a wall between audience and reader. Maybe the emotions can still come through, I don't know. I've been pondering this question for ten years. When you're onstage reading, you forget yourself, and at the same time you're taking possession of a physical space. So you're physically involved but at the same time, you get into an altered state where you're not always aware of your gestures, of how the audience is perceiving you. I can't compare myself to poets who are too shy, nor to the more daring performers, I'm neither. But I'm bothered by this sheet of paper which gives the impression that when you read with it, you're more static than in movement.

TODD SWIFT: I don't accept the division between 'reading' and 'performing'.... My concern is that we can lose sight of the source and intent of a delivery of poetry by concentrating too much on

the vehicle — mode, let's say. If someone passionately reads their work to a live audience, celebrating the oral / aural community of poetry, that is far better than a piss-poor actor dully reciting cold, banal verse from memory. This is why I employ the concept of fusion poetry, where page and stage, reading and performing, are sometimes indistinguishable. What matters is connecting, reaching, moving, touching. Or alienating, if that's your motive.

DAVID GOSSAGE: If someone's up reading a very long poem and a very complex poem that people spend life times studying and learning, then sometimes in a live context it just goes past people.... It's better to keep the shorter jewels, so they can just digest a moment and get enough of the poem.... In a live context with someone reading, the accompanying music's nice, because if it's done well it could try to capture the mood of the poem in another way that you might lose as it's zipping by you. Because they do zip by, they're gone. When you sit and watch poetry, you start going, "Ah," and then it's gone, and you ask the person next to you, "What was it about again?" (laughs) People often, when you do a poetry show, either buy the book or go find the poem.

ANNE STONE: I find that, having done this book tour[18] — where I moved between doing readings and doing spoken word pieces that laid up against the novel, and doing other things — some people were really into it and accepting and open, and they were pretty sophisticated. Because they had an experience of spoken word, they had experience with all sorts of different ways of bringing the work in. I found that in Vancouver, at Bukowski's, they were obviously from a community that's very

vibrant and alive. But in other places people were like, "Wow, if you hadn't read it I really wouldn't have got the inflections." So suddenly the book is stripped because I've done something with my voice, and the sense that I'm going to do the same thing every time with my voice. No, I was in a particular mood today, it came out this way.

MICHEL GARNEAU: What I like about spoken word is that the poets who present their texts have decided they want to do it. Because there's a terrifying tradition of poets who don't enjoy reading in public but they do it anyway. There are people I respect a lot who discourage me in this regard. You go somewhere to present your poetry and next to you there's a poet sighing and saying he hates giving readings. So why choose to take part in the show? When poets feel uncomfortable reading onstage, they should refrain. Because they're going to send the audience a message of non-enjoyment as well. If you recite poems looking like someone who doesn't enjoy it, you're asking the audience to do some strange mental exercise where they have to ignore the fact that you look miserable.... You're going to read your poems with a kind of absence and so you undermine the whole phenomenon.

vi. Memorization: "The text has been eaten"

Some literary writers utilize memorization in their readings; however, it is at this point that the spoken word performance begins to move away from the literary tradition of the last century. The incorporation of the text in the mind of the performer opens up the possibility of movement and gesture on the stage, eye-contact with the audience, and the freedom to improvise.

'Passer dans un car wash à cheval', from The Mucho Gusto CD reissue of L'Infonie album Vol. 3, 1969
Photo by Jean-Patrick Amish

HÉLÈNE MONETTE: L'écran que fait la feuille de papier des poètes, je me demande à quel point ça crée une distance, un mur entre le public et le lecteur. Peut-être que l'émotion peut passer quand même. Je ne sais pas. Ça fait dix ans que je me pose cette question. Quand tu es sur scène et que tu lis, tu t'oublies, et en même temps tu prends possession d'un espace physique. Donc tu t'investis physiquement, mais en même temps tu deviens comme dans un état second qui fait que tu n'as pas toujours conscience de ta gestuelle, de comment le public te perçoit. Personnellement, je ne peux pas me comparer au poète qui est trop timide, ni au performeur le plus audacieux. Je ne suis ni l'un ni l'autre. Mais je suis agacée par cette histoire de la feuille qui donne l'impression que tu es plus immobile qu'en mouvement lorsque tu lis avec.

MICHEL GARNEAU: Ce que j'aime dans le mouvement du spoken word, c'est que les poètes qui présentent leurs textes, ils *veulent* le faire. Ce sont eux qui ont décidé que ça leur tentait. Parce qu'il y a une tradition terrifiante qui est celle des poètes qui n'aiment pas lire en public, mais qui le font quand même. Il y a du monde que je respecte beaucoup qui me découragent parce qu'ils sont comme ça. Tu vas pour présenter ta poésie, puis là, il y a un autre poète à côté de toi qui soupire et qui dit qu'il déteste faire

continued...

[18] Cross-Canada tour to promote *Hush*, spring 1999.

des lectures. Pourquoi a-t-il choisi de participer au spectacle, dans ce cas-là? À mon avis, quand des poètes se sentent mal à l'aise sur scène, ils devraient s'abstenir. Parce qu'ils vont faire que les gens n'aiment pas ça, eux aussi. Si tu récites tes poèmes avec l'air de quelqu'un qui hésite, tu demandes aux spectateurs de faire une pirouette mentale très spéciale: passer par-dessus le fait que tu as l'air malheureux... Tu vas lire tes poèmes avec une espèce d'absence, et tu vas alors desservir tout le genre.

Geneviève Letarte: Au début, quand je faisais mes performances, j'apprenais tout par cœur. Mais parfois j'avais quand même une feuille, parce que je trouvais que c'était beau. Pour moi la feuille faisait partie de la performance, parce qu'elle est le symbole de l'écriture. Je pouvais donc faire des performances d'une heure et demie et je savais tous mes textes par cœur. Mais les textes, à l'occasion, je les lisais, et c'était vraiment voulu parce que je trouvais que de lire, ce n'était pas comme les performeurs, ça amenait un autre niveau. Sauf qu'à un moment donné, c'était devenu absurde et j'ai arrêté de faire des vrais spectacles. C'était beaucoup trop stressant, trop fatigant. Alors je me suis mise à faire surtout des lectures. Je m'y suis habituée. Dans un sens, c'est aussi intéressant parce que je suis quand même capable de performer en lisant. Mais ça reste différent. Je pense que quand tu ne lis pas ton texte, il y a quelque choses d'autre qui se passe, que tu ne peux pas imaginer tant que tu te sers encore de ta feuille. C'est comme les acteurs de théâtre, quand ils répètent avec leurs feuilles au début, et quand ils lâchent leur texte. C'est-à-dire que lorsqu'ils ne lisent plus leurs textes, ils se mettent à bouger. La feuille, ça empêche de bouger.

D. Kimm: Dès le départ, j'ai récité mes textes par cœur. Cela fait que je suis davantage obligée de jouer mon texte, de travailler plus intensément, si on veut. Il m'est déjà arrivé de réciter des textes en les lisant, mais ça m'énervait. Personnellement, je préfère performer sans papiers. Ça m'est facile d'apprendre un texte, mais j'aime surtout l'idée de ne pas avoir de papiers, de sécurité et d'être obligée de me débrouiller. Parfois je le regrette, parfois je suis comme terrorisée. Ça m'est déjà arrivé d'être dans la salle et, cinq minutes avant de monter sur scène, de ne plus me souvenir de la première phrase de mon texte. Panique générale! Je

Catherine Kidd: It really is like a writer writes the story, but then when it's performed, the story writes the writer. It's the words that decide how I'm going to speak them. How I'm going to move, to honestly express them. Silent gesture becomes as significant as spoken voice. I trust the piece more than I trust myself. By the time that I actually perform it, it should feel like I'm getting on a horse, and off we go.

Leah Vineberg: If I hold this paper between you and I, this *is* between you and I. It's like an old acting thing. You can't know the scene or the character or anything until you're off-book.

Geneviève Letarte: When I started performing I used to memorize everything. But sometimes I had a sheet of paper with me because I liked how it looked. For me the sheet of paper was part of the performance because it symbolizes writing. I could give performances lasting an hour and a half and I knew everything by heart. But once in a while I'd read by choice, because I felt that reading wasn't like performing, it added another dimension. But at some point it got ridiculous and I stopped doing long solo shows. It was too stressful and tiring. I started giving mostly readings and got used to it. In a way, it's just as interesting because I can still perform while reading. But still, it's not the same thing. When you're not reading your text, things can happen that you hadn't imagined when you were still using the printed page. It's like actors, at first they rehearse with their sheets of paper, then they let go of their text. When they're no longer reading, they start moving. So the sheet of paper inhibits movement.

D. Kimm: I've always recited my texts by

heart. So there's more of an obligation to act my text, to work more intensely. On occasion I've read while reciting but it annoys me. I prefer performing without my papers. Memorizing is easy for me but I especially like the idea of not having my papers, no security, and having to just deal with that. Sometimes I regret it because I become terrified. It's happened that I've been in the room and five minutes before going onstage, I couldn't remember the first line of my text. Big panic! I didn't have it with me, nothing! And then it came back to me. At my first big show — *Chevale*, with musician Pierre St-Jak, at *La Licorne* — I was so nervous that when I said my first sentence, I realized I'd just skipped three pages of my text. In the end, I caught up. You have to put out, you have to interpret your text, but sometimes when you're acting, you're too far into feelings and suddenly you don't remember what's next... it can get quite intoxicating!

Catherine Kidd: One big difference between doing a reading from the page and doing a performance piece is that the text has been eaten, it's been sort of re-absorbed and I feel much more comfortable that way. Because then if the words have sort of sunk down to gut-level and dispersed into the blood stream, then I just have to plug into that and the piece leads me around by the nose. Reading from the page, I find much more nervous-making.

Buffy Childerhose: I am really dyslexic, and sometimes, particularly when I'm nervous, I can have a lot of difficulty actually reading out loud. I'll stumble over words. I got in the habit of memorizing my work when I was doing creative writing classes and we had to read the poems out loud. I don't want to be reading a poem, which is difficult to do anyway, in front of a group of people, when I'm unaccustomed to that.... When I read from a page, I focus on the words. When I have them memorized and I deliver them, I'm aware of the meaning, in a way. I'm not bound to the cluster of letters the way I am if I'm actually looking at them on a page. And also if you carry the text of it with you, in your person, it allows for a momentum that you can't have if you're reading off the page. Sometimes I'll forget the lines and I'll jump around, but ordinarily it's like, 'Press Play'. The momentum of the piece drags me through. I'm not sure that I would have that if I were actually reading.

ALEXIS O'HARA: When I first did *Vox Hunt*, I had only one piece prepared.... I needed to have three pieces for the slam, if I were to qualify to be in the final round. So I wrote two pieces that day. I, of course, didn't have them memorized. And I recognized immediately that the people who had work memorized were more likely to win than the people who hadn't. So through slam I always memorize. I've performed a lot in the past two years, so I've gotten my performing legs. So if I fuck up I don't worry so much about forgetting things, because you can always just make it up or jump to somewhere else. In that sense I'm more of a performer than a writer, I guess. It's more important for me to give a good performance than to say exactly the words that I wrote because my work is constantly in progress anyway.

JULIE CRYSLER: [Memorization] allows you to respond to the audience. I think your ability to express the words is better, too, when they're deep inside you. The work that it takes to actually memo-

rize the text brings it to another level. The process of memorizing it helps you to understand what you've written even more. I'll notice connections that I didn't really make while I was writing the piece.

ALEX BOUTROS: I felt a fair amount of pressure to memorize early on, too, because a lot of poets in the scene do. It's like you won't be taken seriously if you don't memorize your work. It wasn't a big deal for me, because in classical music you're expected to memorize, too, so it was in the background. A lot of people say it's so uncomfortable to be up there without a paper, to have that barrier taken away, but I didn't feel that.

NORMAN NAWROCKI: The first few shows, maybe for the first year, the big gag was Norman and his music stand. That was my crutch for a long time. And Sylvain Côté[19] just *hated* that. But here's this guy on the stage with a music stand! So eventually I learned how to perform without a music stand. Now, I am no longer embarrassed about reading something in my hand. So it went from performing with a music stand to nothing and now, when I do these spoken word things, I'll hold the book or the text in my hand. It doesn't bother me that it's not memorized, unless I'm doing a whole show. My solo shows, *My Dick And Other Manly Tales* and *I Don't Understand Women*, for example... there are costumes and there's music and there are props and there's everything... there's no paper at all.

TRISH SALAH: I tend to memorize some of my work. In fact, I tend to go to the stage with some pieces ready to perform, and some pieces paper-dependent. That may have to do with the newness of the work, or it may have to

n'avais pas mes textes, je n'avais rien! Et puis c'est revenu. Lors du premier gros spectacle que j'ai fait – *Chevale*, avec le musicien Pierre St-Jak, à La Licorne — j'étais tellement nerveuse qu'en disant ma première phrase, je me rendais compte avec horreur que je venais de sauter trois pages de mon texte. Finalement, je me suis rattrapée. Il faut que tu te donnes, il faut que tu interprètes ton texte, mais parfois, quand tu joues, tu es trop dans l'émotion et soudainement, tu ne sais plus ce qui s'en vient: et ça peut devenir très grisant!

[19] Sylvain Côté, guitarist, Rhythm Activism.

MICHEL GARNEAU: Pour moi, la mémorisation d'un texte est très importante pour un spectacle. Et au niveau historique, il y a plusieurs choses intéressantes. Par exemple, moi, je suis sûrement très responsable du fait que Gaston Miron, à un certain moment, a appris ses poèmes par cœur et les a faits avec des musiciens, en spectacle. Les premières fois que j'ai travaillé avec Gaston, pour lui, il n'était pas question de le faire. Jusqu'à ce que Michelle Rossignol et moi, en 1968, on monte un spectacle qui s'appelait *Parlure, parole, poème*. On a présenté le spectacle partout au Québec, dans des endroits invraisemblables, mais c'était volontaire. Dans des clubs de golf, des salles paroissiales... On avait un tout petit décor, sans éclairages, mais ce n'était pas grave... Tout ce qu'on transportait d'important, c'était une magnifique et très bonne chaîne stéréo, parce qu'on voulait que le monde entende le mieux possible. Le reste, on s'en foutait. La première partie du spectacle était un collage de textes du monde entier à partir des Sumériens, de la Bible – tout était là –, jusqu'aux surréalistes, aux dadaïstes et tout. Ce collage était une tentative de séduction. C'était comme pour essayer d'accrocher les gens, de les amener à la poésie, dans des cas où peut-être même ils n'y connaîtraient rien. La deuxième partie du spectacle, c'était *La Marche à l'amour* de Gaston Miron. On avait demandé à Gaston la permission de lire son texte, et on avait préparé avec lui une version à deux voix. C'est-à-dire que chaque vers était répété une fois, donc le poème était fait deux fois; on avançait, on revenait, Michelle et moi. Il y avait une introduction musicale, puis ça partait et ça durait 35 minutes. Le résultat était assez saisissant, très, très lyrique. On récitait avec beaucoup de passion. Et quand Gaston avait vu ça, à Longueuil dans une petite boîte à chansons, il avait été très troublé. Il m'avait dit: "Là, vous m'avez convaincu, il faut que j'apprenne mes poèmes par cœur." Avant, il arrivait qu'il en sache par cœur, mais il avait toujours ses feuilles. Et plus tard, en 1980, on avait créé *Sept paroles du Québec*. C'était un spectacle qu'on avait fait en France avec Gaston, et qui a été tourné par Jean-Claude Labrecque. On l'avait créé à La Rochelle, puis on a joué à Avignon et à Paris. Il y avait Gilbert Langevin, Gaston, Paul Chamberland, Raoul Duguay, Michèle Lalonde, Yves-Gabriel Brunet et moi. Puis le musicien Dominique Tremblay et sa troupe. Moi, j'étais le metteur en

do with whether I'm interested in direct address. What I mean by direct address is pretty common-sensical, if I don't have paper in hand I'm looking at the audience. I'm hearing myself speak in a slightly different way than I do when I'm reading off the page. I just have that much more autonomy to play with what my voice sounds like, to raise the pitch, to drop it a little bit.... I don't move around a lot. It's not that I employ props or anything much like that, but I find that my body is a better instrument if I'm not focused on reading.

NAH EE LAH: I feel ashamed to go up onstage with paper. It doesn't bother me when other people do it, but it always makes me feel like I can't communicate as much, because I have to look down to see where I am. So I'll be running it through my head, running it through my head. The good thing is that once you put it in your head once, it's there forever.

ANNA-LOUISE CRAGO: I worried about two things, one of which was that I put more work into what I was actually writing than into the package deal of performing the writing. I wanted to transmit more through the words than by the performance of the words. Part of me was afraid that I would take away from the text if I was seeming to be over-dramatic. And I say that about myself because I'm not a natural performator... some people are, so naturally they can have a very dramatic, incredible interpretation which really brings their words to life. I think that in my case people would concentrate so much on how I was being a bad actress that (laughs) they would say, "OK, swallow your saliva, we can't hear the words!"

In Quebec's francophone literary community, the emphasis on memorization and other performative elements had waned from the seventies to the mid-nineties. With the latest generation of writers and performers, this has started to change.

MICHEL GARNEAU: For me, memorizing texts is very important in terms of the 'show aspect'. Historically, all kinds of interesting things have happened in this respect. For example, I'm surely very responsible for the fact that Gaston Miron started learning his poems by heart at some point, and did them with musicians, live. The first times I worked with Gaston, it was out of the question for him to do that. Until Michelle Rossignol and I put together a show called *Parlure, parole, poème*, in 1968. We toured Quebec with this show, unbelievable places, but it was a choice. Golf clubs, church halls.... We had a tiny set, no lighting, but no matter.... The only important thing we carried around was a magnificent and excellent stereo system, because we wanted people to be able to hear as well as possible. We didn't care about the rest. The first part of the show was a collage of texts from around the world, from the Sumerians, the Bible — it was all there — to the Surrealists, Dadaists, etc. This collage was an exercise in seduction. To try to hook people into it, bring them to poetry, in cases where they might not even know anything about it. The second part of the show was *La marche à l'amour* by Gaston Miron. We'd asked Gaston for permission to read his text, and we prepared a two-voice version of it with him. Meaning that each line of verse was repeated once, so that the poem was done twice; we'd go forward, then come back, Michelle and I. There was a musical intro, then it started and lasted 35 minutes. The result was stunning, very very lyrical. We recited with a lot of passion. When Gaston saw this in a little coffee house in Longueuil, he was very moved. He said: "You've convinced me, I have to learn my poems by heart." Before that he used to know some by heart, but he always had his papers. Later on, in 1980, we created *Sept paroles du Québec*. We'd done this show in France with Gaston, and it was filmed by Jean-Claude Labrecque. It premiered in La Rochelle, then we did it in Avignon and Paris. Participants were Gilbert Langevin, Gaston, Paul Chamberland, Raoul Duguay, Michèle Lalonde, Yves-Gabriel Brunet and myself. And musician Dominique Tremblay with his gang. I was directing and I said to everybody: "We're not giving a reading or a recital, we're giving a poetry show. It's a *show*, there's going to be lighting, it's made to seduce people, put them in a good mood, move them, get to them. So I insist that everybody memorize their texts." The poets all agreed, but they were a bit surprised because they'd never thought of this.... Gaston was extraordinary. He said: "Yes, coach, make me work," and I did. After that he found some musicians and organized his own shows.

NANCY LABONTÉ: I know I often give a better performance if I have my sheet of paper with me... even though I know the text by heart. Some texts I've read and re-read over and over and then recited almost by heart, but when you have your text on paper... you're sure not to go astray. I often also write instructions on my page: "Lower on this word," for example. I highlight the text's staging, its 'sounding'.

Michel Garneau in his CBC office, Oct. 15, 1999

PASCAL FIORAMORE: I've done theatre so I'm able to memorize a two-hour text. But when we gave our first show I didn't know my texts. It was the first time I was onstage to do something like this and I'd brought my sheets because I was too nervous. Except that at the same time, this fed into the image of the poet, of the writer with his bunch of papers. And it's funny because the more shows we give — we have 30, 35 texts now – the bigger my pile of papers gets. But now it's become more of a stage prop. Though it also has the advantage that if we want to add a quick text or improvise one — it depends on the event, sometimes we try to do new texts — we can include it or if we're too nervous, take it out. So contrary to concerts, where singers know all their lyrics, I always have my pages with me and I always will. This matters to me because if we get rid of them, we'll fall into a strictly musical space. In terms of representation, when you see somebody with a bunch of papers, it's already much more of the order of declamation and rant than somebody just singing lyrics.

scène et j'avais dit à tout le monde: "Là, on ne fait pas une lecture ni un récital, on fait un spectacle de poésie. C'est un *spectacle*, il va y avoir des éclairages, c'est fait pour séduire les gens, les mettre de bonne humeur, les émouvoir, aller les chercher. Et là, j'exige que tout le monde sache son texte par cœur." Tous les poètes étaient d'accord, mais ils étaient un peu surpris parce qu'ils n'avaient pas envisagé ça... Et Gaston, il était extra-ordinaire. Il a dit: "Ah oui, fais-moi travailler, coach." Et je l'ai fait. Après ça, il s'est trouvé des musiciens puis puis il a monté ses propres spectacles.

NANCY LABONTÉ: Moi, je sais que, souvent, je donne une meilleure performance si j'ai la feuille... même si je sais le texte par cœur. Il y a des textes que j'ai lus et relus et relus puis que j'ai récités pratiquement par cœur, mais quand tu as ton texte sur papier... tu es certaine de ne pas passer à côté. Mais souvent, aussi, je mets des indications sur mes feuilles: "Moins fort ce mot-là", par exemple. Je surligne, il y a des indications de mise en scène, de "mise en son" du texte.

PASCAL FIORAMORE: J'ai fait du théâtre, et je suis capable de mémoriser un texte de deux heures. Mais lors de notre premier spectacle, je ne connaissais pas mes textes. C'était la première fois que je me retrouvais sur scène pour faire quelque chose comme ça, et j'avais amené mes feuilles parce que j'étais trop nerveux. Sauf qu'en même

continued...

temps, ça alimentait l'image du poète, de l'écrivain avec sa pile de feuilles. Et c'est drôle parce que, au fur et à mesure qu'on donne des spectacles, on est rendu avec 30, 35 textes, donc ma pile devient de plus en plus épaisse. Maintenant, mes feuilles de textes, c'est plus devenu un accessoire de scène. Mais ç'a aussi l'avantage que si on veut rajouter un texte rapide ou un texte improvisé – ça dépend des soirées, parfois on essaie de faire des nouveaux textes –, on peut l'inclure, ou si on est trop nerveux pour le faire, on peut l'enlever. Alors contrairement aux spectacles de musique où les chanteurs connaissent tous leurs textes par cœur, moi, j'ai encore mes feuilles dans les mains, puis je vais toujours les garder. Ça, j'y tiens, parce que si on les fait sauter, selon moi, on va tomber dans l'univers uniquement musical. Au niveau de la représentation, quand tu vois quelqu'un avec une pile de feuilles, ça fait déjà beaucoup plus déclamation, déclaration, plus que juste quelqu'un qui chante des textes.

ANDRÉ LEMELIN: Il y a plusieurs niveaux de lecture. Il y a lire un texte sans le savoir, ce que je trouve absolument horrible. Il y a lire un texte qui n'est qu'un support visuel pour la mémoire, c'est-à-dire qu'on sait le texte par cœur, mais on le lit quand même. Déjà, c'est plus dynamique. Il y a aussi savoir un texte par cœur mais le réciter bêtement, ce qui est aussi pire que de le lire sans le savoir. Enfin, il y a évidemment le maîtriser et le réciter librement.

La première fois que j'ai récité un texte sans un support papier, je me suis fait violence littéralement, parce que je haïssais la scène. D'ailleurs, la toute première fois que j'ai fait une lecture publique, je tremblais tellement qu'il a fallu que je mette mes feuilles sur un lutrin. Ensuite, j'ai appris mes textes; à la maison, je me suis forcé à les dire par cœur, avec des notes pas loin. Quand j'avais un trou de mémoire, je reprenais. C'était progressif. Je n'avais pas fait d'école de théâtre et j'étais autodidacte. Maintenant, j'ai un répertoire de textes et je les récite de plus en plus souvent. J'ai acquis une bonne maîtrise de mes textes qui me permet d'être un peu plus ludique. C'est-à-dire que je respecte moins mes textes, j'improvise, je me permets des libertés. Donc, un texte qui était appris par cœur, à la ligne, à la virgule, est presque devenu un canevas... On observe ce processus

ANDRÉ LEMELIN: There are several levels of reading. There's reading a text without knowing it, which I find absolutely horrible. There's reading a text which is just a visual support for memory, meaning that you've memorized the text but you read it anyway. This is already more dynamic. Then there's knowing a text by heart but reciting it flatly, which is just as bad as reading it without knowing it. Finally, there's mastering it and reciting it freely.

The first time I recited a text without my paper it was literally self-abuse, because I hated the stage. The first time I gave a public reading, I was shaking so badly I had to put my papers on a stand. Then I started memorizing my texts, at home I forced myself to say them by heart, with notes nearby. When I had a blank, I'd start over. It was progressive. I didn't go to theatre school, I'm self-taught. Now I have a repertoire of texts and I recite them more and more often. I've gained a mastery of my texts which allows me to be a bit more playful. I respect my texts less, I improvise, I give myself some space. A text that has been memorized, line by line, comma by comma, almost becomes a canvas.... This process can be seen in the story-telling. There's the storyteller who starts with a mental canvas and builds his story by telling it over and over again. After about ten times, he has a finished text and then he retells it almost always identically. So it's like he'd written it, but in his mind. Conversely, there's the storyteller who writes his text, memorizes, rehearses, and after a few shows, goes beyond the form and finds his freedom. And this is where this storyteller connects with the first one. At some point they're both on the same level, although their approaches are quite different....

Memory blanks are a huge fear, but they disappear on two conditions: mastery of your text, and being at ease onstage. And getting used to it is what allows you to feel good onstage. You need to 'master' your nerves.... I remember two readings where I had blanks. Once, I had the text in my pocket so I pulled it out and started over. The other time, I had no text so I went and sat back down — right in the middle of my story! I hadn't mastered my nervousness yet. Nowadays when I get onstage, I always feel stress but if I forget, I'll do something else. I'll reinvent my text because I know the basic canvas.

André Lemelin
Photo by Yannick B. Géinas

3. Theatre versus Spoken Word Performance

As spoken word performance moves away from literary readings by taking on more performative features, it begins in some ways to resemble theatre. Here, Montreal spoken word artists who have experience in theatre talk about what sets their work apart from conventional theatrical performances.

VICTORIA STANTON: In the work that I'm doing now, I'm not trying to inhabit other roles. I'm trying to communicate a whole range of things — emotions, ideas, experiences — in order to create some kind of connection with the audience. My experience of being in theatre was not about that at all. I'm not writing pieces to perform other roles, I'm not setting up scenarios whereby I'm acting. Although I might use some of those tools to perform, and some of the pieces might become kind of theatrical or melodramatic, I don't feel like I'm acting, and for me, theatre is about acting. My intention is not to act, it's to really *be* in that presence. And the *being* in that presence, I find that that's not about theatre.

LEAH VINEBERG: I saw the theatre as one thing, and then I did these little performance pieces or spoken word things as well. But the theatre has taught me about performance and how sacred it is. The stage is a sacred place, and if you're willing to be there, amazing things can happen. I felt that I was avoiding that by staying on-book, so to speak.... I found that there was a very big difference, and my standards went up, also,

for what I was watching in spoken word performance. Suddenly I was pushing for people to stretch a little bit further. It made me very unpopular.

HEATHER O'NEILL: When I started performing my poetry, I thought I'd be much more comfortable with it, because I'd done theater for so long. I was so easy with my body onstage doing theatrical pieces, where you're removed and you're a different person. But spoken word — all of a sudden, when I was first reading, I realized that I was there with myself, I was completely vulnerable and nervous. It was almost a shock, because it was totally different. And I felt ripped-off. Any theatrical training just leaves you and — because you're reading something about yourself — you have to find some way of expressing yourself, of being yourself, but on a performance level.

COREY FROST: I think that I draw on or use the same strategies performing as I do acting in a play. But there's something about the fact that I'm reinterpreting something that also works on a page that makes it different. I had written theatrical monologues and performed them myself. But doing that in the context of theatre was so different from doing it in the context of literature.

BENOÎT PAIEMENT: The basic difference between our stage work and what most actors do in most plays is the presence of the audience. In Ionesco or Molière, the actor obviously knows the audience

dans le conte. Il y a le conteur qui travaille à partir d'un canevas mental et qui, à force de raconter son histoire, la construit. Au bout d'une dizaine de représentations, il a un texte fini et à partir de ce moment-là, il le redit presque toujours identique. Donc c'est comme s'il l'avait écrit, mais mentalement. À l'inverse, il y a le conteur qui écrit son texte, le mémorise et le répète, et qui après un certain nombre de représentations, va au-delà de la forme, et retrouve sa liberté. Et c'est là que le deuxième rejoint le premier.

Les trous de mémoire, c'est une peur épouvantable, mais ils disparaissent à deux conditions: la maîtrise du texte, et être à l'aise sur scène. Et c'est l'habitude qui te permet de t'y sentir bien. En fait, tu dois "contrôler" ta nervosité... Je me souviens de deux lectures où j'ai eu des trous de mémoire. Une fois j'avais le texte dans ma poche, je l'ai sorti puis j'ai redémarré. L'autre fois, je ne l'avais pas, alors je suis allé me rasseoir – en plein milieu de mon histoire. Mais je n'avais justement pas maîtrisé ma nervosité. Maintenant, quand je monte sur une scène, j'ai toujours un stress, mais si j'oublie, je vais faire autre chose. Je vais réinventer mon texte parce que j'en connais le canevas.

Félixe Ross in La Centième fois du silence
Maison de la Culture, May 26, 2000
Photo by Sergio Baptist

BENOÎT PAIEMENT: La différence essentielle, je pense, entre notre travail sur scène et celui de la plupart des comédiens dans la plupart des pièces, c'est la présence du public. Bien sûr, dans Ionesco ou dans Molière, le comédien sait très bien que le public est là, mais il n'y fait pas référence. Tandis que nous, on s'y réfère constamment: "Bonsoir." On commence toujours comme ça: "Bonsoir…"

FÉLIXE ROSS: On s'adresse au public… Brecht faisait la même chose. Brecht, dans ses pièces, annonçait ce qui allait se passer. Mais moi, quand je joue avec le G.P.M., je n'ai pas le sentiment d'être dans la peau d'un personnage; j'ai plutôt l'impression d'être fragmentée en de nombreux personnages et d'évoluer avec plusieurs autres. Et dépendant de l'optique qu'on va choisir, ça va donner une pièce fragmentée à la manière d'un kaléidoscope. On déplace des trucs et ça donne des résultats différents. On explore toutes les possibilités.

D. KIMM: Présentement, je travaille avec Nathalie Derome, et je trouve ça intéressant d'apprendre à faire en sorte que les textes habitent réellement mon corps, que je puisse les livrer sans avoir l'impression de les jouer. Mais je trouve ça difficile, parce que pendant des années, mon style a toujours eu quelque chose d'assez dramatique, avec ma voix grave. Je me rends compte que, pour *La Suite mongole*, je ne peux pas le faire. Je dois revenir à plus de simplicité, je dois arriver à être naturelle. Avec Marcelle Hudon et Maryse Poulin, on improvise, et parfois je fais des choses drôles qu'elles aiment. Ça me fait curieux parce que je ne suis pas habituée à laisser aller cet aspect de moi, mais le spectacle le demande vraiment. Je le fais parce que sinon ce serait capituler, ne pas prendre de risques. Et pour moi, prendre des risques dans ce spectacle, c'est être plus légère, bouger davantage.

is there, but doesn't refer to it. Whereas we do, constantly: "Good evening." We always start with "Good evening."

FÉLIXE ROSS: We talk to the public…. Brecht used to do this; he'd announce what was going to happen in his plays. But when I'm performing with the *Groupe de poésie moderne*, I don't have the feeling that I'm in character; instead, I feel fragmented into several characters and playing with several others. Depending on the perspective we choose, the result will be a piece that's fragmented something like a kaleidoscope. We move things around and get different results. We explore all the possibilities.

NATHALIE DEROME: You have to make the separation between the author and the performer. If you don't kill the author when you perform — when you give it to the people — for me, it's boring. It's like the words are completely lost, because you're not grounded. It's really hard to be grounded with a text when you do it on a stage, because it's grounded by a white page. But the white page has no respiration, has no mouth…. I have my theatrical mentality; it becomes in this case like a trance. After five minutes, I don't listen to the words, but I don't care, because we are floating in a space. Sometimes words bring me to a reality, and I go to the text like *un flotteur*, when you're swimming, and after a while it becomes, "OK, I can swim without it."

D. KIMM: Right now I'm working with Nathalie Derome and I find it very interesting to approach things so that the texts really are embodied, so I can deliver them without having the impression of acting. I find it difficult because for years my style has always been kind of dramatic, with my low voice. I'm realizing that for *La Suite mongole*, I can't do this. I have to get back to more simplicity, learn to be natural. With Marcelle Hudon and Maryse Poulin we improvise, and sometimes I do funny things they like. It's odd because I'm not used to letting that aspect of myself go, but this show is demanding it of me. I have to do it because otherwise, I would be surrendering, not taking risks. In this show, taking risks means being lighter and moving more.

VINCE TINGUELY: Fluffy Pagan Echoes had scripted this whole hour-long thing

Resistance is Reasonable, and we realized that we were contained by it. We couldn't interact with the audience in the same way that we did when it was a Word Circus, where we were just being ourselves. This was much more structured, and I really didn't know how to deal with that. I don't know if anyone in the group did. But when I worked at Playwright's Workshop in 1998, someone came along — he was a theatre person, he had seen our show — and he said he was really inspired by how we broke all sorts of rules, doing this. It was really experimental, apparently. Well, of course we broke rules, in terms of theatre, because we weren't even *thinking* of theatre.

COREY FROST: I thought *Resistance is Reasonable* shook up the *Fringe*, because so much of what happens in the *Fringe*, which is supposedly alternative theatre, is just boring old theatre. That was so much more like anti-theatre, almost.

BENOÎT PAIEMENT: In rehearsal, we work like a theatre company with a director directing actors. But I don't write our texts like a playwright, that is, respecting the characters' evolution in order to get to the end of the story. In this sense

the creation of raw material for the *Groupe de poésie moderne* is closer to poetry and short story writing…. The goal of all this, the stage, is probably somewhere in between poetry and theatre. What we do is very theatrical, but it's not theatre. Because it hasn't been written like a play, the result is different. Our director, Robert Reid, is theatrical. Robert came to the *Groupe de poésie moderne* via theatre, while for me it was via writing. It works because Robert develops biomechanics a lot, which is not an absurd form at all, but one which highlights the absurdity of the texts I write. His work and mine are compatible, complementary.

BENOÎT PAIEMENT: En répétition, on travaille comme une troupe de théâtre avec un metteur en scène qui dirige les comédiens. Mais les textes, je ne les écris pas comme un dramaturge, c'est-à-dire en respectant l'évolution des personnages, pour arriver à une fin. À ce niveau, je pense que la création du matériel de base du Groupe de poésie moderne est plus près de la poésie ou du nouvelliste qui écrit des courts textes…. La finalité du tout, la présentation sur scène, se situe probablement quelque part entre les deux, entre la poésie et le théâtre. C'est très théâtral ce qu'on fait, mais ce n'est pas du théâtre. Encore une fois, puisque ça n'a pas été écrit comme une pièce, ça ne donne pas le même résultat. Robert Reid, le metteur en scène, est théâtral. Robert est arrivé au Groupe de poésie moderne par le théâtre, tandis que moi, c'est l'écriture qui m'y a mené. Alors, nécessairement, ça fonctionne, parce que je pense que Robert développe beaucoup la biomécanique, qui n'est pas une forme absurde, pas du tout, mais qui met en relief l'absurdité des textes que j'écris. Son travail et le mien sont tout à fait compatibles, complémentaires.

Publicity still from La Suite mongole
*(left to right) Maryse Poulin, D. Kimm,
Marcelle Hudon*
Photo courtesy of D. Kimm

4. Pre-performance Rituals

Louise Dubreuil in a cigarette dress, taken at Théâtre LaChapelle June 2000 at an Esse magazine launch
Photo by Guy L'Heureux

An awareness of the physical intensity of live performance results in a number of strategies to control the situation. These range from the preparation of the space, to exercise regimes, visualization and other more idiosyncratic practices. The aim of all these strategies is to be present, in the moment, and grounded.

i. Focusing the mind

Spoken word performance involves both the mind and the body. The mind is prepared for performance through visualization, mantra-like repetitions of prayers, songs or texts, and the inner rehearsal of the performance. This focusing sometimes requires a space apart from the room where the show will happen.

TETSURO SHIGEMATSU: As a mental exercise, I try to first visit the space, scout the location, and if possible get onstage and look out toward the audience. I memorize the image, and then over the days leading up to the performance I continuously visualize the space in order to place myself there. Also, once I decide what I'm going to wear, I wear that particular thing, and I even try to simulate the lights that will be there. Because there's something disorienting about being onstage, if there happens to be a spotlight on you, or bright lights, getting used to all those very curious physical sensations.

GENEVIÈVE LETARTE: When I started I used to have to prepare a lot. This isn't the case anymore. I go, I give my reading. But I have to say that what I'm

GENEVIÈVE LETARTE: Au début, je me souviens qu'il fallait que je fasse beaucoup de préparatifs. Maintenant, ce n'est plus le cas. J'y vais, puis je fais ma lecture. Mais il faut dire que maintenant, ce que je fais, ce n'est plus vraiment de la performance. Quand j'en faisais, ma journée au complet était orientée vers la performance que j'allais donner le soir. Il fallait que je travaille ma voix, que je travaille mon corps. Je faisais des exercices, je mémorisais. Moi, je présentais des spectacles d'une heure... alors ça demandait énormément de préparation. Puis en même temps, il faut que tu sois assez détendu. Finalement, tu dois trouver un équilibre entre l'excitation et la détente. C'était très exigeant. Aujourd'hui, si j'ai moins besoin de tout ça, je pense que c'est aussi parce que j'ai plus confiance en moi.

doing now is not really performance. Back when it was, my whole day was geared toward that evening's performance. I had to work my voice, my body. I did exercises, I memorized. I used to give one-hour shows, so there had to be a lot of preparation. And at the same time, you have to be relaxed. You have to find a balance between excitement and relaxation. It was very demanding. These days, if I don't need all of that as much, it's also because I have more self-confidence.

LOUISE DUBREUIL: The way I like to work is, the day of the performance, I don't have to do anything. I'm not going to clean anyone's house, I have no obligations, so that if I want to, I can lie and do yoga for three hours. I can meditate. I can take a nap. I can be more in touch with how I'm feeling. Just having the day. Whether I need to sleep, or listen to music, or call someone who I know is going to really encourage me. Go for a walk. Whatever. It's not that it's always the same, but the one thing that's constant, what I like, is to have that day.

JASON SELMAN: Prayer. I just focus, remind myself to be honest in terms of performance, be who I actually am — my performance personality is a deviation from my natural performance, I think it's a hyper-extension, it's more intense than what I naturally am, but it's still part of who I am — so I try to say to myself, just be honest in terms of what your essence is, and try to communicate with people.

NANCY LABONTÉ: I don't really have a ritual before performing, but one thing is

80

important and that's feeling balanced. I tend to be a bit aggressive by nature, so before I start reading I need to breathe, to make sure my two feet are firmly planted on the ground. In fact, I get into metaphysics. I have to use the energy from the sky, the earth, I really have to channel that energy, get that juice, so I can project my hologram....

JOSEPH NEUDORFER: My brother David and I live probably forty-five minutes to an hour away from downtown, where most of the shows are, and I'm usually coming from home to go to a show. So I've come to enjoy taking the bus or the metro. It's part of the ritual, the routine, to get to the venue. And time aside, apart, to prepare for the night.

HEATHER O'NEILL: I like to listen to my Walkman. I like to crank up Iggy Pop or something. It's like someone else can give me confidence (laughs), because how can you be weak and neurotic if you listen to Iggy Pop?

DAYNA MCLEOD: For *Wreck Election*[20] I was so incredibly stressed-out. The only thing that calms me down — this is something that I recognize as coming out as a Bruce Springsteen fan — is *Tunnel Of Love.* I just listen to it over and over and over again. Also, the sewing is important.... Once I understand the physical construct of the costume I have to make, the sewing becomes very meditative, and it does feed the writing. The writing and the object evolve at the same time. I like my writing to be quite layered and chocked so full of metaphor that it's pushed to the absurd.... I usually leave a sewing project to the last minute, because it's meditative, but it also charges medita-

tion with stress, because I need to get it done. But because then I'm going over my lines, or going over the piece, or going over the text in my head it's like I'm able to do two things, I'm tricking myself.

COREY FROST: I think that preparation is important, but I find my means of preparation mostly in the writing preparation. The memorization is important for me. The memorization itself is a way of preparing you for what you're going to experience in the performance. So usually, if I'm going to perform, right before I do so, I hide away in a corner somewhere backstage and go over the piece a few times. And just jump up and down a little bit, get the blood running.

MITSIKO MILLER: Usually, I never choose my text beforehand. I take about five or six. Quite often, I try to come as early as possible. Then I read the text, and try to get into the vibe. I check out the scene,

NANCY LABONTÉ: Avant de performer, je n'ai pas vraiment de rituel sauf qu'il y a une chose qui est bien importante pour moi, c'est d'être bien équilibrée. Comme j'ai tendance à être un peu agressive de nature, avant de commencer à lire, il faut que je respire, il faut que j'aie les deux pieds bien ancrés sur terre. En fait, moi, je rentre dans la métaphysique: il faut que je me serve de l'énergie du ciel, de la terre, il faut vraiment que je me branche sur cette énergie, que j'en tire le jus, pour ensuite projeter mon hologramme....

Publicity still from Wreck Election: *Family photo of Bob Loblaw, wife Candy, and daughter Polly Anus (from left, Dayna McLeod, Skidmore, and Alexis O'Hara)* Photo by Susan Moss

[20] Montreal Fringe Festival, June 1999.

81

HÉLÈNE MONETTE: Mes rituels sont surtout d'ordre mental. Pour me motiver, je me répète une phrase de Max (Marcel Décoste) qui dit, mais sans que ça soit guerrier: "La scène c'est à toi, quand t'es là, t'es là." Ou je pense à Bob (Olivier), juste de penser à lui, même s'il n'est pas là, ça m'aide. Mais je n'ai pas de rituel en tant que tel. J'embarque dans ceux des autres quand je les vois faire, en coulisses. Mais il faut respirer, en tout cas. Parfois on n'y pense pas tout le temps, on arrive sur scène.... Une autre chose qui m'aide, moi, c'est de dire une banalité. Mais bien spontanée, pas préparée. D'arriver au micro puis de parler aux gens, dire: "Il a plu toute la journée, une chance qu'il ne pleut pas en dedans." Déjà, en faisant ça, pour avoir une réaction, ça me rapproche du public. C'est comme si j'étais avec eux dans mon salon. Après, je peux commencer ma performance. Ce n'est pas plus compliqué que ça.

John Giorno, 1965
Photo by William S. Burroughs
From www.spress.de/author/giorno

I check out who's there, what they want to hear, what they laugh at. That's why I don't like to be first, because I want to see what they laugh at, what touches them, what they're ready to share with me. Then I go in a corner and I breath like hell. Not because I'm nervous, it's just to center myself. Clear my body. Then I practice my projection, and I try to stay away from people for at least fifteen minutes before. I get a little nervous, just a bit, and then I go onstage.

JOHN GIORNO: I used to be fussy about not wanting to talk backstage, because I was younger. But then, once William Burroughs and I were on tour, I think it was in Copenhagen in the late eighties. A lot of people had come, a lot of friends of William had come and the conversation reached a fever pitch (laughs). The dressing room was so crowded and so loud, everyone was talking at the top of their lungs, and William was being forced to answer every single one of these old friends. I said to Jim Carroll, "Just look at this. This is nuts. All his energy is going now." And Jim screamed, "Everyone out!" They made everyone leave, it became a thing. So we were alone for two more minutes, which didn't mean anything (laughs). From then on I was never fussy about backstage. If they wanted to be backstage, let them be, I'd just go do my own thing. The whole thing is not to allow the difficulties of the situation make you into a worse prima donna.

HÉLÈNE MONETTE: My rituals are mostly mental. For motivation I repeat a sentence by Max (Marcel Décoste) which says, but not in a warrior way: "The stage is yours, when you're there, you're there." Or I think about Bob (Olivier), just thinking about him helps me, even though he's not there. But I have no ritual as such. I get into other people's when I see them doing it backstage. But you have to breathe, for sure. You don't always think of it and then you get up onstage and (gasps for air).... Another thing that helps me is to say something trivial. Very spontaneous, not planned. Like getting in front of the mic and saying: "It rained all day, good thing it's not raining inside." Just by doing this, to get a reaction, I'm already getting closer to the audience. As if I were in my living-room with them. Then I can start my performance. That's all there is to it.

ANNE STONE: I thought about this habitual space that you could occupy, and how that would be one measure of control that you could have over the context of a performance that you might not otherwise be given. Because you're walking into a venue, a room that other people are very much in control of. It's like finding yourself, in some sense, in an audible anthology, and not knowing what the works next to you are going to be, or how you're going to be housed. So you can't always be very tactical about it. I try, in some sense, to blank out my conscious mind, and not think. And I don't hear very clearly. I sit down at a table and I smile, and I seem very malleable, very pleasant. But I basically try to turn off so that nothing can really disturb me. I think about the piece, and I try to find my breathing, or I try to find the place it was written from in the body and go there.

ii. Preparing the Body

The nervous energy of performance demands a response. Whether achieved through exercises and movements, or other improvised means, the aim is to bring the body to a state of calm, which will serve to enhance the performance.

TODD SWIFT: Smoking.

FORTNER ANDERSON: Pacing.

VICTORIA STANTON: Doing yoga before a performance has become pretty crucial for me, and various other breathing exercises. But it seems to start with yoga and then move into the direction of muscle-stretching, and then just breathing. What happens is, when you get nervous you don't breathe, and if you're onstage and you're trying to perform by talking, it's sort of hard to talk when you're not breathing. Time moves weirdly, too, when you're onstage. It seems to expand, a short time feels a lot longer, so when you're just standing there breathing, it feels like you've been doing that for twenty minutes, but you've only been there for thirty seconds. Thirty seconds is not much time. So I've been trying to become more conscious of taking time when I get to a

stage. To just be on the stage, stand there and be with your audience. Just feel what that feels like for a moment.

CATHERINE KIDD: There has to be a bath in there somewhere. I like to sit in the bathtub, I sometimes bring it onstage with me. A lot of the things that I've written feature baths, so I wonder if that's my catch-all metaphor for some kind of birth experience. Maybe there's a kind of religiosity attached to that too. Baths as cleansing yourself of whoever you had been the previous hour, towards who you have to be in the next hour or the next day. [I do a] bunch of voice exercises. I stretch out my jaw and make, "Ki! Ki!" noises or say, "Buttered toast, buttered toast," to get the enunciation down. It helps me feel comfortable with my own mouth, so it's a familiar thing and I'm not tripping over it. Breathe…. All day, before a show, I'm preparing for a show, in terms of settling myself and being private. Meditation and a bath and voice exercises. No coffee (laughs).

LEAH VINEBERG: I always do yoga before I perform, for sure. I have to be extremely grounded. But I'm extremely flighty. I need to feel my feet on the ground, feel my own circulation. I've smoked a lot of cigarettes, and there have been enough times in my life that I wasn't in my body. I find it terrifying to be onstage and suddenly not be able to move because you're just not in your body. It's extremely important to me that it's a mind-body-soul experience. Which is why I do yoga. The out-of-body thing, that just doesn't happen any more.

D. KIMM: I try to relax and focus…. I've been doing Tai Ji Quan for years so I work the tantien, the energy centre. I

D. KIMM: J'essaie de relaxer et de me concentrer…. Je fais du Tai Ji Quan depuis longtemps, donc je travaille le tantien. C'est le centre des énergies. Je n'y pense pas mais il est là quand j'en ai besoin. Alors je n'ai pas vraiment de rituel, sauf que j'essaie d'être bien dans mon corps, d'avoir un bon tonus physique.

BENOÎT PAIEMENT: La concentration est très importante, parce qu'on fait vraiment un travail de précision. Si on n'arrive pas à se bien concentrer, on n'arrive pas à bien performer. Il y a clairement un lien à établir entre la qualité de notre préparation (la demi-heure ou l'heure qui précède le spectacle) et la qualité de la présentation en tant que telle... Donc nous, en guise de rituel, on a développé tout un processus de concentration qui consiste en des exercices physiques très élaborés, et exigeants aussi. Des exercices où on se donne vraiment, comparables par exemple à des *sit-up*, à des *push-up*.

FÉLIXE ROSS: Ce ne sont pas des exercices qu'on fait bêtement. C'est toujours fait dans le but d'amener à une conscience du corps. Être conscient de notre rythme cardiaque, de notre respiration.

BENOÎT PAIEMENT: C'est comme une sorte de visualisation. Et ces exercices, à la limite, peuvent même causer des tremblements des mains ou des genoux. L'effort physique qu'on met en travaillant, en se préparant, calme le corps. Le trac reste là, l'énergie positive reste là, mais le corps s'oxygène. Donc toute notre nervosité est canalisée, ou maîtrisée. En faisant ces exercices, j'ai vraiment l'impression de prendre la nervosité puis de l'embrasser. Et ça fonctionne.

don't think about it but it's there when I need it. So I don't really have a ritual, except that I try to be feeling well, to be in good shape physically.

BENOÎT PAEIMENT: Concentration is very important, because it's really precision work. If you're not focused, you can't perform well. There's a clear link between the quality of our preparation during the half-hour or hour before the show and the quality of the show itself.... So as a ritual, we've developed a whole process of concentration made up of very elaborate and demanding physical exercises. Exercises in which we really put out, comparable to sit-ups and push-ups.

FÉLIXE ROSS: We don't just simply do these exercises. It's always done in order to achieve body awareness. To become aware of our heart rate, our breathing.

BENOÎT PAIEMENT: It's a kind of visualization. And these exercises can cause your hands and knees to shake. The physical effort we put into preparing calms the body. The butterflies remain, the positive energy remains, but the body gets filled with oxygen. So all our nervousness is channeled, or mastered. When I'm doing those exercises I really feel like I'm embracing nervousness. And it works.

JULIE CRYSLER: If I'm all full of energy, then I have to spend some time calming myself down. Sometimes I'm feeling tired and I have to wake myself up. I try to figure out where my body's at before I go onstage. I like to do little vocal exercises, from singing and theatre, to make sure I've not got any cracks in my voice.

BUFFY CHILDERHOSE: I masturbate just to the point of orgasm, until I have all

sorts of energy, and then I stop. Not at the venue. If I can, I'll go to the venue as late as I can, and that's what I do before I go. Because quite often, particularly when I was working a lot, I just had no energy. "OK, I'm stressed out. Maybe if I actually masturbate it'll calm me down." The thing I want to do is cheat myself out of that, and take all that energy and put it into the piece.

JOHN GIORNO: For me, taking a nap. Then I wake up and I'm really rested, like in the morning. And even if you *were* groggy, the real adrenaline kicks in when you're about to go on, and it totally wakes you up.... If it doesn't happen, you know how to make it happen using your internal breathing in a certain way. By hyperventilating, by taking these great breaths that you're letting out and these great breaths you're taking in. If you take in a breath and push it to the bottom of your stomach and keep pushing, you create heat. In Tibetan Buddhism there's something that's called *Tsa Lung*. It's using the breath in a certain way. Another aspect of it is taking breaths in and pushing the air to the bottom to create a vase, manipulating the flow of the internal, subtle rhythms inside the body. I realized that what I was doing onstage was not that dissimilar from this meditation.

TETSURO SHIGEMATSU: For forty-eight hours I refrain from dairy products — I kind of become kosher, in a sense — no meat, no carbohydrates, I watch my diet, drink a lot of water, I tend to save my voice.... I lose all jewelry and accoutrements and identifying markers, in that sense, take off my glasses, rings. I also, I guess every performer could relate to this, I just gather my energy. So externally I probably seem very quiet, maybe even sullen, but I'm just gathering my energy and focusing so I can release it come performance time.

JAKE BROWN: I have to do something physical just before I go on. I do the stretches and jumping up and down, shadow-boxing. I try to think one thought only, which is, "Yes, I really believe what I'm about to say." For real, because if I can't get there, I can't say it. I want to go home, and I have before. I've bailed three times like that. It's a form of cowardice, but I did it. I literally can't speak unless I believe what I'm saying is true. Same thing in front of a classroom, I feel awful otherwise. If I feel like I'm going through a motion, I feel like I should be dead.

iii. Nerves, Fear, Euphoria

The range of emotions performers experience — from nervous energy to feeling physically ill — all point to the reality of the situation; that although text is foregrounded in spoken word performance, the body is also on display. In many cases the intensity of fear points to the fact that spoken word artists arrive onstage without the kind of training that performance artists from traditional disciplines like dance and theatre receive. It also points to the fact that spoken word art involves great risks, as the artists lay bare their deepest thoughts to the audience.

DEBBIE YOUNG: Every performance, I want to throw up (laughs). Every performance, I get insanely nervous. I've noticed that if I get to a performance three hours early then I'm nervous for three hours. So what I do, I try to get there as close to my performance as possible. Because the nervousness is so debilitating, it completely takes over my entire being!

VICTORIA STANTON: Before going on a stage to perform I'm almost unapproachable. I get really really really tired, I feel like I could just fall asleep right there and then. Sometimes I get really nauseous or headachey. Somebody pointed out to me once that my body does this because that's its way of preparing. It's this way of turning inward and focusing.

JOHN GIORNO: I get sleepy... my body closes down. I was in Naples doing this really big performance. They do it differently, everything's *after* dinner. So I was forced to eat dinner first. I eat a little bit, I'm sitting there (yawns). And then of course the adrenaline hits. I love that. For me, that is optimum. You go in front of anything, whether it's fifty people or five thousand people and you get a natural adrenaline rush. It's a sort of a dangerous situation, dangerous in the sense that it's volatile. The unexpected may arise in your voice any time, or whatever. So the adrenaline hits you, just by the nature of these thousand people in front of you. And I can use that adrenaline, and then it's not a problem with me.

BUFFY CHILDERHOSE: I always want to fight as soon as I get offstage. I'm actually incredibly aggressive.

JULIE CRYSLER: It's a very aggressive thing, I think, to stand up onstage and to demand that you're going to be heard. The work that Buffy does and the work that I do, it's latching onto some kind of female power. I think some of my work is about that, I like writing about tough chicks. I think the dissonance between that and your real life is a little bit of an attraction too.

ANNA LOUISE CRAGO: Sometimes I get — this is strange — I get nervous *after* I've performed. I think that it's from when my performing was so personal, and it was so much disclosure. At the time, what I wrote and the stories I would tell would be so much about these major emotional things happening in my life. I mean it's a clichéd thing to say but there's an element of vulnerability in that.

NORMAN NAWROCKI: With *My Dick*,[21] I wasn't nervous as much as I was scared. I was afraid I was going to be beaten up. I was really really afraid. So it was a different kind of nervousness, it was a fear, because I'm doing a show about homophobia that attacks a lot of basic precepts that men walk around with. It's actually like throwing myself to the wolves.... Those are really subversive, surprise shows. The audience members don't know this is a show about homophobia. They come because they think I'm a sexist comedian. That was the scariest show I've ever done, the first show. And nobody attacked me. I fell off the stage, myself. I fell and twisted my ankle.

[21] *My Dick and Other Manly Tales*, one-man show produced in 1998.

CATHERINE KIDD: That's the one thing that emphasizes the artificiality of a performance, for me, is the fact that I never get over nervousness. It helps me feel less nervous that there's a little bit of a remove, ie., I'm not sitting at the table with the people who are listening. It helps me get into my own space, if there's a stage there. By the time I get onstage hopefully I can take that, grab an amplified bunch of energy and put it into the piece. But before the piece it's just learning to house it, to let it flow properly. I wish I were somebody who could just sit down at a table and drink a beer with some people right before they go on, and say, "Oh, that's me," and go up onstage. I'm not! I really look forward to that after the show is over (laughs).

JONATHAN GOLDSTEIN: The payoff is basically like that old Jewish joke: "Why are you hitting your head against the wall?" "It feels so good when I stop."

Norman Nawrocki from
My Dick and Other Manly Tales
Photo from www.nothingness.org/music/rhythm

5. Performing: "What's left after you say the word?"

What does it mean, to perform texts onstage? What kind of experience happens in the time it takes for a spoken word artist to speak to an audience? What effect does music, movement and lighting have? How does the audience figure into the process? At what point does a live performance become a mediated experience?

i. Personae

When the spoken word artist appears on the stage, she might seem to be 'herself', but whether as 'the writer', 'the poet', 'the clown', or 'the spoken word artist', the performer takes on a new, or at least an amplified persona.

D. KIMM: I find that performers sometimes go for easy effects.... I've seen lots of shows, I've been interested in the stage and in spoken word for years, so I'm not impressed when a guy comes on wearing his leather jacket when it's 30° in the room.... I find that performers still do this a lot, the nonchalant rebel trip, which seems to be saying: "I've got my text on a scrap of paper, I just wrote it...." This annoys me, it's very cliché. They don't seem to want to own up to the fact that they enjoy being up there onstage in front of an audience. Or sometimes, there are too many trappings. Even in shows by *La Vache enragée*, some performers put too much emphasis on costumes and everything, and it doesn't make their performance more interesting. What I love to see, on the other hand, and I hope this

will always stay, is real emotion. You're in the room and you feel it, somebody's angry and really living it onstage, this touches me.

LEE GOTHAM: With the movement of words and literature onto the stage, into a theatrical realm, you have this inevitable effect of a foregrounding of the writer / creator's personality. This can be a wonderful, entertaining thing, and it can be a really debilitating thing when it comes to the work itself, to the craft. This fetishizing of the performer before and beyond the work itself, I really feel is characteristic of a lot of spoken word performance now, and not altogether positive in its impact on those performances.

VICTORIA STANTON: But what happens when people create personae? Is that still spoken word? I think it can be. I think if you inhabit the persona, it's not necessarily acting, either.

RAN ELFASSY: I think I'd find it really difficult just to go up and say something without some kind of filter.... It's so much easier to put some kind of filter / persona there, "Okay I'm going to be in performance mode."

AKIN ALAGA: When you see Fela Kuti perform, for me it is disturbing, because I just want to get out of my chair (laughs). Sometimes I don't feel like he's a human being. Or he's a madman. Because he's really *there*! You know? And to be able to do that, in a sense, for

D. KIMM: Je trouve que, parfois, les performeurs ont recours à des effets faciles.... J'ai vu beaucoup de spectacles, ça fait des années que je m'intéresse à la scène et au spoken word, alors ça ne m'impressionne plus de voir arriver un gars avec son blouson de cuir pour lire son texte quand il fait 30 degrés dans la salle.... Et je trouve que les performeurs y jouent encore beaucoup, à l'image du rebelle nonchalant qui a l'air de dire: "Mon texte sur un bout de papier, je l'ai écrit tantôt..." Ça me fatigue un peu. C'est très cliché. On dirait qu'ils n'assument pas le fait qu'ils aiment être là, sur scène, devant public. Ou parfois, il y a trop d'enrobage. Même dans des spectacles de *La Vache enragée*, j'ai trouvé qu'il y avait des performeurs qui mettaient trop d'emphase sur les costumes, et puis, finalement, ça ne rendait pas leur performance plus intéressante. Par contre, ce que j'aime et j'espère que ça va toujours rester, c'est l'émotion vraie. Lorsqu'on est dans la salle et qu'on la ressent, quand quelqu'un est en colère et qu'il le vit vraiment. Ça, par exemple, ça me touche beaucoup.

me, that's the highest thing. There's nothing else, really. To be able to be there, to have direct access to that psychic place right there... and that's why the stage is so sacred, and that's why the page is so sacred, because first of all you're trying to craft out what's going to happen onstage, inside of the limelight.

ANDRÉ LEMELIN: There's an Irish storyteller named Mike Burns — he works in French as well — he closes his eyes when he's telling a story. It's like the story overtakes him, the teller disappears. At one point you're not looking at him anymore; anyway, his eyes are closed. So you do the same, you close your eyes and visualize the story, dive right into it.

COREY FROST: Fortner Anderson talks about spoken word being a medium of truth. Getting the truth out there. But does that mean that the poet is more honest than an actor in the theatre, for example? I was thinking about Maggie Estep, because her stuff is pretty much first-person narrative. But you don't get the feeling that you're actually hearing about someone's experience. You have the feeling that it's manufactured. It's really obvious that she's performing in the role of 'the spoken word artist'. And when she's talking about 'I', she's not really talking about herself, she's talking about this persona. But then I start thinking that maybe that's always the case. If a young Black woman wants to tell other young Black women in the audience about her personal experience, in order to validate them as people in mass culture, is she actually up there being herself, or is she producing a fictional persona that other people can look up to? I'm not saying that's bad. I'm saying that this is unavoidable.... Constantly, every day when you get out of bed, you create your persona.

ANDRÉ LEMELIN: Mike Burns –un conteur irlandais anglophone qui conte aussi en français–, lorsqu'il conte, lui, ferme les yeux. C'est comme si son histoire prenait le dessus, le conteur vient à disparaître. À un certain moment, tu ne le regardes plus; de toute façon, il a les yeux fermés. Alors ça t'oblige à faire la même chose, à fermer les yeux et à écouter, puis à visualiser l'histoire, à y plonger carrément.

ii. "I would do these things spontaneously"

The act of performing onstage can be fairly informal, as are many spoken word events, or it can be as carefully rehearsed and co-ordinated as a dance or theatrical show. Some performers feel that the informality of spoken word performance is the key to its accessibility.

NORMAN NAWROCKI: Sometimes I'm asked to write material for a place and I have nothing and I have to write on the spot. I often get requests, "Can you write something for this strike, can you write something for this occupation? Can you do something for this?" I'll just come up with something. For a long time when Rhythm Activism toured as a duo, one of our specialities was improv pieces. We would arrive on tour... wherever we were going, I would sit down with the organizers of the show, and interview them. And I would write a piece about that city at that moment. We'd go onstage and Sylvain Côté would have an improvised guitar thing and I would perform this piece, and people would just go nuts, totally nuts over it. What I was trying to show was you can take your everyday life situations here and turn them into art, or spoken word, or entertainment.... It's not hard to do, you don't have to spend weeks, months or years on it. I would do these things spontaneously. So now, when I get these requests, it's become easier over the years to just write something about this issue. CBC radio, when the Gulf War first started, called up and said, "Do you have any material about the Gulf War?" I said, "Yeah, we're about to release an album this week, you'll get it Friday."

88

VICTORIA STANTON: Vince and I have allowed ourselves a certain space to just let whatever happens happen…. We might come out onto the stage, and look at each other and go into a spontaneous performance. It might not be text. We pulled one word out of one of our pieces, for a performance, and just started playing with that word or that sentence, and it became part of the performance. We didn't decide to do that beforehand, but it really worked.

VINCE TINGUELY: I find that we're playing with the fact that anything you do onstage is performance. That's a lot of fun, because that's your little envelope of security. Even if you screw up, well, you screwed up onstage, so it's part of the performance.

PASCAL FIORAMORE: Onstage is where our songs get broken in, where we learn to play them, to sing them. That's where I really learn to sing them well, by testing various ways of doing them. This way we always keep an aspect of improvisation. By always presenting new versions of our songs, people don't recognize them. From one time to the next, they don't pay the same attention. Sometimes we'll play the same song for eight, ten shows, and then on the eleventh one people really react, get into it. That means the song has found its ultimate form. Then we can say to ourselves: "OK, from now on we're going to do it like this."

iii. "The music isn't just part of the scenery"

Sound or music is often utilized to accompany spoken word poetry or prose. It's a way to make the work more accessible to an audience, and it also elevates the delivery of the texts, *enlarges the sense that it is a performance.*

ALEXIS O'HARA: I'm really interested in mixing music with performance, because I recognize that that is far more accessible to people than just a person talking. It's like that with humour as well. Humour and music are two ways to get across messages that otherwise people maybe wouldn't get.

DAVID GOSSAGE: There's always been a bit of a stigma about poetry and music, it's sort of highfalutin. There's nothing as unforgiving as bad poetry, with people getting up and feeling like just because they're doing it with music — you still see that to this day, basically wearing their heart on their sleeve. It really can be remarkably self-indulgent, and the craft of poetry isn't there. The whole idea when you're doing something as marginal as this is to bring people in, don't alienate them. The form itself alienates enough people as it is…. With Nietzsche's Daughter,[22] it was very much about the craft of music and

PASCAL FIORAMORE: C'est en spectacle qu'on rode nos chansons, qu'on apprend à les jouer, à les chanter. Moi, c'est vraiment là que j'apprends à les chanter efficacement, en testant différentes manières de les faire. Nous conservons ainsi toujours un côté improvisé. En présentant constamment des nouvelles versions de nos chansons, les gens ne les reconnaissent pas. D'une fois à l'autre, ils ne leur portent pas la même attention. Parfois on va chanter un texte pendant huit à dix spectacles, puis ça va être au onzième spectacle que les gens vont vraiment réagir, embarquer. À ce moment-là, ça signifie que la chanson a trouvé sa "finalité". On peut alors se dire: "OK, à l'avenir, on va la faire ainsi."

David Gossage
Photo by Karine Hunkiar

[22] A music and poetry ensemble active in the late eighties and early nineties.

Geneviève Letarte performing 'Extraits d'un livre chanté' at Espace Go, Montreal, 1987
Photo by Louise Oliguy

(below)
Page from 'Berceuse Indi' by Geneviève Letarte

D. KIMM: Mes textes, c'est un peu comme de la musique. Dans mes spectacles, il y a vraiment un rythme. Et je dirais que l'ordre dans lequel j'enchaîne mes textes est entièrement musical.

GENEVIÈVE LETARTE: Dès le début, il y avait un côté chanté dans mes textes. Déjà, j'en chantais des bouts. Et je pense que dès ma première performance, il y avait aussi de la musique. Par la suite, ça s'est développé, raffiné, complexifié, dépendamment des gens avec qui je travaillais. Je jouais avec des disques pour créer des fonds musicaux, The Ventures, des trucs comme ça. Je faisais des collages sonores. J'intégrais de la musique enregistrée et, parfois, de la musique *live*. J'étais portée vers la musique mais en ayant toujours en tête l'idée que ça puisse servir à alimenter le fait de dire ou de chanter un texte.

PATRICIA LAMONTAGNE: Parfois j'inclus de la musique dans ce que je fais, mais la musique n'est pas qu'un simple décor: elle est ce "quelque chose" qui va propulser le langage, propulser la performance. Je suis guitariste et je peux jouer pour le plaisir, mais sur scène, si j'utilise une guitare, ça va vraiment être dans le but de *créer* des atmosphères.

poetry. The music was very complex, we had up to nine musicians some times. It was all conducted, and Clifford Duffy would rarely read his own poetry. He'd hire actresses to do it, and they'd be coached for weeks and weeks before, how to say this line or this phrase.... We'd have unaccompanied poetry too, in the show. It wasn't always music, we'd stop and do one without the music, and then that one had so much more power. Why did you choose not to use music on this particular poem?... There were some poems, it was literally down to the word, the way the music followed the poem. It wasn't just grooving on the bass, it was word by word. We had to be together or we didn't end up in the same place.

D. KIMM: My texts are a bit like music. My shows have a rhythm and I'd say that the order in which I do my texts is entirely musical.

GENEVIÈVE LETARTE: There's been a sung aspect to my texts from the very beginning. I think there was music in my very first performance. Over time this developed, got refined, more complex, depending on whom I was working with. I was playing with records to create musical backgrounds. The Ventures, stuff like that. I made sound collages. I'd integrate recorded music and sometimes live music. I was attracted to music but always with the idea that it could serve to broaden the fact of speaking or singing a text.

PATRICIA LAMONTAGNE: I sometimes include music in what I do, but it's not just part of the scenery: it's the 'something' that'll drive the language, the performance. I'm a guitarist and I do play for fun but if I use a guitar onstage, it will really be with the intention of *creating* atmospheres.

CATHERINE KIDD: When Jack Beets and I first started out, if he could come to the show, then he would have about seven cassette tapes or digital samples. If I were doing a show somewhere else I

90

would have it pre-recorded on a cassette. Which was hellish! If it's pre-recorded sound, then I have to keep in synch in static time. It's not going to synch itself to me, I have to synch myself to it. That added a little bit of frenzy or hurriedness to the delivery, which never worked very well.

JOHN GIORNO: By the late sixties, I was doing these sound compositions that were meant to be on one of my LP records. Then I would have a performance edit of it, where I would follow it through an earphone. It was precisely done, I would follow it live, using it as orchestration. And not by chance. I knew what I was doing, because it was also highly planned. I always had earphones on, because you can't hear it directly if you're hearing it off the speakers. And then I played with it endlessly. Sound compositions — everyone thinks, "Oh, you use delay, you use reverb." I don't think we ever used reverb or delay. It was one layer of voice over another layer of voice, moved with great difficulty electronically.... With the early electronics, it was very hard to do, really labour-intensive. And nobody even knew that I did it! They would think it was delay! But it didn't matter, that's what I wanted to do. Until 1980 or whenever, when I had enough, and I thought, "Okay, that's that with electronics." For twenty years or more, I did that, using electronics. Then came a point when I ended up making the songs with the band.

iv. "There was smell and sound and light"

John Giorno introduced the concept of 'environment' to poetry readings in the early sixties in New York. This meant bringing in other, extra-textual elements to enhance and intensify the experience of the poetry. Such elements are essential to raising the performance to the level of a popular art, and making it accessible to larger audiences.

JOHN GIORNO: When I started doing these poetry readings, I incorporated the idea of an environment. One phenomenon that was happening in the sixties amongst the artists, was 'environments'. Monumental, conceptual art. Pop art kind of images. In 1966 I did two things with Bob Rauschenberg. One was in the School of Visual Arts, in November of 1966, with Deborah Hay, who was a dancer, Bob Rauschenberg and myself. I had these spotlights on the audience rather than just on the per-

*John Giorno with some of his prints in his NYC studio
June 1999*

91

JEAN-PAUL DAOUST: À un certain moment, j'allais voir beaucoup de concerts rock, et ça m'a fait penser que lorsque je faisais des lectures de poésie, c'était important d'amener de la musique, puis d'incorporer quelques accessoires pour souligner des choses, orienter le texte. Évidemment, un poète n'a pas les moyens du showbiz, mais je trouve que lorsqu'on est sur scène, on fait du show-business, même si on lit des poèmes. La façon qu'on les lit, la voix qu'on a, le corps qu'on a, tout devient une mise en scène, malgré nous. Et moi, j'aime bien en être conscient, et pousser cette idée... Par exemple, lorsque je change d'ambiance –parce que je fais plusieurs sortes de poésie: intimiste, urbaine, éclatée, "dandiste" –, j'aime bien qu'il y ait une musique qui l'annonce, ainsi qu'un changement de vêtements. En 1979, avec la photo tirée du recueil *Portraits d'intérieur* (aux Écrits des Forges), j'étais flambant nu avec une bouteille de champagne sur une peau de zèbre, un peu tramée en rose, ça faisait un peu rétro... Je pense que c'est à partir de ce moment que j'ai voulu, sur scène, présenter des textes qui soient enrobés d'atmosphères. C'est sûr que si on est 15 poètes et qu'on lit chacun deux minutes, à ce moment, on ne peut pas le faire. Mais si je donne une lecture d'une heure, j'ai le temps de m'installer et de créer des atmosphères.

23 In the mid-sixties, Bell engineers collaborated with New York-based artists on a number of projects.

former, trying to dissolve that barrier. A few months later, early 1967, late 1966, at Loeb Street Student Centre at NYU, I lit the whole audience with ultraviolet light. I brought in sound, these Moog sound pieces. It began like that. At one point in 1967 at Saint Mark's Church, I brought in just anything I could think of. There was smell and sound and light. There were these atomizer cans which would emit smells. Dupont had invented this tape, light tape... you could buy it by the hundreds of yards, and they were different colours, the primary colours. So when attached to the light organ, which is what it was called, you'd see these different bands. I draped them over the audience. During one of those, Bell art and technology labs,[23] one of the engineers, said to me, "You know, we can analyze the light content of sound — blue is the low bass, yellow is high, red is loudness with brightness." So he invented this little box for me that would plug in.... In all the performances for a certain number of years, I used this device, and it registered the sound in lights. Quite a few years later it was disco lights! (laughs) It was just dealing with whatever idea there was, to create a situation where the audience wasn't as alienated, could not hear. Not only could not hear, but the poetry that was done in performance was not for performance. It was meant to be read sitting in a chair at night, lit by a candle, when your mind works at a different speed.

TOM KONYVES: My performances never included a lot of live reading; like performance art, I was more interested in action, the poem unfolding through action, not simply reciting. In my videopoems, I try to create a work that is more than the illustration of the poem; as in a poetry performance, the videopoem presents a poem in a visual

context. At its completion, the effect on the audience should be the same aesthetic experience as looking at a painting or sculpture, listening to a piece of music or watching a play. To determine whether a poetry performance or a videopoem works or not, it's useful to ask, "Does the visual context add to the experience of the poem?" The goal is to create a work which uses poetry in a new medium to create a new kind of poetic experience, one which reflects the artist's awareness of the simultaneity of events in our lives.

CATHERINE KIDD: When Jack Beets describes the process, what he talks about is emotion, trusting emotional information. I think that people do that more and more, anyway, trusting instinct and premonition or vibe or mood as a source of information. These are wordless things. To read something made of words in that light, and try to reflect it both in the performance and in the soundscape. OK, so what's the *un*spoken part of this? What's the *un*spoken word of this spoken word piece? And to choose the sounds and the presentation properly.

LYNN SUDERMAN: I wanted to be evocative. I wanted people listening to feel, smell, remember things from their own lives. Sometimes I'd use devices as simple as horror movie tricks, or subtler methods such as telling a poetic story that resembled a classic kid's fable. Or I'd buy *prix de présence* to give away to the audience so they'd have a tactile reminder of a poem.

JEAN-PAUL DAOUST: I went to a lot of rock concerts at some point, and it made me think that when I gave poetry readings, it was important to bring music and to incorporate props to highlight certain things, to slant the text. Obviously, a poet doesn't have show business means but I believe that when we're onstage, it's showbiz, even if we're reading poems. The way we read them, how we use the voice, the body, all of this becomes staging, in spite of ourselves. I like to be aware of this and push the idea forward.... For example, when I want to change the ambiance — because I do several types of poetry: intimate, urban, *éclatée* [fragmented], dandyist — I like using music to announce this, as well as a costume change. In 1979, with the photograph from *Portraits d'intérieur,*[24] where I was bare naked with a bottle of champagne on a zebra skin, lightly screened in pink, the effect was a bit retro.... It was from that moment on that, onstage, I wanted to present texts wrapped in atmosphere. Of course if you have fifteen poets reading two minutes each, you can't do this. But if I'm giving a one-hour reading, I have the time to settle in and create atmospheres.

COREY FROST: I find that more and more I want to do performance pieces that incorporate elements of other art forms. When I did that performance at the McGill Bookstore Café,[25] the stage was in front of the windows. We were watching these people onstage, whose voices were being broadcast on the radio, and yet we were in the position where we could see it live. To me, that made all the difference. So I was watching the performer, and in the background people were just walking by on McTavish Street. And I thought about making films to go with my performances that would be like visual white noise. The way that some spoken word performers will play music, even if it has nothing to do with their piece, because it distracts a certain rational part of your mind while you're listen-

ing. Even something like using a metronome while you're reading can have a really relaxing and intensifying effect. And so I thought make a video, just get a video camera and walk around the streets, film whatever, and then play that on the screen behind your story.

v. "Consciously connecting movements to words"

When the text is memorized, the body of the performer is free to move. Several of the artists we interviewed pointed out the connection between the spoken word and the body's role in performance.

ENDRE FARKAS: Partly the reason why I liked dancing — contact, modern, postmodern — is because I felt there was a close link with poetry reading. It was ephemeral. Once you read the word, it disappears. The dance, you make a gesture, it's gone. So there's a connection with the ephemeral side of it. So what's left after you say the word? What echoes, what remains? What remains after the gesture of the hand is the memory, or the sound. That interested me, that affinity.

NATHALIE DEROME: When D. Kimm tries to play her text, I tell her that language is not only the way you move the mouth, it's also the breath, and if you don't connect the breath with your mouth, even if you speak very well, it won't work. So, for me, writing is OK, but if you want to pull it out of the white page, you have to connect as quick as you can to the body.

JOHN GIORNO: There's this really brilliant young choreographer named David Newman, who has a dance company. He was hired by somebody to do

Nathalie Derome in
S'Allumer contre le vent *at the*
Monument national, 1997
Photo by Luc Senécal

24 Daoust, Jean-Paul. *Portrait d'intérieur.* Trois-Rivières: APLM, 1981.

25 *Reading In The Stacks,* September 1998.

93

some piece I was in a couple of years ago. I was fascinated. What he did to me stayed in my mind, because in a certain way he introduced me to another way of moving my body, by consciously connecting movements to words. Being a poet, I'm not really a dancer, even a rock and roll or even a disco dancer. But on the stage, I'm dealing with breath, and the internal breath generally pushes your limbs around or moves your body. You don't have to think about doing this, you just do it when the phrase comes up.

VINCE TINGUELY: When Victoria and I did the Cabaret — at a *La Vache enragée* benefit[26] — it was the first time we were in this big space. We were stressed, so stressed. We got onstage, and just looked at each other and started running, because we wanted to ground ourselves. So we just ran for thirty seconds or a minute.

VICTORIA STANTON: And that is a direct influence from seeing *Stop Making Sense*, the Talking Heads concert movie. That's what they would do onstage. I learned much later that there's this whole tradition, this non-dance dance tradition in the sixties, of everyday movements being incorporated into dance. And running is one of those things. It was so intuitive. It wasn't because I'd heard about this before, it's because it felt like the right thing to do.

JAKE BROWN: When I first started to perform I was trying to just follow plain instinct, and work some things out. Fewer people liked what I did then, but if you ask me, they might've liked it more. When I was stripping and screaming at the Gay Village for a whole year, gay hipsters liked it, but hardly anyone else. When people asked me,

"Why are you doing it this way?"... I couldn't answer the question myself. I thought, "I can't just do this because I am doing it. There has to be a reason to do it." A huge part of the reason I was doing it was just to find out what kind of effect I could have physically and emotionally on an audience, and what that might mean.

vi. The Role of the Audience: "When others like it too"

The relationship with the audience is both essential, and the source of much of the uncertainty and risk involved in a spoken word performance. It requires a particular kind of focus and doesn't command the automatic respect that conventional theatre or dance receives. Generally, the relationship with the audience is more informal, allowing for a high level of interaction.

FORTNER ANDERSON: Without the audience there would be no performance. You have to pose the question, what brings us to stand before an audience and do this? That brings up a whole series of interesting questions about the psychology of both the performer and the audience. The performers who, in those darkened rooms, gain some kind of satisfaction or pleasure from having the eyes and attention of the audience focused upon them, and the psychology of an audience who would amuse themselves, *pay* to be amused in this way.

COREY FROST: I have an audience in mind when I'm writing any particular piece. And that's what makes it so beneficial to me as a writer, that there exists a spoken word scene in Montreal. Otherwise I probably wouldn't have written much over the last four or five years. When I went to Japan, for instance, I found it really hard to produce anything, because the audience was on the other side of the world. Because I can't write in Japanese, usually in the process of writing I thought about eventually bringing it to Montreal or bringing it to Canada.

ATIF SIDDIQI: I always feel that the listening that people bring to an evening is just as important as the speaking, for my own work or anyone else's. The exchange is very powerful, and I just love being able to be there and have this conversation with an audience.

CATHERINE KIDD: A lot of human energy in the room does seem to be the spark which turns the work from that tired old horse to, "OK, go." The thing that I trust is the work, and I feel like everybody's participating in that.

JEAN-PAUL DAOUST: Sometimes I'm surprised at the audience reaction when I do a reading. I tell myself some people are going to be shocked, that they're going to hate what I do, and then they like it. Go figure.... In any case, I don't have a specific audience in mind when I write, absolutely not. I write for myself first of all and then, I choose texts depending on where I'm reading.

JAKE BROWN: I think the artist should make what they're doing without thinking about the audience that they're performing it for. Ninety-nine per cent of what you put into it should be based only on what you want to do with it, and then try to give it to as many different audiences as you can, and see who responds to it. I have a suspicion that if you make art compelling enough, almost anyone will respond to it. I think it's almost impossible to make it that good, very few people have accom-

Audience at le Cheval Blanc
March 29, 1998
Photo by André Lemelin

plished it, because it's hard to do. Especially now, people are familiar with a wide variety of forms and idioms in art. The odds of someone saying, "Oh, I've seen this before," are much higher than they were even fifty years ago, because you've got a critical mass of information flow.

NANCY LABONTÉ: If I work hard enough to project well, spectators will probably understand the vision I had. This vision is going to transform itself a bit through their own view, each one will feel a personal emotion that won't be the same for everybody. This is true for myself as well: I may feel it differently when I read it on different occasions. This is part of the beauty of poetry. You have to project, but you also have to have the awareness of being heard on the other side. When you're onstage if you're not aware that people are listening to you, it becomes like trying to talk to someone who's not listening. In a case like that, I wouldn't even be able to utter a sentence. All of a sudden, I'd be unable to externalize my ideas, I'd have the impression that communication has

JEAN-PAUL DAOUST: Parfois je suis surpris de la réaction du public quand je fais une lecture. Je me dis qu'il y a des gens qui vont être choqués, qui vont haïr ce que je vais présenter, et puis ils aiment ça. C'est à n'y rien comprendre... En tout cas, moi, je n'ai pas un public dans la tête quand j'écris. Absolument pas. J'écris d'abord pour moi et, ensuite, je choisis les textes en fonction des endroits où je vais les lire.

NANCY LABONTÉ: Si je travaille assez fort pour faire une bonne projection, les spectateurs vont probablement comprendre la vision que j'ai eue. Cette vision va se transformer un peu avec leur propre esprit, chacun va ressentir une émotion personnelle qui ne sera pas la même pour tout le monde. Même moi, je vais peut-être ressentir un texte différemment si je le lis en diverses occasions. Et c'est ça qui fait la beauté de la poésie. Il faut se projeter, mais il faut aussi avoir la conscience d'être entendu de l'autre côté. Si, sur scène, tu ne prends pas conscience qu'il y a des gens qui t'écoutent, ça devient

continued...

comme essayer de parler à quelqu'un qui ne t'écoute pas. Moi, à ce moment, je ne serais même plus capable de formuler mes phrases. Tout d'un coup, je serais incapable d'extérioriser ma pensée car j'aurais l'impression que la communication serait brisée, j'aurais l'impression de ne pas être écoutée. Et c'est ça, je pense, qui fait la qualité d'un texte dit. La conscience d'être écouté. Parce que ce qui est important, c'est la réception. Quand tu récites, tu vis, et quand tu es conscient d'être écouté, il y a comme un lien qui se tisse, une projection qui se fait de sentiments.

HÉLÈNE MONETTE: On cherche à rejoindre le public, on veut que notre performance ait un impact. Je pense qu'il ne faut même pas se demander *pourquoi* c'est comme ça. *Pourquoi* je veux rejoindre? Pourquoi? Pour être aimé? Pour telle ou telle autre raison? Dans un sens, c'est sans importance. On veut toucher les gens, puis parfois ça fonctionne. C'est ça qui est important.

ANDRÉ LEMELIN: Certains de mes textes sont durs, et parfois racontés au "je", à la première personne. Alors, il arrive qu'on ne fasse pas la différence entre la fiction et la réalité. Parfois, on vient me rencontrer à la fin d'un de mes textes et on me dit que j'ai bien réagi dans telle situation de mon histoire. Je m'empresse de répliquer que ce n'était pas moi mais une fiction, mais les gens me répondent: "Mais oui, c'était toi, tu l'as dit, "je, je, je"!" Christine Germain a souvent le même problème. Il y en a qui sont déjà allés la voir en lui disant: "Pauvre petite fille, moi, si j'avais été à ta place, j'aurais fait telle chose..."

Je suis aussi conscient que mes textes ne s'adressent pas à tous les publics. Ça fait quelques fois que je présente mes contes urbains aux *Dimanches du conte*. Au début, mes textes étaient moins bien reçus qu'aujourd'hui... Ça a été comme une forme d'éducation. Parce que dans les contes classiques, on retrouve souvent des princes charmants et des sorcières antipathiques, tandis que mes histoires parlent de prostituées, de clochards, de paumés... Ça passe ou ça casse.

broken down, that I'm not being heard. And I think that this is what makes the quality of a text — the awareness of being heard. Because what's important is the reception. When you recite, you're living and you're aware of being heard, a connection is established, feelings are projected.

HÉLÈNE MONETTE: We want to reach the audience, we want our performance to have an impact. I think we shouldn't even ask *why* it's like this. *Why* do I want to reach them? Why? To be loved? For this or that reason? In a way, it doesn't matter. We want to touch people, and sometimes it works. That's what matters.

The intimate nature of spoken word can lead to confusion in the audience's mind, in recognizing the difference between the performer and the person. Something as simple as the use of the first-person narrative can raise questions about the performer's relationship to her text. This highlights the fact that the audience, no matter how sympathetic, assumes the role of 'instant critic'.

ANNA-LOUISE CRAGO: So many authors are so often attacked — especially when they're young, "Oh, that novel is so autobiographical." Well, my stuff was purely autobiographical, in the sense that most of it was pulled out — at the very least — from emotions that I had lived in my life, if not certain situations. I would let this thing go out there, and then people would be responding, sometimes in very confusing ways. They'd come up and say, "Oh yeah, I've felt that way before." And I wasn't really trying to bond with every member individually over their last heartbreak, right? I wanted them to respond to the work. At the same time it made me feel

frustrated, because I felt like people were withholding creative criticism or even noncreative criticism. Because it was about my life, it becomes difficult to say, "You know, that piece sucked, where you lay yourself so bare, it sucked!" (laughs)

FORTNER ANDERSON: One never knows the effect of the words or the performance. Usually that's not my concern. Given a minimum, then, my concern when I go onstage is to imbue the text with as much emotional nuance and power as I can, during the reading. I'm satisfied when the text flows freely through me, and I'm able to make a communication with the audience.

ANDRÉ LEMELIN: Some of my texts are hard, and sometimes they're spoken in the first person. So sometimes people don't differentiate between fiction and reality. Sometimes people come to see me after one of my texts and tell me how well I handled a certain situation in my story. I reply that it wasn't me, it's fiction, but people say: "Yes it was you, you said I, I, I!" Christine Germain often has the same problem. People have gone up to her saying: "You poor thing, if I'd been in your shoes I'd...."

Also, I'm aware that my texts aren't for everybody. I've presented my urban tales at the *Dimanches du conte* event. At first, my texts were not as well received as they are now. It's been a kind of public education. Because in classic tales there's a Prince Charming and a wicked witch, whereas my stories feature prostitutes, losers, bums.... So it's make it or break it.

DAVID GOSSAGE: Unlike musicians, I think poets aren't used to how an audience is a judge. Often what the poetry people write is very personal, and it's sometimes strange for poets to be judged like that in a live situation. Judged in very subtle ways, shifting their chairs, not being rapt by what you have to say! If you take yourself too seriously, if something is *really* personal to you, it can throw people off.... Everybody has important ideas, some people write them down and some people don't. You can't expect an audience to be as bummed out as you are (laughs).

JOSEPH NEUDORFER: You have to be ready to be in front of an audience that is not very receptive. And it's very easy to take it personally and very negatively. Very early on, you realize you're performing for whoever's listening. You don't concentrate on the silent ears.

Spoken word performances can be tailored to appeal to particular audiences, depending on the message they convey. This raises the question of audience accessibility, and whether performers want to reach a broader public, or a specific community.

ALEXIS O'HARA: When I'm writing stuff that's chick-oriented I'm very conscious of the men in the audience too. I don't want to diss one portion of the audience for another. There have been times when I've written diss-pieces, but they'll be really specific. It's not that I expect everybody to understand what I'm saying, but I give a lot of credit, I don't try to talk down. I'd like to perform to people that aren't necessarily spoken word fans. I think that that's one of my goals, to go for more of the rock crowd, in a sense.

DEBBIE YOUNG: This period of writing — most of my work's looking at the role of Black women — directly relates to me and what I'm trying to find within myself. I've been aggressively ques-

tioned, let's say, on the validity of being so specific. Is our objective as artists to talk to and about everybody? Is our objective to be able to reach masses of people like CNN? I'm not CNN, that's not my objective (laughs). If you want that, you can watch CNN! To be an artist, to be able to subscribe to that terminology, I think that you are allowed to be overtly subjective (laughs).

TRISH SALAH: I've certainly performed or read in spaces — straight literary reading spaces, even avant-garde literary reading spaces — that, on ideological grounds, my being queer and trans has clearly created a huge obstacle between myself and the audience. People have been very cool, and sometimes very polite in a slightly worried way (laughs). As if they might catch something, but they certainly don't want to offend me either. So I'd say queer- and trans-positive, in terms of just an ideological marker, that makes a difference as to my comfort in a space and how I am in it, what people can get out of it.

Trish Salah, 2001
Photo by Chloë Brushwood-Rose

NORMAN NAWROCKI: The best spaces are places where poor people gather. And so, soup kitchens, community halls, those are my preferred places to perform. That's the warmest audience, the most responsive audience. The people really appreciate the work I'm doing the most, and I just feel it from them. And they're not afraid to say anything in the middle of a performance or yell or clap or scream or sing or dance, if that's what the show's all about. So, community venues filled with people from poor neighbourhoods. We've done shows all around the world for all kinds of people, from labour conventions to outside parliament, on buses, on ferries, you name it. But that's the best crowd, for me. The crowd I like the best.

KAIE KELLOUGH: Shows that feature mostly Black performers draw a mixed audience. The shows that feature a majority of white performers draw a white audience. It's a funny way of looking at things. I like culturally-mixed audiences to speak to. An audience that is respectful, but that also participates. One that's willing to participate, to say something, stop you, shout at you, ask a question, that kind of thing.

Vince Tinguely and Victoria Stanton at La Vache enragée, *March 29, 1998*
Photo by André Lemelin

VICTORIA STANTON: In some pieces I think I am writing for a particular audience, that being other young women. But I would like the pieces to work for the other people in the audience, because if I'm trying to figure out something about myself, I don't exist in isolation or in a vacuum. We co-exist with other people. So there's something to be said for developing yourself through a community of people just like you, but then to share that with other communities. It's important to integrate yourself into this larger society that you're part of. So I'd like the work to speak to lots of people. I think accessibility is quite important to me, that I don't want to bewilder people. I think generally speaking, what motivates me to work is communicating with other people. That's what I find exciting about being in a performance situation where people *get* what it is you're doing. And they'll *get* what it is you're doing if it's accessible enough for them to get. It doesn't mean it has to be focused or aimed at the lowest common denominator.

VINCE TINGUELY: I get really annoyed at either end of the spectrum. I hate people who just want the audience to love them, no matter what. So I don't like to do that in terms of performance. On the other hand, I don't like people who are so obscure that you pass out, because they're being too far out or too difficult to grasp. So I tend to try to communicate in the vernacular, and I really like writing in the vernacular. I like using swear words a lot, because they're in the *Oxford Concise Dictionary*. They exist. Why not use them? People use them all the time, so I like to put that into what I would call the canon. It's not even revolutionary. It was revolutionary in the fifties and sixties, it shouldn't be an issue any more.

JASON SELMAN: It's nice when you have people in the audience who don't know you.... It's one thing to preach to the converted. It's nice to have people who you respect, fellow poets, you do a show and they say, "That was a good set," that means a lot. It's another thing when people you don't know at all... come to you and say, "That was good." That's a separate experience.

HÉLÈNE MONETTE: I like it when other performers give me compliments. We compliment one another because there are certain people you like, you like their style. But when total strangers come to see me to share their comments, I love it.

GENEVIÈVE LETARTE: An ideal audience is when there's no one I know in the place. No friends. No friends if possible. Maybe a few friends onstage with me, that, I don't care. But when there's no friends in the room, it goes really well... otherwise, it's horrible. Especially in Montreal, because I've always lived here and obviously, I know a lot of people. This is one of the reasons why, at some point, I stopped doing shows. I couldn't take it anymore.... Am I going to do that all my life? Perform in front of my twenty-five friends? I found the situation really absurd. But maybe I didn't love them enough. Maybe that's the explanation, in the end. You really have to love your friends to give shows in front of them. It's not so straightforward. What I want most now is to travel. I don't travel a lot, but I have performed abroad and felt so free, so loose! So good....

As well as particular demographics, spoken word artists distinguish between the different moods or dispositions which an audience can present. Some audiences are quiet and attentive, others are rowdy and ready to respond vocally to the performance.

DEBBIE YOUNG: When you do a show, you can have a quiet audience but you feel the energy, you can feel what's happening. I've had a couple of shows like that at Isart where the audience was dead quiet, you could hear a pin drop, but I was reassured because my spirit felt the energy. I've also had quiet shows that I have not been able to read at all, whether people were feeling me or not appreciating the work. I think the most comfortable setting for me are shows where people are involved, loud and involved. Focused, focused on the word. I think that's my most comfortable audience, just because you can overtly gauge what's going on, what people are thinking (laughs). It makes me feel like I'm not talking *at* people.

DAYNA MCLEOD: In terms of audience and in terms of venues, the bars were ideal for me. The cabaret space was perfect, because the stuff I was doing was maximum fifteen, twenty minutes. And you knew immediately if you had them in the bar or the cabaret, and immediately if you didn't, because then they yell at you. The best place to do anything, in terms of feedback, in terms of a working project, is for a drunk audience. If I have anything to test out, that's what I test it out on. I've done some performances in galleries, and the audience comes loaded with all these preconceptions of what it is.

PATRICIA LAMONTAGNE: My ultimate goal in all my shows is to go beyond the norm, beyond logic, beyond political correctness, beyond the limit. So I enjoy performing for crazy people! I like performing for people who aren't afraid to follow me into my madness. Who aren't

Patricia Lamontagne, June 1999

HÉLÈNE MONETTE: Lorsque d'autres performeurs me complimentent, c'est bien. On se complimente entre nous parce qu'on aime certaines personnes, on aime leur style. Mais quand de parfaits inconnus viennent me voir pour me faire part de leurs commentaires, j'adore ça.

GENEVIÈVE LETARTE: *An ideal audience is no one I know in the place. No friends. No friends if possible. Maybe a few friends onstage with me, that, I don't care.* Mais quand aucun de mes amis n'est présent dans la salle, ça va très bien à ce moment-là... Sinon, c'est horrible. Surtout à Montréal, car je vis ici depuis toujours et, évidemment, je connais beaucoup de gens. Et ç'a justement été une des raisons pour lesquelles, à un certain moment, j'ai cessé de faire des spectacles. Je n'étais plus capable d'endurer ça... *Am I going to do that all my life? Perform in front of my 25 friends?* Je trouvais la situation vraiment absurde. Mais peut-être que je ne les aimais pas assez. Peut-être que c'est à cause de ça, au fond. Il faut vraiment aimer ses amis pour donner des spectacles devant eux. Ce n'est pas évident. Maintenant, moi, ce que je veux le plus, c'est voyager. Je ne voyage pas beaucoup, mais il m'est arrivé de présenter des spectacles à l'étranger, d'y dire mes textes et de me sentir tellement libre, tellement dégagée! Tellement bien...

PATRICIA LAMONTAGNE: Dans tous les spectacles que je présente, mon but ultime est de dépasser la norme, de dépasser la logique, de dépasser la

continued...

Pascal Fioramore: Au Cabaret Juste pour Rire, en septembre 1999, il n'y avait presque personne quand on a fait notre spectacle. La salle avait l'air vide. Après notre prestation, des gens sont venus nous voir et nous ont dit : "C'est vraiment un très bon spectacle qu'on a vu. Comment faites-vous pour être précis et pour vous donner autant alors qu'il y a rien qui se passe dans la salle?" À ça je réponds: "*The show must go on.*" Ce n'est pas parce qu'il n'y a que quatre personnes devant toi que ton spectacle doit être moins bon. Ces personnes se sont déplacées pour toi et tu te dois de leur donner le meilleur de toi.

Pascal Desjardins: Puis dans le fond, on le fait aussi pour notre simple plaisir.

27 Quebec Drama Federation's year-end performance event.

afraid if I take them into a world where there are few markers. The spectators' degree of culture doesn't matter to me. What does matter is that they're in the same state of mind as I am. Because people who are very sophisticated may know everything that's going on in Montreal, culturally-speaking, be in the underground, go to all the openings, and yet be unable to make that leap to the other side of things.

Catherine Kidd: If I'm reading late, well, I want to emphasize the funny bits, because that's usually where people are at by the end of the night. The audience definitely affects the delivery, whether it's more somber or more humourous, more irreverent or earnest. A lot of that happens automatically, not even consciously, depending on the kind of vibe you're getting from this human organism that you're a part of.

Sometimes, spoken word performers encounter audiences that aren't ideal, either in terms of size or in terms of being receptive. Here, a few artists discuss their strategies in dealing with difficult audience situations.

Tetsuro Shigematsu: My favourite audience at one point happened to be at the *Celebration '93.*[27] It was the toughest audience I've ever had to play. There was a lot of young people; it wasn't tough in that respect, but in the fact that they were all half-drunk, or fully drunk, and simply not paying attention. It was more like a party, people were milling about on the rafters, and it was like being in a cock-fight or some illegal boxing match. The person who went on previously was some poet, and he was reading and nobody was paying attention to him. And when it got to be my turn on the stage, I remember not

knowing quite what to do. So I really didn't do anything, I was just standing there, feeling very alone in the spotlight. I said nothing, and I know now what I didn't know then, was that there are few things as powerful as being absolutely still on the stage. Once I had a sufficient amount of attention — people were still milling about — I began. But I very much knew what my objective was, and that was to capture the attention of this audience, to tame them, and to bring them in. I gave a performance that was probably a little bit esoteric in terms of the delivery and other technical aspects, but in my mind I had thrown this metaphysical lasso around this huge beast, this unruly beast, and with all my strength I was pulling them in and I was pulling them in.... By the time I got to my last line, and indicated that the performance was over, people started hooting and hollering and stamping their Doc Marten boots against the floor, people began banging on chairs. It's probably the most wonderful sound of approval that I've ever heard, simply because in that one moment I knew that it was sincere.

Pascal Fioramore: At the *Cabaret Juste pour rire*, in September 1999, the room was almost empty when we gave our show. Some people came to see us after and said: "That was a really good show. How can you be precise and give so much of yourself when there's nothing happening in the room?" My response was: "The show must go on." Just because there are only four people in the place doesn't mean your show should be lame. These people came here for you and you owe them your best.

Pascal Desjardins: And at the end of the day, we also do it for our own enjoyment.

EDWARD FULLER: I prefer many rather than few people. But, sometimes I've felt that even if there's a negative situation happening, in terms of low attendance, you can turn that around into a positive element that gets you to explore what you've been doing — you give it something extra, in a way you might not if there were a lot of people. Occasionally I worked at the Phoenix Café,[28] cleaning or baking. Sometimes I would do an impromptu show, singing. They had this installation exhibit of coloured plastic pigs that would spin around on sticks (laughs). One night there was this guy (that I knew in passing, as someone who'd seen me perform before) with his family eating there.... There was one other table of people there that night... but I was singing to the family's table, and moving the pigs around as I sang (laughs). And days later the guy said to me that his parents told him they'd never taken hallucinogens before, but they felt like it would probably be like that (laughs). I felt that was a great compliment. That was a successful performance — giving people a sense of an altered state of consciousness, beyond anything they'd experienced before.

ATIF SIDDIQI: It tells me a lot about the piece, whether the audience is attentive or not, if I'm connecting or not. When I had done a reading from *M*[29] for *YAWP!*, I lost the audience halfway through. I found that the material in that reading *was* a bit didactic. That material is no longer in the piece, it's all been edited out.

JULIE CRYSLER: I did a show at the *Union Française* in the summer of 1995. It was some kind of benefit, kind of a rock and roll show. I was into the idea of playing rock and roll shows. It was not so long after *Lollapalooza*, and I remember

Maggie Estep got bottles thrown at her, but I was like, "I'm tougher than her, I'll take them on." So I agreed to take the show, and I show up, and poor old David Jaeger and Todd Swift are standing up reading their poems and people are talking over them because everyone is there to see Grime from Chateauguay! And then I have to follow Grime! So I go up onstage, and the image that I had in my head at that point was this evangelist preacher who I had seen when I was in high school. He had managed to quiet this whole crowd of unruly teenagers who were only really there to eat the free pizza in the end. He was making these broad gestures. So this was the idea that I had in my head: the way I was going to control the crowd was by coming out and speaking really loud at the beginning and having my hands up like a fucking evangelist. And it worked.... They totally shut up through the whole thing. I think that was one of the days when I got a comment like, "I'm not really into poetry, but your stuff's pretty cool." So you're opening people's minds to the possibility that writing can be interesting and good.

There is a debate among spoken word artists about how much or how little they should court an audience's approval. Where does the responsibility lie, in the nature of the performance itself, or in the audience's willingness to listen?

TETSURO SHIGEMATSU: I've played for audiences that are hot or cold and so forth, but I guess my tendency is to put the onus of responsibility on myself. That if they're cold and unresponsive, it's not because they're *inherently* cold and unresponsive, but I just have to change gears. I have to try something else, I have to change tactics and find

Poster for Rising Son, *written and performed by Tetsuro Shigematsu*

[28] A vegetarian co-op restaurant that operated between 1992 and 1996.

[29] *M: Mom, Madonna, The Millennium and Me,* performed at Cabaret Music Hall, September 1998.

101

what they will respond to. So it's true, every audience is different, and I tend to, when I'm onstage, treat and sense the audience as a collective, singular consciousness.... A chemistry is formed between the audience as a singular entity and yourself as a performer. So whenever I come across a challenging situation, I try to assess the audience. It's just like meeting another person for the first time.

Once you learn to perform, and once you're writing, you develop almost a sixth sense about what will work and what will not work. The final test — for me — is always to put it in front of an audience. That's the critic I trust most, a collective audience that doesn't have a lot of people, that is not packed with friends and relatives, and has enough strangers in it. That's the final litmus test because in my mind the audience is always right.

JAKE BROWN: If you're the biggest idiot on earth, and then you say something smart, people are happy to hear it because they don't feel like you're acting like you're on top of them. That's really my schtick, that's the substitute-for-teaching angle. It certainly works as show business, in the sense that the concrete arbiter is that the people are paying money to go see it. Teaching in a university, you'd never know for the rest of your life what the students really thought of you, because you have institutional authority and they'll suck up to you even when they don't know they are. In an audience situation, no way. It instantly changes with the same person. So a student may think, "Ah, this professor, he's great," and yet the same person one night later seeing me perform will go, "Why should I listen to this guy?" That's the challenge that was addicting to me, still is. It fits with one of my main

philosophical principles, which is that credibility should accrue *only* on the content of the message given. On no other criterion; not fame, not wealth, not institutional authority, not pre-held perceptions about what you're seeing and what you're looking at.

"Why not be high?"

When performing onstage, spoken word artists are aware of the energy the performance creates. In the best circumstances, this energy flows from the artist to the audience and back, and can bring about an altered state of consciousness.

VINCE TINGUELY: The first time we did the show with Fluffy Pagan Echoes, it was such a rush. It was like a drug. I worry when I don't get a rush, that maybe I'm getting jaded. You're not getting paid to do these small events, but it's definitely a motivation if you have that little rush.

JOHN GIORNO: By 1968, I started giving out free drugs at *Johnny Guitar* and all the many other readings. Because I knew Owlsley, as well as a lot of the acid dealers. I guess they all made a lot of money, so they gave me the acid free. At Saint Mark's Church, or other places, we'd make these LSD punches with that pure Owlsley sunshine acid. We'd get a lot of grass and give away hundreds of joints. The acid punch would be in a place that if you wanted it, you took it. If you wanted to smoke a joint, you did. The idea was, since I was high, everyone else could be high. At rock concerts people were high, so why should it be this pruny little academic thing where you're supposed to sit with a necktie in a poetry reading? Why not be high?

VICTORIA STANTON: There's a lot of energy put into being present in the performance and being focused on what you're doing. Making sure that you're in your feet, you're on the ground.... It's a weird thing when you're doing a *long* performance. A lot of stuff happens in an hour: there are moments of being terrified, moments of just feeling kind of sleepy, moments of being distracted, moments of being hyperaware of what you're doing, and these moments of pure bliss. And sometimes, depending on what it is I'm doing, moments of being very sad. I've had moments where I'm comfortable with being onstage as a performer, but able to step outside of that performance. I'm taking on this dual role of being me as performer, and then being me as myself watching me as performer. And actually giving that a voice. Some really wonderful things have happened through that, and that's where I find lately I get the rush. When I'm in the middle of a performance, and then I actually comment on what it is I just said or did. That's when people get it, you almost feel this physical ZZZT! connection happen.

COREY FROST: I definitely get a rush from performing, but I think that the rush itself is caused by the fact that my mind works on more levels and on higher levels than it usually does. Because when I'm onstage, first of all I'm thinking about my performance. Or I'm in the persona that I'm performing, so I'm thinking about the words of the performance. But then there's another level at which I'm analyzing that performance, and making small adjustments as I go along. You know, the 'me' inside the persona who is directing the persona.... But then there's another level entirely where I'm not thinking about performance, and my mind is just sort of wandering. So there really are three levels of thought. I don't get that on a daily basis (laughs).

There is an argument that spoken word is an intimate experience, and that the best way to perform spoken word is in close proximity to the audience. Even technology as simple as a microphone can disrupt the immediacy of the art. However, there is also a desire on the part of many artists to reach larger audiences. Here, the ramifications of that desire are discussed.

VINCE TINGUELY: At the beginning, a small audience is best, because you're just learning your craft. The informality really makes it special, because a lot of the people in the audience are other performers, or they're just people out for a good time. It's not heavy. But I think that there's this evolution going on where people become better and better at what they do. At that point a small venue becomes no challenge at all. I

Corey Frost at the Impure *benefit, November 2000*
Photo by Juan Guardado
from www.madgenta.com

ANDRÉ LEMELIN: Du côté anglophone, les performances ont toujours eu tendance à être beaucoup plus rythmées que du côté francophone. Je pourrais même dire que de notre côté, on a longtemps fait abstraction de la forme – de la performance – pour se concentrer davantage sur le contenu. Ce n'est pas que les textes des performeurs anglophones ont moins de contenu, je crois plutôt que ces derniers ont une plus grande conscience de la forme, de la mise en scène et de la représentation. Dans le milieu du conte ce phénomène pourrait être expliqué en partie par notre tradition, par l'image folklorique du conteur qui donne ses histoires devant les gens, sans distance aucune, et qui est très accessible. En tant que conteurs québécois francophones, on est probablement un peu pris avec cette vision qui est profondément ancrée en nous. Et comme pour beaucoup d'autres conteurs, ce fut un idéal pour moi que de ne pas créer une distance, en dépit même du fait que je me retrouvais sur une scène avec des éclairages et un micro. C'est comme si nous essayions de nier le fait que nous n'étions pas au même niveau que les gens qui nous écoutaient... On travaille là-dessus lors des *Dimanches du conte*, qui deviennent alors une espèce d'école laboratoire. Avant on organisait des soupers dans des cuisines et, en mangeant, on racontait des histoires. Ces soupers étaient à la fois ludiques et expérimentaux, parfois improvisés. Et cette expérience, cet idéal de la non-représentation, de la non-distanciation, dans une cuisine, ça fonctionnait. Mais dans un autre contexte, pas toujours. Quant à moi, j'en suis sorti avec l'idée que lorsque je suis sur une scène, je suis systématiquement en représentation.

VICTORIA STANTON: Penses-tu que ça vient de l'influence du milieu anglophone du spoken word?

ANDRÉ LEMELIN: Je l'ignore. Mais je crois certainement qu'il y a une question de formation qui entre en ligne de compte. Je me demande à quel point les performeurs anglophones

30 Hakim Bey. *T.A.Z.: The Temporary Autonomous Zone, Ontological Anarchy, Poetic Terrorism*. New York: Autonomedia, 1985; Hakim Bey. *T.A.Z.* CD. Laswell, Bill, producer. Island / Axiom Records, 1994.

think that in that sense, spoken word can get to a higher level of drawing a larger audience. It's possible.

VICTORIA STANTON: There's an essay by Hakim Bey.[30] The larger the space — even if you're performing live — the more mediated it appears to be. If you're in this huge space, which means that most of the audience is looking at you from a very large distance, then you're not really connected to the audience in the same way. But I think, although I prefer working in smaller spaces, one of my goals is to be able to be comfortable in any kind of space. I don't think that it's a bad thing for spoken word artists to become household names, and for spoken word performers to perform in really large spaces.

ANDRÉ LEMELIN: On the anglophone side, performances have always tended to have much more of a beat than on the francophone side. I could even say that on our side, we've tended for a long time to disregard form — performance — to concentrate more on content. I'm not saying anglophone performers' texts lack content, but I do think they're more conscious of form, of staging and representation. In the storytelling scene, this phenomenon could be explained partly by our tradition, by the folk image of the storyteller narrating his stories in front of people, with no distance, very accessible. As French-speaking *Québécois* storytellers, we're probably a bit stuck with this image, which is deeply rooted in us. And like for many other storytellers, it was an ideal for me not to create a distance, despite the fact that I ended up on a stage with a microphone. It's as though we tried to deny the fact that we weren't at the same

level as the audience.... We work on this during *Les Dimanches du conte*, which in this way becomes a kind of laboratory-school. Before, we used to organize suppers in people's kitchens and tell stories while eating. Those suppers were both playful and experimental — and sometimes improvised. This experience, this ideal of non-representation, non-distancing, can work in somebody's kitchen, but not always in another context. I came away with the idea that when I'm onstage, I'm systematically in representation.

VICTORIA STANTON: Do you think this comes from the influence of anglophone spoken word?

ANDRÉ LEMELIN: I wouldn't know, but I think training certainly comes into it. I wonder to what extent anglophone performers have taken detours via theatre, or other more visual kinds of representation. This didn't used to be the case for francophones but now, a lot of poets and storytellers I see in representation have made this theatre detour, or at least stage work, directing, rehearsing... and their example is obviously going to inspire others. I go to *Les Dimanches du conte* often and I see that storytellers are more and more aware of being in representation. Maybe not in performance, but aware that they're onstage, that there's an audience in front of them.

DEBBIE YOUNG: I studied theatre in Jamaica, my mom sent me to theatre school before I went to high school. You know theatre spaces — bare, props, you, your body — that's it. You had to use your voice. You had to project. You talk to the person at the back of the hall.... People notice that I don't perform with a microphone. It's not because of any style of mine, it's because I'm scared of the damn thing! It's loud and it gives feedback and you can't hear yourself realistically. So bigger venues force me to use microphones, and it feels like it affects my performance.

LEAH VINEBERG: I did 'Chronicles of Miss Dietka Blue' as part of this live broadcast at Isart, called *Solo*.[31] But it was going to be a live performance as well, and I went in a full costume, for a very small audience... and the radio. Suddenly any gestural work was lost to the radio. And also, I couldn't move. I had to put it all in my voice for the sake of the radio. But this was a very interesting exercise. I think the distinction between spoken word and performance art is the microphone. There's something about having to put everything into the microphone.

vii. Collaboration: "It's really team work"

Traditional writing practices are by and large a solitary art, with particular 'authors' identified with particular texts. While many spoken word artists follow a similar route, by its nature the practice allows for greater collaboration between artists as well. In this section, we look at some of the collaborative strategies between members of spoken word groups, and between spoken word artists and musicians or sound artists.

The Vehicule Poets and Endre Farkas

In Montreal's first great era of spoken word experimentation, The Vehicule Poets worked together on collaborative performance poetry. Ken Norris explains how he and his fellow poets approached this idea.

KEN NORRIS: My performance work really was kind of a thing apart, and it was mostly me participating in somebody else's work, or writing something collaboratively for the occasion. With the collaborative performance work I was always like Tonto or Sancho Panza, along for the ride. So it would be Tom Konyves, Opal L. Nations, or Endre Farkas who would be setting up the enterprise, and I would be chiming in when my turn came. I was a member of the band, kind of like George Harrison having to field a Lennon-McCartney song. OK, the song is written, or maybe it needs a few lines here, but why don't we use a sitar on this one? I tended to contribute to atmosphere when I wasn't contributing text. But I always felt like an integral member of the performance band.

On the *Sounds Like* LP[32], I'm the third voice on Farkas' 'Er / Words / Ah'. I liked doing it, and actually contributed quite a lot to the performance of the

ont emprunté des détours par le théâtre, par d'autres formes de représentation plus visuelles. Chez les francophones, avant, ce n'était que peu le cas, mais maintenant, beaucoup de poètes et de conteurs que je vois se donner en représentation ont fait ce détour par le théâtre ou du moins le travail scénique, la mise en scène, les répétitions... Et c'est évidemment leur exemple qui va en inspirer d'autres. Je vais souvent aux *Dimanches du conte* et je m'aperçois que les conteurs prennent davantage conscience qu'ils sont en représentation. Peut-être pas en performance, mais ils sont conscients qu'ils sont sur scène, qu'il y a un public devant eux qui écoute leur histoire.

[31] November 1998.

[32] Various artists. *Sounds Like — sound poetry by eight Montreal poets* LP, Farkas, Endre & Norris, Ken, producers, Véhicule Press, 1980.

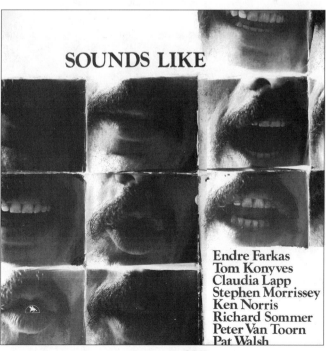

poem, really stretching it in a kind of Four Horsemen direction. But I didn't write a word of that poem. My participation was in interpretation, in performance. When Konyves and I wrote 'See / saw', that was really more of a fifty-fifty thing, both of us writing text. And I wanted to dress up in an admiral's costume, because I'd been the admiral in a fifth grade production of *HMS Pinafore*. In that case I brought both text and costumes to the production. When we did 'Drummer Boy Raga', there were, I believe, six or seven of us generating a rather surrealistic text.

Artie Gold[33] was always giving me shit for participating in these performances. He thought that I should know better. He wouldn't have anything to do with this stuff. I was mostly an 'on the page' poet in my own work, but I liked having these outside projects, or winding up in the middle of someone else's work. The degree to which the Vehicules were a communal enterprise has really tended to be overlooked.

An Evening with the Muses' Company: *Geneviève Raymond and Endre Farkas*
Photo courtesy of the artist

33 One of the Vehicle Poets.

While Endre Farkas began his collaborative career with the Vehicle Poets, he soon branched off into more rigorous work with dancers, actors and musicians.

ENDRE FARKAS: With the Vehicle Poets, there was rehearsal, sometimes. But rehearsals often fell apart as they tend to do. I started to get more structured when I was working with a smaller group of two, three people. Where I was writing most of the pieces, and they were dancers, actors who came in. Their contribution was to respond, whether it works in their medium or not. I would love going into dancers' studios — because they had nice big spaces — and watch them go through warm-ups and then discussions, and as we're doing it we're making the piece. I would come in with a text and then by the end of the afternoon the text would be in shreds and it would be somewhere else. I learned in the process how to write for a different medium.

For dancers, I wrote it knowing that the sound itself was going to go through changes as they got tired, as they got bent, shaped. Other times, it was theatrical, as I was moving more towards the stage, which is what I'm interested in now. It's dialogue in chorus, so I would have the actors, sometimes two of them, say the same text, the third one counterpointing, and it would come back and forth. So, still, it's not straight theatre, it's performance-influenced theatre, but it does have a story-line. It's almost like a libretto. The composition almost dictates itself, to suggest the kind of flow, the kind of language, the kind of interaction. That's part of the creative process. And when it's done, you feel good and relieved, hopefully, but the process is still what it's all about.

Fluffy Pagan Echoes

Fluffy Pagan Echoes came together without a conscious intention to perform collaboratively, but at their first performance they composed an 'exquisite corpse' text to open the show. Their interest in performing as a group evolved throughout their first year of existence, and culminated in an hour-long show at the 1995 Fringe Festival. In addition, the group served as an ongoing writing and performance workshop, and a social club.

*Fluffy Pagan Echoes
October 1994
(from left) Scott Duncan, Justin
McGrail, Victoria Stanton, Ran
Elfassy, Vince Tinguely*
Photo by Scott Duncan

VINCE TINGUELY: I was definitely not a performer when FPE started in 1994. In fact I couldn't even perform socially with people any more. Scott Duncan wrote really good poetry. I didn't understand it, but I couldn't understand anyone's poetry at that point. I remember looking at Ran Elfassy's and at Justin McGrail's poetry, and I couldn't read it. I couldn't absorb what it meant. It took six or eight months of being in the group before I started to pick up on what they were actually saying, which was just my own particular state of mind at the time. So I felt really challenged by the situation. Every month there were new pieces.

VICTORIA STANTON: This was an excuse to write more regularly, because one of our goals — at first unspoken, and then it became decided — was to never perform the same piece twice. Every month, whether they were good or not, we'd have new pieces, so that there'd always be something new for the audience. Because we did three or four rounds in each show, we each produced three or four new poems a month.

VINCE TINGUELY: Justin memorized impossibly long pieces, and he did it consistently. Ran was the closest, I would say, to the idea of a *Lollapalooza* performer. Very influenced by popular culture and by rock music, very brash. Very punk, in the sense of being deliberately abrasive, and deliberately trying to alienate the audience. And the audience just ate him up, he was certainly one of the most popular performers in the group because of that. Scott was a storyteller in a way, a sort of *raconteur*, and he would test the limits of people's patience with his particular stories. Which I thought was kind of interesting. And Victoria would say, "I'm not a poet, I'm a performance artist." So I felt I had to catch up with this somehow. Learn how to perform, basically. It was almost like a workshop, in the sense that you had these different kinds of performers.

JUSTIN MCGRAIL: We learned about each other through our poetry, and in a way that lent a larger degree of trust, because we were trusting each other based on our art. I think that is what radiated to the audience. Almost anything we ever did was accepted, and it

107

wasn't because we were brilliant, it was just because we were quite obviously human and weren't really on the stage. There wasn't that whole barrier / audience thing.

VICTORIA STANTON: The group really served many purposes, not just for our own creative work, but for our social skills. And boosting my confidence as a social person. There's strength in numbers, and I could feel secure in that group.... We started to influence each other's styles and subjects. Again, this happened very organically. We thought group pieces could work really well with the structure of the performance evening. That started out with one person writing a group piece, one piece in five voices. At that point it became easier and easier to write for each other, because we got used to what each other wrote about and how each other sounded and performed.

SCOTT DUNCAN: To create FPE pieces I often worked from a concept and an idea of a space. Because there were five of us, it was always important to consider the space we performed in. The concept was most often a reaction to something we'd experienced in the scene in Montreal. The group taught me that art could be fun and in fact has to be fun to create in order for an audience to enjoy it. The group set me free to think about things in a wider context than some sort of beatnik / traveller paradigm, which had been central to my artistic output from high school right up to the time we started.

VINCE TINGUELY: What I found from being in FPE was that nobody had the same style, and nobody wanted each other's style, but there was something about being with other people doing

stuff onstage where you would realize that you can up the ante on these things a lot. I think that in our particular group we learned a lot from each other that way. That's why we kept reaching new levels, in a sense. The first piece in my memory, where it really clicked for us as a group, was when we did the group piece which Justin had written, at the Concordia Visual Arts gallery. He choreographed this piece. He was talking about the architecture of the space, because it was L-shaped. How the group could move around and also how the group could *command* the audience to do things such as, "You stand over there, and you stand over there." The whole piece was about authority, and [that] because you're a performer you can tell the audience to do anything, and they'll do it.

JUSTIN MCGRAIL: As time went on we were more familiar with each other. By the time *Resistance Is Reasonable* was done, and by the time we did our last show — 'Layers Of Caked-On Grime' was the last poem I wrote for all of us — which wasn't really hard because I knew what everyone's voices were. So we could write for each other in a fairly precise way.

Groupe de poésie moderne

This poetry ensemble has a more disciplined, theatrical structure than either The Vehicle Poets or Fluffy Pagan Echoes. Robert G. Reid directs the group, and of its two writers, Benoît Paiement and Bernard Dion, only Paiement performs with them. The other members have changed over time, and are generally actors who collaborate with the writers and director to create the phenomenon of the Groupe de poésie moderne.

BENOÎT PAIEMENT: La structure qu'on a présentement – quatre comédiens sur scène avec un metteur en scène – c'est temporaire, mais je crois que cette façon de fonctionner est la plus efficace, en ce qui concerne les textes. Avec ce que j'ai écrit, une fille et trois gars, ça me semble être l'équipe idéale.

BENOÎT PAIEMENT: Our current structure — four actors onstage plus a director — is temporary, but I believe this way of operating is the most efficient one, as far as the texts go. With what I've written, one girl and three guys seems the ideal team.

COREY FROST: There was such a great difference between Fluffy Pagan Echoes and the *Groupe de poésie moderne*, even though they were doing similar things. Composing poetry out of bits of sound. Yet the way that they did it was so theatrical, so rigidly choreographed. That was really valuable, because they could do things that you couldn't do otherwise, unless it was very carefully rehearsed, with that exact timing of the performance. But what FPE was doing, I saw it as much more English culture (laughs). I hate to say this, but it was more American in a sense. More independent, more anti-traditional, irreverent. It definitely broke the barrier between the performers and the audience, because when FPE performed it was beautifully sloppy, in a sense. There was a real casual connection to the audience that's not there with the *Groupe de poésie moderne*.

BENOÎT PAIEMENT: Our entire repertoire fits into two notebooks. Hundreds of pages of text, generally very short, the longer ones are up to a page and a half or two pages. We have these texts, we choose a few of them, sew them together and then rehearse. We know most of them well, so we can perform them easily.... We've been doing them for eight years, so they can be done in a conventional way, in a traditional way, so to speak. Or we can interpret them completely differently, depending on the context we place them in, which texts come before or after. Their meanings can change depending on the order they're assigned. And as they're rather short, we can integrate a lot of them into a one-hour show, maybe about twenty, which allows multiple possibilities. And this is where Robert Reid comes in. It's his job to take these texts and organize them, with a general idea in mind, or with a clear idea of certain parts of the show. And as the texts are sewn up together, parts of the show take shape, *tableaux* which are then sewn to other parts. But the important thing that unites all of it is form. The style we've developed, our way of saying sentences very rhythmically.

BENOÎT PAIEMENT: On a un répertoire qui tient dans deux cahiers. Des centaines de pages de textes qui sont en général très courts, les plus longs pouvant aller jusqu'à une page et demie ou deux pages. Ces textes sont à notre disposition, on en choisit quelques-uns, on les coud les uns aux autres, et à partir de là, on les répète. Pour la plupart, ce sont des textes qu'on connaît bien, qu'on peut interpréter facilement... Comme ça fait quand même huit ans qu'on les joue, ces textes peuvent être interprétés d'une certaine façon convenue, d'une façon traditionnelle, en quelque sorte. Ou on peut aussi les interpréter d'une tout autre manière, en fonction du contexte dans lequel on les place, c'est-à-dire en fonction des textes qui les précèdent ou qui les suivent. Ainsi, selon l'ordre dans lequel ils s'enchaînent, nos textes peuvent revêtir des significations différentes. Et puisqu'ils sont plutôt courts, dans un spectacle d'une heure on peut en intégrer beaucoup, soit environ une vingtaine, ce qui donne lieu à une multitude de possibilités. Et c'est là, essentiellement, qu'intervient Robert Reid. C'est à lui qu'il incombe de prendre ces textes et de les organiser, en ayant en tête une idée générale, ou une idée de certaines parties du spectacle. Et à mesure que les textes sont cousus les uns aux autres, il se crée des parties de spectacle, des tableaux qui sont à nouveau cousus ensemble. Mais à la base, il y a une chose très importante qui unifie le tout, et c'est la forme. Le genre qu'on a développé, cette espèce de façon de dire les phrases d'une manière très rythmée.

Groupe de poésie moderne *at the* Impure *benefit*, November 2000 *(from left) Félixe Ross, Francis Neron, Christophe Rapin, Benoît Paiement* Photo by Juan Guardado

FÉLIXE ROSS: In fact I believe the essence of our work is in the rhythm. Not only the rhythm each actor imparts to the text, but also the rhythm that comes from each actor getting on the other's wavelength, which creates the ensemble rhythm.

BENOÎT PAIEMENT: It's really team work, four actors playing like hockey players. Each one tries to score goals. But if each one plays inside his or her little world, if we forget to make passes, what happens? We get beat 7-0. So there has to be cohesion.

FÉLIXE ROSS: Understanding the other person's rhythm and making room for each one is crucial. Without necessarily being able to see each other, we have to feel each other's rhythm to be able to pick up on it or bring one in yourself. When I 'play' I sense my three partners, I know where they are, I know one of them is about to move to a certain place, etc. It's almost esoteric.

David Neudorfer
of the Rhythmic Missionaries

Rhythmic Missionaries

Rhythmic Missionaries differ from the previous three groups discussed because the members are both poets and musicians. Like The Vehicule Poets and Fluffy Pagan Echoes, the group serves not only as a performance vehicle, but as a poetry workshop for the members.

JASON SELMAN: There was no growth, no direction to the poetry at all until the Rhythmic Missionaries came together as a group. I would've just been writing in isolation, and I don't think I would've gotten anywhere. I wouldn't have realized the sense of tradition, or performance and what that carries with it. When I'm doing something with the Rhythmic Missionaries, it's different than if I was doing something in another band. Then I might get more nervous, because I have to know certain things. With us, we're pretty free, because it's very improvisational. There are no charts, we never write anything down. Just loops and stuff, and little melodies here and there, and that's about it. "What key are we in?" Those kinds of things. I enjoy it the most when we're all together — to me it's the ultimate. Every poet has their own spotlight on them and gets their moment when we do a set. If we're doing a musical piece and I'm reading, then I'm running the show. If David Neudorfer is doing a piece he's running the show. He's the conductor, we're following him.

Les Abdigradationnistes

Les Abdigradationnistes *started out with the two Pascals: Pascal Fioramore generating the texts, and Pascal Desjardins providing musical accompaniment on a keyboard. A totally performative enterprise, the duo deploys costumes, props, satirical ditties and a running barrage of pseudo-poetic commentary to skewer all that is kitsch and* kétaine *in Québécois culture. The duo became a quartet in 1998.*

PASCAL FIORAMORE: *Les Abdigradationnistes* are made up of us two [the 'Pascals', Fioramore and Desjardins] with a scratcher and a violinist. They've been part of the group for at least two years, but when we first started, we were doing shows in little bars, they weren't with us. Nowadays we always play together. Their presence has really improved our shows. Not just on the musical level but also onstage.

PASCAL DESJARDINS: Now that there are four of us onstage, we have to reorganize what goes on because the dynamic is different. Since they've been with us, we're becoming aware of a whole lot of things about staging.

PASCAL FIORAMORE: We want to do more of it. We're thinking about using sets more, and costumes, doing choreographies.... In fact we want to transmit a spirit of unity. Even while continuing to say and do what we want — whether it's very vulgar, or ridiculous or even if it all sounds very chaotic — if in some way what we're offering is coherent, spectators will be more receptive.

Les Abdigradationnistes: Simon Paquet, Pascal Fioramore, Pascal Desjardins, Warner Alexandre Roche
Photo by Galilé Marion-Gauvin

Collaboration with musicians

The marriage of words and music brings spoken word into the terrain of the songwriting craft — in fact, with musical accompaniment, spoken word can share the stage with singers and bands — but there are important differences between the two. Ian Ferrier has said that he seeks an equilibrium between the words and the music, so that one doesn't overwhelm the complexities and resonances of the other. This is the challenge facing all spoken word artists working with musicians.

IAN FERRIER: The sound's really part of how to imagine these things. The timing of it, and how things are said, enunciation and the sound.... The really nice thing for me is I was interested in both, music and writing, ever since I was ten or eleven or twelve. I ended up doing much more writing than I did music, just because I thought I was better at it. But I never lost the interest. It's nice to be able to think that way, and to be able to work with really good musicians, and

PASCAL FIORAMORE: Les Abdigradationnistes se composent de nous deux [Pascal Fioramore et Pascal Desjardins], puis d'un scratcher et un violoniste. Ça fait deux ans qu'ils font partie du groupe, mais au début, quand on donnait des spectacles dans des petits bars, ils n'y participaient pas. Aujourd'hui, on joue toujours ensemble. La présence de ces nouveaux membres est vraiment venue enrichir nos spectacles. Et pas seulement sur le plan musical, mais également sur le plan scénique.

PASCAL DESJARDINS: Maintenant qu'on est quatre personnes sur scène, on doit réorganiser ce qui s'y passe, car la dynamique est différente. Depuis qu'ils sont avec nous, on prend conscience de beaucoup d'éléments par rapport à la mise en scène.

PASCAL FIORAMORE: On veut l'exploiter davantage. Graduellement, on pense accorder plus d'importance aux décors, aux costumes, monter des chorégraphies... En fait, on désire transmettre un esprit d'unité. Même

continued...

D. Kimm and guitarist Alexandre St-Onge at La Vache enragée, *January 1998*
Photo by André Lemelin

en continuant à dire et à faire ce qu'on veut, que ça soit très vulgaire, que ça soit ridicule ou que l'ensemble sonne chaotique, si à quelque part ce qu'on propose se tient, nos spectateurs vont être plus réceptifs.

D. KIMM: Je travaille toujours avec des musiciens. Je ne peux pas monter un spectacle littéraire sans qu'il y ait de musiciens, car ce sont eux qui me permettent d'avoir vraiment une trame pour le spectacle, d'avoir un concept.... J'intègre parfois des danseurs, des chanteurs et des comédiens. Mais j'aime beaucoup entendre les écrivains lire eux-mêmes leurs textes. Il y a là une musique particulière, une intensité touchante. C'est très different d'un comédien qui peut s'appuyer sur sa belle voix ou sur des techniques théâtrales.

34 Kidd, Catherine. *everything I know about love I learned from taxidermy* cassette / book. Montreal: conundrum press, 1996.

be able to have an exchange where we say, "Oh yeah, this works, that doesn't work. What are we gonna do next?" Have that be an understandable conversation.

D. KIMM: I always work with musicians. I just can't organize a literary event without musicians, because they're the ones who allow me to have a framework for the show, a concept.... I sometimes integrate dancers, singers and actors. But I love listening to writers reading their texts. There's a specific music there, an intensity that's touching. It's very different from an actor, who can rely on his or her nice voice or stage technique.

DAVID GOSSAGE: In a collaboration, you just decide as you're doing it. Some texts lend themselves better to having more music, or having music as a counterbalance to it. You take a poem about a specific thing, and you make a music that is completely contrary to it, just to make some kind of statement about the poem and about the music. When you listen to the whole thing, there's something that's gnawing about it that you want to listen to again.... With poetry, the music's a lot tighter in on the poem. With theatre, it's generally a lot more blanket-type things underneath it.

CATHERINE KIDD: I read the piece to Jack Beets, do it simultaneously with memorizing the piece, or absorbing it, as I say. Then we brainstorm on the emotional information that it has. On the page it has a story line. With Jack, with sounds, they're prelinguistic information. So we try to find where it's spindly and sparks, where it's very swollen and we need to find something that sounds like plate tectonics or like lava. Do we need something oceanic sounding? How does it

make you feel here? Because Jack and I know each other very well, drawing metaphors for the kind of sounds that we need comes very easily. It's very kinesthetic, because our media merge. We can talk about the pitch of a colour or the shape of a paragraph. After we've come up with that, and Jack has made the initial notes on the written text, he keeps it around and looks at it all week.... Then we do our archeology of sounds. "We need something that sounds like an incubator for eggs." Sometimes they're movie soundtrack bits, and sometimes they're found sounds. For 'Global Warming', we needed (makes a wave sound), oceanic. We didn't want to take it from one of those environmental records, because there would be seagulls in there or something. We took a very old recording of the bath sounds in 'Core Assembly' on *taxidermy*.34 We took little bits of that recording, and noticed that the sound of water is melodic. You just take one little phrase of it and slow it down, "Da-da-da, diddle-dum." So, loop those and find tunes. Or plate tectonics, we'll take two cobblestones and grind them together and slow that down, so it doesn't sound like two small stones, but two continental stones (laughs). The movie soundtracks are usually jokes or irony, something in the text suggests something ironically, so we need Hitchcock in there, or we need Cecil B. DeMille or a spaghetti western.

And then we both have to make generous open edits and concessions to the other medium. Sometimes whole sections of sound will start one place, and then be moved somewhere else in the text. The speed of the delivery has to be absolutely in synch with the sounds, and so if you're talking way too fast there, either take out some of that text because it's not going to work, or vice versa. It's a give-and-take until it integrates as seamlessly as possible.

PASCAL DESJARDINS: Usually, Pascal arrives with a text, and we take it from there.

PASCAL FIORAMORE: Sometimes Pascal has me listen to music he's found, I look through my texts (flips through his sheets) and spontaneously answer: "Great, tomorrow we're gonna turn this into a song for the show. Good night!" …. I stock up on songs while over there Pascal is creating a bank of music, and at a certain point we try to mesh our creations. But sometimes he suggests tunes for which I don't have a text yet. Then I keep the melody in mind and try to write texts in relation to the music, something that would correspond to the ambiance.

DAVID GOSSAGE: Clifford Duffy was initially wanting to do a lot of improvised things. The collaboration of music and text would be purely an improvisational thing, because he wanted to do the free conscious poetry thing, we'd make stuff up. We started doing a bit of that, but that didn't work out so well (laughs)…. It's funny, because later on at *Round Midnight*, with rappers, that was all improvisational. But that's the nature of rap. From a musician's point of view you can't improvise with a structured poem because you just walk all over it

ENDRE FARKAS: I was working with this contemporary musician where he basically — this was before computers were simple — he wanted to hook me up, he wanted my body as a sound-source. He wanted to program into the computer a chance element, so that at any time, of eight, nine sound sources, only two, three click in at random. We did a couple of months of research, going to various institutes around the city for how to pick up sound from the body. I got to the point where, half-naked, I had electrodes attached to my head, I had a nose microphone, I had a throat microphone, and I had these microphones inside half-cut tennis balls. It looked like I had leech things…. So this was his composition called 'Close Up', and my text for that was more about how I feel about this kind of intrusion… but you never knew what part of it was going to come out. There were times that my text was drowned out because it clicked in the heartbeat sound — "Badum, badum!" because I was nervous. Or when I clenched my fist onstage, this muscle contraction sounded like ocean waves. Each performance of the text was different. Then, when we were on tour, the bright technician ended up sending the disc through these X-ray machines, so that screwed it up. There we were, opening night in Edmonton, and this thing wasn't working! It ended up with the technician coming onstage with me and manipulating the sound. So you got a two-person performance. He wasn't a smoker — he liked his dope — so he ended up baking hash cookies and grass cookies. He would eat a couple before a performance and you never knew what was going to happen!

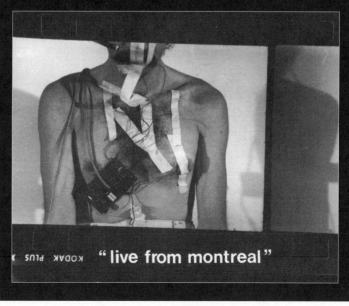

"live from montreal"

Pascal Desjardins: D'habitude, Pascal arrive avec un texte, puis on travaille à partir de ça.

Pascal Fioramore: Mais il arrive aussi que Pascal me fasse écouter une musique qu'il a trouvée, que je regarde dans mes textes puis que je lui réponde spontanément: "Parfait, demain on va en faire une chanson au spectacle. Bonne nuit!"… J'emmagasine des textes tandis que Pascal se monte une banque de musiques qu'il travaille un peu de son côté, et à un certain moment on essaie de juxtaposer nos créations. Mais parfois il me propose des airs pour lesquels je n'ai pas de textes. À ce moment-là, je garde les mélodies en mémoire, puis je tente d'écrire des textes par rapport à la musique, quelque chose qui concorderait avec l'ambiance.

Hélène Monette: Avec chaque personne, il y a toujours une manière différente et implicite de travailler. Avec Bob Olivier, même si je n'ai aucune connaissance musicale, je pouvais faire des suggestions à ce niveau. Et parfois, c'était le contraire. Bob pouvait me dire: "Ne change pas ton texte, garde ton rythme, reste dans la musique de ton texte." Et à ce moment-là, lui, il rentrait dans mon territoire pour venir y ajouter des ambiances sonores. Mais lorsque je travaillais avec Max (Marcel Décoste), c'était complètement différent. Le plus souvent, soit il arrivait avec de la musique déjà toute composée et je mettais un texte dessus, soit on travaillait en même temps, en cherchant en même temps. Quant à Sylvie (Chenard), je la laisse aller. Mais c'est toujours un échange, une écoute mutuelle. Par exemple, si je me sens mal avec une musique, je le lui dis, on en discute et on essaie de trouver une autre perspective.

(laughs). You don't know what they're going to say!

Hélène Monette: There's a different and implicit way of working with each person. With Bob Olivier, even though I have no musical knowledge, I could make suggestions at that level. And sometimes it was the opposite. Bob would say: "Don't change your text, keep the rhythm, stay with the music of your text." At that moment, he'd be coming onto my territory to add sound ambiances. It was completely different when I worked with Max (Marcel Décoste). Most often he'd either arrive with music already composed and I'd put a text on it, or we'd work at the same time, searching together. As for Sylvie (Chenard), I let her go. But it's always an exchange, reciprocal listening. For example, if I feel uneasy with a piece of music, I tell her, we talk, and we try to find another approach.

viii. Slam style: "The competition is for the audience"

While the slam poetry form of spoken word must be recognized for bringing the performative aspects of memorization, accessibility and popularization to the forefront, there is also a fear expressed by some performers that slam poetry is too competitive. The argument is that by placing poetry in a competitive framework, it creates a 'lowest common denominator' mentality that degrades the work. The debate highlights the underlying uncertainty about spoken word performance's credentials as an art form, and the common criticism that it is merely entertainment.

Todd Swift: Scott Duncan once said on camera to the CBC, the first night that *Vox Hunt* did a slam, that it introduced competition into the field of poetry. I reminded him that the initial poet laureates were from Greece, and they got their laurel leaves from poetic competitions, and in fact it was a shame that poetry and rhetoric and acting was dropped from the Olympics… because it used to be a spiritual and philosophical competition as well. Philosophers would debate. I see nothing wrong with competition in the arts. That's how we get our grants, after all, a lot of really positive things come from that.

Buffy Childerhose: I think having a slam bar come into a city can be a positive thing. I really liked the slams at first, and then I started seeing more and more work that I found was really cheap. You knew there were a lot of people who figured out how easy it was to play a slam, and how to win a slam. It just made me think of bad open mic nights when I was working at the student bar at Concordia. It's a shame, because you see somebody like Patricia Smith perform — and certainly not that the poetry has to be heavy and serious, but — it was nice to see her do these short pieces that were still really potent and viable. They didn't go for the cheap, quick response. I found that slam ended up being a lot about the cheap response, the cheap line, the laughter.

John Giorno: Sometimes I think that slam poetry's origins are the worst of what I did back in the sixties and seventies. Absolute aggression wins the prize (laughs). I was, in those years, the most aggressive poet. Somehow the combination of alcohol and my own energy, I was more aggressive than anyone. And everyone appreciated that. You know, I was pouring sweat in Saint Mark's Church, and in Paris, France, and people then would say, "Oh, isn't he great?" Because I was the most... most! And I think to myself, well, that's not necessarily the best (laughs). Poetry is not about aggression, the best poet isn't necessarily the most aggressive poet. And then in New York in those poetry slams, through winning a draw, it becomes just spontaneously writing poetry. Where you get a category and inside that, poetry on the spot (snaps fingers), you have to write and you're judged bad or good.... I'm not necessarily that kind of poet. On the spot, I'm not so clever about inventing things, in terms of repartee, which is what that's about.

ALEXIS O'HARA: The thing is that there are good poets who consistently lose slams, and the drag is that there is this flash that gets people. That people will always go for poetry that's memorized, poetry by poets who are comfortable in their bodies. That's the rule, but there are many exceptions to the rule. When we did the slam where there were a lot of francophones, the woman who took second place was a forty year old secretary who was totally shaking. But her work was so gorgeous that people just couldn't not like it. I think that there is a structure, but that structure does not connote content at all.

The competition aspect of it is stressful, but it's only three minutes out of the day, and then you can spend another two hours doing something else. That's what I think a lot of people don't realize. Even at the slam, somebody comes and slams, and if they win a slam, then the next time they come to the show they can take fifteen minutes as a feature performer. And sure there's

a whole reward system there, it's all very subjective — maybe something that won't win this month is something that in a year from now will be all the rage.

JULIE CRYSLER: For a slam to work, everybody involved has to realize the competition is a joke. It's a ploy, and it's pretend. When you forget that, I think the attitude really changes. I remember being down and slamming in New York. I was sitting with Taylor Mali and Eileen Reyes, and he says, "Oh, you're slamming against Paul Bibeau, he's really good." And Eileen said, "She's not

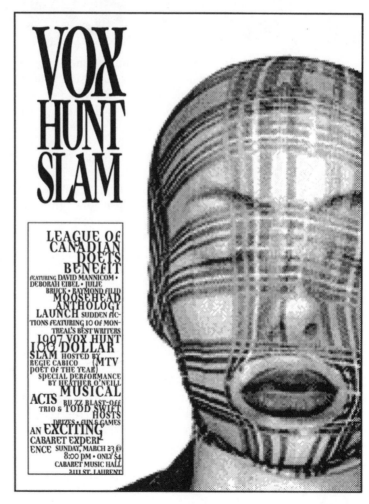

Alexis O'Hara
Photo courtesy of the artist

slamming *against* him, she's slamming *with* him." The competition is for the audience, and to create a framework for the show. It's not a real thing where people get focused on the idea of, "I want to *win* a slam," as opposed to, "I want to reach an audience."

HEATHER O'NEILL: I didn't find slamming that much different from other readings. Some people say, "Oh, getting the mark, how can you stand that?" But every time you perform you're getting evaluated by the audience.

ALEXIS O'HARA: Whether or not you're going to be getting a score at the end of your poem, or whether there's gonna be three other girls that are gonna perform that night, and one of them is gonna do better than you in your mind, we're always competing. Whether or not we like to admit it or not, there's a competitive aspect in everything we do. I try to work against that. That's what's kind of

ironic about me running the slam — it's a competitive thing, but I'm always encouraging people, I'm always trying to figure out ways to help things get better. It's very hard, I just feel completely schizophrenic when I start talking about it because I can see both sides, and I understand. I've been to the Nationals[35] and I've seen how ugly it can get. That day in Connecticut when I did that thing that didn't go very well, the whole Syracuse team was sitting in the front row like this (arms crossed), stonewalling me. That kind of shit exists. But it's just a microcosm of the world, really. A lot of people would say, "That's why I want to avoid it, because its a microcosm of all the evil, competitive stuff." But there's so much camaraderie.

I'm interested in the convention aspect of it. There is no performers' convention. You can go to *South By Southwest* if you're a musician, or you can go to different music festivals, but there are no spoken word festivals, really. In Europe there are, but not in North America. The slam is the only one. And there are a lot of people that go to the National Poetry Slam that aren't even competing. They just go there, they have their books to sell, they're going to perform two or three times and meet people and hang out.... There are a myriad of day events and late night events, where you can perform for seven minutes, where you can wear a costume, where you can build a set if you want. That's what I try to emphasize with other people too, what a great opportunity it is.

35 The National Poetry Slam takes place annually in a selected city in the United States.

AN ORAL HISTORY OF MONTREAL SPOKEN WORD

Part 1. THE QUIET GENERATION

VII

"It *is* possible to say poems"

A performative form of poetry began to appear in Montreal in the sixties. Its roots can be found in the Québécois folk tradition of storytelling, and the experimental work of poets like Claude Gauvreau and Paul-Marie Lapointe. The incendiary and galvanizing effect of Paul-Émile Borduas' Refus Global manifesto on Québécois artists in the fifties, led to the blossoming of the heady and politically-charged atmosphere of the Quiet Revolution in the sixties and seventies. Experimental and theatrical forms of poetry were practiced by such major Québécois artists as Gaston Miron, Raoul Duguay, Jean-Paul Daoust and Michel Garneau. We asked Michel Garneau to tell us about his memories of performative poetry in Montreal in the sixties.

MICHEL GARNEAU: At the end of the forties, in Quebec, there was very well-written poetry, like Alain Grandbois and Saint-Denys-Garneau. Then around 1963, during the first FLQ [*Front de Libération du Québec*] wave, Gaston Miron appeared on the scene; he used to grab people on street corners and *say* his poems to them. All of a sudden, Quebec poetry connected with the oral tradition, it tapped into its sources again. At the time there was a bar called *Le Perchoir d'Haïti*. It had been opened by a Haitian Montrealer as a place to play music and sing songs in Creole, in French. Like *Québécois* people,

Haitians have a strong oral tradition because they were illiterate for a long time, which necessarily helps the spoken word. The owner of *Le Perchoir* was a very joyful, very generous man, and he realized he could fill his place up by organizing poetry evenings. So a lot of sixties' poets, Gilbert Langevin, Pierrot Léger, Gaston Miron and many others, discovered this place where they could go and say their poems. Another good place was *La Poubelle* [The Garbage Can] (laughs). Officially, it was a *boîte à chansons* [coffee house / folk club] but there was also jazz and more or less improvised poetry evenings. And *La Poubelle* never closed, so we went there often. But I was still only a spectator then....

"Ah! Poetry — nobody's interested!"

For Garneau, radio was an obvious medium for the transmission of the spoken word. A radio host for over forty years, he has always struggled to bring literature to life through readings and performances on air, despite the obstacles thrown in his way by those less enlightened.

MICHEL GARNEAU: I started doing radio at fifteen, in Trois-Rivières. I went to see the station manager and said: "I'd like to do a special kind of evening show, with music and texts." He said the same thing many station managers said for years: "Go ahead if you want to, but you won't get paid more (laughs)."

THIS HISTORICAL OVERVIEW OF SPOKEN WORD PERFORMANCE IN MONTREAL IS NEITHER COMPLETE NOR DEFINITIVE. RATHER, IT PROVIDES A BACKGROUND TO OUR DISCUSSION, BASED SOLELY ON WHAT WE WERE TOLD BY THE ARTISTS WE INTERVIEWED. THE HISTORY OF QUÉBÉCOIS PERFORMANCE POETS IN THE SIXTIES AND SEVENTIES IS PART OF MAINSTREAM CULTURAL DISCOURSE IN THE PROVINCE, BUT WE HAVE TOUCHED ON IT FOR THE BENEFIT OF READERS OUTSIDE OF QUEBEC WHO MIGHT BE UNFAMILIAR WITH IT.

Part 1. GÉNÉRATION TRANQUILLE

"C'est possible de dire des poèmes"

MICHEL GARNEAU: À la fin des années 40, au Québec, il y avait de la poésie qui était très bien écrite, comme celle d'Alain Grandbois ou de Saint-Denys-Garneau. Puis vers 1963, durant la première vague du FLQ [Front de Libération du Québec], Gaston Miron est arrivé sur la place publique; il accrochait des gens au coin de la rue et leur *disait* ses poèmes. Et soudainement, toute la poésie québécoise s'est rattachée à la tradition orale, elle y a retrouvé ses sources. À cette même époque, il y avait un bar qui s'appelait Le Perchoir

continued...

d'Haïti. Cet endroit avait été ouvert par des Haïtiens montréalais pour y faire de la musique et chanter des chansons créoles, en français. Comme les Québécois, les Haïtiens ont également une importante tradition orale, car ils ont longtemps été analphabètes ce qui, forcément, aide la parole. Donc, le patron du Perchoir d'Haïti, un monsieur très joyeux, très généreux, a découvert qu'il pouvait remplir sa salle en organisant des soirées de poésie. Alors beaucoup des poètes québécois des années 60, Gilbert Langevin, Pierrot Léger, Gaston Miron et plusieurs autres, ont découvert cet endroit où il était possible de dire leurs poèmes. Un autre endroit qui était intéressant s'appelait La Poubelle (rires). C'était officiellement une boîte à chansons, mais il y avait aussi du jazz et des soirées de poésie plus ou moins improvisées. Et comme La Poubelle ne fermait jamais, on s'y retrouvait souvent. Mais de mon côté, à cette époque-là, j'en étais encore au stade du spectateur.

"Ah! La poésie, il n'y a personne qui s'intéresse à ça!"

MICHEL GARNEAU: J'ai commencé à faire de la radio à 15 ans, à Trois-Rivières. Je suis allé voir le gérant de la station et je lui ai dit: "J'aimerais faire une émission un peu spéciale, le soir, avec de la musique et des textes." Il m'a alors répondu ce que d'autres gérants m'ont répondu pendant plusieurs années: "Si tu veux, mais tu ne seras pas payé plus (rires)." À cette époque, la radio privée était beaucoup moins obsédée par le commerce qu'elle ne l'est aujourd'hui. À Trois-Rivières, si tu voulais faire une émission le soir et que tu ne demandais pas d'argent pour la faire, on te donnait ta chance. J'ai donc travaillé à Trois-Rivières, et ensuite à Rimouski où, pendant des années, j'ai fait des émissions de poésie. J'ai alors longtemps bénéficié de cette avenue pour dire mes propres textes quand j'en avais, et aussi pour donner des textes d'autres poètes. Et c'est quelque chose que j'ai commencé à faire très jeune. Dès l'âge de 15 ans, jusqu'à l'âge d'à peu près 25 ans, la radio était mon gagne-pain. J'ai travaillé à Radio-Canada à partir de 1960 et, par la suite, je me suis toujours arrangé pour avoir une

Michel Garneau in his CBC office, 1999

At the time, private radio was much less obsessed with business than now. In Trois-Rivières, if you wanted to do an evening show and didn't ask for any money to do it, they'd give you the opportunity. So I worked in Trois-Rivières, then in Rimouski where I did poetry shows for years. I took advantage of that avenue to read my own texts, and other poets' texts too. Very young, starting at fifteen until I was about twenty-five, radio was my bread and butter. I started working for Radio-Canada in 1960 and then always managed to have a show. I'd understood one thing: I never said I was going to do a poetry show. I'd find euphemisms, I'd propose a title, I'd always say: "There's going to be music and texts." Because when I used the word 'poetry', people would react: "Ah! Poetry — nobody's interested in poetry!" You can still hear people say the same thing today.... In 1961 or 1962, on Radio-Canada, on Saturday night, I hosted a show called *Blues et insomnie*. The title had nothing to do with poetry but the show was mainly jazz and poetry. So I was very interested in what was going on in Montreal, but only as a spectator.

"Lay claim to the showbiz aspect and get pleasure out of it"

Perhaps the most important aspect of performative poetry in Montreal in the sixties was a series of large public readings organized to raise funds to defend Pierre Vallières and Charles Gagnon, founding members of the FLQ. These events, called Poèmes et chansons de la résistance, *served not only as a focus for rising nationalist sentiments, but also helped launch the careers of a whole generation of* Québécois *poets. They eventually led to the first "Nuit de la Poésie" in 1970, which was immortalized in Jean-Claude Labrecque's documentary film of the same name.*

MICHEL GARNEAU: In 1966, there was an event which, in terms of the place of poetry in society and of poetic forms, was a landmark: the first *Poèmes et chansons de la résistance*. That year a committee, of which I was a part, was formed to find ways of raising money to pay lawyers for Pierre Vallières and Charles Gagnon, who were accused of being the leaders of the first wave of the FLQ and whose trial was dragging on. These two men were very committed, they had political ideas, they wanted to fight for Quebec independence, but they had not placed bombs or done anything to warrant such a trial. Members of the Vallières-Gagnon committee wanted to do two things for them: find money to get them good lawyers, and politicize their trial, because it was biased and gave the impression they were dangerous criminals who belonged behind bars. So we started asking sympathizers for five or ten dollars apiece. One day, Jacques Larue-Langlois, Robert Myre and others thought of organizing a benefit show. I was asked to be part of a show called

Poèmes et chansons de la résistance and immediately said yes. It was held at *La Comédie canadienne*, now called the *TNM [Théâtre du Nouveau Monde]*. Paul Chamberland was there, and Pauline Julien too I think, and Gilbert Langevin. We were a little worried, as I recall, wondering if anybody was going to turn up... because the advertisements mentioned a few singing stars were taking part, and the rest was poets. Also, some participants were thinking they might end up preaching to the converted. But contrary to all our expectations, there was a capacity crowd. And curiously, the content wasn't very political, because the show had been put together so quickly. In the end, one of the only political poems was one of mine, only because I'd happened to write one just a few days earlier. But everybody in the show was aware that it was a political gesture, that all the profits were going to the Vallières-Gagnon committee. I think some people came to see the stars, heard some poems and were very surprised. On the other hand, I remember Chamberland, who had just come back from studying in Europe, and who was completely taken aback to see the audience standing up shouting, screaming during his poem. The reactions on that evening are easier to understand now, with historical perspective. Because it was part of something that was slowly rising, this whole identification phenomenon, of saying: "No, we're no longer francophones, we're *Québécois*. We don't know how far we're going but we want to go there, we want independence, we want social justice." There were people saying this onstage during the show, and others in the audience wanted the same thing, so there was this mutual recognition. It was fabulous. It ended up being this great *fête de la parole* [feast for the spoken word].

After Montreal, the show was presented in Trois-Rivières, Hull, Québec City and Sherbrooke, I believe. We redid it again the next year because trials such as that one were held for many years. So the *Poèmes et chansons de la résistance* shows continued until the seventies.

Jean-Claude Labrecque's movie on Quebec poetry was inspired by these song and poetry shows. In 1970, he had the brilliant idea of organizing the first *Nuit de la poésie,* figuring he'd film what went on. He spoke to various people, including Gaston Miron and a guy who worked with Gaston in publishing who had also organized demonstrations at the *Bibliothèque nationale*, on Saint-Sulpice Street where, in the sixties, there were a lot of demonstrations, concerts and poetry events. For the staging, Michelle Rossignol and I got together, chose some poets, and thought we'd present a big poetry fest from 8:00 PM to midnight. But Quebec was just chock-full of poets, so we invited others to come too, and then we'd see how late things went on. Jean-Claude Labrecque agreed with this plan. So the first part of the show was more formal, we'd organized the stage a bit, but the second part was total madness. Poets would come and tell us they wanted to go on, we'd put them on in order of arrival, with no pre-selection at all. Which led to some absolutely stunning moments. I remember one poet all dressed in red — his name was Pierre Bertrand — who gave an anti-marijuana speech — while right in front of him there was this thick blue cloud (laughs). Obviously, he got booed! I never saw anything like it again, ever. A big tall guy who said his poem in a big voice got ousted by the audience. His topic was so unpopular and ridiculous, it was insane! What a divine moment. Unfortunately, it didn't get into the movie, because Labrecque had had to

émission. J'avais compris un truc: je ne disais jamais que j'allais faire une émission de poésie. Je trouvais des euphémismes, je proposais un titre, et je disais toujours: "Il y a avoir de la musique et des textes." Car lorsque j'employais le terme "poésie", je voyais que le monde réagissait: "Ah! La poésie, il n'y a personne qui s'intéresse à ça!" Comme on entend encore souvent aujourd'hui... En 1961 ou 1962, à Radio-Canada, le samedi soir, j'animais une émission qui s'appelait *Blues et Insomnie*. Le titre n'évoquait pas la poésie, mais l'émission était essentiellement composée de jazz et de poèmes. J'étais alors très intéressé par ce qui se passait à Montréal, mais toujours en tant que spectateur.

"Réclamer la part spectaculaire et en retirer du plaisir"

MICHEL GARNEAU: En 1966, il y a eu un événement qui, dans le domaine de la place de la poésie dans la société et des formes poétiques, a été marquant: le premier spectacle *Poèmes et chansons de la résistance*. Cette année-là, un comité dont je faisais partie avait été formé pour trouver des moyens de payer les avocats de Pierre Vallières et de Charles Gagnon, qui avaient été accusés d'être les leaders de la première vague du FLQ et dont le procès s'éternisait. Ces deux hommes étaient des gens engagés, qui avaient des idées politiques, qui voulaient lutter pour l'indépendance du Québec, mais qui n'avaient pas posé de bombes ou fait quoi que ce soit pour se mériter un tel procès. Et les membres du comité Vallières-Gagnon désiraient faire deux choses pour eux: trouver du financement pour qu'ils aient de bons avocats, et politiser leur procès, car ce dernier était biaisé et donnait l'impression qu'ils étaient de dangereux criminels et qu'il fallait les mettre en prison. Alors, dans un premier temps, les membres de notre comité ont demandé à des sympathisants de donner cinq ou dix dollars. Puis, un jour, Jacques Larue-Langlois, Robert Myre et quelques autres ont pensé à monter un spectacle bénéfice. Alors, quand on m'a demandé si je voulais participer à un spectacle qui s'appellerait *Poèmes et chansons de la résistance*, j'ai accepté tout de suite. Le spectacle s'est tenu à La Comédie Canadienne, qui s'appelle maintenant le TNM [Théâtre du Nouveau Monde]. Paul Chamberland était là, et je pense

continued...

stop shooting by then, he had no film left. Despite the fact that he'd stuffed the truck with film. He'd taken everything the NFB [National Film Board] gave him, and stolen some as well. Three cameras were filming. They started shooting at 7:00 PM, before the show, for

From the Poèmes et chansons de la résistance *album*

atmosphere, so by 4:00 AM.... Jean-Claude said: "We don't have any left and we're not going to call and ask the Board for some at this hour, they're gonna kill me (laughs)!" There were some funny moments, like that poet's performance, but there were also extraordinary moments of connection with the audience, of discovery and dialogue. Some of these are in the movie. Sometimes now I meet young people and this is all they know about poetry because their teacher showed them the movie. But two other films were made on the *Nuits de la poésie*, in 1980 and in 1990. If they've been shown thousands of times, it's thanks to the fact that the first *Nuit de la poésie* had such an impact. In 1970 at the *Gesù*, not only were the 1600 seats taken, but the hall was full of people and about a thousand people outside wanted in! To avoid a possible riot, Jean-Claude thought fast and reacted immediately. Big monitors were set up in the hall, with loudspeakers, and more monitors put on each side of the stairs, outside. Some people stayed outside watching the monitors, even though it was fall and rather cold. Quite astonishing. The room was 'dangerous' because a lot of people were smoking pot. I kept thinking that if a fire broke out, it would be a catastrophe. Even the aisles were full of people sitting down. While shooting, Jean-Claude, who was the only one of the three cameramen with a mobile camera, wanted to move around at some point but he couldn't budge. There was just *no* way to get around. He wanted to change place and I don't know how it happened but the crowd carried him from one side of the room to the other. I saw Jean-Claude Labrecque go across the room riding the crowd, with his camera! The atmosphere was very beautiful. This event created quite a phenomenon, people all over the place started holding poetry nights, lots of them. I organized quite a few myself.

PATRICIA LAMONTAGNE: In the early seventies, Claude Péloquin, an ultra-extrovert, organized happenings. And when you watch the movie of the first *Nuit de la poésie*, you can see that other poets, such as Claude Gauvreau, felt the urge to do performance through poetry, but it was at the embryonic stage. For example, in the movie you see Paul Chamberland dressed in very bizarre fashion, but this didn't change his relationship to orality. There's Denis Vanier too, he was eighteen then, reciting a very rant-like kind of poetry, very powerful, like: "Fuck the cops." But even then, it was still very close to the page.... There were women like Michèle Lalonde, for example, with her poem 'Speak White', which in fact was a political manifesto. So there was an eagerness to *perform* vocally. But the poets had their sheets of paper in their hands and as I see it, were still really clinging to their text.

MICHEL GARNEAU: In *Poèmes et chansons de la résistance*, we presented a text by Michèle Lalonde titled 'Panneau réclame' [Billboard]. It's a piece for three voices which is in the 1970 film of *La Nuit de la poésie*. Because it was spoken by Michèle Lalonde, Michelle Rossignol and Michel Garneau, it started like this: "My name is Michèle. My name is Michelle. My name is Michel. Our name is Michel(le). Yes." This was the most formally theatrical text in our shows. It was a very grave poem, but rendered with a lot of humour; we incorporated our own sound effects, like factory sirens, at a time when poetry was still considered something very serious. When I started, in the sixties, humour was bad form. Poetry was seri-

ous stuff — or else it was romantic, or metaphysical, or political. It could be all of that but it could *not be* funny. This was one of my first problems as a poet, because philosophically speaking I've always thought that, if there's no humour in how we see the world, it makes no sense. Humour allows for fluidity and relativity in human relationships. For me humour is something infinitely important but at the same time, it's a hard one to argue. And with the 'three Michel(le)s' text, people looked at us kind of confused. Today it can seem trivial but historically, after the October Crisis, this text had enormous impact and enormous influence. That text made it possible to lay claim to the showbiz aspect and enjoy it, and simultaneously make people laugh while being politically coherent and consistent. People suddenly realized it was possible to be onstage and *embody* the poems, because when we said the text, even though we used lecterns, we knew it by heart. And before that, for another show of *Poèmes et chansons de la résistance*, the three of us together had worked on a text by Michèle Lalonde titled 'Outrage au tribunal' [Contempt of Court] which was also recorded... but without me because I had hepatitis which I caught in prison (laughs)!

I ended up in jail in 1970. I was there for thirteen days which, technically, is not a lot. But for someone like myself who is well aware of always having respected every form of legality, whose crime was participating in *Poèmes et chansons de la résistance* and being a militant for Quebec independence, landing in prison was quite serious. Like 544 other people, I was arrested at about 5:00 AM, awakened by a machine gun poking me in the stomach, with a soldier on the other end

continued...

1970, il a eu l'idée brillante d'organiser la première *Nuit de la poésie*, en se disant qu'il allait filmer ce qui allait s'y passer. Il s'est donc adressé à différentes personnes, entre autres à Gaston Miron et à un gars qui travaillait avec ce dernier dans l'édition, puis qui avait aussi organisé des manifestations à la Bibliothèque nationale, sur la rue Saint-Sulpice où, dans les années 60, il y a eu beaucoup de manifestations, de concerts et de soirées de poésie. Et pour la partie mise en scène, Michelle Rossignol et moi on s'est réunis, on a choisi des poètes, puis on pensait présenter un gros spectacle de poésie de 20 h à minuit. Mais on se disait également qu'étant donné que le Québec regorgeait de poètes, on allait en inviter d'autres à venir après, puis on allait voir jusqu'à quelle heure ça durerait. Et Jean-Claude Labrecque était d'accord avec ça. La première partie du spectacle a été un peu formalisée, c'est-à-dire qu'on avait organisé un peu la scène, mais ensuite, ç'a été le délire total. Des poètes sont venus nous dire qu'ils voulaient monter sur scène, et on les avait mis dans l'ordre où ils étaient arrivés, sans faire de sélection. Ce qui a donné lieu à des moments absolument étonnants. Je me souviens d'un poète tout habillé en rouge – il s'appelait Pierre Bertrand – qui est venu faire un discours contre la marijuana. Et puis devant lui, il y avait un gros nuage bleu (rires). Évidemment, il s'est fait huer! Je n'ai jamais revu ça dans ma vie. Un grand gars fort, qui dit son texte avec une grosse voix, mais qui se fait sortir par le public. Son propos était tellement impopulaire et ridicule, ça n'avait pas de bon sens! C'était un moment absolument divin. Malheureusement, ça ne s'est pas retrouvé dans le film, parce qu'à cet instant, Jean-Claude Labrecque avait dû arrêter de tourner, faute de pellicule. Pourtant, il avait bourré le camion de pellicule. Il avait pris toute celle que l'ONF lui avait donnée, et il en avait même volé un peu. Trois caméras tournaient. Ils avaient commencé à tourner à 19 h, avant le spectacle, pour l'ambiance, alors rendu à quatre heures du matin... Jean-Claude a dit: "On n'en a plus, et on ne va pas aller en demander à l'Office à cette heure-là, ils vont me tuer (rires)!" Il y a eu quelques moments comme la performance de ce poète qui étaient drôles, mais aussi des moments extraordinaires de rapport avec le public, de découverte ou de dialogue. Il y a de ces grands moments qui sont dans le film et qu'on peut revoir. Moi,

yelling at me to get up. The situation was so absurd that I started laughing, I thought it was a joke. But the guy with the gun wasn't laughing... he was very threatening and serious. I had a lot of trouble understanding what was happening to me and especially, tolerating it. You end up in prison without knowing why, and getting out of your cell or calling a lawyer is out of the question. You're in jail, period. You have absolutely nothing to do, you can't even see the other prisoners. So from one cell to the next, people would identify themselves: "Doctor Serge Mongeau, Family Planning Clinic," "Charles Prévost, biologist, professor at the Université de Montréal" (laughs). We spent five days talking to each other like that, recognizing each other by our voices. In addition to this there was the acoustics, the echo in a prison, very special. In the morning we'd be woken up by two different radio stations, one at each end of the hallway; CKVL at one end, CKAC at the other. When the news came on, the guards would shut the radios *off*! Silence. Then they'd come on again. So we'd hear the two stations at the same time, very loud. But throughout all of this, an analysis was evolving. At some point two guys, two fervent chess players, started playing together — from one cell to the other, no board, no nothing, just in their minds and their voices. Except that because they were politically committed, they were renaming everything. For example, the bishop [in French, *fou*, fool or idiot] was Bourassa (laughs), and so on across the chessboard. We'd listen to them play, and laugh. The more it went on, the more people could visualize the board so some people started making suggestions, commenting on the game (laughs). It was completely insane. We'd tell each other stories and more

seriously, discuss the situation. There was a historian among us and at some point he said: "Judging from what is happening, I think the government must have proclaimed the War Measures Act. It's a law created for a situation such as this, and it allows the suspension of civil liberties because there's a fear of insurrection." We couldn't believe it, we were rebelling because we thought we were living in a democracy! He replied: "The only explanation for the fact that we're in here, that we're not getting any explanations, and that we have no lawyers and no visitors... the only legal possibility is that law." One morning the guards turned the radios off too late and a sentence slipped out: "Pierre Laporte's body." [Quebec Transport Minister in Bourassa Liberal government]. And then the discussion started up incredibly intensely, so they decided to let us out of our cells, to let us go down into one of the rooms where there were tables with chessboards painted on them (laughs). So we all met there and the discussion went on: "What does that mean, 'Pierre Laporte's body'? Why did he die? Who killed him? Is it the FLQ? If so, what do we think of this?" There were about ten of us who said: "If the FLQ killed him, it's because the FLQ exists as a coherent, violent revolutionary group who goes all the way. It's regrettable, but we support their action." Others replied: "No. We refuse violence, you're not allowed to do that, it's a crime." And physically, we separated. The ten supporters at one end of the table, the other thirty at the other end. The guards let us keep talking for a while, then put us back in our cells. And there I started writing, I'd managed to get some paper and a pencil. 'AGM24' was both the title of my poem and my ID number: left wing

[*Aile Gauche*], Mezzanine, cell 24. I worked on it for two or three days. A text about that situation, a text that was both political and lyrical. Days went on and still we knew *nothing*! When you have no information, your mind starts playing tricks on you.... We could see part of the Parthenais Street parking lot from the mezzanine. At one point we saw a crowd of people and immediately thought it might be a demonstration. When somebody asked if the crowd had gotten bigger, somebody answered: "No, it's soldiers doing manoeuvres and passers-by are watching." That, I think, was the most depressing moment of the whole affair.

We were royally bored. In the afternoon, after lunch, there was usually a sort of naptime when everybody was really quiet. So I'd decided to read my poem then and at some point I said: "Gentlemen, I'd like to read you something." And I read my poem: "Four rows of bars get in my face every day..." [trad: SLH] With the prison echo, it resonated very loudly (laughs). When I finished there was a long silence. Inside I sort of fell apart, I thought everybody was embarrassed for me, that I'd just made

a fool of myself and should never have read my poem. These were the thoughts going through my mind when a voice said: "Read it again." I felt relieved so I read it again. There was another big silence, then another voice said: "Thank you." And I started to cry. Because as a poet, what you seek is to become the voice of your fellow humans. Taliesin, the bard, said it: "My voice is cast in silver, for it is the voice of my people." [trad: SLH] And in prison, this takes on a huge importance.

A while later I witnessed something extraordinary: seven, eight people sitting at the tables writing my poem very small, on cigarette paper, rolling it, carefully inserting it into Lifesavers packets and distributing them to all the prisoners. The first guy who'd be let out had the mission of taking it to people who would publish it. In the end, two of my poems got out of prison this way, while I was still inside. 'AGM24' was published in *Point de mire*, and 'Petit matin' [Little morning] appeared in *Quartier latin*.

That was a landmark event for me because it reinforced my desire to speak on behalf of others. I wanted to take

je rencontre des jeunes qui ne connaissent que ça de la poésie, parce que leurs enseignants leur ont montré le film. Mais deux autres films sur les *Nuits de la poésie* ont été tournés en 1980, puis en 1990. Et si ces films ont été projetés des milliers de fois, c'est parce que la première *Nuit de la poésie* a connu tout un impact. Lors du spectacle donné en 1970, au Gesù, non seulement les quelque 1 600 sièges étaient-ils occupés, mais le hall était plein de monde, puis dehors, il y avait à peu près 1 000 personnes qui voulaient rentrer! Et pour éviter une éventuelle émeute, Jean-Claude a pensé vite et a tout de suite réagi. Des gros moniteurs ont été installés dans le hall, avec des haut-parleurs, puis d'autres moniteurs chaque bord des escaliers, dehors. Il y a des gens qui sont restés dehors à regarder les moniteurs, même si c'était l'automne et que la nuit était plutôt fraîche. C'était assez étonnant. Et la salle était "dangereuse" parce qu'il y avait beaucoup de monde qui fumait du pot. Moi, je me disais que si le feu prenait, ça allait être une catastrophe. Même les allées étaient pleines de monde assis. Et durant le tournage, Jean-Claude, qui était le seul des trois cameramen à disposer d'une caméra mobile, à un certain moment il a voulu se promener mais ne pouvait même pas. Il n'y avait *aucune* possibilité de circuler. À un certain moment il a voulu changer de place et je ne sais pas comment c'est arrivé, mais la foule l'a transporté d'un côté à l'autre de la salle. J'ai vu Jean-Claude Labrecque traverser la salle sur la foule, avec sa caméra! L'atmosphère était vraiment très belle. Cet événement-là a donc créé tout un phénomène. Par la suite, des gens d'un peu partout se sont mis à faire des nuits de la poésie, et il y en a eu beaucoup. Moi, à cette époque, j'en ai organisé plusieurs.

Names of people jailed in October 1970

PATRICIA LAMONTAGNE: Au début des années 70, Claude Péloquin, qui était très extraverti, a fait des genres de happenings. Aussi, en regardant le film sur la première *Nuit de la poésie*, on peut constater qu'il y avait d'autres poètes, comme Claude Gauvreau, qui avaient déjà une certaine volonté de faire de la performance à travers la poésie. Mais c'était vraiment embryonnaire. Par exemple, dans ce film, on voit Paul Chamberland habillé d'une façon bizarroïde, mais ça ne changeait pas son rapport à l'oralité. On peut aussi y voir Denis Vanier, alors âgé de 18 ans, réciter une poésie très déclamatoire, très puissante, du style: "*Fuck the cops*." Mais encore là, c'était très près de la feuille... Il y avait aussi des femmes comme Michèle Lalonde, par exemple, avec son poème *Speak White*, qui était en fait un manifeste politique. En somme, à cette époque, il existait une volonté de *performer* vocalement. Mais les poètes avaient leurs feuilles dans les mains et, à mon avis, ils demeuraient réellement accrochés à leur texte.

MICHEL GARNEAU: Dans *Poèmes et chansons de la résistance*, on avait présenté un texte de Michèle Lalonde qui s'appelait "Panneau réclame". C'était un texte à trois voix, qui se retrouve d'ailleurs dans le film *La Nuit de la poésie 1970*. Étant donné qu'il était récité par Michèle Lalonde, Michelle Rossignol et moi-même, il commençait comme suit: "Je m'appelle Michèle. Je m'appelle Michelle. Je m'appelle Michel. On s'appelle Michel(le). Oui." Et dans les spectacles qu'on donnait, ce texte était la chose la plus formellement théâtrale. C'était un poème très grave, mais rendu avec beaucoup d'humour; on y intégrait notre propre bruitage, des sirènes d'usine, par exemple, et ce, à une époque où la poésie était encore perçue comme quelque chose de sérieux. Moi, quand j'ai commencé, dans les années 60, l'humour était très mal vu. La poésie, c'était sérieux. Ou bien c'était amoureux ou métaphysique, ou politique. Ça pouvait être tout ça, mais ça ne *pouvait pas* être drôle. Et ç'a été un de mes premiers problèmes en tant que poète, car j'ai toujours pensé philosophiquement que si, dans notre vision du monde, il n'y a pas d'humour, ça n'a pas de sens. C'est l'humour qui permet la souplesse et la relativité des rapports humains. Pour moi, l'humour est quelque chose d'infiniment important, mais en même temps, ça se défend mal. Et avec le texte des trois Michel(le)s, le monde nous regardait d'un air perplexe. Maintenant ça peut paraître anodin, mais historiquement, à ce moment, après la crise d'Octobre, ce texte a eu énormément d'impact et énormément d'influence. Ce texte permettait de réclamer la part spectaculaire et d'en retirer du plaisir, en même temps que de faire rire tout en étant politiquement cohérent et conséquent. Et tout à coup, les gens ont réalisé qu'il était possible d'être sur scène et d'*incarner* les poèmes, car lorsqu'on disait le texte, même si on utilisait des lutrins, on le savait par cœur. Puis avant, pour un autre spectacle de *Poèmes et chansons de la résistance*, encore les trois ensemble, on avait travaillé un texte de Michèle Lalonde qui s'appelait "Outrage au tribunal" et qui a aussi été enregistré... mais sans moi, car j'étais atteint d'une hépatite que j'avais attrapée en prison (rires)!

En 1970, je me suis retrouvé en prison. J'y suis resté 13 jours, ce qui, techniquement, n'est pas beaucoup. Mais pour quelqu'un qui est parfaitement conscient d'avoir toujours respecté tout forme de légalité, dont le crime avait été de participer à ôter *Poèmes et chansons de la résistance* et d'avoir milité pour l'indépendance du Québec, de me retrouver en prison, j'ai trouvé ça assez grave. Comme 544 autres personnes, j'ai été arrêté vers 5 h du matin, en me faisant réveiller par une mitraillette qui me poussait dans le ventre, avec un militaire au bout qui me criait de me lever. La situation était tellement absurde que je me suis mis à rire, je croyais que c'était une farce. Mais l'autre avec sa mitraillette n'entendait pas à rire... il était très menaçant et très sérieux finalement. J'ai eu beaucoup de difficulté à comprendre ce qui m'arrivait, puis surtout à l'admettre. On se retrouve en prison sans savoir pourquoi, et il n'est pas question de sortir de cellule, ni d'appeler un avocat. On est en prison, point. Et on n'a absolument rien à faire, on ne peut même pas voir les autres détenus. Alors d'une cellule à l'autre, les gens s'identifiaient: "Dr Serge Mongeau, Clinique de planification familiale," "Charles Prévost, biologiste, professeur à l'Université de Montréal" (rires). Pendant cinq jours, on s'est parlé comme ça, on se reconnaissant par nos voix. Rajoute à ça l'acoustique, l'écho d'une prison, c'était très spécial. Et le matin, on se faisait réveiller par deux postes de radio différents, un à chaque bout du couloir; d'un côté c'était CKVL, de l'autre, CKAC. Et quand les nouvelles arrivaient, ça *coupait*! C'était le silence. Ensuite, ça repartait. On entendait les deux stations simultanément, et le volume était très fort. Mais à travers ça, tout un discours s'organisait. À un moment donné, deux gars, deux grands joueurs d'échecs, ont commencé à jouer ensemble – d'une cellule à l'autre, *no board, no nothing, just in their minds and their voices*. Sauf qu'étant donné qu'ils étaient politiquement engagés, ils renommaient tout. Par exemple, le fou, c'était Bourassa (rires), et ainsi de suite pour tout l'échiquier. Pendant qu'ils jouaient, on écoutait puis on riait (rires). Et plus ça allait, plus certains pouvaient visualiser l'échiquier, alors il y a des gens qui ont commencé à faire des suggestions, à émettre des commentaires sur la partie (rires). C'était complètement dément. On se racontait aussi des histoires et, plus sérieusement, on parlait de la situation. Parmi nous, il y avait un historien, et à un certain moment il nous a dit: "D'après ce qui se passe, je crois que le gouvernement a dû proclamer la Loi des mesures de guerres. C'est une loi qui a été créée dans telle circonstance, et qui permet la suspension des libertés civiles parce qu'il y a insurrection appréhendée." Et on n'en revenait pas, on s'insurgeait parce qu'on pen-

Michèle Lalonde

SPEAK WHITE

Les murs ont la parole
L'HEXAGONE

sait vivre dans une démocratie! Il nous a répondu: "La seule explication du fait qu'on est ici et qu'on ne nous donne pas d'explication... puis qu'on n'a pas de possibilité d'avocat ni de visites... la seule possibilité légale, c'est cette loi-là." Et un matin, les gardiens ont arrêté les radios trop tard, et ils ont laissé passer une phrase: "Le cadavre de Pierre Laporte." À cet instant, ça s'est mis à discuter incroyablement, et ils ont décidé de nous laisser sortir de cellule, de nous permettre de descendre dans une salle où il y avait des tables, et au bout desquelles des jeux d'échecs étaient peints (rires). On s'y est tous rencontrés, et la discussion s'est poursuivie: "Qu'est-ce que ça veut dire, "le cadavre de Pierre Laporte"? Pourquoi est-il mort? Qui l'a tué? Est-ce que c'est le FLQ? Si oui, qu'est-ce qu'on en pense?" Là, on était environ 10 qui ont dit: "Si c'est le FLQ qui a tué Pierre Laporte, c'est que le FLQ existe en tant que groupement révolutionnaire violent, cohérent, et qui va jusqu'au bout des choses. C'est regrettable, mais on endosse leur geste." Les autres ont répliqué: "Non. Nous, on refuse la violence, on n'a pas le droit de faire ça, c'est un crime." Et physiquement, on s'est séparés. Les 10 qui endossaient à un bout de la table, puis les 30 autres qui n'endossaient pas à l'autre extrémité. Les gardiens nous ont laissé discuter un certain temps, puis ils nous ont retournés dans nos cellules. Et là, je me suis mis à écrire, car j'avais réussi à obtenir du papier et un crayon. "AGM24", c'était le titre de mon poème et mon numéro matricule: aile gauche, mezzanine, cellule 24. J'ai travaillé sur mon poème pendant deux, trois jours. Un texte sur cette situation, un texte politique et lyrique. Les journées passaient, et on ne savait toujours *rien*! Et quand on n'a pas de nouvelles, notre imagination peut nous jouer des tours... Depuis la mezzanine, on pouvait apercevoir un bout du stationnement donnant sur la rue Parthenais. Et à un certain moment, on a vu un attroupement de monde. Tout de suite on a cru que ça pouvait être une manifestation. Et quand quelqu'un a demandé si l'attroupement avait grossi, un autre a répondu: "Non, ce sont des militaires qui font des manœuvres et il y a des passants qui regardent." Ce fut, je pense, le plus grand moment de dépression de toute cette affaire.

Donc on s'ennuyait royalement. Et durant l'après-midi, après le dîner, généralement, il y avait une espèce de sieste où tout le monde se tenait bien tranquille. Alors moi, j'avais décidé que j'allais lire mon poème aux gens. À un moment donné, j'ai dit : "Messieurs, j'aurais quelque chose à vous lire." Et j'ai lu mon poème: "Quatre rangées de barreaux chaque jour me rentrent en pleine face..." Avec l'écho de la prison, ça résonnait fort (rires). Quand j'ai eu fini, il y a eu un long silence. Je me suis alors intérieurement écroulé, je me suis dit que tout le monde était gêné pour moi, que je venais de me couvrir de ridicule et que je n'aurais jamais dû lire mon poème. J'en étais à ces réflexions quand une voix a dit: "Lis-le encore." Ça m'a soulagé, alors je l'ai relu. Ensuite, il y a eu un autre grand silence, puis une autre voix a dit: "Merci." Et là, je me suis mis à pleurer. Car ce qu'on cherche comme poète, c'est à se faire la voix de nos semblables. Le barde Taliesin l'a dit: "Ma voix est d'airain, car c'est celle de mon peuple." Alors dans une prison, ça revêt une importance toute spéciale.

Un peu plus tard, j'ai été témoin de quelque chose d'extraordinaire. J'ai vu sept, huit personnes assises aux tables en train d'écrire mon poème en tout petit, sur du papier à cigarettes, le rouler, l'insérer méticuleusement dans des rouleaux de Life-Savers, puis distribuer ces rouleaux à chacun des détenus. La première personne qui était libérée avait la mission d'aller porter le poème à des gens qui le publieraient. Finalement, deux de mes poèmes sont ainsi sortis de prison, tandis que moi j'y étais encore. "AGM24" fut publié dans la revue *Point de mire* et "Petit matin" parut dans *Quartier latin*.

Cet événement a donc été extrêmement déterminant pour moi, car il a renforcé mon désir de parler au nom d'autrui. J'avais envie d'agir, et d'autres ont ressenti ce sentiment chez moi. Quelqu'un du groupe est venu me dire: "Quand on va sortir d'ici, moi, je rejoins ma bande puis on va former une cellule du FLQ. Veux-tu embarquer avec nous?" Je lui ai alors demandé ce qu'ils avaient l'intention de faire, ce à quoi il m'a répondu: "La révolution." Et lorsque je lui ai demandé s'ils iraient jusqu'à tuer du monde, il m'a dit que s'il le fallait, ils n'hésiteraient pas à le faire. Ils avaient déjà commencé à s'organiser. Son groupe disposait d'une ferme à la campagne, ils avaient cambriolé plusieurs banques pour se procurer des armes et comptaient récidiver jusqu'à temps qu'ils se considèrent bien armés. Mais il ne savaient pas encore ce qu'ils feraient après. Alors je lui ai demandé si je pouvais réfléchir un peu (rires)... Je savais que je ne pouvais pas lui répondre par un simple "non"... Le lendemain, je lui ai dit: "Honnêtement, je ne peux pas faire ça, car je n'y crois pas. J'essaie de concevoir que la violence a eu un rôle historique dans l'histoire du monde, mais j'en suis incapable. Peux-tu me nommer la mort de quelqu'un qui a servi à quelque chose? Puis à part de ça, essentiellement, je suis écrivain." Tout de suite après, il y a eu un moment merveilleux. Mon interlocuteur m'a regardé, puis a dit: "T'es écrivain, ben t'es mieux d'écrire, mon maudit (rires)!"... Quand je suis sorti de prison, j'ai essayé d'écrire le plus possible, en me rappelant que mon travail devait essentiellement servir à ce à quoi il avait servi l'après-midi où j'ai dit mon poème à mes compagnons de prison, à qui j'avais donné une voix et qui, en le transportant dans leurs rouleaux de Life-Savers, avaient décidé que ça faisait partie de leur parole à eux aussi. Je pense que c'est ça, en tant qu'écrivain, qu'il faut essayer de faire. Et le message n'a pas toujours besoin d'être politique, il peut se situer dans le social, ou dans le plaisir, et avoir la même portée.

125

action and others felt this in me. Somebody from the group came to see me and said: "When we get out of here, I'm joining up with my gang again to form an FLQ cell. D'you want to come aboard?" I asked him what they intended to do and he said: "Revolution." When I asked if they'd go as far as killing people, he said that if they had to, they wouldn't hesitate. They'd already started organizing. His group had a farm in the country, they'd robbed several banks to buy weapons and intended to keep doing it until they felt they were sufficiently armed. But they didn't know what they were going to do after that. I asked if I could think about it a bit (laughs).... I knew I couldn't just say, "No." So the next day I said to him: "In all honesty, I can't do it, I don't believe in it. I'm trying to conceive of a way in which violence has played a historical role in the history of the world, but I can't. Can you name a single person whose death has served a purpose? And anyways, basically I'm a writer." The moment that followed was wonderful. My discussion partner looked at me and said: "You're a writer, well then you better write, damn you (laughter)." So when I got out of jail I tried to write as much as possible, reminding myself that my work essentially had to serve the same purpose it had the afternoon I read my poem to my fellow prisoners, to whom I'd given a voice and who, by carrying it in their Lifesavers rolls, had decided that it was part of their shared political expression as well. I think this is what writers must try to do. The message doesn't always have to be political, it can be social, or be about pleasure, and have the same impact.

36 Nadel, Ira B. *Various Positions: a life of Leonard Cohen*. Toronto: Random House of Canada, 1996, pp. 52-53, 62-64.

"The counterculture movement is obviously American"

At the same time Québécois *nationalism was creating a surge of creative energy in the francophone milieu, the influence of the cultural revolution in the United States was also being felt. The Beat writers who had struggled in obscurity through the forties and fifties were lauded in the sixties. Bob Dylan admitted to being profoundly influenced by Jack Kerouac and Allen Ginsberg. Leonard Cohen was so impressed by the Beat poetry scene in New York, he began reading his own poetry backed by jazz ensembles in Montreal nightclubs in 1958.*[36] *Poetry was hip, not only in Quebec, but everywhere.*

HUGH HAZELTON: The sixties was a pretty accelerated time. People were experimenting with all sorts of things that kind of got overwhelmed in the late seventies and the eighties by the conservative backlash.... I heard Ginsberg several times and I really liked what he was doing with the spoken word. And LeRoi Jones, too, who I never heard perform, but I had all his books. I really liked what he was doing, anything was part of the poem.

JOHN GIORNO: What makes poetry great or any poet great is that poetry — and that's prose writing too — is absolute wisdom. It's not just discursive knowledge, it's not just a nice essay. It is absolute wisdom that liberates people. That's the nature of what a poem is. One interesting example, I think, is *Howl* by Allen Ginsberg.... In 1956 a friend of mine said, "John, I've got something that's gonna blow your mind." I said, "Yeah, OK. Great." He must've mentioned Allen's name, and said, "Here are three joints, I'm leaving you the book." I put it in the drawer and forgot about it. A couple of weeks later, which is now early May, the weather's changing, it's springtime. (Snaps fingers) I remembered the joints! So I went, "Ah!" I opened the drawer and I smoked a joint and there was this book. I read *Howl*, and it totally blew my mind. I'm a gay man; in 1956, there's nothing gay in literature. *Howl* was a reflection of my mind. I couldn't believe that somebody had actually written these words. I was nineteen years old. I ran out into the streets, I ran down into Riverside Park, just so I could scream. And it wasn't about howling, it had nothing to do with that. I just ran screaming at the top of my lungs, weeping with joy. Tears running down my face, running and falling, and then getting up and running again and falling. Then I noticed that my pants were torn, and liquid was coming from up here (points to his forehead)... because I had scraped my forehead and there was blood running down. It didn't matter, it wasn't hurting. It was joy, absolute joy. That's an example of a poem being wisdom. I'm that very generation that was transformed by Allen and that poem.

PETER BRAWLEY: Let's face it, there are great roots. The Beats and all this jazz, that's where spoken word comes from. We like to think of Ginsberg and Kerouac and all these guys as being so cornball. Believe me, when they read they were passing around wine and screaming and yelling, and jazz bands in the background. We think of it as Grandpa Allen up there doing 'Howl'. Well, it wasn't like that. It was kinetic and wild and nutty, with live music going on.

JOHN GIORNO: You hear, "Why was 'Howl' such a great poem?" It's because it really liberated a generation. I told this story, to some kid who interviewed me for a newspaper column in Illinois somewhere. And he says to me, "John, it's great that that happened to you, but you know, I've had three classes since high school where we studied 'Howl'. It's a nice poem, but it doesn't do that for us." (laughs)

Véhicule Press postcard with Peter Brawley (R) and friend, 1973. Poem by Peter Brawley
Photo by Stephen Lack

Allen Ginsberg performed his poetry at Sir George Williams University in the late sixties, and in the early seventies John Giorno performed in Montreal for the first time, along with Ginsberg and William Burroughs. It was in this supercharged cultural atmosphere that poet Jean-Paul Daoust began making his mark. He was part of a whole new generation of Quebec poets and writers whose work embraced the vernacular and pop sensibilities of the times.

JEAN-PAUL DAOUST: I lived partly in the United States, I spent my summers in Michigan for many years and I was necessarily influenced by that country's literary culture. That's where I discovered the whole counterculture movement, Ferlinghetti, Ginsberg, Bukowski. I felt he was writing about a kind of disgust-

"Le courant contre-culture, évidemment américain"

JEAN-PAUL DAOUST: J'ai vécu en partie aux États-Unis, j'ai longtemps passé mes étés dans le Michigan, et forcément j'ai été influencé par la culture littéraire de ce pays. C'est là que j'ai découvert tout le mouvement de la contre-culture, avec Ferlinghetti, Ginsberg, Bukowski. Lui, je trouvais qu'il racontait une sorte de réalité urbaine dégueulasse, mais qui était prémonitoire de ce qui ce passe maintenant... Et pour moi, *Le Festin nu* de Burroughs a aussi été une révélation du point de vue de l'écriture. J'aimais également Walt Whitman, qui a écrit des phrases comme "*The United States themselves are the greatest poem.*" C'était alors incroyable de lire une phrase comme ça. En fait, toute cette forme de littérature m'impressionnait et me plaisait beaucoup. Ça me fascinait, c'était complètement différent de ce qui m'était enseigné au collège, au cours classique. Alors qu'ici souvent

continued...

on parlait de la France, moi je parlais de l'Amérique. Avec des gens comme Lucien Francœur, entre autres. Le jet qui passe là [Daoust parle d'un avion qu'on entend passer pendant qu'il parle], je pouvais désormais l'écrire, alors qu'avant, on n'aurait pas pensé à en faire un poème.

La première fois que j'ai été publié, c'est au début des années 70, dans des revues très marginales qui s'appelaient *Hobo-Québec* et *Cul-Q*, pour "culture québécoise". Ces revues publiaient justement les gens qui n'étaient pas encore connus, comme Denis Vanier, Yolande Villemaire et Claude Beausoleil. Mais elles publiaient aussi des gens un peu plus connus, tels que Paul Chamberland. Et l'esprit de ces publications était très audacieux, ça se voulait un peu contre la morale, contre toute la répression, etc., donc très contre-culture, finalement, de par la nature des textes et de la mise en page. Par exemple, on pouvait faire un montage et y inclure une feuille de cannabis ou un sexe d'homme ou de femme. Et au plan du langage, c'étaient des textes qui voulaient casser la baraque, qui amenaient plein de sujets dont on n'avait jamais entendu parler avant, à travers l'écriture. Que ce soit la drogue, le sexe, le rock'n'roll, bref, des choses du vécu, mais qui passaient dorénavant au niveau de la littérature. Alors ces nouvelles thématiques, on les amenait, et on faisait des mises en page très éclatées. À ce moment, le texte était important, mais tout l'emballage visuel qui l'entourait lui donnait des allures de performance sur la feuille. C'est sûr qu'il y avait des limites, parce que le support était une feuille de journal, mais ça demeurait complètement marginal. C'est à partir de là que j'ai commencé dans le milieu, en rencontrant des gens et en travaillant avec eux. Ces deux revues ont fait naître des amitiés, et des genres d'écoles qui se sont développées.

ing urban reality, but which was foreseeing what's happening now... Burroughs' *Naked Lunch* was also a revelation in terms of writing. I also liked Walt Whitman, who wrote things like: "The United States themselves are the greatest poem." It was amazing to read a sentence like that then. That form of literature made a deep impression on me and I enjoyed it a lot. It fascinated me, it was completely different from what I was taught in college, in the *cours classique* [Humanities]. Whereas here we often talked about France, I was talking about America — with people like Lucien Francoeur, among others. The jet that's flying over us [Daoust is referring to a plane we can hear as he speaks] was now something I could write about, while it wouldn't have been considered suitable for poetry before.

I first published in the early seventies, in very marginal publications like *Hobo-Québec* and *Cul-Q*, which stands for *Culture québécoise*. They featured writers who weren't known yet, like Denis Vanier, Yolande Villemaire and Claude Beausoleil. But they also pub-

lished people who were a bit better known, like Paul Chamberland. Their spirit was very bold, they stood against morality, all forms of repression, etc., so very countercultural in the kind of texts and the page layout. For example, you could do a montage and include a cannabis leaf or male or female genitals. In terms of language, the texts really wanted to shake the foundations and break the rules, they tackled topics we'd never heard about before in writing: drugs, sex, rock'n'roll, all of these everyday things were now becoming the stuff of literature. So we brought in these new themes and designed some pretty wild pages. The text was important but the whole visual packaging gave the page the look of a performance on paper. There were limits, of course, because the support was newsprint, but it was still completely marginal. So this is how I got started on the scene, meeting people and working with them. These two publications gave birth to friendships, and what could be called schools of writing developed.

Jean-Paul Daoust wears the American flag
Photo courtesy of the artist

Part 2. THE VÉHICULE GENERATION

On the anglophone side of Montreal, the sixties were dominated by those two titans of Canadian literature, Leonard Cohen and Irving Layton.

ENDRE FARKAS: Leonard Cohen was not of performance poetry but of performing poetry. He and Layton were really the two public figures. They went after that idea that poetry should be not only written but performed. Back to the bard and the oral tradition.

"Actively cultivating a conscious radicalism"

While Leonard Cohen read poetry backed by jazz musicians, and then went on to pursue the bardic tradition as a soulful troubadour and Columbia recording artist, his career didn't spark a movement in performative poetry. For the most part that aspect of poetry remained dormant in anglophone Montreal until the rise of the Vehicle Poets in the seventies. What follows is a brief chronicle of their activities between 1973 and 1981. For a more thorough overview of their theory and practice, check out Vehicle Days — An Unorthodox History of Montreal's Vehicle Poets, *edited by Ken Norris,*[37] *and* Poetry in Performance *by Tom Konyves.*[38]

ENDRE FARKAS: I'd been writing, and I had started to go to some of these coffee house events as an observer, like the Yellow Door. In the late sixties, early seventies, George Bowering became the writer-in-residence at Concordia. He started bringing in Canadian poets, which was a revelation to most of us. Because here, other than Cohen and

Layton, it was American influenced. I took my MA in Creative Writing, and the teacher was Richard Sommer, who was... into the Dadaists and Surrealists. Tristan Tzara and Alfred Jarry and those people. So I got a good background in the history of it, what these people were doing, why they were doing it. I think Tom Konyves was in that class, and John McAuley, who later on became part of the Vehicle Poets.

PETER BRAWLEY: Before the big exodus to Toronto and New York, the Main was a huge booming art scene in the seventies. You had Tom Dean and Steve Lack and Andy Ducovitch and Lee Plotek. They're all quite well recognized artists

Endre Farkas at Véhicule, 1976
Photo courtesy of the artist

now. They had 'meet the artists' nights, and they had tours around the lofts with parties going on.

ENDRE FARKAS: Visual artists of my generation were finding that there were no places to exhibit their work, because they were beginning to do things that

[37] Various authors. *Vehicle Days — An Unorthodox History of Montreal's Vehicle Poets.* Norris, Ken, ed. Montreal: Nuage Editions, 1993.

[38] Konyves, Tom. *Poetry in Performance.* Montreal: The Muses' Company, 1982.

Claudia Lapp, 1972
Photo courtesy Ken Norris

Claudia Lapp and Michael Harris at the first poetry reading at the Véhicule gallery, December 1972
Photo courtesy of Ken Norris

39 A famous jazz club in the forties and the fifties.

were different, that weren't necessarily museum pieces.... Young writers of my generation were finding that there was no place for them to read. And a group of people, mainly visual artists — I wasn't part of the first group — got this space, Véhicule, on Sainte-Catherine near the Main. It used to be a second-floor nightclub next door to restaurants visited by hookers and down-and-outers.

SIMON DARDICK: In 1973 I had been out of work for a while. A friend, who knew I had published magazines, came along one day and said, "There's some people down at Véhicule Art Gallery... they're looking for somebody with some printing background. Maybe this would be interesting to you." So I showed up and never left. I went down to the gallery and became the press manager, and learned how to become a typesetter. Here I was, a university drop-out interested in literary stuff, and had been a painter. Guy Lavoie, one of our partners — who designed the Véhicule Press horse logo, actually — he was a graduate of the Museum of Fine Arts School. We were all a motley group of artists, writers, painters, and university drop-outs

that learned trades. Guy went to College Ahuntsic and became a printer. We all learned how to become printers, so we could do the production.

The press was run as a co-op, situated in the back of Véhicule Art Gallery, in the kitchen of what used to be the Café Montmartre.39 We did printing for political groups, community groups, artists, we did a lot of printing for Powerhouse Gallery, we used to do posters and invitations for a lot of galleries. But at the same time we printed our own books, mostly poetry and artist's books. Because we were attached to the gallery it was really an interesting kind of cross-fertilization thing happening, where you had visual artists and writers getting together and coming up with really interesting books. They loved the idea of multiples, so we would end up doing art books. With the artist's books, they would come and we would sit down over coffee or wine and have these long discussions. The authors were very much involved in the design of the books. That was really a lot of fun. We had light tables set up, and people would do their own lay-out in some cases, because we were using the old waxers, putting it down and rolling it on. The visual artists had the concept of making some sort of printed multiple of their work. It was really interesting working with them, because they have a different thought process than just a totally verbal, word-oriented person. So they would come in with certain visuals. It was really great working on someone's book like that, and discussing it with the writer and coming up with something that you felt was a work of art.

The first book that was really published by the press was Bob McGee, Robert McGee, now living in New York. It was a book called *Three Dozen*

Sonnets & Fast Drawings. It was a little saddle-stitched book done with many different colours and screens. And then *Honey* by Claudia Lapp. *Contacts* by Bill Vazan — who's a sculptor — which was an artist's book. And *Hitchhike* by Fred Vitale and Stephen Lack. Allan Bealy was really important for us at the press. He grew up here, but he's been living in the States for many many years now. He was a visual artist, for whom the printed word was extremely important. He had a broadside series that he brought out that elicited a lot of interest at the time. In 1973, the first of his broadside series came out.

IAN FERRIER: I guess when I first ran into a Montreal poetry scene, it was at the turn of the sixties, beginning of the seventies, when Véhicule Press was just starting up. And they used to do a reading series and chapbooks and litmags and all kinds of stuff.

SIMON DARDICK: Allan Bealy had a chapbook series called Eldorado Editions. Ian Ferrier was one of the first people in that.[40]

PETER BRAWLEY: I ran into Allan Moyle and Stephen Lack, who were just starting work on *Montreal Main*, their first film. That's in 1973. The way we wrote *Montreal Main* and *The Rubber Gun*[41] was — what exactly was it everybody was saying? Was it 'docudrama'? Because we were a real gang of troubled kids involved with narcotics, and that's *The Rubber Gun*, you know? It's about how we're all arrested. But that's how we scripted a lot of it, as more of an improv thing. I was always influenced by Frank O'Hara and early Warhol stuff like stoned-out list-making. So I got to have a bit of a rep in the film scene with these little lists I'd send people. I was really

*Eldorado Editions poster, 1974
Pictured are (from left) Claudia Lapp, Tom Ezzy, Endre Farkas, and Ian Ferrier
Courtesy of Endre Farkas*

influenced by that format, and I've always had a talent for the witty, understated line. Then we started doing things for Véhicule, doing the alternate magazines... where we'd publish more automatic things. The lists, and memos of Allan, stoned-out memo things.

SIMON DARDICK: Parallel to that there was a reading series that was happening, coming out of the gallery. So on Sundays you had all these events happening. It was all together, it was one pot of things bubbling away. The first series was organized by Michael Harris

40 Ferrier, Ian. *From Yr Lover Like An Orchestra*. Montreal: Davinci Press, Eldorado Editions, 1974.

41 *Montreal Main*, director: Frank Vitale, 1973; *The Rubber Gun*, director: Allan Moyle, 1976.

and Claudia Lapp, and then after that it was taken on by people like Endre Farkas and Artie Gold and other poets.

ENDRE FARKAS: I ended up meeting Claudia Lapp, who was living with a visual artist who was one of the members of Véhicule Art Gallery. Claudia invited me down to Véhicule, where she and Michael Harris had started a reading series. That was in 1973, 1974. I went to this space, this strange place run by visual artists, sculptors and poets. It was really a kind of freedom. Since nobody really knew what they were doing, you were free to do whatever you wanted to do. After a year of running the series with Michael, she asked me if I wanted to run it. I didn't know anything about it, so I said, "Sure." By that time I was with Carol Harwood, a dancer. She helped out and showed up on Sunday afternoon and put out the few little mimeo books that we had and the coffee and donuts we put together that people paid for. Ken Norris started to hang out to hear the people. Basically I just invited anybody who had a poem. It was a very quiet time; Leonard Cohen sort of dominated, and then he disappeared, and there was kind of a lull. There were some others who were more serious poets, and we were the young know-nothing know-it-alls that decided to run the reading series. So we just said that every Sunday afternoon we would have a reading, and word got out. Ken Norris showed up and Artie Gold showed up and Tom showed up, John showed up, Stephen Morrissey showed up. What we had in common was basically that we were not of the mainstream, we were young, and we were interested in stuff that [wasn't] necessarily for the page. Although at first we were all writing.

SIMON DARDICK: We seriously started publishing, I think, really in 1975 and 1976. I would say we published a lot of people... Michael Harris, Richard Sommer, Claudia Lapp.... In most cases, these people performed before we published them. So they were known quantities.

KEN NORRIS: When I came back to Montreal in 1975 I'd spent the previous two years playing in a rock band in New York. So I had no problem at all signing up with a poetry band. And that's what the Vehicule Poets were after a while, something of a poetry band. Not too much of that stuff wound up in print, but there were numerous performances of really odd texts. And I really loved that stuff. We were bringing Dada and Surrealism to Montreal, which really needed some loosening up at the time.

SIMON DARDICK: It was always very multidisciplinary... there were so many influences coming. There was definitely European influences. You'd have someone like Italian performance artist Vito Acconci coming in and doing something really amazing and crazy. And that evening you'd have Françoise Sullivan doing a dance piece. Two days later you would have poetry readings on Sunday, or bagels and then poetry. Many people, like Endre Farkas, were always extremely performance-oriented. It wasn't just enough to stand up and read your work. You tried to do something else with it. That made it really very interesting.

ENDRE FARKAS: Carol, my wife now, was one of the first members of the Contact Improvisational groups that started up in Montreal. She danced with an all-woman's group called Catpoto. People like Marie Chouinard were hanging out there, using the space. Richard Sommers' wife Vicky Tansy was dancing, Margie Gillis was there occasionally. So I got involved with the dance community, because I liked the kind of freeform. They asked me if I would write something for them, mix text and movement? I started to work with dancers and movement and the idea of text as movement. That kind of thing interested me. Also, I was interested in collage and chance poetry. I started to do some of that kind of stuff, because Contact is chance, it's improvisation. So I cut up text and mixed it up and pulled from it and put together text.... At the same time Steve Morrissey was hanging out with Pat Walsh, and he was interested in concrete poetry. So he was actually doing installation pieces with Pat Walsh, bringing huge rocks into the gallery (laughs). I thought, "OK. Concrete." You know? John McAuley was working with some sculptors who got interested in his stuff, they plastercasted him. And Tom Konyves started to come to the readings. He read, and his early stuff was terribly conservative love poetry. He got really pissed off because we didn't want him at first. He disappeared for a while, went to New York, came back and was a changed man.... He was interested in doing some Surreal and Dadaist kind of things like collaborative writing, chance poetry. I'd done this one voice piece, 'Er / Words / Ah'. I ended up first doing it by myself, then recording voices in three of my voices, then using other people, so it started to grow. One of the things that Véhicule was very important for, was that it offered the sense of collaboration.

TOM KONYVES: In the late seventies, as a poet at the artist-run Véhicule Art Gallery, I had the opportunity to see the

Ken Norris and Tom Konyves *reading from* Poetry in Performance *at Paragraphe Books, 1982*
Photo courtesy of Endre Farkas

(opposite page, from top) cityflowers *by Artie Gold,* Everyman His Own Football *zine,* CrossCountry *Montreal issue, 1975*

Ken Norris at Paragraphe Books, 1982
Photo courtesy of Endre Farkas

work of many performance artists. Performance artists were mostly visual artists, not poets. Art in public places was also becoming popular; I performed Ezra Pound's poem, 'In A Station of the Metro', in the Berri Metro station.

KEN NORRIS: I did a lot of collaborative work with Tom Konyves, which led me into performance. Then Tom and Endre Farkas and I toyed with becoming a performance group called ETC., but that didn't last long. They wanted to do very different things, and I was the guy stuck in the middle, who was really the least interested in performance poetry. I didn't really want to become an 'actor' of texts. When the Vehicule Poets were doing performance poetry we were being influenced by Dadaists like Hugo Ball and Tristan Tzara, the Surrealists, bill bissett, Gerry Gilbert, the Four Horsemen, and the Beats. Those strike me as being the primary influences on that stuff. Alfred Jarry too.

133

SIMON DARDICK: Véhicule Gallery would have people come up from the States, and come from all over the world, and that was really terrific. People would come from across the country, because the gallery was extremely active in inviting people. In most cases though, there were mostly local writers at the reading series. This meant the local writers had a chance to meet other artists and performance people, and how do you know how that will influence people? Sometimes you can't put your finger on it, but you just know that it has to.

ENDRE FARKAS: The Vehicule Poets were the bridge between the solely literate world and the visual — television, cinema, radio — explosion in the sixties. One of the things that happened in the sixties and seventies was that the artists actually started to *use* the media, as opposed to just listening to it. You now control, as opposed to it controlling you.

A recent photo of Artie Gold and Ken Norris
Photo courtesy of Sonja Skarstedt

KEN NORRIS: We were actively cultivating a conscious radicalism. We were poet-rebels. And poetry in Montreal at that time was really conservative, and mostly has been for about thirty years now. So we went out of our way to be agent provocateurs.

ENDRE FARKAS: Marie Chouinard did her piss in the bucket piece. At first it shocked the world but Montreal didn't care (laughs). We did things that were outrageous for the times. One year Brother André's heart was stolen[42] — we didn't steal it! — so Véhicule Art Gallery had an exhibition where it was all Brother André stuff, and invited the thieves to bring back the heart. People were dressed up as priests, and we had confessional booths. Artists did documentation, they snuck into the Oratory and had sex on the altar and photographed it and displayed it. There was this huge crucifix with a huge erection.

SIMON DARDICK: Depending on the printing jobs, sometimes the Véhicule Press would have to work late at night. We would be there because we had to work, and we would see the performances. But I also felt that we were the running critics. We'd say, "What is this shit?" or, "This is really cool!" And sometimes it was literally shit. It would be somebody with little cones of feces, a collection of feces throughout the whole gallery under little clear cones. You never knew in the morning when you arrived, if we didn't go to the performance the night before, what was going to be there. So in a sense the poets were almost the straight guys to what was happening with some of the other performances.

ENDRE FARKAS: The gallery got some video equipment, the old portable reel-to-reel three hundred pound shit. Tom started to videotape the readings, and the readings became more and more boring for all of us. At Michael Ondaatje's reading, there was an installation of about a hundred lambs' legs on the floor. So Tom is shooting that while Ondaatje is reading *Dainty Monsters* or something. Tom didn't want to do

[42] Brother André's heart is a relic kept in a glass case at Saint Joseph's Oratory in Montreal.

straight documentary stuff any more, so he started playing around with video, he went into what he labeled 'video poetry'.

TOM KONYVES: I wrote and produced a short video, 'Sympathies of War', in 1978 using three quarter inch colour video, and called it a 'videopoem'. It was a performance recorded on video. I added a scrolling text, but the performance was unedited. I wanted to show it to the director of The San Francisco Poetry Film Workshop — he was in Montreal supplying most of the entries to McGill University's *Poetry Film Festival* — but he had a difficult time talking about video as a format for poetry. He made it sound like film was the only acceptable format for visual poetry. I personally didn't care about the distinction between film and video other than being surprised at what I thought was his display of a rude class distinction — poets who work with film as opposed to poets who can't afford to — when I was really, genuinely interested in the content of the visual poem, not the type of recording device used in the process.

"It's good to be called the mafia"

After the first few anarchic years of its existence, Véhicule Gallery became somewhat more organized in 1977. Relationships that had been loosely defined were formalized. The poets who gathered around the weekly poetry readings became directly involved in the editorial board of Véhicule Press, and they became known as 'The Vehicle Poets'. According to Vehicle Days, *the Vehicle Poets were Endre Farkas, Artie Gold, Tom Konyves, Claudia Lapp, John McAuley, Stephen Morrissey and Ken Norris.*

ENDRE FARKAS: The Véhicule printers were always running these bloody machines on Sundays during poetry readings. One day I got pissed off and yelled at Simon and then he said, "Well, why don't you join, and become an editor of Véhicule Press?" So I said, "OK." Artie, Ken and I became the first editors of Véhicule Press.

SIMON DARDICK: The main reason for forming an editorial board was because we wanted to qualify for Canada Council money.... Ken Norris saw 'The Vehicle Poets' as being simply the people who read at Véhicule Art Gallery. In fact a lot of them don't have anything in common, except for the fact that they read at the gallery. It was amorphous, and then it became codified a bit. Once you have a book out, it's the Vehicle Poets.

ENDRE FARKAS: It was a derogatory term... it was some people who felt that we were the mafia, the Vehicle Poets, because we ran the reading series, we ran the press, we ran events at Véhicule. We put out anthologies, and some people didn't get in.... The people who had been published by Delta like David Solway, Michael Harris, the so-called Delta Poets, and Antonio D'Alfonso, who later started Guernica Press, called us the mafia. Although we were friendly, it wasn't vicious. He said, "It's good to be called the mafia," but in Italian.

SIMON DARDICK: As Véhicule Press, we did a number of anthologies over the years. We did the first book edited by Ken and Endre. It was the Montreal scene, old and young, you had everybody from Frank Scott to first time poets.[43] Then we brought out a book called *Cross/cut*,[44] and we've done a few over the years. Just looking to see what there is at the time. Every time

The Véhicule printing press

43 Various authors. *Montreal English Poetry of the Seventies.* Farkas, Andre & Norris, Ken, ed. Montreal: Véhicule Press, 1977.

44 Various authors. *Cross/cut: Contemporary English Quebec Poetry.* Norris, Ken & Van Toorn, Peter, ed. Montreal: Véhicule Press, 1982.

*Michel Bonneau and Endre
Farkas at the launch for*
Murders in the Welcome Café
Photo by Ben Soo

part of the menu, and the back part of the menu is in the back. It's this murder that takes place, and it's a poem, but it's a sort of concrete poem. It was quite a lovely book. At the time, the American Library Association gave it three stars... for innovation or something, and we went into a second printing, because we sold out the first 300 copies. And so we sold another 150 copies in the States. It was really unbelievable. It was a best-seller, 450 copies. So there I see a real direct connection between somebody who's been active in the performance, spoken word, reading aspect of the gallery, and a book. That book didn't come out, per se, for that specific performance, or anything that he did. But it came out of his sensibility.

ENDRE FARKAS: I had a small chapbook called *Murders in the Welcome Café*, which evolved from just a text to a two-person performance to a videotaping, with editing, music and the whole thing.

SIMON DARDICK: In 1979-80 Endre and Artie and Ken ceased to be our editors. I think our view of Véhicule Press as publishers began to mature somewhat, and we wanted to do more than poetry.... I know at Véhicule Art, at one point there was a putsch, basically. People took over, and people left. And we were the press that was in the middle, because we had furniture! We had equipment. Our sympathies were with the group that left, so we had to be

you do that, you formalize things a little bit. It was very general and amorphous, and then it became specific. But I don't think when we were in the midst of that, we saw that that was happening.

We published a book of Endre's called *Murders in the Welcome Café*.[45] When we'd moved from the gallery to Chinatown proper, 1000 Clark Street, there was the Welcome Café, which was a real greasy spoon Chinese restaurant. The back of the cover is the actual table-cloth which has cigarette burn holes in it. The frontispieces are really the front

45 Farkas, Andre. *Murders in the Welcome Café*. Montreal: Véhicule Press, 1977.

136

incredibly diplomatic. It took us a while — a year — to leave, I think. And people really did hive off. I mean the video section became PRIM. People went off into various different things, other galleries were formed... sometimes by the people who were originally involved with Véhicule Art.

ENDRE FARKAS: After we started to go separate ways, Ken said, "You know, for about the next ten, fifteen years nobody'll give a shit about you. And then in the nineties it'll start picking up again. Some of this stuff will become interesting for people two generations away from us." The Vehicule Poets were important for the work they did, but also for the community work they did. Setting up the press, setting up the gallery, setting up the reading series, and the sense of believing in collaboration. You need that in a performance community, you need the sense of community, because you work with other people. You don't just get up there and read your poem.

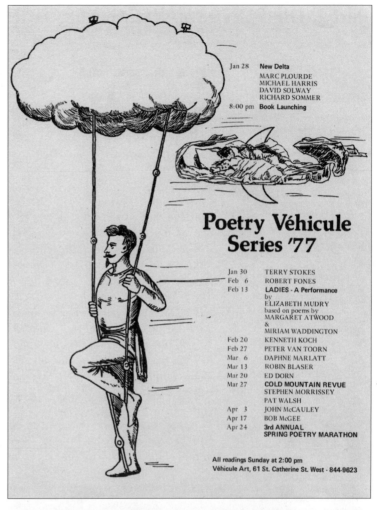

Jan 28   **New Delta**
MARC PLOURDE
MICHAEL HARRIS
DAVID SOLWAY
RICHARD SOMMER
8:00 pm   **Book Launching**

Poetry Véhicule Series '77

Jan 30	TERRY STOKES
Feb 6	ROBERT FONES
Feb 13	**LADIES - A Performance** by ELIZABETH MUDRY based on poems by MARGARET ATWOOD & MIRIAM WADDINGTON
Feb 20	KENNETH KOCH
Feb 27	PETER VAN TOORN
Mar 6	DAPHNE MARLATT
Mar 13	ROBIN BLASER
Mar 20	ED DORN
Mar 27	**COLD MOUNTAIN REVUE** STEPHEN MORRISSEY PAT WALSH
Apr 3	JOHN McCAULEY
Apr 17	BOB McGEE
Apr 24	**3rd ANNUAL SPRING POETRY MARATHON**

All readings Sunday at 2:00 pm
Véhicule Art, 61 St. Catherine St. West - 844-9623

The Véhicule Press offices, 2001
Photo by Andy Brown

Part 3. THE PERFORMANCE GENERATION

JEAN-PAUL DAOUST: Il y a plus de 25 ans que je fais des lectures. Les premières que j'ai données, c'était à la Casanous, chez Janou St-Denis, en 1975. [NDLE: Janou St-Denis est décédée le 11 mai 2000.] On lisait dans un bar enfumé, avec de la musique, et là, il *fallait* que le texte passe, sinon les gens dans la salle pouvaient aller jusqu'à lancer leurs bouteilles de bière sur la scène. Dans le temps de la Casanous, j'ai aussi lu à la Galerie Dazibao. Mais Chez Janou St-Denis, on pouvait au moins y aller une fois tous les trois mois, et il était possible d'y lire les temps qu'on voulait; cinq minutes, une demi-heure, une heure, c'était très ouvert. Ç'a été un tremplin. Et à cette époque, comme la performance commençait à apparaître, on en profitait pour monter des spectacles, ça nous donnait la chance d'élaborer nos lectures...

Puis en 1976, j'ai publié un premier livre qui s'appelait *Oui, cher*, aux éditions Cul- Q. C'était un livre-objet. Par exemple, un sein de femme qui s'ouvrait, avec un poème à l'intérieur. Ou encore on ouvrait un paquet de cigarettes, et il y avait un poème dedans. Le livre était composé de plusieurs trucs comme ça. Ensuite, j'ai fait un autre livre, *Chaises longues*, également publié aux éditions Cul-Q. J'étais allé à Sainte-Lucie, dans le Sud, avec mon copain du temps, et durant notre voyage, on avait envoyé des cartes postales à nos proches. Quand on est revenus, on a ramassé ces cartes et on en a fait un petit livre. On se moquait un peu de toute l'atmosphère tropicale, les noix de coco, les fleurs exotiques, etc.

Toujours en 1976, je crois, au Musée d'art contemporain – dans le temps qu'il était à la Cité du Havre –, il y a eu un événement qui a rassemblé des performeurs durant toute une fin de semaine. Moi, j'avais justement fait une performance à partir des cartes postales que j'avais écrites à Sainte-Lucie. On avait déversé trois tonnes de sable sur le site, dans lequel on avait planté des cartes postales un

46 Janou St-Denis died May 11, 2000.

"Things that struck me"

In 1981, after Véhicule Press and The Vehicle Poets had parted ways, Véhicule Gallery itself ceased to exist. In the nine years of its existence, a number of francophone artists remembered the space for its nurturing of experimental art forms. Michel Garneau read at Véhicule Gallery, and one of his books was translated by Robert McGee and published by Véhicule Press. Jean-Paul Daoust remembered the poetry posters which The Vehicle Poets had installed in city buses. Still, the performance poetry scene at Véhicule Gallery remained largely anglophone, and in the seventies the francophone and anglophone poets and performers of Montreal were usually isolated from each other. It is interesting that Jean-Paul Daoust's work was equally as intent on blurring the lines between disciplines as any of the Véhicule artists.

JEAN-PAUL DAOUST: I've been giving readings for over twenty-five years. The first ones were at the *Casanous*, hosted by Janou St-Denis, in 1975.[46] We were reading in a smokey bar where there was music, so the text *had* to get across, otherwise the audience might throw beer bottles up at us onstage. Back in the Casanous days I also read at *Galerie Dazibao*. But with Janou St-Denis you could at least go every three months, and you could read as long as you wanted: five minutes, half an hour, an hour, it was very open. So this was a launching pad. And performance was beginning to appear at that time, so we took advantage of this to organize shows, it

gave us an opportunity to make our readings more elaborate....

In 1976 I published my first book, *Oui, cher* [Yes, dear] at the *Editions Cul-Q*. It was an artist's book. For example, it had a pop-up woman's breast with a poem inside it. Or a cigarette package would open up and there'd be a poem inside. The book had several such things. Then I did another book, *Chaises longues*, also with *Cul-Q*. I'd been on holiday in St-Lucia with my then-boyfriend and during our trip, we sent postcards to our close friends. When we came back, we collected the postcards and made a little book with them. In it we were kind of mocking the whole tropical thing, coconuts, exotic flowers, etc.

And in 1976 too, I think, at the *Musée d'art contemporain* — back then it was located on Cité du Havre — there was an event bringing performers together during one whole weekend. I did a performance using those St-Lucia postcards. We had three tons of sand dumped onto the Ile, we planted the postcards in it here and there, and I walked around in my bathing suit with my boyfriend. We were drinking champagne and I was improvising poems, texts. We saw all kinds of things like this over the three days, performances by artists from here and elsewhere. I remember Claude Beausoleil climbing a ladder to recite poems about stars. Maybe that was the Golden Age of performance, there was really a lot of it. Personally, that's when things clicked for me....

Three years later, in 1979, I published a first book of poems, *Portraits d'intérieur*. These poems were a bit more structured than the earlier ones, more linear. But as I said earlier, it also contained a picture of me lying naked on a zebra skin with a bottle of champagne. At the time I felt that Quebec literature, because it was preaching the political side so much, was forgetting the individual. With my book I wanted to go against this trend, to show there were also *individuals* in Quebec who were experiencing various things.

Actually, at the start, I didn't want to do performance but I believe that because my poetry has always been very oral, I think it naturally took me there.

While Daoust came from a literary background, many emerging francophone performers were inspired by both the text-based and the visually-based performance art then springing from the art galleries in Montreal.

NATHALIE DEROME: I studied in theatre but I didn't do theatre. There I met Sylvie Laliberté and we started to work together. We saw performances in Montreal in those years [1980]. Véhicule Art organized many performance events and invited a lot of artists: Bob Wilson, Richard Foreman, Meredith Monk, Marie Chouinard, etc. We saw a lot of performances. It was really hot. We wanted to make our own stuff also, and not wait for somebody to call us. But it was not like, "We are doing performance!" It was more like, "We are doing something." With Sylvie Laliberté we called it '*Performance variétés*' because our preoccupation was Dadaist and early 20th Century. That *théâtre de variétés* aspect, *boulevard*. The early Expressionist thing. This was where we started.

GENEVIÈVE LETARTE: When I went to Paris in 1975, I was twenty, and I saw a show that really impressed me. It was Brigitte Fontaine, whom I didn't know at the time. Her performance knocked me out. I'd never seen anything like it, she was inventing something, that woman.... She arrived onstage with Jacques Higelin, who was carrying a little bongo drum, they walked hand in hand, then she started talking.... It was very theatrical and very simple at the same time, absolutely incredible. Plus, here was a couple working together. I

peu partout, et je me promenais en costume de bain, avec mon copain. On buvait une bouteille de champagne, et j'improvisais des textes, des poèmes. Et durant trois jours, on a vu plein de choses comme ça, des performances données par des artistes d'ici et d'ailleurs. Je me souviens entre autres que Claude Beausoleil grimpait dans une échelle en récitant des poèmes sur les stars. Cette période-là était peut-être l'âge d'or de la performance, car il y en avait beaucoup. Personnellement, c'est vraiment à ce moment que j'ai eu un déclic...

Trois ans plus tard, en 1979, j'ai publié un premier recueil, qui s'appelait *Portraits d'intérieur* [Trois-Rivières, APLM, 1981]. Les poèmes qu'il contenait étaient un peu plus structurés que mes précédents, dans le sens qu'ils étaient plus linéaires. Mais comme je l'ai dit plus tôt, ce recueil renfermait aussi une photo où j'étais tout nu sur une peau de zèbre, avec une bouteille de champagne. À cette époque, je trouvais que la littérature québécoise, à force de prêcher autant le côté politique, en venait à oublier l'individu. Alors avec mon recueil, je voulais un peu aller contre ce courant, montrer qu'il y avait aussi des *individus* au Québec qui vivaient telle chose et telle chose.

Finalement, au départ, je ne voulais pas faire de la performance, mais je crois qu'étant donné que ma poésie a toujours été très orale, ça m'y a naturellement amené.

GENEVIÈVE LETARTE: Quand je suis allée à Paris en 1975, j'avais 20 ans, et j'ai vu un spectacle qui m'a vraiment marquée. C'était un spectacle de Brigitte Fontaine, que je ne connaissais pas à l'époque. Sa performance m'avait renversée. Pour moi, c'était du jamais vu, cette femme inventait quelque chose... Elle était arrivée toute seule sur scène avec Jacques Higelin, qui trimballait un petit bongo, ils avaient marché en se tenant par la main, puis elle s'était mise à parler... C'était à la fois très théâtral et très simple, puis complètement incroyable. En plus, un couple qui travaillait ensemble, je vénérais ça. Je trouvais ça vraiment beau. D'ailleurs, plus tard, j'ai eu un copain musicien avec qui j'ai fait plusieurs spectacles. Alors ensemble,

continued...

Sylvie Laliberté with Nathalie Derome, Beauté-Boeuf, *1984*
Photo by Benoit Bourdeau

on formait aussi cette espèce de combinaison: femme écrivaine, musicien éclaté.... *Brigitte Fontaine* m'a probablement beaucoup influencée. Et évidemment, d'autre part, il y avait sa collègue américaine Laurie Anderson. Quand elle est venue à Montréal pour la première fois, c'était dans un local sur l'avenue des Pins, et il y avait une femme qui l'assistait, qui jouait avec des bandes. C'était vers la fin des années 70 ou au début des années 80. Je me souviens que j'étais allée la voir avec des amies et qu'on étaient sorties de sa performance en se disant qu'elle était rien de moins qu'un génie! Comme Brigitte Fontaine, je crois que Laurie Anderson m'a fortement inspirée. Ces deux femmes ont été très importantes pour moi. Puis en tant que Québécoise, francophone, Nord-Américaine, c'est comme si je me situais entre les deux....

JEAN-PAUL DAOUST: Je me rappelle que Laurie Anderson m'avait énormément frappé. Avec tous les changements de voix qu'elle faisait et les gadgets qu'elle utilisait, elle est peut-être la première performeuse à m'avoir vraiment ébloui, parce que je l'ai vue au début de ce courant, vers la fin des années 70, dans des petites salles à Montréal. Ses textes étaient très songés, tantôt c'étaient des poèmes, tantôt c'étaient des chansons, et parfois pour un même texte c'était les deux à la fois. Et je trouvais extraordinaire qu'elle joue ainsi avec ses textes... Après l'avoir vue, j'ai réalisé qu'il y avait plus de possibilités que je ne le croyais.

GENEVIÈVE LETARTE: C'est justement vers la fin des années 70 que je suis devenue poète-performeuse. J'avais déjà fait de la musique de rue, avec des fanfares, puis à ce moment j'étais dans un groupe de femmes qui s'appelait Wondeur Brass. Avec ce groupe, on faisait aussi des poèmes et un peu de théâtre, on jouait avec des textes... Et c'est quand j'étais avec Wondeur Brass que m'est venue l'idée de faire des performances avec de la poésie. À un certain moment, ça s'est clarifié, je voulais prendre mes propres textes puis les performer sur scène, et il n'y avait personne d'autre que moi que ça intéressait. C'est pour cette raison que j'ai quitté le groupe Wondeur Brass et c'est ainsi que je me suis retrouvée sur scène. Et à ce

venerated this, I felt it was so beautiful. Later on I had a musician boyfriend too, we did lots of shows together.[47] Together we made up the same kind of combination: woman writer, unconventional musician.... So Brigitte Fontaine probably influenced me. And obviously there was her American counterpart Laurie Anderson. The first time she came to Montreal, in a place on Pine Avenue, she had a woman assisting her, playing with tapes. It was in the late seventies or early eighties. I went to see her with some friends and when we left that performance, we felt she was nothing short of a genius! So these two women are very important to me. As

a *Québécoise*, francophone, North American, I'm sort of situated in between these two....

JEAN-PAUL DAOUST: I remember that Laurie Anderson really struck me. With all her voice distortions and her gadgets, she may be the first performer who really dazzled me because I saw her early on, at the end of the seventies, in small venues in Montreal. Her texts were very insightful, sometimes they were poems, sometimes songs, and sometimes both within one text.... After seeing her I realized there were more possibilities than I thought.

GENEVIÈVE LETARTE: I became a performer-poet at the end of the seventies. I'd already done music with brass bands, and at the time I was in a women's group called *Wondeur Brass*. We did poems as well as theatre, we performed texts.... It was when I was with *Wondeur Brass* that I got the idea to do performances with poetry. It became clear to me that I wanted to use my own texts onstage, but nobody else was interested. So I left *Wondeur Brass* and ended up onstage doing what I wanted. With the exception of Louise Guay, I don't think I'd seen anybody else do anything like this in Montreal at the time. It didn't really exist and I wanted to do it, it was visceral. Writing was one thing, but as I'd done theatre and street music, I knew the high you get from playing live in front of people. This is what I wanted to do more than anything. I gave my first performances

Hélène Monette with musician Daniel Roussel at a Happening, Café Instantané, La Prairie, 1981
Photo by Pierre Grimard

47 Serge Boisvert.

140

around 1980, the first one was at Powerhouse Gallery, I think, then it continued on in various forms.

HÉLÈNE MONETTE: I got started on the scene in 1983, 1984, during the *Montréal poésie ville ouverte* event which was held simultaneously in various cafés. Janou St-Denis, who ran the Casanous — she didn't know me — found me quite insistent and wondered if I could really write. I'd just arrived from Trois-Rivières and in those days I was really impulsive, willful, borderline annoying…. I eventually met Paul Chamberland, and I felt his view of society had things in common with mine. He gave me the impression of being the teacher and I was the student. So I started with him: he'd say his text and once in a while, I'd say these ten-second bits.

ENDRE FARKAS: In the eighties was the first referendum. It was quite a heavy thing here. The irony of it was that the English writers didn't feel much sympathy for the English population of Quebec, because the English population of Quebec couldn't give a flying fuck about the English art here. Historically, when you look at it, the English controlled Quebec through the economy, not the arts. The artists were ignored. In some ways, we were a lot more sympathetic to the francophones, but in a sense we weren't connected, because of language. The bridge was dance. That's why dance is big in Montreal, because you need body language. The dancers were English and French, working together no problem. It's different for your audience when you read poetry. Most of them were either unilingual English, or unilingual French, or smatterings of French / English…. We were sympathetic towards the struggle of the francophones because we as English artists were struggling in very little recognition here. We were an island within an island within an island.

moment, à part Louise Guay, je pense que je n'avais vu personne d'autre présenter quelque chose du genre à Montréal. Ce n'était pas vraiment quelque chose qui existait, et si je voulais le faire, c'était vraiment parce que je sentais que c'était viscéral. J'avais vraiment le sentiment qu'il fallait que j'amène mes textes sur scène. Écrire, c'était une chose, mais comme j'avais fait du théâtre et de la musique de rue, je connaissais la griserie que procurait le fait de jouer *live*, devant des gens. Et à ce moment, j'avais plus envie de le faire que n'importe quoi d'autre. J'ai commencé à faire mes premières performances de poésie vers 1980. La première c'était, je pense, à la galerie Powerhouse. Puis après, ç'a continué, en prenant différentes formes.

HÉLÈNE MONETTE: À Montréal, j'ai commencé dans le milieu en 1983, 1984, lors du festival *Montréal poésie ville ouverte*, qui se tenait simultanément dans plusieurs cafés de la ville. Et Janou St-Denis, qui était propriétaire de la Casanous - elle ne me connaissait pas -, me trouvait insistante et se demandait si je savais réellement écrire. Moi, j'arrivais tout juste de Trois-Rivières. Dans ce temps-là, j'étais très impulsive, puis très volontariste, à la limite d'être fatigante… Et finalement, j'ai rencontré Paul Chamberland, de qui je trouvais que le regard qu'il posait sur la société s'apparentait au mien. Il me donnait l'impression qu'il était le maître, et que j'étais l'élève. C'est avec lui que j'ai commencé: il disait son texte et, de temps à autre, moi j'en disais des petits bouts qui duraient environ 10 secondes.

A performance of Endre Farkas' Mise au Jeu / Face Off
Photo by Christian Knudsen

Part 4. THE FOUFOUNES ÉLECTRIQUES GENERATION

"We weren't punks, we were simply riffing on it"

In the eighties, the punk and underground music scene in Montreal lent new energy to spoken word performance. Poets performed in punk music venues, and performers like Ian Stephens, Clifford Duffy and Norman Nawrocki managed to carve a niche in both the poetry and the music scene at the same time. In a sense, performance poetry in the post-Véhicule days had to start from the bottom, without government funding, and based in the rock and roll bars of the era.

FORTNER ANDERSON: Clifford Duffy and I despised the Vehicle Poets, because they had resources and money and essentially were established and worked at the time. Clifford Duffy and I did a number of shows with a poetry group called the Punkitariat in 1979. I remember conversations where we believed that punk actually existed for perhaps several months, at that time, in England. It had a very precise expression, and we weren't punks, we were simply riffing on it. We would play at the punk shows put on at 364 Saint-Paul West [Gallery 364], between shows by the Normals, Arthur's Dilemma, Chromosome 64. The entryway was under this pig's head and a curtain of chicken legs. I'd created these huge collage-paintings that we hung up on the walls. We papered the floor with the front cover of a magazine that Clifford and I had published. And then the concert people would come in and Clifford and I would be doing poetry between punk bands. People would spit at us, punks would jeer, throw beer bottles as we did our work. We'd perform *Blue Dog Plus*,[48] his book, and a couple of others. I did a couple of small pieces, but it was mostly Cliff's work and improvisations off Cliff's work.

Then we did a bunch of different shows and installations in Old Montreal, and then St. Denis Street. There was also

Fortner Anderson from No More Fun / Pu de Fun *poster*

48 Duffy, Clifford. *Blue Dog Plus*. Montreal: Dromotexte, 1984.

the company I put together called Dromotexte, which published Cliff's books... and a book called *Schizotexte*, which was a group of Montreal poets: Michael Toppings, Anne-Marie Weiss, and a guy named John Reiger. *Dial-A-Poem* was a long project that I did in the early to mid-eighties, where I recorded several hundred Montreal poets and visiting poets, and people would dial up the word THE POEM on the phone, and hear each day a new poem.

At the same time Fortner Anderson was publishing and performing, Ian Stephens was engaged in much the same sort of activity.

PETER BRAWLEY: I met Ian Stephens through the early eighties. He was a big fan of *The Rubber Gun*. I couldn't believe that somebody'd noticed the film work, because as far as I was concerned it was all over. Ian had started a magazine called *Xero*, and I read with him at the *Xero* launch, in 1984. Actually, I was quite flattered to find a place with all those kids because I was on the run, then, from the old days. They were always so great, treating me like the old uncle of the whole scene.

October 1978. Thin, pale, and twenty-two, my slightly flared jeans longer than my worn-down Earth shoes, I helped my friend Scotty struggle into 364 St. Paul street with my Fender Bandmaster atop his Peavey bass stack. Our first show in front of people.... The room was an empty store front rented by a mild-mannered studenty type who looked more sloppy than punk, but even this, at the time, meant something. Anything that wasn't overtly granola was vaguely exciting.

[The Normals] played after the Punkatariat Poets. I was surprised at the aggression of the audience towards this spoken word stuff. It was totally new to me and I was willing to just watch it, even if I didn't like it. But the people that had crowded into the place were suddenly ignited into a screaming and spitting frenzy. It came so out of nowhere, it seemed scripted. "Fuck you," they shouted good naturedly. Someone threw a beer. It then dawned on me what these kids were doing. They were acting out what they'd heard punk was, what the TV reports were. As soon as they left this place they'd be back to what they were (something similar to what I was), but here they could be those nasty, swearing, spitting, bottle-throwing kids shown in clips on the news. It was something like a very contained sports riot, except from what I could tell, they weren't at that point even drunk. It was a sober riot.

– excerpted from 'Snub - Part 4: *Trop fort pour le système*' by Rob Labelle, in *Fish Piss # 5*, 1999.

(left) Gallery 364 with papered floor
Photo courtesy of Fortner Anderson

(right) Schizotexte by Michael Toppings, Anne-Marie Weiss, and John Reiger (Dromotexte, 1986)

143

Red Shift s'associe plus facilement au 'dance' agressif. Ian Stephens, chanteur et parolier, implore et gronde des textes qu'il qualifie de poésie urbaine. Trois musiciens l'accompagnent avec une musique essentiellement électronique.

– from 'Montréal Foisonne', *Québec Rock*, July 1984.
No byline.

IAN FERRIER: I would run into Ian Stephens. He had a band called Red Shift that he'd work with, and I saw him do stuff with them. We're about the same age, and we came from the same kind of background. The MA program at Concordia was busy trying to flunk him out. The great thing about him was that he was always so completely himself, and refused ever to be anything different than that. Regardless of what anyone would say or do or tell him.

Red Shift
Ian Stephens foreground
Photo courtesy of Alex Espinosa

IAN STEPHENS: ...I went to England at twenty-one and I was living with a boyfriend and it was really cheap to go to plays. It was the early stage of punk and this had ramifications on theatre there. A friend of mine doing a writing program at Concordia told me to come and study here. I came back. I had a hell of a time there. They had told me that they were a student's university but they were just as antiquated as everybody else. I was writing gay themes and of the experiences I had had in Europe.... At Concordia I kept having straight professors. Robert Martin, an ally, sent my work to Michel Tremblay and Tremblay said, "I'll work with you if you want." So I did that for a year at his house in Outremont....

– from 'Dark and Sexy Places' by Gaëtan Charlebois, *MTL Attitude*, November 2, 1995.

PETER BRAWLEY: He hyped Michel Tremblay into helping him with a play. I think at one point in his Masters he was thinking of acting. He should've acted, Ian. If I was him, with the kind of amazing family Ian was from, I would've gone right to Hollywood. I used to kid him about it like that. "With your looks, Ian? Why don't you just go cruise down Sunset Boulevard? What's with the radical, revolutionary trip?"

FORTNER ANDERSON: Clifford Duffy had huge fights with Joy Glidden and Ian Stephens. I imagine that right before that time was when we met. I think I saw him read a couple of times, which was very early on. Ian was working at Psyche Industry at that time. I know I used to meet him down there. He was published in *Xero*, and that was probably right before he started his rock and roll band Disappointed A Few People.

IAN STEPHENS: I liked the collective creativity of [being in a band]. In a way, you're more lucky if you can't support yourself as a writer because it forces you to get into other social situations. The band scene, bar scene, the buddies, drugs, sex and so on was all very useful for me. In a way, it filled that bucket of memory a little. I wouldn't have been a better writer staying at home.

– from 'Dark and Sexy Places' by Gaëtan Charlebois, *MTL Attitude*, November 2, 1995.

"Putting a backdrop to spoken word"

Ian Stephens
Photo courtesy of Alex Espinosa

Ian Stephens had been performing with Red Shift since 1982. Close on his heels, both Clifford Duffy and Norman Nawrocki started combining music and spoken word. Such a move would have seemed obvious at the time: text-based artist Laurie Anderson, and poets Anne Clark and John Giorno were touring with bands, while rock and roll icons like Lydia Lunch, Exene Cervenka and Henry Rollins had all undertaken spoken word tours. Working with a band was one strategy for an artist to reach a larger audience than could be found at a poetry reading.

DAVID GOSSAGE: Clifford Duffy and I basically met in the scene around Bar Saint-Laurent in the early eighties. Stephen Barry was a big figure, there were blues shows and people playing at parties. There were a lot of poets and writers and painters just sitting and talking; it was a much smaller gang of people, it seemed, at that point. Poets

JEAN-PAUL DAOUST: Aux Foufounes Électriques, on a donné une performance où on écrivait des textes à partir de ce que nous inspirait la peinture en direct, réalisée par des peintres comme Bob Desautels, entre autres. Ça, c'était très intéressant. Il y avait vraiment un échange. Alors, un peu à la manière d'un cadavre exquis, je pouvais prendre le texte d'un autre, le continuer, puis il était imprimé, il circulait dans la salle et il était lu. À la fin, il y avait un encan dans lequel des toiles étaient vendues, de même qu'un livre où tous les textes de la soirée avaient été rassemblés. Cet endroit nous permettait, en tant qu'écrivains, d'aller côtoyer d'autres formes d'art en direct.

HÉLÈNE MONETTE: En 1986, on avait écrit une pièce de théâtre collective qu'on avait présentée aux Foufounes Électriques. C'était du théâtre poétique, et il y avait notamment Patricia Lamontagne et Danielle Roger qui avaient participé au projet.

*Rhythm Activism
(from left) Luc Bonin, Sylvain
Côté, Norman Nawrocki*
Photo by Michel Laplante

49 An anarchist café that operated
during the eighties.

are usually the first people to tell you that they're poets (laughs), so Clifford told me he was a poet. Clifford and I were just talking about collaborating one night at Bar Saint-Laurent. I was playing jazz and also writing music for theatre pieces. It's essentially the same sort of thing, from where I come from, putting a backdrop to spoken word.

NORMAN NAWROCKI: In the summer of 1985, somebody told me about a local poet, Peter Bailey. He's a Black poet, originally from Halifax. He was really important to Montreal at that time, in the early eighties. He was doing lots of performance poetry. He was doing work with tapes and loops and things, before other people were doing it. I invited him to my place and we drank beer. He read me his poetry, and I said, "You know, I got some of these things in a shoebox." When I brought them out and started reading he said, "We should do a show together." I woke up the next morning with a terrible hangover and wondered "What have I done?" We went to the Café Commun-Commune,[49] there was a crowd of about thirty people, I got *really* pissed because I had no

idea how I was going to do anything onstage, I had never performed in front of anybody before. And people loved it, they asked me if I had any books or albums or cassettes or videos or whatever, and I'm like, "Holy shit."

Foufounes électriques

In the mid-eighties, many of the new generation of poets, spoken word artists and text-based performance artists performed at Foufounes électriques. Founded in 1983, it was an alternative bar that hosted punk, post-punk and other underground rock bands. It quickly became the central location for local performers to play. Foufounes is still in operation today.

JEAN-PAUL DAOUST: At Foufounes électriques, we gave a performance where we wrote texts inspired by live-action painting by artists like Bob Desautels, among others. This was very interesting, there was really an exchange. In the manner of 'exquisite corpse', I could take somebody else's text, keep working on it, then it got photocopied, it circulated around the room and was read on the spot. At the end there was an auction where the paintings were sold, as well as a book containing all the texts written during the evening. That place allowed us writers to get in touch with other forms of art produced live.

NORMAN NAWROCKI: I got a phone call from somebody who ran the poetry club at McGill who said, "We understand you draw a big crowd and we would like you to perform at the Foufounes électriques with a band." A band!? Luckily I bumped into a friend who played bass and she showed me how to put words to music, she practiced with me for a few weeks, then we did the show at the Foufounes électriques. That was my second show and there were a few hundred people there, and they loved it.

HÉLÈNE MONETTE: In 1986, we presented a collectively-written play at Foufounes électriques. It was poetic theatre. Patricia Lamontagne and Danielle Roger were among the participants.

DAVID GOSSAGE: Foufounes worked out because we had a following of people who came to our show, a literary following. It was funny, because when we played the Foufounes électriques we'd finish early and then all the punks would start coming in *afterwards*. We had a pretty big cross-section of people, but it wasn't the rock scene in the eighties. I was studying music, and the music was all written down, my musicians were always McGill graduates. You'd come in and there'd be music stands!

PETER BRAWLEY: With Ian Stephens reading and Ava Rave and Joy Glidden and all these people, that was a big post-punk scene. The real art-punk vanguard types. They were into spoken word. They did a few performances at Foufounes, and then I started to read with Ian at the Folie Du Large, this crazy obscure nightmare of a place on Bleury. The bathrooms had all the poetry written on the walls, and cheap beer and weirdo people, the whole nine yards. Ian would play. He actually wrote a poem about it, that poem I always read of his, "Stumbled in, sorely sauced, the Folie Du Large."

JOHN GIORNO: One of the great sequence of places to perform in Montreal was Foufounes électriques. I got invited up to do several gigs there, I remember, over the years, with my band. I must've

performed there a half-a-dozen times over a ten year period. I wasn't just coming in to play a gig, the way William Burroughs might. William was invited as a famous artist, or Allen Ginsberg for that matter. But when I was invited, because I wasn't famous, it was more as a poet to participate in what was a larger festival of what was happening in Montreal.

PETER BRAWLEY: Laurie Anderson and Burroughs and Giorno did a tour way back in the early to mid-eighties that really got away from rock and roll and into spoken word. I saw them in New York with that show. It was amazing. It was the first time that I noticed that it had become like a rock show. It was packed, it was at a big rock venue. And Giorno, I couldn't believe how radical he was.

FORTNER ANDERSON: We invited Giorno up a couple of times. He came up twice with his band for the first and second

Alan Lord at Ultimatum, *1985*
Photo courtesy of Ian Ferrier

Ultimatum poetry festivals. Alan Lord worked essentially to put on the first festival, which took place at The Foufounes électriques.[50] *Ultimatum* was interesting because it attempted to put forward

50 May 1 to 5, 1985.

DE NEW-YORK
JOHN GIORNO BAND
$8
11 NOVEMBRE 21H
les Foufounes électriques
97 EST STE-CATHERINE

Monette, setting it up at Le Milieu, which is up on Saint-Laurent, it's been transformed into a Spanish church. It ended up with most of the poets not being paid, and Alan having to move into a one-room apartment on St-André for two years, to hide out from the creditors. It was a complete financial disaster.

NORMAN NAWROCKI: I was in that one, *Ultimatum II*, when the organizer left with all the money. It was a big scandal, everyone wanted to kill him. The cheques for John Giorno bounced and everything else. I took an ad out in the paper to denounce him. There was a lot of shit. That was a real bad period.

Disappointed a Few People

Ian Stephens and his band launched the Disappointed a Few People album in 1986. The name of the band is taken from the title of a poem that appeared in his first chapbook. Although he seriously pursued a career as a musician and lyricist for the next eight years, Stephens never stopped writing poetry.

English and French poets. There were people brought in from Vancouver, New York... it was grandiose, the dream. Psyche Industry Records put out the *Ultimatum* album. Alan and I worked on the *Ultimatum* festivals and events. During the year the focus changed to bringing people up from New York; people like Kathy Acker, David Rattray, and Sylvere Lotringer from Semiotexte publishers. But there was no audience during the year for people like that. We would invite Kathy Acker up to the Foufounes, it would cost several thousand dollars, and thirty people would show up. The second festival, which Alan Lord tried to put on in 1987,[51] was a grandiose event. I worked with Hélène

PETER BRAWLEY: That was really the glory days of the garage scene. Three O'Clock Train and DaFP, the Nils, all that stuff. Ian started to really take off with the DaFP album. Disappointed A Few People. Always a tricky title. With a dead bird logo with the arrow in its heart. They did lots of great stuff with it, they did nice t-shirts and the whole nine yards. Ian's significant other, Alex Espinosa, is also an amazing fashion designer. DaFP once had a huge opening at the Spectrum for the album, and Ian did a whole big glamour rock night. He threw dayglo crucifixes out to the crowd. He had the style of a latter-day svengali with a punk heart of gold, where he

[51] September 11 to 19, 1987.

148

always really looked the part. He and Alex would come in there, and Alex would be carrying his little Pekinese doggie. Ian would have all the clothes for the band, he had that flair of seeing how it all looks. Ian threw everything he had into it. He was on the case twenty-four hours a day, there was nothing like the guy.

IAN FERRIER: I have a copy of a forty-five with a crushed bird on the cover kicking around somewhere. I also remember his Mom talking about how hard it was to boast to her extended family and grandchildren that he'd just done *Fuck With Christ* (laughs).

LYNN SUDERMAN: I knew Ian through the music scene first when he was with DaFP. He was a rather intimidating figure: handsome as anything — all that blond hair — over six feet tall, great build, charismatic performer. Then, off-stage, he was very laid-back. Almost shy. He was curious and focused, and had all the time in the world for everyone.

PETER BRAWLEY: He also brought out a little zine of his own called *La Flèche* with all the crazy ultra-queer collage work all over it. He was quite a collage maniac, also good at design.... I think he was a real pioneer. But I think he had a bit of a nihilist streak, Ian. He didn't have the kind of faith I have, but he had an incredible faith in what he was doing. I think he was a kind of latter-day Gestaltist, he loved to just get out there and do it.

(above) DaFP launch poster
(below right) Ian Stephens performs at DaFP launch
Both courtesy of Alex Espinosa

La Flèche chapbook by Ian Stephens
Courtesy of Peter Brawley

Part 5. THE *GAZ MOUTARDE* GENERATION

NANCY LABONTÉ: C'est Jean-Sébastien Huot qui a été le fondateur de *Gaz Moutarde*, en 1989. Jean-Sébastien était alors étudiant au cégep et il avait 17, 18 ans. Comme il écrivait de la poésie et qu'il était très attiré par la contre-culture, il avait décidé de faire une petite revue de poésie, tout seul – en fait c'était plutôt une plaquette qui rassemblait quelques-uns de ses poèmes et qu'il avait fait circuler parmi ses amis. Quand on l'a vue, ça nous a donné l'envie de faire une vraie revue de poésie. La plaquette de Jean-Sébastien a été le numéro zéro de *Gaz Moutarde*. Ensuite un des professeurs de Jean-Sébastien, Mario Cholette, avait été très intéressé par ce qu'il avait fait et il s'est joint à lui pour débloquer des fonds auprès de la direction du cégep afin de soutenir la revue. À partir du numéro deux, le cégep supportait *Gaz Moutarde* en mettant à notre disposition les presses, le papier fluo, et l'infrastructure. Puis ils nous ont prêté une salle pour faire le lancement du premier numéro. On vendait de la bière de courtoisie, ce qui nous permettait d'amasser un peu d'argent pour payer l'envoi de communiqués de presse et la distribution. Tranquillement, on s'organisait, et ça allait bien. Pour le numéro deux, le lancement s'était tenu aux Foufounes Électriques mais dès le numéro trois, le lancement a eu lieu au cégep du Vieux-Montréal, où environ 200 personnes sont venues. Beaucoup de poètes y étaient, dont Gaston Miron, Paul Chamberland et Bruno Roy, puis certains ont par la suite commencé à publier dans *Gaz Moutarde*, comme Denis Vanier et Josée Yvon. Dans les numéros suivants, on a eu toujours une tête d'affiche de la scène de la poésie québécoise. Et à chaque numéro qui sortait, on organisait 'des gros lancements', et il y avait toujours plein de monde du milieu littéraire. C'était des lectures qui commençaient à 19 h et qui se terminaient quand les gardiens de sécurité nous sortaient (rires).

En général, le maître de cérémonie était Mario Cholette qui avait peut-être 28, 29 ans quand *Gaz Moutarde* est né, et il était vraiment dans le mouvement avec nous. Le groupe comportait des gens de deux générations.

En août 1990, il n'y avait toujours pas de *Nuit de la poésie* de prévue.

"It was explosive"

After the failure of Ultimatum II, *any sense of a cohesive spoken word scene had largely ceased to exist. The following eight years, from 1986 to 1994, were characterized by fragmentation. In the eighties, young francophone writers were less interested in performance; many of them were publishing narrative works instead. Individual performers and small groups practiced here and there, somewhat like the rise of city states in Europe after the fall of the Roman Empire. The most successful of these groups in that era was a new generation of francophone poets that sprang into being, bonded together by the grassroots poetry zine* Gaz Moutarde.

NANCY LABONTÉ: Jean-Sébastien Huot was the founder of *Gaz Moutarde* in 1989. He was a college student of about seventeen or eighteen. He wrote poetry and was very attracted to the counter-culture, so he decided to produce a little publication all by himself — actually it was more like a booklet with some of his poems in it which he circulated among his friends. When we saw it, it made us feel like producing a real poetry review. So Jean-Sébastien's booklet became issue number zero of *Gaz Moutarde*. Then one of Jean-Sébastien's teachers, Mario Cholette, was very interested in what he'd done, and joined forces with him to get some funds from the Cégep administration to help our publication. So starting with the second issue, the college supported *Gaz Moutarde*, by making the presses available to us, the dayglo paper, and the infrastructure. Then they let us have a room to hold the first launch in. We had beer company sponsorship, which allowed us to collect a bit of money to pay for things such as sending press releases and distribution. Slowly we got organized, things were going well. For the second issue, the launch was held at Foufounes électriques. But starting with number three the launch was held at *Cégep du Vieux-Montréal*, and about 200 people came. There were lots of poets there, such as Gaston Miron, Paul Chamberland and Bruno Roy, and some of them started publishing in *Gaz Moutarde*, like Denis Vanier and Josée Yvon. So in the following issues, we always had a big name on the Quebec poetry scene. We held mega-launches for each issue, and they were always packed with Montreal literary people. The readings went on forever — we'd start at 7:00 PM and stop when the security guards threw us out (laughs).

The MC was usually Mario Cholette, who was about twenty-eight or twenty-nine when *Gaz Moutarde* was born, and he was totally into it with us. The group included people from two generations.

In 1980, Jean-Claude Labrecque had made a second Nuit de la poésie *film. However, Nancy Labonté describes how it took the enthusiasm of the* Gaz Moutarde *poets to inspire the filmmaker to make a third film in 1991.*

NANCY LABONTÉ: By August 1990, there were still no plans for a *Nuit de la poésie 1990*. Nobody had thought of organizing it, and we decided there had to be one in September. We rented the Lion d'or, which at the time wasn't a popular place to have shows in yet…. It hadn't been used for shows for about five years, it was really dusty. So we had to do a big clean-up, but we did get it for 300 dollars.

Then a girl who was working in cinema came to set up the stage, she'd designed a really solid set. The show featured the *Gaz Moutarde* crew, in addition to the usual group of francophone readers you'd see everywhere, and also some young ones who were new on the scene. In all there were about thirty poets. CIBL community radio was also in on it — they broadcast the show live.

VICTORIA STANTON: So the event was organized by *Gaz Moutarde*?

NANCY LABONTÉ: More or less. In fact, it was me and Pierre Bastien, who's now with *Exit*, who sort of kick-started the project. Bastien hadn't published in *Gaz Moutarde* yet but he'd become friends with the group. He was a bit older than us, a filmmaker, and he was the one who convinced us to organize *La Nuit de la poésie 1990*. During the time we were organizing it, sending press releases, selling tickets, etc., Jean-Claude Labrecque, who had filmed *La Nuit de la poésie* in 1970 and in 1980, started organizing his own *Nuit de la poésie 1990*. So obviously we rebelled against him, and in the end we won, he changed all his posters and then he made *La Nuit de la poésie 1991* (laughs)! And *Gaz Moutarde* was invited to take part in this big poetry event, but not the whole group. Only two people were chosen — Jean-Sébastien, who founded the publication, and me because I was 'the girl' in the group. This happened often when *Gaz Moutarde* was invited; either the whole gang could go together, with Mario

Cholette and David Hince, which was perfect, or only two of us, and it was always the girl and the founder (laughs) …. So obviously it was problematic.

And during that famous evening, that's exactly what happened. We were getting something like a hundred dollars each — the *Union des artistes* fee — to make a public appearance and be filmed by the NFB. And because of the honoraria, invitations were limited. Mario and David were angry because once again they hadn't been invited…. Finally, the wave broke and the whole group went up onstage. It was about 2:00 AM, everybody was drunk, stoned, we were all completely wound up because of the situation. Plus, because the show was being put on film, the whole evening had been run like clockwork. Labrecque allowed five or three minutes per poet, no more. And when somebody went overtime, he'd literally go up and get them off stage. He even interrupted Josée Yvon and Janou St-Denis, living monuments of Quebec poetry. True, both women read for a long time, but they deserved respect! So

Gaz Moutarde #6
cover art by Eric Godin, 1991

Personne n'avait pensé à en organiser une, et nous on avait décidé qu'en septembre, il fallait qu'il y en ait une. On a donc loué le Lion d'Or qui, à l'époque, n'était pas encore une salle populaire pour faire des spectacles… Quand on l'a loué, ça faisait environ cinq ans qu'il n'y avait pas eu de spectacle, c'était tout poussiéreux. On avait donc dû faire le grand ménage de la salle, mais on l'avait eue pour à peine 300 dollars!

Puis une fille qui travaillait en cinéma était venue monter la scène, elle avait conçu un décor vraiment solide. Le spectacle mettait en scène toute l'équipe de *Gaz Moutarde*, en plus de la brochette classique des lecteurs francophones qu'on voyait toujours, et aussi quelques jeunes nouveaux dans le milieu. Au total, l'événement devait réunir une trentaine de poètes. On avait aussi mis CIBL dans le coup — la station avait retransmis le spectacle en direct sur ses ondes.

VICTORIA STANTON: Donc l'événement avait été organisé par *Gaz Moutarde*?

NANCY LABONTÉ: Plus ou moins. En fait, c'est moi et Pierre Bastien, qui est maintenant lié à *Exit*, qui avions donné le coup d'envoi au projet. À l'époque, Bastien n'avait pas encore publié dans *Gaz Moutarde*, mais il était devenu ami avec le groupe. Il était un peu plus vieux que nous, et c'était un cinéaste, puis c'est lui qui, à un certain moment, nous a convaincus que nous devrions organiser la *Nuit de la poésie 1990*. Il en a été le catalyseur. Puis pendant qu'on était en train d'organiser l'événement et qu'on commençait à envoyer des communiqués de presse, à vendre des billets, etc., Jean-Claude Labrecque, qui avait filmé les *Nuits de la poésie* en 1970 et 1980, a commencé à organiser sa propre *Nuit de la poésie 1990*. Alors évidemment on s'est insurgé contre lui, et finalement on a gagné, il a changé toutes ses affiches puis il a fait la *Nuit de la poésie 1991* (rires)! Et *Gaz Moutarde* a été invité à participer à cette grosse nuit de la poésie, mais pas toute l'équipe. Seulement deux personnes avaient été choisies, dont Jean-Sébastien, le fondateur de la revue, et puis moi, parce que j'étais 'la fille' du groupe. Cette situation arrivait souvent dans des soirées où *Gaz Moutarde* était invité; soit on pouvait

continued…

y aller tout le groupe ensemble, avec Mario Cholette et David Hince, ce qui était parfait, soit seulement deux personnes du groupe étaient invitées, et c'étaient toujours la fille puis le fondateur (rires)... Alors évidemment, c'était problématique.

Et lors de cette fameuse soirée, c'est justement ce qui s'est passé. Je pense qu'on recevait 100 dollars chacun – le cachet de l'Union des artistes – pour faire une présentation publique et être filmés par l'ONF et à cause du cachet, les invitations étaient limitées. Et Mario et David étaient fâchés parce qu'une fois encore ils n'avait pas été invités... Finalement, la vague a déferlé, puis toute l'équipe de *Gaz Moutarde* est débarquée sur la scène. Il était peut-être 2 h du matin, tout le monde était saoul, tout le monde avait fumé, on était tous crinqués à cause de cette histoire. Et de surcroît, comme le spectacle était filmé, toute la soirée était très chronométrée. Labrecque allouait trois minutes par poète, pas plus. Et quand quelqu'un dépassait son temps, il allait carrément le chercher sur la scène pour le sortir. Ainsi, il a même été jusqu'à interrompre Josée Yvon et Janou St-Denis, des monuments de la poésie québécoise. Elles lisaient longtemps, j'en conviens, sauf que c'étaient quand même des personnes à respecter! Tout ça a fait qu'il y a eu une espèce de mouvement de hargne et de ressentiment en coulisses, puis à un certain moment, ça a éclaté. Nous, quand on est débarqués sur la scène, ç'a vraiment eu l'effet d'une bombe au gaz moutarde (rires). C'était l'enfer! Mario Cholette s'est presque complètement déshabillé pendant que tout le monde lisait en même temps. Il y avait même des gens dans l'assistance qui couraient dans les allées en gueulant de la poésie. Ç'a dégénéré en un super spectacle dada-anarchique (rires)! Puis là, on a voulu nous sortir et on a résisté! Et c'est comme ça, à cause de notre rage, que s'est construite la 'légende' de *Gaz Moutarde* !...

Après cet événement, quand on nous invitait dans des lectures ou des festivals, les organisateurs s'attendaient à ce qu'on sème un peu la pagaille (rires). Et quand on ne le faisait pas, les gens étaient un peu déçus. Alors ils nous payaient plein d'alcool pour qu'on soit saouls et qu'on se mette à délirer. Ça, c'étaient les belles années de *Gaz Moutarde*. *Gaz Moutarde* était devenu une image.... C'était explosif. On aime beaucoup la poésie, mais on aime aussi s'amuser. Moi, j'adore la

all of this created a groundswell of animosity and resentment backstage, and at one point it all came to a head. When we hit the stage, it was just like a mustard gas explosion (laughs). It was hell! Mario Cholette got almost completely undressed, everybody was reading at the same time, there were people in the audience running around shouting poetry. It degenerated into some kind of Dada-anarchist super-spectacle (laughs)! And then they wanted to get us off the stage and we resisted. So the 'legend' of *Gaz Moutarde* grew out of our rage!

The impact of the Gaz Moutarde gang on Nuit de la poésie 91 made them a popular attraction in the Québécois poetry scene. Naturally, this popularity caused the initially incendiary scene to become more and more established.

NANCY LABONTÉ: After that, whenever we were invited to readings or festivals, organizers sort of expected us to cause a stir (laughs). When we didn't, people were disappointed. So they'd buy us tons of drinks to get us drunk and out of control. Those were the good old days of *Gaz Moutarde*.... *Gaz Moutarde* had become an image, it was explosive. We love poetry but also we love to have fun. I adore poetry, but every time I go to a *soirée de poésie* I find it really dull. With *Gaz Moutarde*, you had to be noisy, and it was great fun.

Then, as soon as nobody in the group was still in college — I wasn't in college when I joined the group anyway — we started asking for grants. When we started getting them, we continued producing issues the same way, and things started going downhill. The atmosphere was dif-

Gaz Moutarde #5
cover art by SAMOVAR, 1990

ferent. We had to make financial reports, we'd get to meetings feeling not necessarily in the mood.... We'd smoke pot, drink, we didn't give a damn about numbers. And we weren't getting along, some wanted the review to continue being photocopied while others preferred glossy paper, so we started quarreling.

I think things really started to degenerate when we went to glossy paper. Jean-Sébastien Huot was really the spirit of *Gaz Moutarde*, he had founded the movement, he was the core of the team. But when the review changed format, even he felt like he was falling into a black pit. From then on we couldn't go back, we were sort of stuck in a mould. He left the group and it was like a suicide, the group dissolved.

Ever since the *Gaz Moutarde* adventure, poetry readings have proliferated on the francophone side. Sometimes I feel like we democratized poetry, we brought it closer to people. During the *Gaz Moutarde* years, Jean-Sébastien Huot barely knew how to write — he'd bring us his texts written phonetically, with no verb agreements, words missing, it was nuts. But *that* was poetry, *that* was *Gaz Moutarde*. Even though the poetry was written, it had an oral aspect.

PATRICIA LAMONTAGNE: I think that, on the francophone side, a stronger desire to do performance emerged thanks to *Gaz Moutarde*. I worked with them a bit, José Acquelin and Pierre Bastien. They all had a very unique relationship with the stage, a little aggressive sometimes. It was really rebellion, revolt. Very few of those poets ever read, and if they did, they'd perform as well.

poésie, mais chaque fois que je vais dans une soirée de poésie, je trouve ça vraiment plate. Avec *Gaz Moutarde*, il fallait faire du bruit, il fallait que ça bouge, et c'était plaisant.

Puis à partir du moment où il n'y a plus eu personne du groupe au cégep – d'ailleurs, moi, je n'étais pas au cégep quand je suis entrée dans le groupe – on a demandé des subventions. Lorsqu'on a commencé à en recevoir, on a continué à faire des numéros de cette manière, puis ça s'est mis à moins bien fonctionner. L'ambiance était très différente. Il fallait faire des rapports financiers, et on arrivait au meeting plus ou moins disposés… On fumait du pot, on buvait, on s'en foutait, nous, d'écrire des chiffres. Et puis on ne s'entendait plus, certains voulaient que la revue continue d'être photocopiée, d'autres préféraient qu'elle soit imprimée sur papier glacé, alors la chicane a éclaté.

Je pense que c'est quand la revue est passée au papier glacé que ça a réellement commencé à dégénérer. C'était vraiment Jean-Sébastien Huot qui était l'esprit de *Gaz Moutarde*, c'est lui qui avait fondé le mouvement, et c'était lui le noyau de l'équipe. Et même lui, quand la revue a changé de format, il a eu l'impression de tomber dans un entonnoir. À partir de cet instant, on ne pouvait plus retourner en arrière, on était comme pris dans un moule. Alors il a quitté le groupe, et ç'a vraiment été comme un suicide. C'est là qu'on s'est dissous.

Depuis l'épopée de *Gaz Moutarde*, du côté francophone, les lectures de poésie pullulent. Parfois j'ai l'impression qu'on a démocratisé la poésie, qu'on l'a aidée à devenir plus près du peuple. À l'époque de *Gaz Moutarde,* Jean-Sébastien Huot savait à peine écrire et quand il nous remettait ses poèmes, c'était écrit au son, sans accords de verbes, parfois il manquait des mots, ça n'avait pas d'allure. Mais c'était ça, la poésie, c'était ça, *Gaz Moutarde*. Même si la poésie était écrite, elle avait un caractère oral.

PATRICIA LAMONTAGNE: Je pense que là où on a vraiment senti du côté francophone une volonté plus claire de faire de la performance, c'est à partir de ce que présentait l'équipe de *Gaz Moutarde*, avec qui j'ai travaillé un peu, comme José Acquelin et Pierre Bastien. Tous ces gens avaient un rapport très unique avec la scène, un peu agressif, parfois. C'était vraiment la rébellion, la révolte. Et parmi tous ces poètes, très peu de gens lisaient, et s'ils lisaient, ils donnaient quand même une performance.

Gaz Moutarde #16
cover art by
Mathieu Beauséjour, 1993

Text by Nancy Labonté

Part 6. THE DORMANT GENERATION

"In my gang of friends"

"Dans ma gang d'amis"

GENEVIÈVE LETARTE: Dans mon groupe d'amis d'Ambiancess magnétiques, personne ne côtoyait d'anglophones. . Jamais. Puis la situation a changé doucement quand j'ai eu un copain anglophone... Quand j'ai commencé à sortir avec lui, mes amis trouvaient ça étrange, c'était vraiment une affaire bien nouvelle dans mon entourage. Et comme mon copain était aussi un artiste, il connaissait également des gens dans le mileu. Ça m'a permis de découvrir un autre monde, tranquillement. Je peux dire que jusqu'à ce que je rencontre cette personne, je ne connaissais à peu près pas les écrivains anglophones. Et la scène spoken word, pour moi, ça n'évoquait absolument rien.

PATRICIA LAMONTAGNE: En 1985, à 25 ans, j'ai fait ma première performance à l'occasion d'un spectacle pour *La Semaine des périodiques culturels*; cinq revues littéraires présentaient chacune cinq poètes, et moi je passais à la toute fin. Il y avait des poètes très connus à l'époque – Charron, Roy, etc. – et tous arrivaient avec leur feuille à la main, et ils récitaient. Moi, personne ne me connaissait, ou très peu, car j'avais quand même déjà publié dans des revues. Et après ma performance, j'ai eu une ovation debout! Sur le coup je ne comprenais pas cette réaction, mais aujourd'hui, avec le recul, je pense que c'est parce que j'étais venue combler un besoin. Les gens étaient ouverts, ils étaient prêts à ce qu'on leur présente autre chose. Alors moi je suis arrivée, puis j'étais en rupture très radicale, je pense, avec les baby-boomers, les poètes de la maison d'édition Les Herbes rouges. Mais Jean-Paul Daoust avait aussi une certaine volonté de présenter quelque chose de différent, et je crois qu'il a développé ça, justement, par la suite. Cela dit, même dans les années 80, je ne trouve pas qu'il y a eu une grande évolution en ce sens. Il y a eu Pauline Harvey et certaines autres petites tentatives, mais sans plus.

After the collapse of the rock club scene in the mid-eighties, the problems facing spoken word performers and poets multiplied. They operated in small pockets, each isolated by particular issues of language, race, politics, lack of support or recognition by the traditional arts establishment, and the lack of event organizers committed to the form.

HUGH HAZELTON: When I came to Montreal I got to know Latin-Americans, because I worked as a translator. And then I started reading with them, because I often wrote in Spanish. So, basically, I started reading with them rather than with anglophones or even francophones. I'd been reading at Janou St-Denis' *Place aux poètes*. That goes back to, I don't know, 1986, 1987. Janou had been doing that for all those years... she would have open mic after the read-

Hugh Hazelton, May 12, 1999

ings, and she was real friendly to the Latin-Americans. About twice a year she would ask us to organize a Latin-American night, we'd have to read half in French and half in Spanish.

GENEVIÈVE LETARTE: In my gang of friends from *Ambiances magnétiques*, nobody hung out with anglophones. Never. The situation changed when I got an anglophone boyfriend.... When I started going out with him, my friends found it strange, it was really something very new in my circle. And given that my boyfriend was an artist too, he also knew people in the milieu. Over time, this allowed me to discover another world. Until I met this person I barely knew any anglophone writers, except the very well-known ones. And the spoken word scene meant nothing to me.

PATRICIA LAMONTAGNE: In 1985, at twenty-five, I did my first performance for the show during *La Semaine des périodiques culturels*; five literary periodicals each presented five poets. I was on at the very end. There were some very well-known poets — Charron, Roy, etc. — and they all came with text in hand and read. Nobody knew me, or just a little, as I had already published in a few periodicals. After my performance, I got a standing ovation! I didn't understand this reaction at the time, but today, with the distance, I think it's because I filled a need. People were open, ready for something else. I came along and was making a radical break, I believe, with the baby-boomers, the *Herbes rouges* poets. But Jean-Paul Daoust also had a certain desire to present something different, and I think he developed this afterwards. This being said, even in the eighties, I don't feel there was much evolution in that direction. There was Pauline Harvey and a few other brief attempts, but nothing more.

NORMAN NAWROCKI: It was in the mid-eighties, from 1985 on, that I became a part of the 'scene', so-to-speak. But I was never really inside, I was always on the outside. If that scene was marginalized, because of what it was, then the work I was doing with Sylvain Côté and other people, was outside of that even. We were marginalized on that margin because our work was 'political', and it wasn't straight poetry either. People couldn't really put a finger on us.

In the mid-eighties, Jillian DeGannes, Dee Smith, Amuna Baraka and Tisca Pratt got together during a summer writing workshop, and performed at the Montreal Afro Festival. At the time, tensions were growing in the Black community, with the shooting of Anthony Griffin and other Black youth by the Montreal police. Tensions peaked when Marcellus François was killed. Students formed AKAX, a militant protest group that included dub poet Michael Pintard in its ranks. Pintard joined DeGannes, Smith, Baraka, Pratt, and Anthony Bansfield to form the Diasporic African Poets, a troupe that performed frequently at community events.

ANTHONY BANSFIELD: I moved to Montreal in 1986. At that time, I was living out at NDG, and there were these guys living in the same building as me, who became the rap group Shades of Culture, Justin and Orion. Those guys were doing some interesting stuff, and we would just sit back and listen to records. I had a little poem I did for them one day, and they said, "Oh yeah,

that's good. You should do some more of that." It was like hip-hop poetry, so they enjoyed it. I guess it was at that point that I started to do it in public. When I was at Concordia, I bumped into a group of people who had a little poetry group that they were forming, the Diasporic African Poets, so they asked me if I'd like to come. Michael Pintard was the guy that started that. In the beginning, we were doing these poems that were associated with a political purpose. Some might call it agit-prop. Then, some of the stuff was on themes of love and relationships, and some were funny, not all of them had a political purpose to them, or a point that was overt. I don't think at that time there was really a spoken word scene. I don't think that term had really begun to be used that much when I was doing stuff. But we knew that there were Black people doing interesting poetry. I saw it as doing some performance poetry, and doing some rapping.

"There wasn't really a spoken word scene per se"

Venues available to performers were few and far between. The idea of performance of texts had faded away in (white) anglophone circles to some extent, while poetry readings remained in traditional spaces or were closely tied to McGill and Concordia universities. Todd Swift exhibited a prescient sense of the importance of bringing writers out of academia and into the streets of Montreal when he inaugurated The New McGill Reading Series. *The Folk Night series at Reggie's Pub in Concordia's Hall Building was another regular venue where young musicians, poets and spoken word artists like Will Kenny, Leah Libin, and Torrey Pass could test the stage.*

Poster for New McGill Reading Series by Billy Mavreas

155

The Yellow Door Coffeehouse, established in the early sixties, had an ecumenical atmosphere which lent spoken word artists a venue during these lean years. Jeremiah Wall's poetry and performance events at Hillel House were small-scale, but it was through his efforts that a number of writers and artists, including Golda Fried and Victoria Stanton, had a place to develop their skills before emerging as key players when the Montreal spoken word scene rose like a phoenix in 1994.

TODD SWIFT: I first became aware that little was happening on the reading scene in Montreal in 1987. I had been in Belfast to research a book called *Map-Makers' Colours*. What struck me was just how much the poets there were part of a community. When I came back, I wanted to start a reading series. There had been no hipster reading series in Montreal that also connected with the 'high art' crowd. At that point Bill Furey and I, with Graham Finlay, were very much inspired by what Louis Dudek had done in the forties with his *McGill Reading Series*. We looked for a venue. At first we had the Alley at McGill — I was a Concordia student, but I'd want-

ed to call it *The New McGill Reading Series* to refer to Dudek's series — but we quickly thought it would be better to put it on the Main. To me it is the central mythic place for literature in the city. So we did one year at Antigone, and another year at Bistro Duluth, which was just off the Main. These were wildly successful events, even by today's standards, in the sense that, even in the dead of winter, easily 200 people would come. Interestingly enough, the poster-maker for the series was Billy Mavreas, who of course later worked with Jake Brown and *YAWP!* It is important to recall how significant my actions were at this time — how unsettling and establishing to the anglo community; since I was openly and loudly driven to create an English Quebec Literary Renaissance modeled on the work of Yeats, and fueled by Pound's tactics. Since that time many of my ideas have become commonplace: that Montreal was a scene like Berlin or San Francisco, for instance; that cabarets should feature poetry. We had a lot of really fine writers at that point, people like Michael Ondaatje. *NMRS* also featured playwrights and novelists, like Tomson Highway and Neil Bisoondath. And we had support from the Canada Council. The philosophy then, as it is now, for me, was to have a very famous or well known writer and then an emerging or very young writer on the same bill, each given equal time. So that went on for about three years.

JUSTIN MCGRAIL: The first time I ever read poetry was at Reggie's bar in Concordia during the *Folk Night* happy hour thing. I was the only poet, I read three poems and they dug it! I got beers bought for me, whoo! This was the whole drinking poet thing, when I was still drinking.

Todd Swift reads at Reggie's for Writes of Spring, 1990
Photo courtesy of the artist

VICTORIA STANTON: At Reggie's, most people who went up with their poetry stood where the microphone was, which was at the side of the stage, reading in a quivering voice, and everyone was drunk and no one would listen. And this infuriated me, infuriated me! So after going for a couple of months, I memorized one of my pieces and I went there and I was so nervous. I got up onstage. I said, "First of all, I'm not using the microphone, and I'm not gonna stand on the side of the stage, I'm gonna stand in the centre of the stage." I started to talk, and people were still chattering. I just stood there really quietly, then I said, "I have something important to tell you!" This woman up at the front of the stage said, "You really need attention, don't you?" I said to her, "Why else does anybody get up onstage?" So I did this piece, and people listened! I realized at that moment that this is what gets people's attention. You know your piece and you perform your piece and people will listen.

LEE GOTHAM: In the late summer of 1989, I quickly got myself involved in the publishing and editing of a literary journal, *Pawn To Infinity*, and the first readings I was doing here in town were at places like The Yellow Door. There wasn't really a spoken word scene per se. After finishing up my degree I went straight back to my old habit, travelling around the world. And only after three more years of that rhythm, did I get the notion to start up a more animated performative series.

VICTORIA STANTON: There were the writing workshops at The New School[52] facilitated by a fellow student, and that's where I started writing on a semi-regular basis.... My first public reading

was actually an open mic at the Yellow Door in 1989, while I was at The New School.

ANTHONY BANSFIELD: The one show I put together, back when we were doing our stuff with the DAP, was at the Yellow Door (laughs). I always wanted to do a show at the Yellow Door. It had such magic to it, and it was a nice little show we did down there. It wasn't a huge show, but people really enjoyed it. That was 1989, 1990. That was the kind of thing that you associated with a poetry space, but otherwise you were just anywhere.

JEREMIAH WALL: When I came back from the States in 1987, I found the poetry scene was mostly just readings. I began shortly thereafter to [organize] a reading here and there. The scene was not traditionally in bars at that time. It was really galleries. Places like Gallery Sekai down in St-Henri or Café Prague, on Bishop Street. There was always an energy around, it wasn't so much where you'd go as what had been there only ten or twenty years before.

Hillel House had this concert series for many years, they had a coffee house called *The Golem*. The Yellow Door always had literature and folk music. So I thought because I did both that it would be good to have both, to have beat-style coffee houses where you knew there'd be the bongo guy and people doing the stuff. And I tried to do that at Hillel for several years. I probably did fifteen to twenty shows there. *Dracaena* magazine started when Karen Reynard met me at Hillel and I'd just done a show, so I'd say I did the first few shows in 1988 and 1989, and by 1990 was calling it *Café Vilna*.

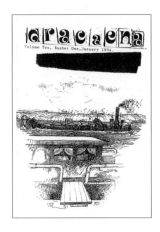

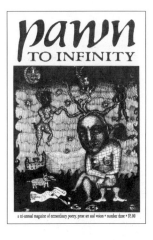

52 An alternative educational program at Dawson College.

"Une belle collaboration"

D. KIMM: Le premier spectacle que j'ai fait, c'était *Chevale*, en 1990. Je n'avais aucune formation, je m'étais lancée dans le projet tête baissée. Mon texte était écrit, et je voulais en faire un spectacle. J'ai commencé par demander à Pierre St-Jak – qui est un très grand musicien – s'il voulait travailler avec moi. Je pensais qu'il refuserait, étant donné qu'il ne me connaissait pas, mais il a accepté. Ensuite j'ai demandé une bourse, et je l'ai obtenue. Puis j'ai demandé l'aide d'un producteur, et je l'ai eue aussi. Tout le monde acceptait mes requêtes, alors j'étais obligée d'aller de l'avant... Mais à chaque fois, j'espérais que quelqu'un me dise non.... Finalement, c'est donc arrivé un peu par hasard, tout ça.

HÉLÈNE MONETTE: J'ai rencontré le musicien Bob Olivier vers 1990. Et ç'a été le début d'une belle et importante collaboration puisque depuis ce temps, on n'a jamais arrêté de travailler ensemble. Bob est très polyvalent, il s'adapte facilement aux gens. Et comme il a déjà été dans des groupes rock, il sait occuper le devant d'une scène, il est plein d'énergie. Alors il m'accompagne tandis que je chante. J'ai également travaillé avec un autre de mes amis, Max – Marcel Décoste – avec qui c'était complètement le contraire. Max est un chansonnier qui s'est produit dans les bars partout en province, et avec lui, on composait les chansons ensemble pour que lui les chante.

J'ai aussi travaillé avec Sylvie Chenard deux ou trois fois. À la blague, on se faisait des gageures. Par exemple, dans un party, sur un coup de tête, on s'est dit: "OK, on monte un spectacle." Et c'est ainsi qu'on s'était *bookées* au Bistro 4, en novembre 1992. Danielle Bérard jouait de la batterie, moi je chantais, et Sylvie était la *lead* guitare, c'était elle qui coordonnait la musique.

"A fine collaboration"

The performing of texts remained as much a rarity in the francophone milieu as in the anglophone. Geneviève Letarte continued working with her 'gang d'amis' at Ambiances magnétiques, and released an album, Vous seriez un ange, *in 1992. Hélène Monette was writing and performing, and in 1990 D. Kimm was able to mount a one-person show, her first. It is interesting that, while these three women were something of an anomaly in the francophone arts community, their work was supported financially and artistically, nonetheless.*

D. KIMM: My first show was *Chevale*, in 1990. I had no training, I threw myself into the project head first. My text was written and I wanted to turn it into a show. I started by asking Pierre St-Jak — who's a great musician — if he wanted to work with me. I thought he'd refuse, because he didn't know me, but he agreed. Then I asked for a grant and I got it. Then I asked a producer for help and got this too. Everybody was saying yes to me so I had to go forward... but each time I asked I was hoping somebody would say no.... So it all happened a bit by chance.

HÉLÈNE MONETTE: I met musician Bob Olivier in about 1990. It was the beginning of a fine and important collaboration, we've never stopped working together since then. Bob is very versatile, he adapts to people easily. And he's been in rock bands so he knows how to command the front of a stage, he's full of energy. So he plays while I sing. I've also worked with another friend, Max — Marcel Décoste — with whom it's the opposite. Max is a songwriter who's played in bars throughout the province; with him, we wrote songs together for him to sing.

I also worked with Sylvie Chénard two or three times. We used to make bets, as a joke. For example, at a party, on a whim, we said: "OK, we're giving a show." This is how we booked ourselves into Bistro 4, in November 1992. Danielle Bérard played drums, I sang, and Sylvie was lead guitar, she coordinated the music.

D.Kimm
Photo by Eva Quintas

Up and Down The Main

In the early nineties, English spoken word performance — including poetry reading — was beginning to happen on or near St. Laurent Boulevard. The Off The Boulevard *series presented readings by Ian Stephens, Peter Brawley, Bill Furey and Darius James, among others. It started in the old Powerhouse Gallery space on St. Dominique, and later moved to Stornoway Gallery on Bleury. Two important venues, the Café Phoenix, a vegetarian co-operative restaurant, and Bistro 4, a small café, began hosting sporadic poetry readings and small musical events. From the beginning, Bistro 4 offered its space to both francophone and anglophone event organizers for free. In addition, poets, rappers and hip-hop artists began practicing their art at acid jazz events organized by District 6 at upscale clubs like Savoy and DiSalvio's. Interest in people performing their texts seemed to be on the rise again. In December 1992, about a year after finishing* The New McGill Reading Series, *Todd Swift organized a marathon poetry reading on the Main.*

TODD SWIFT: *Capacity 101* it was called, for political reasons, but also because that WAS the real seating capacity of the venue, Hell's Kitchen. I organized it with un-sung genius Daniel C. Mitchell. It is still one of the great moments in Canadian literary history. We had over thirty poets perform, including four Governor General's winners, plus a jazz band, for over twelve hours.

District 6 produced the Round Midnight *acid jazz nights on a weekly basis. For a time, Swift got star billing, and the series offered a new opportunity for*

Maxianne Berger
Cathy A. Coley
Deborah Eibel
Endre Farkas
Doug Isaac
Jim Infantino
Steve Luxton
Phil Moscovitch
Ryk Mcintyre
Mary di Michelle
Erin Mouré
William Neale
Esther Ross
Robyn Sarah
Eric Sigler
Todd Swift
& more ...

Capacity 101

Live Readings
Live Jazz
Open-mike Contest
Book Giveaways
Cheap Beer
& The World's
Most Lyrical
Band

An Illustration of Jazz & Poetry

Wednesday, December 2, 1992
2$ 7:00 pm   12:00 pm
Hell's Kitchen, 4650 St. Laurent

spoken word artists to perform with musical backing.

TODD SWIFT: I first started working with music, and a stage setting, when I met Tom Walsh in 1992. I did some gigs for him at Club DiSalvio, *Round Midnight*, and got to work with great jazz / soul singers, rappers, DJs and other musicians. People danced to my poems. This turned into Swifty Lazarus, which has been Tom's and my pet project.

DAVID GOSSAGE: When we were doing the *Round Midnight* things in the nineties, we had a lot of people come up and do poetry. There were DJs, there would always be a DJ scratcher who would spin discs and scratch. Usually two rappers, and myself and whoever happened to come on. There would usually be a saxophone player, often a percussionist. The cool thing about that was it became much more of a spoken word thing. I don't think Victor Schiffman[53] knew that *Round Midnight* was going to be so much of a rap, poetry thing. They had intended it as an acid jazz thing, but the rappers are rabid. If there's anybody in the room who's into the culture,

Poster for a reading at the Café Phoenix, 1992

53 Victor Schiffman was a producer for District 6.

159

the audience beforehand, to give them some cultural or historical reference to what we were doing. That worked out really well, and became very spoken word. It was like the fifties, because it was a jazz group underneath and the guys rapping. The only difference was this time the musicians were white and the rappers were Black (laughs). It used to be the other way around!

"We were in our last phases"

In 1993, Toronto's dub poetry scene was booming. Members of the Diasporic African Poets, notably Michael Pintard and Anthony Bansfield, soon decided to move there in a search of greener pastures for their skills.

they're jumping up onstage. *Round Midnight* was at DiSalvio's, too, so that was kind of a strange thing to have there, to have all these rappers in, and the beautiful people on one side going, "What is this? I think it's cool, is it cool?" Basically scaring them. It stayed at DiSalvio's for two years, and it switched over to *Squeeze — So What* at Metropolis. When we did *Squeeze*, we had line-ups of guys to get up and rap. Bang-bang-bang, it was incredible. Spoken word can have a life of its own. If people who don't have anywhere to do it find venues to do it, it can take over. It's pretty infectious for the people who have it — there's a disease analogy there somewhere — literally, the rap scene would get bigger and bigger every week.

One of the nicest things we did with the *Round Midnight — So What* thing is we went to Ottawa and did the jazz festival there. We had a bad experience at the Quebec jazz festival, people didn't know what the hell it was. Literally, the audience left. We were still booked to do Ottawa, so we tried to explain it to

ANTHONY BANSFIELD: You had dub poetry coming on the scene, and Lillian Allen in Toronto, and Clifton Joseph and Michael St. George. Pintard set something up and eventually we hooked up with them. Meeting them and working with them was another layer for us, another level. Because we had been meeting as a group and just doing our poetry, just talking to each other and talking over ideas. When The Diasporic African Poets met the Toronto dub poets, the next thing was to perform at an international dub poetry festival. The dub poetry festival was 1993, in Toronto. That was amazing! Because then I met people like Mutabaruka, Sister Jean Breeze, of course the other Toronto people like Afua Cooper and Makeda Silvera, Dionne Brand and so on. They were doing all kinds of stuff, publishing and performance and writing. At that festival you had the dub poets, you also had people coming from Jamaica and Trinidad. Brother Resistance is this guy from Trinidad who came up, and

Kariega Mandiela. People from Dominica, from Jamaica, and from England, and South Africa. Mzwake Mbuli was out there. So for us, that was a real inspiration. We did some performances as part of the festival, but just being on panels and talking, or just informally hanging out with these people, and seeing their performances, was a real jolt for a lot of us. At that time, the group — we were in our last phases. Lillian Allen and Clifton Joseph, they're the ones who really put me on for moving to Toronto. They always really supported me, and Michael St. George too. It was Lillian who said, "Hey, you should come to Toronto and see what's going on, and try a few things." That was a good move, actually, at the time.

Ian Stephens released a CD, Wining, Dining, Drilling,54 *in 1993, which featured both songs and spoken word pieces. Stephens, along with Julie Bruck, Geneviève Letarte and Anthony Bansfield, was one of the Montreal artists invited to contribute to MuchMusic's* Word Up *spoken word video series, curated by Jill Battson.*

The birth of Wired on Words

Ian Ferrier and Fortner Anderson formed Wired on Words in 1993 to record Montreal spoken word artists, and to broadcast the recordings on CKUT FM. The project would go on to win a Standard Broadcasting Award in 1994.

IAN FERRIER: Montreal was beginning to feel all the energy from stuff happening in the rest of North America. The poetry slam scene and all that. It was as if everybody woke up, all at the same time, from 1993 on.

FORTNER ANDERSON: In 1987, after *Dial-*

This CD [*Wining, Dining, Drilling*] is no easy listen. Cuts like 'Diary of a Trademark' and 'I Started to Get Sick in New York' explore themes that run deep. "Everything from alienation to schizophrenia, subjects like AIDS or HIV, being queer, going nuts in this society. I hope there's some black humour there too.... I think clarity and honesty are part of what will lessen the tragedy of this disease, and also the tragedy of existence. That allows you to have a sense of humour, I think. If you can laugh at yourself — cajole yourself into a closer, true perspective — that's the whole point of humour.... I realized a long time ago that if you don't have a sense of humour, you'll just die. I think people who commit suicide have lost their sense of humour. That's why a lot of teenagers kill themselves. They don't have a sense of perspective...."

Stephens is speaking from experience. His own attempt came at age seventeen. "It was tough. Rural Canada is not very queer. There wasn't much in terms of role models."

Maybe Stephens is the role model now. "On a one-to-one level I don't mind it," he says. "But I don't want to be a sort of cut-out figure. I don't see myself as a teacher. I just see myself as a writer, that's all I want to do."

– from 'Ian Stephens', by Kevin Press, *Chart*, April 1994.

A-Poem, I got tired of being tied to the phone and was looking for other ways to put the work out there. And so I started the radio show *Dromotexte*.55 The whole premise of the show was to present spoken word recordings in kind of a top-forty format, with little commentary. Just play the work. And the happy idea came about that we were going to record the Montreal poets, similar to *Dial-A-Poem*, and put them on the air. Using the recordable cart strategy, and working as a first step in the long journey to the creation of the CD.56

IAN FERRIER: Part of the reason that I got into the spoken word scene was I always liked doing studio stuff, recording stuff. We started the first *Wired on Words* series in the summer of 1993. Fortner and I were walking up the street one day, and I was telling him

54 Stephens, Ian *Wining, Dining, Drilling* CD. Producer: Kevin Komoda. Montreal: EnGuard Records, 1993.

55 On Radio McGill, later CKUT FM.

56 Various artists. *Millennium Cabaret* CD, Anderson, Fortner & Ferrier, Ian, producers, Wired on Words, 1998.

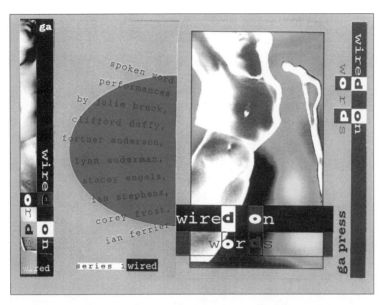

Wired on Words cassette case design by ga press

four-track. Everything was perfectly smooth from beginning to end, and everybody was really helpful. I was totally amazed, I'd never actually run into a place where there was no resistance to new stuff. We ended up doing maybe twenty pieces on carts.... Ian Stephens, Lynn Suderman, Ann McLean did a piece for it, Bill Furey did one, Julie Bruck did a piece for it, or two. Most people would do two or three. Fortner Anderson too. Clifford Duffy had a couple, but they were prerecorded. His stuff was pretty complex. It was stuff he did with David Gossage, as Nietzsche's Daughter.

LYNN SUDERMAN: I had written a few poems, and asked for some feedback from a Vancouver-based spoken word poet named Judy Radul. She was a very talented performer and poet, and told me that my humble attempts at the genre were rather puerile. I went back at them, toyed with them, kicked them around, then got to talking with Ian Stephens. He was very encouraging and asked me to participate in the CKUT *Wired on Words* radio poem project. I did, and lo and behold, one of the poems went to number seven on the charts.

that I'd just heard the Governor General's award winner for poetry had sold three hundred copies of their book that year. We just went, "Oh, God. It's a dead art!" I said, "You know you could really cheaply put spoken word on the air, you could just record it on a cassette and people could play it like songs." He said, "OK, let's do that."

The *Wired on Words* series was recorded in CKUT. It was mostly on quarter-inch, but there was some on

Fortner Anderson at Reggies, September 1999

Ian Ferrier with Sam Shalabi and Will Ezilini at Reggie's September, 1999

Part 7. THE *ORALPALOOZA* GENERATION

"Finding dynamic ways of presenting words"

In the spring of 1994, a number of anglophone writers and performers began to come together. One loosely-defined group was largely drawn from the ranks of graduating Concordia creative writing students interested in innovative means of presenting literature to their generation. These people created ga press, a chapbook publishing house, index, *a free monthly literary magazine, and* Ouma Seeks Ouzo, *a performance troupe. A second group, which became known as the Fluffy Pagan Echoes, was made up of five writers, poets and performance artists who were disenchanted with the format of the traditional poetry reading.*

ga press

ga press was Corey Frost and Colin Christie. They became enthusiastic about chapbook production in the spring of 1994, publishing the For Example *anthology, and co-publishing the second* Hence *anthology. The pursuit of excellence in small-press publishing went hand-in-hand with a growing interest in the performative possibilities of text.*

COREY FROST: The first performance, the first public reading that I did was the launch of the *For Example* chapbook, which happened in 1994. Concordia, my second year there, is where I met most of the writers that I now consider my colleagues or peers or friends. I met Colin Christie and Catherine Kidd in the same class, and it was with Colin

that I really started getting involved with doing small publishing, which led to involvement in 'the scene' at large. There were about fifteen people in the creative writing class, I think, and everyone was invited to submit their favourite piece of work to *For Example*. It wasn't juried or anything, it was participatory. And Colin Christie and I assembled it.

TRISH SALAH: I went the workshop route and switched from theatre into poetry and prose fiction, got interested in literature and literary theory. I started thinking about what it might mean to complicate what I understood to be the traditional genres of writing — playwriting, poetry and fiction — with nonfictional, theoretical, parafictional forms. That's what I did for quite a while, and then eventually found myself involved in things like editing magazines — *The Moosehead Anthology, Pawn to Infinity*. I did readings probably as early as 1992, but in a very traditional format.

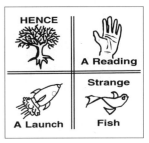

Poster for Hence *launch
by ga press*

*ga press: Colin Christie and
Corey Frost, 1994*
Photo by Tammi Downey

Poster from first Fluffy Pagan Echoes Word Circus, June 22, 1994

Fluffy Pagan Echoes at Bistro 4, August 1995 (from left) Justin McGrail, Vince Tinguely, Ran Elfassy, Victoria Stanton, Scott Duncan
Photos by Joyce Abrams

COREY FROST: The *For Example* launch was actually a joint launch at Bistro 4 with the first *Perhaps* magazine. At that event I was just reading a text, in a sense, but the text I read did have performative elements to it. It was actually the first piece that I wrote about spiders. It was the grain of the novel I'm working on now. And so it was already tending towards finding dynamic ways of presenting words. The experience of having the audience in front of me, interacting with my work, encouraged me to develop ideas of performance.

TRISH SALAH: I guess I had a feeling that things were starting to happen in the spring of 1994. That's when I became conscious of something besides poetry open mic nights.... I thought, "Oh, maybe I should have a hand in organizing such things." That's around the time Michelle Power and Corey Frost collaborated on the second *Hence* chapbook. ga press were starting to bring out chapbooks fairly regularly. I had seen Steve Edgar's and liked it a lot, and got interested in that idea. Corey was also starting to put together the idea for *The*

Sentence That Thought Life Was Simple,[57] which was a collaboratively-written meditation on writing, and letters always reaching their destination. Around that time I was starting to memorize my own work; not all of it, but specific pieces for performance. And I was starting to write with performance in mind. At the *Hence* launch, I had memorized my work and was very much interested in what it would mean to have my body at my disposal, rather than occupied with reading words.

Fluffy Pagan Echoes

Fluffy Pagan Echoes came into being largely through the efforts of Scott Duncan. He found his interest in organizing a 'different', more animated reading series was shared by other writers he met in Montreal's literary scene. In June 1994, he formed Fluffy Pagan Echoes with Ran Elfassy, Justin McGrail and Vincent Tinguely. Their first show took place at the Phoenix Café on June 22. Justin McGrail suggested the 'Word Circus' format, where

each performer presented a poem in a series of three or four sets.

JUSTIN MCGRAIL: Well, what I remember about that reading was that we, Scott and I especially, were *drinking* heavily.... As I recall, Ran was on, and Ran was doing a Ran poem, which — especially the first time I'd ever heard them — were just peeling my head open. So I got up and did my Shakespeare poem. I remember that was fun because I was drunk, and I got off stage and wandered around. That was great to immediately establish that we didn't need to be on the stage, that we were free of that. Here I am at a poetry reading and I'm actually doing my own arrangement of a bunch of Shakespearean lines and... people loved it.

VINCE TINGUELY: There were probably thirty people in the audience, but it wasn't a big space so it felt like *all these people had come to see us!* When it ended and we passed the hat, we each had eight dollars. We went across the street to drink at La Cabane, thinking, "This is amazing. This is what we've been looking for, something really exciting."

After their first show, questions were raised about the all-male line-up of Fluffy Pagan Echoes, so the group decided to seek another member.

VICTORIA STANTON: I ended up getting together with Scott at La Croissanterie on Hutchison to talk to him about his project.... I got up on the table and I started performing. He's like, "You're in!" (laughs) I said, "Well, I'm performing next week. Why don't you come and check it out...." This was a *Moveable Feast* reading.[58] I ended up going to the next Fluffy Pagan Echoes meeting, and I realized that these were kindred spir-

Phoenix Café on the Main, 1995
Photo by Vince Tinguely

its. We had different concerns in our writing, we had similar concerns in wanting to stir things up in the poetry scene. We wanted to make exciting, interesting events around performing our texts. I was actually really excited about being involved in something, being *part* of something.

SCOTT DUNCAN: And then we went on to do a series of performances at the Phoenix for almost a year, ten months.

57 Various authors. *The Sentence That Thought Life Was Simple.* Montreal: ga press, launched October 13, 1994.

58 *The Moveable Feast* was a writing workshop active in the mid-nineties.

Victoria Stanton at Bistro 4 for a Moveable Feast *reading, July 11, 1994*
Photo by Scott Inniss

165

Oralpalooza *by ga press*

"A rock music ambience"

On July 13, 1994, auditions were held to select spoken word performers for the Montreal leg of Lollapalooza, *the travelling rock festival. Spoken word artists who had worked in obscurity for years suddenly gathered en masse at the auditions, held at the Phoenix Café. The potential for a Montreal spoken word scene was made concrete by the sheer number of performers. The artists selected at the audition performed at* Oralpalooza *with some of the American spoken word artists touring with* Lollapalooza, *and then at the festival itself, in 'Reverend Samuel Mudd's Spoken Word Revival Tent'.*

The audition

FORTNER ANDERSON: The *Lollapalooza* people contacted me looking for someone to put it together. And in the end, I think it was clear that they found Montreal to be one of the most exciting events. Not only the *Oralpalooza* event that showcased them the day before, but then at *Lollapalooza* itself.

COREY FROST: I didn't know what to expect, really. I got this call out of the

blue from someone who I didn't know, and they didn't know me. But someone had given the Montreal organizers my name. It was weird because they were basically suggesting that I do exactly the thing that I wanted to do right then. I was so excited by this possibility.

GOLDA FRIED: I guess I was just pulled into it. Corey Frost literally saw me on the street. We were in the poetry class together at Concordia. "There's an audition for *Lollapalooza* in five minutes. Do you want to read?" I was like, "OK." I've always been into rock music, and I was like, "*Lollapalooza*, oh my God!" A free ticket. It was thirty bucks or something, and L7 and Nick Cave were playing. I told him, "Of course I'll do it, do you think I could get in?"

VINCE TINGUELY: A lot of people we've talked to pointed out that *Oralpalooza* was where everyone got to eyeball everyone else who ended up being part of the scene later on. I didn't know anyone in the room, really, except for Fluffy Pagan Echoes. But a lot of these people came back when the spoken word scene started really happening.

COREY FROST: I did a piece about spiders. There was a narrative to it and I had props. I had an eight ball which was supposed to represent the spider's eyes. And a broken umbrella with no fabric on it that I opened and closed to look like a spider. I stuck a sparkler on the end of it that I lit during the performance. I went a little bit overboard, but I was excited.

JUSTIN MCGRAIL: Well that was the first time I ever saw Corey Frost perform. I'd seen Corey around, he was a hard guy to miss. And when he did his spider poem I remember being on one hand amazed,

but on the other hand I felt sort of hostile to it. I recognized later, and it's something which I also recognized when I did the slams, that you could have a competitive streak in you even if you didn't think about it. My initial feeling was, "Oh my God, how long have all these other people been doing this? I feel terribly unqualified. Where did they all come from?" Scott Moodie was hurling himself against the wall at one point, and I remember just thinking, "What the hell is this?"

BENOÎT PAIEMENT: Yes, *Groupe de poésie moderne* was at the audition. It wasn't the finest thing we did, it was very noisy and it's hard for us to perform when it's noisy. It was a rock music ambience, but we got to be interviewed and perform for *MusiquePlus*, which was good for us.

JUSTIN MCGRAIL: With *Oralpalooza* of course, when we did the math — they had a mandate where they had so many poets, it was going to be gender equity, and then they had a youth emphasis. So it worked out that if you were an above-twenty-year-old male poet, there were three spots, and there were fifty people reading for it.

VINCE TINGUELY: I didn't actually audition. My thinking was, "Oh, I'm too old for this kind of *Lollapalooza* thing." Because I had done campus radio shows for so long and had played spoken word — from Anne Clark, Joolz, Henry Rollins' spoken word, Lydia Lunch, Exene Cervenka — I had this idea that it was these rock stars, that's what spoken word is. As it turned out, the actual line-up of *Lollapalooza* was a lot more interesting than that. Both the people touring, and the people from Montreal who took part.

*Christophe Rapin
and Benoît Paiement
April 1999*
Photo by Robert Beaudoin

COREY FROST: I didn't really have any idea about what I was getting into at the time. I don't think I would have known at the time who Henry Rollins was. I was just doing whatever came naturally.... Fortner Anderson was up there onstage being a total talk show host lunatic. The impression was absolutely the opposite of the impression I have of him, in regular conversation, now. But in a way, that turned me off of the whole event, because I thought to myself, if spoken word was all about this hilarious grandstanding, then it wasn't really what I was interested in. But I got a big rush doing it.

JONATHAN GOLDSTEIN: The first time that I'd ever read in public was at the auditions. I was so nervous, I drank a whole bottle of red wine in the alley before the thing started. I had finished a piece, and people laughed and people seemed to like it and I couldn't believe it. I was like a big spazzy kid who was being accepted by the popular kids. The adrenaline was so strong, I went over to one of the open windows because everyone was honking and screaming. I think Brazil had won the World Cup. They didn't

Golda Fried, 1997

Cover art by Howard Chackowicz

have air conditioning there and the windows were open... so I went over to the open window behind the stage, and I started yelling just for performance value, at the people in the street, to shout out that people were reading poetry up here and it was really important and everything. But I was so drunk that I felt myself sway and almost fall right out the window. Which just totally sobered me. I was completely lucid, I went back to the microphone — white.

Victoria Stanton: I was struck by the number of people who were doing performance poetry, in French and in English. There was some costume-based performance, very visual performance, highly-choreographed performance, rap performance. The thing that all these had in common was that, yes, these were *performances.* And none of them were held together by music, especially where the rap performances were concerned, and the very musical text pieces. I didn't realize that there was *so much* going on, and I wondered where all these people came from. I was very excited, because I realized that, wow, there's a lot of stuff going on in this city. People in their own little pockets.

Corey Frost: I remember being impressed by the rap group, At Random. I knew that kind of stuff existed, but I was so impressed at the skill that it required.... I was just flabbergasted that there was so much going on. But I think that a lot of the people, maybe not everybody, but a lot of the people there had the same feeling. They all thought that they were finding out about something, but in fact it was just starting.

Oralpalooza and Reverend Samuel Mudd's Spoken Word Revival Tent

At Oralpalooza, which took place at Club Bowling, the Montreal spoken word artists selected at the auditions had the opportunity to perform alongside the American artists touring with Lollapalooza. The performative emphasis of the American spoken word poetry helped create an awareness of the possibilities inherent in the form.

Feelings were mixed about the main event; it was exciting to be part of a travelling rock festival, but the audiences were largely indifferent to the local performers.

Golda Fried: Immediately it was like we were superstars, they were asking us for CKUT interviews. I slept through the interview and felt like shit, but I was so happy. It was such an ego thing.... Andrea Clark — who later died — was reading, she was amazing. She did a rap thing. Victoria was great.... And Regie Cabico was reading. It was all so connected.

Jonathan Goldstein: They had a comics thing happening beside the spoken word tent that Howard Chackowicz was at, and we were so excited. He put together a comic and I put together the chapbook which he did the cover for. We really thought that this was going to be our generation's *Woodstock*, you know? So I went out to the photocopy place and I made a hundred copies of my chapbook, and I was afraid that might not even be enough. I really thought that we were just going to be mobbed, it was just going to be insane, you know. And I think I sold three copies.

VICTORIA STANTON: They had their head-lining acts, these were the touring poet performers who had travelled with the festival from coast to coast. So the big names would draw the crowds, because they would be listed in some schedule or other. Which I never actually saw, but people seemed to know because they would show up, and then Maggie Estep would appear! So someone was in the know, it wasn't us (laughs). Then she'd finish and they'd disappear. And then the local performer poet would get up onstage to maybe five people, usually the other performers.... That was a very disappointing day. But interesting to be a part of none-the-less, because there were these poet stars from the States.

"Oh my God, there's all these venues"

The energy from the Oralpalooza *experience continued to build in various directions. While some projects, like Jonathan Goldstein's spoken word band Blowhard, were shortlived, there was a growing number of young artists seeking outlets for creative expression of text, both in performance and in print. Fluffy Pagan Echoes'* Word Circus *was building its audience on a monthly basis, and a new weekly series for performance,* The Bard's Gauntlet *sprang into being at Fokus, a small gallery on Duluth. In addition, spoken word was happening at the* Urban Wanderers *reading series, at cabaret events in Stornoway Gallery, which had moved to a larger space, at* The Yellow Door, *and on the street.*

COREY FROST: I started doing performances and I started publishing chapbooks at the same time. At *Oralpalooza* I performed, but I also put together that anthology, a chapbook that contained all

of the performers, called *Oralpalooza*. And then that fall was the busiest for ga press. We did five or six books that fall, and almost each time, we had launch events, which was another way it was obvious that the two domains were converging. At first, I thought of it as being two parallel activities, parallel and separate... they felt different. The performances were what established me in a social sphere, that was the direct connection to other people in Montreal. The chapbook-making was a more isolated process in some respects. Even though our particular brand of publishing was pretty integrated in the social sphere too, because it was hands-on publishing. We invited people to participate, content-wise. But also it was a social activity in that the actual making of the books — which is what I think of as the performance of the book — often involved a lot of people. When we'd get the pages back from the photocopier and were stapling the books together, we'd invite people to come over and staple with us.

JONATHAN GOLDSTEIN: I had a spoken word band. Sam Shalabi played guitar, and Howard Chackowicz played drums. We basically set to music the poems from the chapbook from *Lollapalooza*, which was called *Blowhard Poems*. And then we called the band Blowhard. We played at Dawson and at Concordia... no spoken word venues, but we did Purple Haze and Club Rage. Then, we just stopped. It seemed so ridiculous — like the kind of thing you would do with a pair of longjohns on your head, and bouncing on your parents' bed for your sister and brother.

PASCAL FIORAMORE: Before the *Abdigradationnistes*, we had a first group called *Les Lazy Boyz* (everyone laughs). Performance-wise it was very similar to

*Blowhard flyer
art by Howard Chackowicz*

PASCAL FIORAMORE: Avant les Abdigradationnistes, on avait formé un premier groupe qui s'appelait Les Lazy Boyz (rires). En ce qui a trait à la

continued...

VICTORIA STANTON: Fluffy Pagan Echoes did this poem, 'Song For The Industrial Life Building' in November, 1994, on McGill College, in front of the building. That was part of my independent study for Concordia's Interdisciplinary Studies program.

VINCE TINGUELY: We did it at a lunch hour.... We went to the building, this high rise, and we were screaming at the building. Because that's how you respond to something that big, if it's going to hear you, you have to shout at it.

RAN ELFASSY: The audience was the eight people who were leaving the building, as well as the security guard. That was ideal, I think that was a great audience. We were just basically provoking them.

VINCE TINGUELY: Halfway through this pretty short performance, the security guard came out and told us to go away but we kept doing it. He said, "I'm calling the police," and he left. We finished the poem, and then we zipped around to the back of the building, where there's a Van Houtte. We were having coffee, when our sound man Neil Wiernik showed up. He was going to record this, but he hadn't made it in time. "Well, we had to leave the space because the police were coming." He said, "Yeah, I know, I was there when they came."

VICTORIA STANTON: Then we did another piece for the Decarie Expressway in December 1994.

RAN ELFASSY: The audience were the cars whizzing by — they just saw five people for a moment, making a gesture...

JUSTIN MCGRAIL: The September Fluffy Pagan Echoes show was packed, and a real breakthrough. Where all the material that we brought, we sort of stepped it up a little. I think in *Episode One*[59] actually reflects that. I remember I was on a cloud after that show. After that it was, "This is for real." It kind of took off from there. That was when we started getting gigs elsewhere.

COREY FROST: It served a purpose to the community, to have the Fluffy Pagan Echoes around, because if anyone was trying to decide whether or not there was a spoken word scene developing, you could at least point to these five people and say, "Those are spoken word artists."

VICTORIA STANTON: I think what was so enchanting about it, too, is that it wasn't decided, "This is our goal." We just did it because it was fun. It wasn't forced or deliberate or contrived.

performance, c'était très représentatif de ce qu'on fait actuellement. Pascal et moi avions déjà fait de la peinture ensemble, mais outre ça, notre premier travail commun au niveau de la musique et de l'écriture, ç'a été Les Lazy Boyz, de 1994 à la fin de 1995. En fait, on était quatre.

PASCAL DESJARDINS: Il y avait aussi Simon, alias dj DLT, qui est maintenant *scratcher* dans les Abdigradationnistes, et Frédérique Pierre. Lui, il n'est plus avec nous aujourd'hui, il a été remplacé par Alexandre Roche, qui est violoniste.

what we do now. Pascal and I had already done painting together, but other than that, our first collaborative work in music and writing was *Les Lazy Boyz* from 1994 to the end of 1995. There were four of us.

PASCAL DESJARDINS: There was Simon, alias DJ DLT, who's now the scratcher with the *Abdigradationnistes*, and Frédérique Pierre. He's no longer with us, he was replaced by Alexandre Roche, a violinist.

Ran Elfassy, March 1999

The Bard's Gauntlet

Local poet Will Kenny began to organize The Bard's Gauntlet*, a weekly series, at Fokus, a tiny gallery on Duluth Street, near St. Laurent.*

TORREY PASS: I'd read at Fokus... Bistro 4... although it wasn't a regular event there, they would have interspersed nights of what was starting to be called spoken word at that time. I would never miss a Fluffy Pagan Echo performance (laughs). But I think in that era, I was brushing shoulders with the spoken word scene in the sense that a lot of people were preparing work in the specific interest of performing it to an audience in an attractive and energetic way. So I'd be tag-teaming with people who would be doing performance poetry or spoken word. Whereas I think I was more just reading poems.

ZOË WHITTALL: At the time I felt like there was a really close-knit scene of people that went to each other's shows. I guess it mostly revolved around Fluffy Pagan Echoes, from what I remember. In the fall of 1994 Fokus had *The Bard's Gauntlet* every Wednesday, an open stage with one featured reader. I thought that was really good. It got lots of people who never read coming. It was really small and encouraging. I had a lot of fun. That's where I first saw Ian Stephens and David Jaeger.... Fokus was the first thing I ever did, where I got up and read my first poems. I read at Fokus with Torrey Pass and Corpusse and Ian Stephens. I was so nervous and I was such a little kid.

TORREY PASS: Ian Stephens read at Fokus in December 1994, as well, with Leah Libin. I remember Leah was nervous, because she wasn't sure if he was aware that he'd be sharing, that he wouldn't necessarily be the sole performer. So she was worried about stepping on his toes.

LYNN SUDERMAN: Ian was very inclusive, very encouraging to young writers. His comfort level onstage, no matter how intense the performance, was so obvious.

Diary of a Trademark

The publication of Diary of a Trademark[60] *marked Ian Stephens' return to the literary pursuits he'd set aside for a career in music. He performed his poetry frequently in the following months, and was one of the stalwarts of the nascent Montreal spoken word scene.* Diary of a Trademark *was launched at Stornoway Gallery in November 1994.*

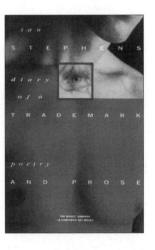

IAN STEPHENS: Some people, when they find out they're HIV, go crazy. They start having wild sex, doing wild drugs, don't keep up with their medication, get tired and die rather quickly. I made a very conscious decision to work on my health and remain monogamous, and to concentrate on my writing.

– from 'Living to write about it', by Matthew Hays, *XTRA!*, March 17, 1995.

ENDRE FARKAS: Someone whose stuff I liked, I didn't always get but I liked, was Ian Stephens. I liked his attitude and some of his text. I think he was also more literary-based, although running to performance, but he was coming out of a literary background. I was publishing the Muses' Company at that point, and I asked Peter Van Toorn to put together an anthology of new writers called *Sounds New*. He had seen a

59 Fluffy Pagan Echoes (Scott Duncan, Ran Elfassy, Justin McGrail, Victoria Stanton & Vincent Tinguely). *Episode One – A Word Circus*. Montreal: Egg Sandwich Press, 1994. Launched in October, 1994.

60 Stephens, Ian. *Diary of a Trademark*. Montreal: The Muses' Company, 1994.

Lynn Suderman
Photo courtesy of the artist

poem by Ian he really liked, and he finally tracked him down and got it. I got in touch with him, and he sent me a manuscript. I liked it, and I spent about six, seven months working with him on it. I finally published the book, and got to know him in the process.

IAN STEPHENS: There are new styles of poetry that have been coming for a while, and Montreal is only catching up to it now. Leonard Cohen is good but why are we stuck with this icon haunting all our poetic sensibilities? This scene needs to be blown out of the water. I don't think my book is a major cachet of nitroglycerin or anything, but that's what needs to be done.

– from 'A queer and haunted landscape', by Juliet Waters, *The Mirror*, October 17, 1994.

LYNN SUDERMAN: Ian worked very hard on his material. I remember one piece, 'Diary of a Trademark', he worked on for a long time, tuning each word and thought. If you read 'Trademark', Ian's philosophy comes out: life isn't about safety nets and careful planning. It's about intense joy and pleasure, and equally intense pain. This was a man who felt and experienced life intensely.

PETER BRAWLEY: Ian and I had the greatest friendship for the on-the-phone brainstorming, we'd talk for hours. He was very plugged into it, too. He had ideas all the time. Even when he got sick he kept on working. I said, "You've got to stop working," he said, "Are you crazy? I'm writing a book. I've gotta get a book out." You could tell he really meant it. And what a stunning book, it

really is an amazing poetry book... a landmark in literature. Of course, Ian, with the Masters degree, I could see he wanted to do a real book, after years of chapbooks like *La Flèche*.[61] Despite all his punk pretensions, and his nihilism and his fashion stuff, he's really a good poet.

FORTNER ANDERSON: It was only quite late that I actually began to appreciate what he did. The stuff in the early eighties, it didn't capture me. It was only a few years after the *Ultimatum* poetry festival where I was captured by it. I was always impressed by Ian's ability to read the work. He imbues each word with a nuance, so that you can capture the meaning and the emotional subtext to what he's saying. He was a master of reading his own work. The texts themselves, some of them I found to be good, very good. His book has maybe a dozen very strong poems. Poems where he's captured at once the uniqueness of his life, his vision, and expressed it in a language and form which match it.

ENDRE FARKAS: Ian Stephens and I went on tour, the *Quanglo* tour.[62] So I got to know him there. I remember we were having this talk. He was at one point really frustrated, he said, "Everybody just thinks of me as a queer poet. I don't want to be thought of as a queer poet, I want to be thought of as a writer." That's one of the reasons that he was happy that I published him, because I was straight! (laughs) That I wasn't pushing the queer angle. I liked him. At the end we had a bit of a falling-out, because I think he just felt that the world owed him more than it was giving him.

61 Stephens, Ian. *La Flèche.* Montreal: Sidewalk Press, 1987.

62 *Quanglo* tour, with Julie Keith, Joe Fiorito, Linda Leith, Edeet Ravel, Mark Abley, April 1995.

IAN STEPHENS: This world is so beautiful and it has to be cherished. I just love existence. I adore it. Every inch of it. That's what sort of makes me angry. I would love to be old and sit with a dog and look out at the lake, but in fact that won't happen — so I cherish each moment.

— from 'AIDS poet cherishes each moment', by Philip Marchand, *The Toronto Star*, March 21, 1995.

The Wired on Words cassettes

Wired on Words produced three spoken word cassettes between December 1994 and March 1995. For their first cassette, Wired on Words, *an anthology, ga press published a booklet that was attached to the cassette case.*

It was launched in conjunction with CKUT's Seasonal Hoop-la-la-la *at Stornoway Gallery on December 17, 1994.*

IAN FERRIER: The Wired on Words radio carts started to climb the charts, something we didn't expect. They got played a lot and people were talking about them and they liked them. When we put out a tape, a lot of people came to buy that.

FORTNER ANDERSON: Another motivation for Wired on Words was the thought that Ian Stephens should be recorded as much as possible before he passed away. My personal thought was that it was a matter of some urgency. He'd already started to get quite ill, the disease was progressive. We had the opportunity to record him, and so went forward with it.

IAN FERRIER: All of the pieces came from that book, *Diary of a Trademark*. The cassette got recorded in two parts because he got really sick in the middle of recording. He just stopped because he was so tired. But then he used to go up and down, up and down. The last stuff was recorded in January 1995, the year before he died.

The Ian Stephens cassette was launched at Building Danse, March 1995. In April, Stephens was voted Best Spoken Word Artist at the Montreal Independent Music Industry awards.

FORTNER ANDERSON: I'm quite proud that we did that. We'd like to re-issue it on CD. I think that's a document for posterity, in that Ian's public is much reduced. To think that there would be a public for him outside of Montreal, that's the work of decades. But I believe in the strength of his work.

Interior of Diary of a Trademark *cassette, Wired on Words, 1994*

Ian Ferrier, September 1999

Fear and Loathing at Bistro 4

It is Monday night again. I leave my incredibly brown apartment on Rivard to go Main-lining. I am still recovering from the words. I am still remembering the performance virgin who toppled from the heat, caught by the arms of the audience like a lover. He regained his balance and heroically continued. Or the night that it was so crowded that someone sat on me, spilling water and orange juice into my lap quietly, because we couldn't interupt, couldn't interpret. It is time to watch the window, the people going by, looking in at us looking out. To them, we are the show, but we know otherwise....

Loaded up on anti-depressants and red dye number 4, I find a group of regulars and claim to misunderstand the question when they ask why I'm stuffing my face with Twizzlers. I claim it was the benzedrine in my tea, the filtered water left haphazardly in the fridge.

Lee Gotham stands before the mic. He drawls. The man with the comic book name speaks like the wake of a sailboat finally reaching shore; his radio-friendly voice strains to find superlatives. Strains to avoid cliché between the acts: *and remember... every drink... you purchase... contributes to this... wondrous event. Enjoy... with pleasure... a whole whack of impromptu stuff.* Enough said. On with the show. I stuff another Twizzler into my mouth as a way of denying any Freudian psychosis. Those onstage have their microphone, after all. I have an urge to blurt out to the enthralled room that the coffee everyone is drinking is in fact only a legalized drug.

A room full of ears getting pierced. Letters dangling from lobes. Me with my Twizzler, the red dye number 4 giving me confidence. Perhaps I will sign up for the open mic, perhaps I can ad-lib a story about a woman who shoots up time but grows old too quickly.

A friend at the table asks me what is wrong. There is a break between performers. The Fluffy Pagan Echoes are next. Their members fill the corners of the room kissing cheeks. The silence has subsided. I do not mention the red dye. I tell her I am suffering from "solipsistic vibrosis." I think I may have heard it somewhere, from someone holding a page in a hand that quivers like an insect in a haiku. Too much coffee, I reckon.

There is an Echo trying to make me believe I am watching television but I am not fooled. The newscaster announces that poetry is the art of trying to get laid in a public medium. I suck another Twizzler and cross my legs. "All anyone can ask is to perform in a café with their ex-lover there." I think the audience is a roomful of ex-lovers although none of them are mine. This gives me further confidence to perhaps put chalk in hand and sign up for that unapproachably open mic. Alas, I have not the courage.

Meanwhile there are people making faces at me through the window; they are not trying to tell me anything although I wish they would. And Lee is back but I can't understand him. What's wrong? my friend asks again, and there is a woman with an exposed belly-button giving birth to mangoes. She really likes mangoes. While the camera points at us from the Main where the garbage truck is picking up yesterday's failed poetry. And I am out of Twizzlers so I slink away from the table... through the den of style complete with a crowd high on brown drugs... another Monday night and my mind is stuffed as full as the garbage truck and equally fecund. Enough said.

— by Andy Brown, *index*, April 1995.

Enough Said

Lee Gotham's Enough Said series can rightly make the claim of being the catalyst which put the new spoken word scene in Montreal on the map. Soon after its inception, the media became aware of the phenomenon, and spoken word artists appeared in the local entertainment weeklies, newspapers, on radio and on television. The series played the crucial role of creating a general awareness of the art form, and offered a weekly meeting place for all the players.

JUSTIN MCGRAIL: Once we'd started getting asked by people to do shows, we realized, "Oh my God, there's all these venues." It seemed within months that all of a sudden there were all these places we could read.

VINCE TINGUELY: At that time there was the Fokus show, there was *Enough Said* and there was Fluffy Pagan Echoes, all within a block.

LEE GOTHAM: I guess I became aware of the potential for a spoken word scene... at the end of October, in the fall of 1994. It was right on the tail end of the *Urban Wanderers*[63] reading series at Bistro 4, they were closing shop. It was far from an animated and performative orientation, for the most part they were stock readings. And I thought, "Well shit. There's probably room for improvement here." Or at least room for change. So I spoke to Daniel[64] right there behind the counter at Bistro 4, and arranged to take over that vacant Monday night slot. It took two or three weeks to re-establish an audience. It wasn't for the most part the audience the *Urban Wanderers* had had, but it only took those two or three weeks for a buzz to get around.

JUSTIN MCGRAIL: I think the *Enough Said* series was really important.... What Fluffy Pagans talked about at our first meeting was, "We hate poetry readings." And Lee Gotham was definitely in that same mindscape, that poetry readings suck the way they are.

LEE GOTHAM: The early days were really a fun and surprising success. I think it was gathering momentum quite quickly, a lot of people took the initiative to get in contact with me, so I was doing less beating of the bushes looking for talent. I just exercised a general criteria of performativity, but not swinging to either extreme of either singer-songwriters and stand-up comedians at the one end of the spectrum, and staid conservative literary offerings at the other end of the spectrum. I tried to exclude those two ends, but include everything else. All the grey matter, all the grey area in between. And exploit it to its fullest as well!

JASMINE CHÂTELAIN: *Enough Said* was so regular. It would finish, and two days later Lee would be walking around telling people who was going to be up in the next six days. You always knew where you could go on Monday. Aside from being a regular event, it was a social event. And you started seeing the same people perform and the same people going. And to me that constitutes a scene. It wasn't sporadic or spontaneous or flukey any more.

LEE GOTHAM: Even before having a regular experience of hosting an event like that, I thought the frequency was fairly important — if I wanted to develop a lot of interest quickly, and an interest that might endure. In other words, get something of a community aspect brought to the forefront. I mean commu-

nity sounds a bit pretentious but there was just as much creativity taking place *between* the sets, and between people's performances, just in conversations.

MITSIKO MILLER: I was really into the French-language scene. I went to French school. I went to French university. I didn't really know what was happening on the 'other side'. I'd been to French poetry readings that were really stale and boring, and the great thing about *Enough Said* was that it was very vivid. It took me a while before I actually did the open mic.

LEE GOTHAM: Basically the notion of doing the series in the first place was to provide a middle ground between the academic lectern approach, the literary *soirées* that were only distinct from a gathering on the shelves of the library or some other place at school inasmuch as they'd chosen a different venue, and the rock and roll thing or the punk aesthetic or the real street-level experience. The open mic was a compliment to the more laboured and prepared literary offerings.

Lee Gotham, August 1997

63 *Urban Wanderers* reading series ran from 1993 to 1996.

64 The proprietor of Bistro 4.

175

'Slampapi's Slam Philosophy'

... You're reading this page because I created a show in Chicago at The Green Mill called *The Uptown Poetry Slam*.... It has played to over fifty thousand faces, tongues, and pairs of ears. It has pissed off a lot of people and made others feel divine.

A regular feature of this grab bag, variety show, which mixes together an open stage, special guests, musical and dramatic acts, and lots of audience interaction, is a mock competition between poets scored by judges selected from the crowds that pack the place every Sunday night. Even though *The Uptown Poetry Slam* has always placed more emphasis on the performance aspects of this cabaret styled show, the competition, because of its gimmickry and dramatic nature, has been the media-generated cause for its spread to a couple hundred cities worldwide. Is this a good thing? Sometimes I think no.

But the Slam does not belong to me. It belongs to the thousands of people who have dedicated their time, money, and energy to this Chicago-born, interactive format for presenting poetry to a public that has a zillion other barks and belches and flashes to hold its attention. Am I proud of the community that has grown from my small efforts? Yes, and I hope that it continues to grow in accordance with a few philosophies that have become what I consider to be the back bone of what we call the 'Slam Family':

The purpose of poetry (and indeed all art) is not to glorify the poet but rather to celebrate the community to which the poet belongs. (This idea is paraphrased from the works of Wendell Berry). The show and the show's effect upon the audience are more important than any one individual's contribution to it. The poets are not the point, the point is poetry (Alan Wolfe). The performance of poetry is an art — just as much an art as the art of writing it. NO audience should be thought of as obligated to listen to the poet. It is the poet's obligation to communicate effectively, artfully, honestly, and professionally so as to compel the audience to listen. The Slam should be open to all people and all forms of poetry. With respect to its own affairs, each Slam should be free from attachment to any outside organization and responsible to no authority other than its own community of poets and audience. NO group, individual, or outside organization should be allowed to exploit the Slam Family. We must all remember that we are each tied in some way to someone else's efforts. Our individual achievements are only extensions of some previous accomplishment. Success for one should translate into success for all. The National Slam began as a gift from one city to another. It should remain a gift passed on freely to all newcomers.

Such philosophies might sound a high tone in your head and leave your cynical self muttering "What Bull!" Sometimes it is. The idealism and cooperative forces of the Slam are in constant conflict with the competitive and self-serving appetites of its ambitious nature. This struggle has taught us much, but threatens to obliterate all that has grown to be. I, as surely you have guessed, am on the side of idealism and hope....

Idealism and hope. That's me. Along with whiny, jealous, bitter, "Where's mine," "Who's she think she is,".... "F_ _ _ it, I quit." If you're in Chicago on Sunday night stop by The Green Mill , 4802 N. Broadway, knock me on the noodle and say hello. Show starts at seven. Bring five bucks.

– Marc Smith (so what!)

The Montreal Poetry Slam

Slam poetry had its beginnings in Chicago in 1987, when Marc Smith organized events at The Green Mill as a response to the inaccessibility of academic poetry in the United States. Although there were various attempts to organize slams in Montreal, it wasn't until the Vox Hunt *team of Jasmine Châtelain, Dan Mitchell and Todd Swift began organizing in 1995 that the form became popular.*

TODD SWIFT: I think it was in 1993 that I was a semi-finalist at the Boston slam... I had gone down to Boston, to the CanTab Lounge which was then the heart of slam territory in the States. The Boston team was the best, two years in a row. National champions. Patricia Smith, who is an African-American journalist, was really the driving force, as well as her husband Michael Brown, who edits the international slam newsletter. And I stayed with them for a while and did some research there.... I'm always interested in learning from other cultures and bringing them back here. I'm an internationalist and a regionalist at the same time.

JEREMIAH WALL: The first so-called 'slam' I witnessed was organized by FEWQ,[65] at the old Lux nightclub. That's defunct, poetry is bad for business. At the *Café Vilna* location I did a slam, one time. The slam movement that occurred in Montreal later was certainly not in existence. We did an open stage but it was in the form of a slam. Golda Fried was there, a lot of interesting people were there. It was all female judges, and they gave the award to Hugh Hazelton. It was a cash prize.

TODD SWIFT: In 1995, I was ready again. I'd slammed. Lee Gotham had a series which focused on people like Adeena Karasick. My friend at the time, Jasmine Châtelain, had written this piece which I thought was really quite wonderful and I showed it to Lee and he said it wasn't good enough to be published in his magazine. I just got really annoyed. So one night, Jasmine and I and Dan Mitchell are sitting in a bar, Maître Renard,[66] and I said, "Well, let's start our own reading series, and blow the socks off of Lee." Of course, he'd been my friend for years, and it was kind of a fun thing — so that was the acrimonious birth of *Vox Hunt*. It was called *Vox Hunt* because Maître Renard was a bar that had a picture of Renard fox outside. I was thinking of fox hunt, and we made that little dumb pun.

JASMINE CHÂTELAIN: The first slam was in March, 1995. We thought about it in February, and I think three weeks later we put on this event. We had no intention of doing it more than once, and didn't even know if more than ten people would show up at it. Something like a hundred and fifty people showed up. What spurred me on was that out of seventeen people — we had spots for ten and seventeen people signed up — I knew one person. Sixteen of them were people I had never met. And I was really pleased by that. So we decided to keep going.

TODD SWIFT: Slam is a genuinely American art form, like jazz, which whether we like it or not, is developing. And it creates a whole different kind of poetry, which is designed to be three minutes or less, and has democratic, immediate impact. It's in your face and it reaches an audience, and it's not elitist, and it's not academic. The metaphor that Dan

Mitchell came up with was a television show without the cameras. Give people the feeling that they're seeing kind of an Ed Sullivan show. It's live but it's not being filmed.

JULIE CRYSLER: I went down to New York and was hanging out with Shut Up Shelley.... She hosted a night at the Nuyorican, so through her I met Boni Joi and Regie Cabico and Bob Holman, this whole gang of New York people. I was completely blown away by what I saw. There was a heightened level of energy over what I had seen in the university circle and open stages. It was really very inspiring, so I started getting on people's cases to bring these people up! I joined the Montreal slam team.... The first time I got booked on the Plateau was after the slam. I started getting booked after that.

EDWARD FULLER: *Vox Hunt* was a contest to be in the spoken word championship in the States. I had done other contests. I had done Elvis contests and other singing contests, as a lark and a comedy exercise. For me it was an extension of stand-up comedy. So I was used to going out and doing contests just to try something new, to try something different. I went to the very first *Vox Hunt*. It gave me an outlet to express deeper ideas that I had but wasn't doing anything with, as I had stopped doing stand-up at that point. Though I often placed, I had to face the fact that if I wanted to win *Vox Hunt*, on any level, I would have to memorize some of the work (laughs). That was part of why I wasn't winning (in all humility, not the only part). It was good that I didn't win right off the bat, because it forced me to write more, and perform more often. I started writing about subjects that otherwise I might not have written about,

Jasmine Châtelain in Toronto, October 1999

[65] Federation of English Language Writers of Quebec.

[66] Venue of the *Vox Hunt* slam 1995-1996. Located on St. Laurent Boulevard.

177

Montreal was the only Canadian team to compete in the Nationals. Alex Jacobs, representing the Mohawk Nation, competed in the individuals as did Torontonian R. David Stephens. Jill Battson, originally English but now living in T.O. (T.O. SLAM organizer and producer of *Word Up* on Virgin Records[67]) was also there, but mysteriously without a T.O. team. Strange, since the team advertised in the handbook. Rumours flew. Perhaps she poisoned the lot of them with Earl Grey tea on the trip down; or maybe she found a tall tree and left them hanging and dangling from various shades of white stockings. But let's talk winners.

Patricia Smith from Boston won the Individuals for the fourth time with pieces she's been performing for five years, and Asheville, North Carolina won the team competition in light of their nationalist fervour. "America! America! America!" doesn't quite turn my poetic crank, thank you very much, but then, neither does America (ignorance is piss).

The Montreal team I competed with placed 24th out of 27 team entries. So why did we fare so poorly? Well, perhaps it had something to do with content. We did not speak of love (a real SLAM seller), nor did we speak of racial anger (it seems that being a young, angry white woman is not the American way). Profanity didn't go over too fucking well, which left me at the bottom of the barrel smuggling booze into non-alcoholic environments.

– from 'Poultry Olympics — The 1995 National Poetry SLAM (Aug 9 - 12, Ann Arbor, Michigan)', by Deborah Ann, *Brazen Orality*, May 1996.

index magazine MONTREAL
literature/performance listings

april 1995

Laura Killam • Richard Sanger • Ian Stephens
Fear and Loathing at Bistro 4

67 Various artists. *Word Up* CD. Battson, Jill & Kulawick, Geoff, producers. Virgin Music Canada, 1995.

kind of writing for the audience, to appeal to the audience's sensibilities.

The first Montreal slam poetry team, which consisted of Julie Crysler, Sabrina Mandell, Deborah Ann and David Jaeger, travelled to the National Poetry Slam in Ann Arbor, Michigan, in August, 1995.

EDWARD FULLER: I went as a judge to the Ann Arbor National Slam Championships, and so I wasn't on the official team. Ann Arbor is a liberal college town, from what I understand. It seemed like a vibrant community, though maybe that impression was due to all the spoken-word performers that

were in town from all over North America. They had a couple of open mics and I performed, but it was just informal. The venues were packed, and I saw lots of dynamic performances at all the different levels of competition.

Ouma Seeks Ouzo and *index*

In the early spring of 1995, a floating collective of people began an automatic writing workshop called Ouma Seeks Ouzo. Almost simultaneously, a number of them gained control of index magazine, a publication that had previously been focused on the more traditional poetry community in Montreal. This gave the spoken word scene it's own publication, and also briefly brought it into conflict with the 'establishment'.

JULIE CRYSLER: I don't even know how I fell into this, but I started doing *écriture en directe* with Corey Frost and Catherine Kidd and a whole bunch of people. We were doing a lot of Dadaist and Surrealist exercises. We would yank out a line from a book and we would all write from that. We would do exquisite corpses.

COREY FROST: Ouma Seeks Ouzo started off as an automatic writing workshop. It was basically the editorial collective of *index*. It wasn't like school where you critiqued people's pieces, it was meant to generate material.... So we decided to do this live because it was fun when we did it in private. Ouma Seeks Ouzo did two independent shows, and also appeared a couple of times at benefits. At the independent shows we would take suggestions from the audience for words and then do automatic writing on that for a couple of minutes, and then perform it live. It wasn't that dissimilar from stuff that Fluffy Pagan Echoes did.

JULIE CRYSLER: I can't imagine that our shows were entertaining, actually (laughs). They were fun for us. There was a Bistro 4 one we did that actually turned the whole audience pretty much into part of our group. We did one also at Lion D'Or, for the *index* show.[68] We had all written poems that were based around a single line. We were conducted by Nick Carpenter, a playwright. So we were all lined up, and he would direct us to speak louder or softer. I remember it ending with Corey Frost saying, "Behemoths… eels… behemoths… eels (laughs)." Again, I don't know how anyone would be able to parse the meaning of what that was about, but it was more sound poetry than anything else, at that point.

SCOTT DUNCAN: In the spring of 1995 there was *Enough Said*, there was *Vox Hunt*, there was the stuff that Fluffy Pagan Echoes were doing, there were all the Concordia creative writing students, and Trish Salah's crew, Ouma Seeks Ouzo…. So there were five or six or seven regular features every month, and every week there were other events, and people coming to town and reading. It was amazing. That to me was the height — it was a few months where that was really what was happening.

COREY FROST: In the spring of 1995… I took over *index* magazine. That came out of the blue. It had existed for a year as a literary events listings thing, and then FEWQ — that I had briefly done some design work for — called me up and asked me if I wanted to get involved. They were looking for an editor, because Stephanie Blanshay — who had edited it — decided that she wanted to leave, but didn't want to see it die.

When they asked me, I thought, "Well, I don't want to continue doing what they've been doing," because it was very insular. It was Westmount-centered, and it was basically publishing a lot of people who I didn't think were really interesting at all. So I resolved that I would surreptitiously take it over and make it into something that I thought was positive, and more centered on the emerging spoken word scene. Then Trish Salah got involved with that too, and then Laura Killam and Dana Bath.

TRISH SALAH: I went away to New York in the summer of 1994 but was dissatisfied with that. I heard that Corey and Colin were taking over at *index*, so I came back to Montreal. Corey asked me if I wanted to become the prose editor at *index* at that point and I started doing that.

ZOË WHITTALL: Trish Salah interviewed me for *index*. I remember sitting at the Phoenix with Trish and getting asked these questions. I was like, "I don't know. I don't know! I don't know who Hélène Cixous is. Sure!" I was so intimidated and so unbelievably shy, but at the same time so honoured to be included.

ANDY BROWN: I did a writing group with Dana Bath and Corey — Ouma Seeks Ouzo, and that got me more into the scene. *index* started going again, and I saw, back-stage, all that Corey and Colin were doing. *index*, for me was job-training as it was for a lot of people. We had to teach ourselves how to do lay-out and advertising and editing. And it had to come out every month.

COREY FROST: It became primarily a listing of spoken word events and some articles about spoken word, and we

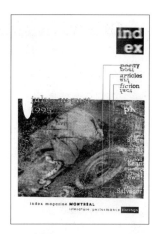

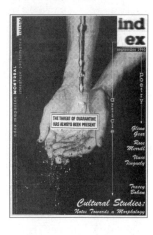

68 *index* benefit cabaret, June 1995.

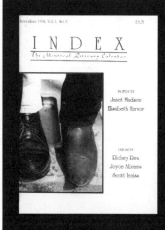

After Frost took over, Blanshay stayed on as publisher. So did Carmine Starnino as poetry editor. Starnino also filled in as acting prose editor and in that capacity solicited an excerpt from Montreal author David Homel's third novel, *Sonya & Jack*, just published by Harper Collins.

That's also when the new prose editor, Patrick Salah,[69] took over from Starnino. Salah, a graduate of the Concordia Master's program in creative writing, decided that Homel's fiction did not fit his editorial vision. He called Homel and told him that the piece was "not queer enough."

For Homel, this was an exclusivity issue. A member of the Federation of English-language Writers of Quebec (FEWQ), Homel attended its annual general meeting in April to ask that FEWQ not distribute the new *index* to its membership as it had planned to do. FEWQ passed that motion, but tabled another motion about future support for the magazine through monthly advertisements.

"It's a question of access and democracy," Homel said later. "An organization for writers shouldn't fund events which, by their very nature, exclude members of that organization. The Writer's Union of Canada sponsored an event last year — the Writing Thru Race conference — and it was very destructive. All I was trying to do was make sure FEWQ didn't suffer the same kind of internal damage."

Salah disagreed: "This is not about exclusivity. Nothing could be further from the truth. I don't have any intention of not publishing people based on who they are, but on how I feel about their writing. That's a pretty standard job description for an editor."

Salah also points out that the term "queer" applied to fiction no longer has to do with whom you sleep. It refers, instead, to anything outside the mainstream. "The rumor is that we're only publishing gay male fiction," Salah said. "Anyone who's seen the first issue knows that's not true."

— from 'The young, the restless, and other anglo misnomers', by Joel Yanofsky, *The Montreal Gazette*, Saturday, May 6, 1995.

published a lot of people who were doing stuff in the scene at the time.

SCOTT DUNCAN: When the article came out in *The Gazette*, surrounding the new *index*, Joel Yanofsky took everybody down a peg. Which means two things. One, he's got an outside perspective, so it's respectable just in the sense that he's seeing it differently and his view is worth something. But at the same time, it obviously meant enough for him to bother.

ANDY BROWN: There were all these people who were hungry and living on the edge... and wanting to promote an alternative. But these people who'd been around for ages were saying, "It's always been *this* way." And Corey was saying, "That's just it, I don't want to do it that way." And you've got to respect Corey for doing that. They probably just saw him as some young brash kid who didn't know anything. They didn't realize what was going on, I think.

CATHERINE KIDD: It might have something to do with the fact that English-language publishing in this province has perhaps reason to feel a little bit defensive to begin with. So when there's a whole other thing going on that they don't really feel a part of in any way, then maybe the suspicion comes from that. Which means unfortunately that it's not suspicion based on anything very real.

COREY FROST: I went to Japan in the fall of 1995. I basically only worked on six or seven issues, and then more people got involved and gradually took it over.

[69] Transsexual writer Trish Salah used to be known as Patrick Salah.

Other Muses

Julie Crysler recognized the prominent role female performers were playing in the spoken word scene, and hosted the Other Muses *series at Bistro 4 in May 1995 to showcase their talents. Zoë Whittall, Buffy Childerhose and Catherine Kidd were some of the new performers who were featured.*

JULIE CRYSLER: I was putting together *Other Muses*, this reading series, and I remember being so excited about it. I was driving my room-mate nuts. I remember psyching myself up to call Erin Mouré, I'd gotten her number from somebody, (whispers) "Will you come and do my reading?" She's like, "Sure!" It was really exciting.

BUFFY CHILDERHOSE: I think I probably became aware that there was some sort of community — although I take issue with that word, and certainly my place in it! — at the show that Julie had organized. Because I saw so many people I had known over the years, who I had run into in many different places, either performing there, or sitting there.

JULIE CRYSLER: What I really wanted was to pay people. I wanted to recognize the amount of effort that goes in. These shows are not really profitable, and we had a pay-what-you-can. I went around to all the local bookstores and asked for free books to give to the readers.

"The year when spoken word invaded the *Fringe*"

Three spoken word collectives mounted experimental performances at the 1995 Montreal Fringe Festival. Groupe de poésie moderne *produced* Le Principe, *Fluffy Pagan Echoes produced* Resistance is Reasonable, *and members of the Ouma Seeks Ouzo workshop produced* (BOOK) Title Goes Here.

BENOÎT PAIEMENT: Our Fringe show was called *Le Principe*. The play was basically what *Groupe de poésie moderne* had always been doing. But there was a little something that joined the whole thing together this time. It was basically a suite of short stories, but we tried to make it as unified as possible, to make one whole thing. And that's when 'the principle' came in, to cement the whole story. The principle created characters and situations, and as the play went along we found out that things weren't possible any more. So we had to eliminate our characters. Within this we were as usual working on the rhythm, on the basic words and the sentences

Groupe de poésie moderne *in* Le Principe, *Fringe Festival*
June 1995
Benoît Paiement,
Catherine Ego, Michel Vallières,
Christine Picard, Bernard Dion,
Sandra Thorton,
Paule Tremblay
Photo by Hubert Simard

181

and the absurdity of the language and of the situations.

SCOTT DUNCAN: This allowed *Groupe de poésie moderne* to work on two levels. The level of the characters, and then the level of the text. Which was a fundamental difference from basic theatre.

BENOÎT PAIEMENT: Exactly. When one of our characters was talking, he was talking or she was talking to another of our characters, and to the public at the same time. This was not like the usual theatre, where the character is within its own world.

COREY FROST: The Fringe festival show, *(BOOK) Title Goes Here*, was kind of the theatre arm of ga press. It was Colin and I, with the addition of Laura Killam and Trish Salah. Fluffy Pagan Echoes were in the show, occasionally (laughs).

VINCE TINGUELY: (Laughing) Nightly! There was definitely a carry-over from the kind of work you did with Ouma Seeks Ouzo and what happened onstage at the Fringe, I think.

Sound poem schematic for Fluffy Pagan Echoes by Ran Elfassy

TRISH SALAH: There was also a carry-over of text and bodies! (laughs) It was a ga production, but of course ga was first and foremost a chapbook publisher, which I certainly wasn't a part of. So, there were these interesting partial belongings, or these bizarre vectors whereby one project encroached upon and enabled another in some ways, while leaving a part of itself behind.

COREY FROST: It was about the time of the *Fringe* show when, in my mind, the two streams of chapbook-making — which is a kind of design performance — and then stage performance, converged. At first it didn't occur to me that they were similar, but it's become a kind of tenet of my artistic sensibility that they are basically the same activity. My experience with the performance of text onstage enhanced my idea that text is always a performance, and that in turn fed into my ideas about publishing. At that point Colin and I had started doing performances together as a duo who called itself 'ga'. At *Enough Said*, they had a ga press night. We did this thing where we had TVs, and our faces were on the TVs, doing the talking. We were just holding the TVs in front of our heads. It would be the author being present but not present, and I didn't even realize at the time that's what it was about. I was really excited about the things we were doing, even though to a lot of people it seemed like absolute childish nonsense. Like when Colin and I sat around and just threw out all of the inane phrases that were stuck in our memory banks from childhood on, that we picked up from advertising or from TV shows or the news. But I was so exhilarated at doing that, because it was pure language, in a sense. But not even pure language, it was pure discourse. It was taking snippets of official discourses, like from the news or

S	(WHISPER) FOUR		OOOOR	ODOUR	POWER	POWER · POWER
Im		FOOOOOOOO R		(WHISPER) FLOUR	FLOWER	ROAR · OAR
Vc	FOUR · FOUR · FOUR		FLOOR · FLOOR	FLOOR · FLOOR	FLOWER	WOW · YOW
R		FOOOOOOOOOO R		(WHISPER) FLOWER	OR-NOR OR-NATE	ORNATE · OR NEW

SILENCE 10 SEC

S	POW!	POW!			BEEP · BEEP	BEEEEEE
Im	ROAWR!		(WHISPER) OW ·			BUZZ · BUZZ
Vc	OW!	OW!		BEEP	WEEP · WEEP	WHEEEEE
R			(WHISPER) WOW			ZZZZZ

S	SLEEEE	SLEEP · SLEEP		RE · ZOW	(YAWN)	HUH · HUH
Im	ZZZZ	ZZZZ	ZOW		LOW · LAW	LOW · LOW
Vc	SHEEZE		SHE · SHAW	LLL · OW	RE · SO	ENOUGH
R	SSSSS	TK · TK · TK	SEE · ZOW	EE · SHAW	EE · NO	REE · SON

from advertising, which are meant to have a specific purpose, and ironizing them. And that's what I wanted to do with the *Fringe* show. So as much as it seemed like playful nonsense, for me there were pretty serious theoretical intentions there. For me, it's the material, whether it's writing or performance or whatever, it's the material that's the most intellectually-informed. For a lot of people, theory is a bad word. A theoretical background is a turn-off. But for me that's the work that's the most fun, because of the liberation that's involved in it. Because it allows an escape from your assumptions about what should constitute a piece of theatre... it really — as far as I was concerned — subverted the conventions of the *Fringe* theatre show. As did the Fluffy Pagan Echoes show. That was the year spoken word invaded the *Fringe*, in a sense.

Photo by Joyce Abrams

word show, that breaks the theatrical illusion. It's much more interactive... because it comes out of a sensibility of talking to someone, rather than talking *for* someone. But our show was definitely not much like talking *to* someone. It was collage.

JUSTIN MCGRAIL: For the Fluffies, it totally makes sense that we worked towards *Resistance Is Reasonable*, the idea of a sixty-minute poetry play. It had all the elements of the group's evolution: in our first act the individual poems were all so different; and then the second act where there was a duet, a trio, a quartet up to a quintet. And similarly, you can see where elements in *Resistance Is Reasonable* came from. Engaging the audience outside the venue and asking them for content, totally followed from the things we had done when Fluffy Pagan Echoes performed outdoors.

COREY FROST: There was really a palpable difference, for me, between the theatre people shows and the shows that were done by spoken word people. It's not like there's a strict demarcation between the fields, and people can do both, but there's a different interaction with the audience, for me, in a spoken

TRISH SALAH: We were involved in this recursive rewriting of the text of our performance, our performance being making chapbooks using text from audience members.

COREY FROST: I thought it was hilarious, a lot of the stuff we did. To be fair, I think that we enjoyed doing it a lot more than the audience enjoyed watching it, most of the time. Certainly on the 'buzz board', the mainstream reaction was not very positive. "This doesn't make any sense!" The *Fringe Festival*'s a lot like poetry slams, really, because people have a certain expectation of the personae that they're going to run into. Each show has a persona, has a personality... just like the poetry slam is usually won by someone who suits the role of the slam poet. But the one comment I remember is that someone said they thought *(BOOK) Title Goes Here* was the most intelligent show at the *Fringe*.

The Last *Word Circus*, The First *YAWP!*

By the end of the summer of 1995 the Montreal spoken word 'scene' had begun to enter a new phase. Fluffy Pagan Echoes lost a member, and became much less active as a group. Scott Duncan organized Big Mouths, Small Stage *for the Montreal* Mirror's *tenth anniversary celebration at Club Metropolis. Vincent Tinguely and Victoria Stanton also started to organize events outside of Fluffy Pagan Echoes, beginning with a live broadcast of spoken word for CKUT, at the Mont-Royal Street Fair in August. The* Enough Said *series was winding down. At the same time, Jake Brown emerged as the host of* YAWP!, *an extremely popular spoken word cabaret.*

VINCE TINGUELY: Most of our poetry or performance was pretty personal, so we found ourselves almost unwittingly becoming really emotionally involved with each other. It wasn't just a professional thing. So when there was a breakdown during the *Fringe*, that was the end of the group as it had been. We had a final *Word Circus* in August. Justin McGrail had graduated with his Masters degree, he'd been here for eight years, and he didn't want to be around anymore.

JAKE BROWN: Concordia got hit with a funding cut in 1994-95, and they cut the bottom fifty per cent off their part-time lecturing faculty, based on seniority. So I was temporarily out of a job. Suroosh Alvi asked me to write an article for *The Voice Of Montreal* about spoken word.[70] When I talked to Ian Ferrier, especially, it sounded by his description that things were rolling *right now*, and that was part of the excitement that I sensed amongst all of these performers. I got so excited by everyone I met that I wanted to throw a party to thank them all. I came by that last Fluffy Pagan Echoes show. I came in the window and Victoria read a flyer right away, advertising my first show ever.[71] So I rented a PA system and decided I might as well perform. There were more than three hundred people, because these artists were good, obviously. I was addicted instantly, because to me it was like everything that thrilled me about teaching a university class, except wild.

Billy Mavreas, May 28, 1999

[70] Brown, Jake. 'Slam This! Montreal's Punk Poets Can't Be Held Down', *The Voice of Montreal*, September 1995.

[71] August 1995.

BILLY MAVREAS: I went to the first *YAWP!*, which was in a warehouse space in Old Montreal.[72] When I got there I saw big naked Jake and I thought, "Hey! What's going on here?" I knew Jake from McGill. But my first impression was that everybody was quiet on the floor, sitting down, listening intently to what I thought was laughable. So I was very curious as to what people were getting from this. I wanted people to stand up and mill around, I guess I wanted a party. But then later on I started appreciating their work.

LEE GOTHAM: I view *Enough Said* as having offered a spectrum of what was possible for a spoken word event. And since then, different elements of that spectrum were taken up and exploited by different events. With the advent of the slam event came a more carnivalesque and more raucous aspect of what took place. I always avoided the competition side of it, and money was never an issue, it was always a free event. The cabaret side of it, the smokey caffeinated café setting and the rhythm of a variety of performances brought up and animated by a single host figure, that took off in a big way with Jake's thing, *YAWP!*. I think *Enough Said* was a catalyst and an instigation, because at least two very determined personalities saw the ultimate benefit, and interest out there for the spoken word.

[72] Patti Schmidt's loft.

Generic Yawp! *poster by Billy Mavreas*

8a. THE *VOX-YAWP!* GENERATION

Three portraits of Jake Brown by Billy Mavreas

The inception of Vox Hunt *had taken spoken word in Montreal to an unprecedented level of popularity. The crowds that hadn't appeared at Lollapalooza's spoken word tent, turned out in droves for the slam series. Jake Brown's YAWP! series was quickly able to capture audiences of similar size, and for the next three years these two series dominated Montreal's anglophone spoken word scene.*

"Giving the Montreal scene a whirl"

After Enough Said *ended, Jake Brown took over the Monday night slot and began presenting YAWP! at Bistro 4. Through the YAWP! open mic, new performers like Heather O'Neill, Iz Cox, Thoth Harris and Emily S. Downing gained notoriety in Montreal.*

TODD SWIFT: The demographic that Jake had pigeon-holed was the under-age crowd, the fifteen to twenty-five crowd. *Vox Hunt* was more interested in the twenty-five to thirty-five, 'been there, done that' crowd. We were Apollo to his Dionysus. He always talked about his Dionysian dancing with the devil and his madcap rituals and his nakedness. It's the punk aesthetic. He always talked about DIY.

RAN ELFASSY: As a waiter at Bistro 4, I don't think I missed even one *YAWP!* show. For me the regular cabarets were good nights, not because I was a performer, but because the tips would be pretty good. It was usually full and often times packed, literally to the ceiling. I remember scrubbing Doc Marten footprints, salted in the winter, from the stainless steel bar.

BILLY MAVREAS: I noticed that Jake was using, for the first few events, the same image on his posters. So I just went up to him and I gave him my phone number and I said, "I'll do posters for you, man. I could do a new poster each time." And of course at that point, there was no question of doing it for money or anything like that. After he saw what I was doing, he basically gave me carte blanche. So I just went haywire after that, and Jake encouraged me to do just that. As long as the information was clear enough, I could do whatever I wanted. And that's where I would say the rock and roll imagery started trickling in.

JAKE BROWN: The two main things that my show was supposed to do, if it was doing it right, was to find new talent, and then to showcase the best of that talent in big venues where they're going to have big audiences.

BILLY MAVREAS: I became a co-producer of *YAWP!* with Corrina Hagel, Mary McDonald and Rachel Demoskoff as the team, and Jake as the masthead or whatever. So I would go to each show. I would try to recruit talent or my friends that were doing something a little bit different. My role, I think, in the beginning was to try to get the spoken word shows a little more chaotic. It's OK to have a fire juggler, it's OK to have something a little off, because it was a variety show more than an 'orthodox' spoken word show.

RAN ELFASSY: I remember when a one man show calling himself 'Knurl' came on. Knurl followed Jake's shouted introduction, making allusions to Plato and the world of the real. Knurl did not

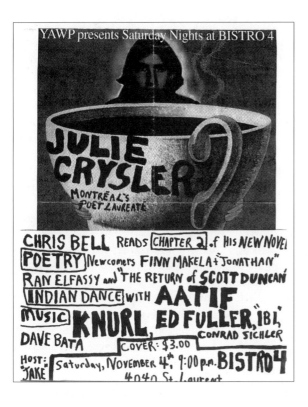

speak, his act was simply a prolonged clap of distortion made by impressively amplifying the sound of metal against metal. The audience reaction was to clamp their ears shut, screaming and — some — smiling. In the quiet that reigned right after the ten minute long industrial tears of feedback, the much diminished MC needed only to murmur the name of the next performer. And how the audience listened! This is when I realized that *YAWP!* was as much about bringing people together to listen, as it was to seduce voices to speak. Within a few months, it was clear to me who were fans of poetry as such and who were simply the curious giving the Montreal scene a whirl. I think that about one third of the audience was familiar faces glued to the idea of a spoken word show.

BILLY MAVREAS: *YAWP!* was stressful at times, but it was fun. I didn't allow myself to be involved too much in what could be called the politics of it. I was able to observe everything and analyze and critique the way people were moving in and out of each other, how spoken word performers were relating, what their politics were. But I wasn't putting any emotional investment in it, so it was very interesting because you could see things without trying to get onto the hill of beans for yourself. But also, my duties at *YAWP!* were ones in which I'm counting money or I'm stamping people's hands, so often I was just in and out of the place. I didn't last too long. I just went back to doing posters because I felt more comfortable behind the scenes.

(left) Yawp! *poster design by Jake Brown*
(right) First Yawp! *poster by Billy Mavreas*

187

RAN ELFASSY: Jake's postering ability was spectacular... ubiquitous *YAWP!*. Here a *YAWP!* There a *YAWP!* Everywhere a *YAWP! YAWP!*.

MARTA COOPER: We started seeing *YAWP!* posters up and went to a *YAWP!* and went, "Oh my God, what is this?" Because I was expecting something like a *Scrivener* reading, and it definitely wasn't what was going on.

BILLY MAVREAS: The only thing that I was doing for a long time, was *YAWP!* posters. And that's how I was recognized in the *bande dessinée* community. Before that it was very small, just a few punk rockers that knew who I was.

73 Childerhose, Buffy. 'Sounding a Barbaric *YAWP!*', feature on Jake Brown, *Hour*, February 13, 1997.

TORREY PASS: Jake Brown was one of the things that scared me away from the performance scene. Because it was becoming sort of like a circus. I got the impression that if you weren't going to cover yourself in slimey white stuff and jitter and scream, then you had no place being there (laughs). I felt, how can I go up and read after that? His stuff's really interesting, I really like it, but it did really change the face of the spoken word scene in Montreal. When he came it was a definitive separation between it being a friendly, everyone's-on-the-same-level kind of thing, to being something that was more like a rock show.

RAN ELFASSY: *YAWP!* was a social event. Like all galleries, one couldn't possibly be pleased with everything. Many recitations were delivered in that New York rage à la Beat. Of course there was booze and sex! Either you got hooched, mooched, or smooched. *YAWP!* was a best-of album. Everything was sincere, production levels were almost always superb, and there was always something for everyone. Naturally, when the performer was good enough to notice I would leave tables waiting.

Vox Hunt *joined forces with* YAWP! *for an* Agent *benefit in July 1996, and a successful show at Club Soda in August. Both* Vox Hunt *and* YAWP! *carried on* Enough Said's *mandate of bringing in spoken word artists from other cities. The first season of* YAWP! *culminated in 'An Evening With* YAWP!' *in Toronto, at the Rivoli, in May 1996. It showcased a number of Montreal's spoken word artists. By the spring of 1997,* YAWP! *was the dominant spoken word show in Montreal; Jake Brown was featured on the cover of the English-language weekly* Hour,73 *and in large articles in the*

English-language daily The Gazette.74
Here he talks about how he brought in
various out-of-town acts.

JAKE BROWN: Todd Swift had success in bringing up some of the New York people. Taylor Mali and Regie Cabico in particular were very successful at their shows. Dan Mitchell wrote bill bissett a letter, asking for a submission for his *Agent* chapbook. He was happy to send it. Todd brought him in for the *Agent* launch75 we did together at Isart. I worked with bill five times after that, in Toronto and here. I just phoned him and asked him to come perform. If other people knew how easy it is, they could do it. For John S. Hall, we e-mailed him from the website, he e-mailed us right back and said he was interested in coming, told us how much he would charge, and he came. Dan Webster got a call from Michael McClure's agent saying that they were touring with a spoken word piano combo with Ray Manzarek. Dan jumped on it. He put on a show for them in Toronto, and then he and I did it here. DKD bankrolled the show, which came just ahead of breaking even, plus five or six hundred bucks on the show. I was scared shitless about that show. A twenty dollar *YAWP!*? But Ray sold the tickets. I tried to book beatnik-style people. It's a very *manly* thing, the beatnik-style, so I booked Fortner Anderson and Scott Duncan and Lee Gotham. It worked fine, it was a beautiful show. There were people there who would never ever go to *YAWP!*, or know what it was. There were people there who had never gone to a poetry show or even seen somebody reading poetry, ever.

TODD SWIFT: I thought *YAWP!* was a disaster... Jake's alliance with the music industry was going to be counter-productive for the spoken word scene. I thought that unfortunately, tragically, *YAWP!* was going to become quite corporate, because it was allied with Donald K. Donald, in a sense. It was gonna be more and more like *Lolla-palooza*, which helped some of the performers that were a part of it, but at the same time the spoken word was off to the side in a small tent. It was never on the grand stage. I told Jake, continuously, that the spoken word should be pre-eminent, but that's not what he wanted to do. So I thought that the *YAWP!* would devolve into a music show, with periodic poetry acts.

Jake Brown at YAWP!
Lee's Palace, Toronto, 1996
Photo courtesy of Jake Brown

Ray Manzarek at YAWP!
Cabaret Music Hall, 1997
Photo courtesy of Jake Brown

The posters on the following two pages are by
Billy Mavreas. Note that the Jim Carroll show
never actually happened.

74 Lepage, Mark. 'Could this be Year of *YAWP!*? — Spoken word — musical cabarets edge toward mainstream', *The Gazette*, January 23, 1997.

75 December 1996.

189

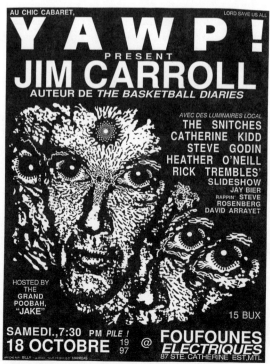

8b. THE *VACHE* GENERATION

"L'importance de la tradition orale, peu importe le langage"

Sylvain Fortier: Le premier spectacle qu'on a fait avec la revue *Zéro de conduite*, c'était le 1er avril 1995, à la Casa Obscura [à l'époque, sur l'avenue Mont-Royal]. Ça s'était décidé très rapidement; on voulait présenter de la poésie et de la musique, et ça s'était organisé tout aussi vite, de trouver les gens pour monter sur scène. On présentait un spectacle dans un endroit où il y avait 40 places assises, maximum, et à notre grande surprise, 200 personnes étaient venues! C'était dément. Ç'a très bien marché, et particulièrement pour moi, qui performais mes textes sur une scène pour la première fois. Ce soir-là, j'ai vraiment assumé que j'étais un artiste.... Un peu plus tard, j'ai perdu mon emploi, et quand est venu le temps de prendre la décision à savoir si je me cherchais un autre travail ou si je me lançais, j'ai décidé de me lancer.

J'avais écrit plusieurs poèmes pour *Zéro de conduite*, j'avais rencontré des gens du milieu, ensemble on avait décidé de faire un lancement-spectacle pour la revue. Ensuite, à chaque nouveau lancement, pour chaque nouveau numéro, il y avait un spectacle, et j'y participais....

Par la suite, un autre projet s'est rajouté. L'équipe de *Zéro de conduite* a commencé à tenir des soirées de poésie-musique un peu libres, qu'on pourrait rattacher à la tradition du spoken word. Ça s'appelait *Les mots-dits mercredis*, et ça se passait au bar Le Hasard [rue Ontario est]. Ces soirées ont débuté en avril 1996 et on en a fait pendant un an.

André Lemelin: Avant les soirées de *Zéro de conduite*, il y eu Alain-Arthur Painchaud et Daniel Brisson qui avaient mis sur pied *Les mardis du hibou*. Une fois par semaine, il y avait de la lecture de poésie. Au départ, c'étaient des soirées inégales car elles étaient trop souvent constituées de poètes saouls qui lisaient platement leurs textes. Sauf que progressivement, d'autres personnes se sont greffées à ces soirées. Il y avait des chanteurs, des auteurs-compositeurs qui venaient jouer, et puis tranquillement, ça s'est diversifié et ç'a créé un courant qui s'est comme imposé

"The importance of the oral tradition, no matter which language"

Although Groupe de poésie moderne *frequently performed in the anglophone venues, the French and English performers remained largely oblivious of each other until Mitsiko Miller began a bilingual series on Sunday evenings at Bistro 4, in the fall of 1995. Her series eventually became known as* Cabaret de La Vache enragée, *and featured writers with an interest in performance and 'oralité' like Geneviève Letarte, Hélène Monette and André Lemelin, and new performers like Sylvain Fortier, Stéphane Despatie, and* Les Abdigradationnistes, *who had already started to make their mark on the francophone poetry scene.*

Sylvain Fortier: Our first show with *Zéro de conduite* was on April 1, 1995, at the *Casa Obscura* [then on Avenue Mont-Royal]. It all happened very

quickly; we wanted to present poetry and music, and found the people to go onstage very quickly. There were forty seats in this venue, max, and to our great surprise, 200 people turned up!

It was insane. Things went really well, especially for me. I was performing my texts onstage for the first time. That night, I really owned up to the fact that I'm an artist.... A while later I lost my job and when the time came to decide whether to find another job or take the leap, I decided to take the leap.

I'd written several poems for *Zéro de conduite*, I'd met people in the scene, together we'd decided to do a show for the publication launch, then after that with each new launch, for each new issue, there was a show and I was in it....

After that came another project. The *Zéro de conduite* team started holding poetry-music evenings, sort of free-style, that could be linked to the spoken word tradition. They were called *Les mots-dits mercredis* [puns on 'damned Wednesdays' and 'spoken-words Wednesdays'], and took place at *Le Hasard* bar. They started in April 1996 and went on for a year.

André Lemelin: Before the *Zéro de conduite* events, Alain-Arthur Painchaud and Daniel Brisson had organized *Les mardis du hibou*, weekly poetry readings. At first they were uneven, because too often it was drunken poets just reading their texts. But progressively, other people came aboard. Singers, songwriters who came to play, and slowly things diversified, a trend was created and sort of naturally imposed itself. Here was a public place where you could intervene as a performer, the evening wasn't really defined. Anybody could come up and take some space. Sometimes a Russian would do word-plays in French. The first few minutes were brilliant, but after ten minutes, it got awful. But every now and then he'd start singing in Russian, and the room would literally sit up. There was Julie Laforme, who did poetry and really impressed me, because everybody else read with their pages but she recited by heart. I saw the difference it made, to be on the high-wire without a net. I loved it and it really inspired me. These evenings were a kind of catalyst for me.

PASCAL FIORAMORE: Towards the end of *Lazy Boyz*, in October 1995, I was still writing texts. One day, a guy who was organizing poetry evenings at the *Porté disparu* café asked me if I'd like to take part. I said yes because... I was 'naïvely' interested in doing just about anything. I'd never been to those events. So one night I went... and I was horrified. Badly organized, a real fiasco. I didn't read that night, but I promised I would the following week. During the week, I wrote seven texts in one hour. While I was rehearsing them, Pascal came over and offered to play keyboards when I read them in public. I thought: "Why not?" So that evening or the next, we gave the show together.

PASCAL DESJARDINS: And the surprise is that we got applause! It was completely absurd. We had a good laugh that time.

PASCAL FIORAMORE: We expected to get *booed*. Ripped apart. But the opposite happened. We went back the next month and maybe did only one or two texts more. This is how the *Abdigrad-ationnistes* slowly started getting around, often with the same texts. But people still wanted to hear those texts.... Audiences seeing us for the first

Mitsiko Miller
Photo by Susan Moss

time had heard about certain texts and those who knew them wanted to hear them again. And this is still true now.

VICTORIA STANTON: So it wasn't pre-meditated?

PASCAL FIORAMORE: Not at all. It was totally on impulse. And it has always been this way ever since we've been doing shows. We've never invited our-selves to be in a show. People hear about our performances, they call us and we go. This is how we discovered plenty of different events. As for anglo-phone spoken word, we mostly had access to it through the evenings orga-nized by Mitsiko Miller, with *La Vache enragée*.

MITSIKO MILLER: After *Enough Said*, Daniel from Bistro 4 asked me to do a show, a French show. I didn't really want to at first but when I went to see different French shows — and I don't want to be mean, but — it was pretty boring. So I decided to do a show, but I'd rather it be bilingual. So that's how it

naturellement. C'était un endroit public où on pouvait intervenir en tant que performeur, et il n'y avait pas vraiment de définition de la soirée. Tout le monde pouvait venir occuper l'espace. Parfois un Russe venait faire des calembours en français. Les premières minutes c'était génial, mais après 10 minutes, ça devenait horrible. Or de temps en temps, il se mettait à chanter en russe, et là, la salle levait littéralement. Et il y avait Julie Laforme qui faisait de la poésie et qui m'avait impressionné, parce que tout le monde lisait avec ses feuilles, et puis elle, elle récitait de mémoire. J'ai vu la différence que ça faisait; d'être sur la corde raide, sans filet. J'ai adoré, et ça m'a beaucoup inspiré. Ces soirées, pour moi, ont été une espèce de catalyseur.

PASCAL FIORAMORE: Vers la fin des Lazy Boyz, en octobre 1995, j'écrivais encore des textes. Puis un jour, un gars qui organisait des soirées de poésie au café Porté disparu m'a demandé si ça me tentait de par-ticiper à l'une d'elles. Et j'ai accepté, parce que... j'étais "naïvement" intéressé à faire n'importe quoi. Je n'étais encore jamais allé à ces soirées. Je m'y suis alors rendu, juste pour voir de quoi il en retournait... et j'ai été horrifié. C'était mal organisé, un vrai fiasco. Je n'ai pas lu lors de cette soirée, mais j'avais promis que je le ferais la semaine d'après. Et à un certain moment, pendant la semaine qui a suivi, j'ai écrit sept textes en une heure. Puis pendant que je me pratiquais à les dire, Pascal est arrivé et il m'a proposé de jouer du clavier quand j'allais les lire en public. Je me suis dit: "Pourquoi pas?" Et, le soir même ou le lendemain, on est allés faire le spectacle ensemble.

PASCAL DESJARDINS: Et la surprise, c'est qu'on a eu une ovation! C'était complètement absurde. On a beaucoup ri ce soir-là.

PASCAL FIORAMORE: Nous, on pensait se faire *huer*. On pensait se faire démolir. Mais c'est totalement le contraire qui est arrivé. Le mois d'après, on y est retournés, et on avait peut-être fait seulement un ou deux textes de plus. C'est ainsi que Les Abdigradationnistes ont

continued...

193

tranquillement commencé à rouler leur bosse, mais souvent avec les mêmes textes. Sauf que les gens voulaient quand même les entendre... Ceux qui nous voyaient pour la première fois avaient entendu parler de certains textes, et ceux qui les connaissaient déjà voulaient les réentendre. Et c'est encore comme ça aujourd'hui.

Victoria Stanton: Donc, ça n'avait pas été prémédité....

Pascal Fioramore: Pas du tout. C'était totalement une impulsion. Et depuis qu'on donne des spectacles, ça s'est toujours passé de cette façon. Jamais on ne s'est invités à participer à des soirées. Les gens entendent parler de nos performances, ils communiquent avec nous, puis on y va. C'est de cette manière qu'on a découvert plein de soirées différentes. Et pour ce qui est du spoken word anglophone, c'est surtout grâce aux soirées organisées par Mitsiko Miller, avec *La Vache enragée*, qu'on a eu accès à ça.

Mitsiko Miller: ...*No matter what, had it been in French or English, what really mattered was the musicality, and also* la nouveauté, et l'importance de la tradition orale, peu importe le langage.

Hélène Monette: L'expérience de *La Vache enragée* est venue éliminer la barrière qui existait entre les poètes francophones et anglophones. Lors de ces soirées, on donnait simplement un spectacle ensemble. Je crois que le travail qu'a fait Mitsiko Miller à ce niveau est très important. Les spectacles de *La Vache enragée* ont démontré une belle ouverture vers autre chose, et je trouve que c'est très encourageant.

La vache enragee			23 mars 97	
8:45	F'ting	10 min		musik
9:00	Pascal Fioramore	15 min		poésie
9:15	Groupe de poésie	25 min		poésie
9:30	Valérie Donnelly	15 min		chant
9:45-10:00	Break			
10:00	F'ting	10 min		musik
10:10	Alex Boutros	15 min		poetry
10:25	André Lemelin	15 min		conte
10:40	PJ Côté	15 min		poésie

started, it was really, *yicky yicky*, you know — *broche à foin* as we say in French [last-minute]. It didn't really have a name, because I didn't think it would last.... I think the first, initial impulse was to make each, anglophones and francophones, discover different forms of literature that were more oriented towards *oralité*. I had a lot of different influences, and I noticed how there were two clans, two different perspectives of poetry, two different views. I didn't do it thinking, "Oh my God, I will bring French and anglos together, oh I will bring electronic music and rap together." That was not the concept. It was really... a selfish image of my taste, and I wanted to share it with other people. It's just that it ended up having a political aspect, which I didn't think about, by bridging the gaps between the two communities. No matter what, had it been in French or English, what really mattered was the musicality, and also *la nouveauté* [novelty] and the importance of the oral tradition, no matter which language.

Hélène Monette: The experiment conducted through *La Vache enragée* eliminated the barrier between French and English poets. During those evenings we simply gave shows together. I think Mitsiko Miller's work in this respect is very important. The *Vache enragée* shows demonstrated a fine opening

Leah Vineberg at La Vache enragée, *Jan. 1998*
Photo by André Lemelin

towards other things, which I found very encouraging.

In it's second year, La Vache enragée *relocated to Le Cheval Blanc, on Ontario Street East. The series had quickly established itself as a popular venue for highly performative work in both French and English. Mitsiko Miller's brash personality gave the event an energetic and exciting tone, where the audience could never know what would happen next. In May 1997, the first* La Vache enragée anthologie *was published by Revue Stop.[76] Like the series, it included both French and English texts.*

MITSIKO MILLER: I was pushy. I couldn't give the performers money, but somehow it was '*bien coté*' in the French scene. So that everybody wanted to perform at *La Vache*. I could give criteria. They would come up to me and say: "I'd like to read," and I'd say, "You know, this is very performance-oriented." They're like, "Ya ya sure, no problem." So they made an effort to be at *La Vache* because they knew it's like, glitter. And I found it was good for them because, Jesus, the usual readings are so boring. Its popularity was really because of the content as well. And we got credibility, I'm glad it got some good reviews.

"Wanting and eager and anxious to read and perform"

While the scene was anchored by three regular series, Vox Hunt, YAWP! *and* La Vache enragée, *performers also practiced in non-traditional theatre, performance art, and one-off cabaret events. The cabaret format has long been a tradition in Montreal's live performance community, and spoken word found itself welcome there, along with musicians, dancers, performance artists and actors. The dynamic interactions between all of these venues kept the scene vibrant and unpredictable, offering a variety of opportunities for both new and experienced artists.*

A new performance poetry troupe, the Rhythmic Missionaries, formed at the beginning of 1996. Like many of the other young spoken word performers at the time, they had begun practicing on their own before being drawn to the larger scene.

DAVID NEUDORFER: Members of the Rhythmic Missionaries all went to elementary and high school and CEGEP together.

JASON SELMAN: We were all writing separately, and not really sharing what we were doing with each other, and then one day we just started to show what we had. I think in the fall Joseph and David took a poetry course, and they started writing intensely. And then from their interest, I think that's where it started.

JOSEPH NEUDORFER: We started writing, and then within six months we started performing. It was just very natural. The written word was connected to the spoken word.

Joseph Neudorfer

[76] Various authors. *La Vache enragée – anthologie 1996-97.* Miller, Mitsiko, ed. Montreal: Revue Stop, 1997.

DAVID NEUDORFER: A couple of guys in our group, the Rhythmic Missionaries, their families are from Barbados. There's Jason Selman. There's Lindsey Mayors, and Michael Woodsworth. We had an amazing storyteller, a harmonica player, a saxophone.

JOSEPH NEUDORFER: Blair, the storyteller played congas. Jason plays trumpet and performs his own poetry as well. Lindsey Mayors, who plays the drums, also performs his own poetry. And there's a new bassist, Phillipe Colprun. Before we started performing at different venues, my brother and I would invite people over. We'd have thirty people in our basement, it was a very intimate setting, with everybody wanting and eager and anxious to read and perform whatever they had. And then we realized that there was this larger community or larger possibility to perform in front of greater audiences. So it was very natural.

DAVID NEUDORFER: I remember an event, *Rough Trade*, with Ian Stephens at The Stornoway.

JOSEPH NEUDORFER: That was the first show we went to. I think Todd Swift hosted.

DAVID NEUDORFER: There was a dub poet — Dee Smith. And I remember seeing Jake there. I didn't know who he was, but he just stuck out. He had huge eyes, looking around for possible next poets. And then we were asking around, "How can I start reading my poetry out loud?" And somebody referred us to Jake. The first event Rhythmic Missionaries performed at was *YAWP!*[77]

Rough Trade – The Death of Ian Stephens

Rough Trade *was organized in December 1995 by Jasmine Châtelain as a tribute to Ian Stephens, who by then had become seriously ill. Although he'd been invited, no one expected him to attend until he walked through the door, shaking snow off the blanket thrown over his shoulders. The reading he gave was to be his last performance.*

IAN FERRIER: Ian Stephens died in March of 1996.

FORTNER ANDERSON: As he grew more and more ill, there were performances that were harrowing, because he expended so much physical effort to appear onstage, and was so visibly sick.

IAN FERRIER: The thing that knocked me out most about Ian Stephens wasn't performance at all, actually. It was when 'A Weary State of Grace' appeared in the *Mirror*.[78] I was totally astonished by that. It was so real, so vivid, and so

77 According to Rhythmic Missionaries member Jason Selman, the first performance by the group was at the Ethnic Origins bookstore.

78 May 5, 1994.

right on the edge, hanging onto existence. I thought it was the strongest piece he had ever done. I thought that when he recorded it, it was still the strongest piece he had ever done. He was so angry about a lot of stuff, so things would come out in fits and starts. I think he was angry about the way culture treated alternative culture, and he was angry about the fact that he was dying. I always got the feeling with his performances that he was trying to punch his way out of something. It had that kind of intensity.

SCOTT DUNCAN: For a long time, Ian Stephens was the god, the king. To me, our quality of production, our output, to some extent comes from who you look up to, and how seriously you take them. I know in Montreal one of the defining moments was when Ian Stephens died, because he was that character.... And maybe it was a center that doesn't exist any more.

IAN STEPHENS: I have no apologies for anything I did. I was just unlucky to get AIDS. I am not chastened by the events in my life. I think when we find a cure we should continue that philosophy to its next level, in terms of sexual mores and a joy in sex and kindness to each other and a celebration of intimacy.

— from 'Dark and Sexy Places' by Gaëtan Charlebois, *MTL Attitude*, November 2, 1995.

Mahalia 'Miss Thang' Verna
Photo courtesy of the artist

Isart and *Coco Café*

At the beginning of 1996, Clement Grant and Carole Faubert opened a new performance space and art gallery, Isart, on Saint-Antoine in Old Montreal. With a conscious mandate to promote grassroots art practices, Isart especially encouraged young Black producers to coordinate DJ nights, hip-hop events, and performance series. Inobe Stanlislaus, Mahalia Verna and Tanya Best were among the first people to organize shows at Isart. They went on to form Inobe Productions, which continues to produce the Coco Café *spoken word series today.*

MAHALIA VERNA: I think it all started when I was studying at Concordia, and I started looking for an extra-curricular activity or implication. I saw that Isart was looking for volunteers, so I started working with the people at Isart back then. I was helping them organize their art exhibits, and that's where I met Inobe.

Inobe Stanislaus
Photo courtesy of the artist

INOBE STANISLAUS: One day Clement Grant was at La Huerta, before it burnt down, and Atif Siddiqi's show[79] was happening there, I think Rima Bannerji was performing. I knew Clement was starting his art gallery, so I had this crazy idea for him — ask artists across the city to define what a diva was, through their own medium, and the show was called *Que es Diva*. He just looked at me and said, "Okay, do it." I felt kind of challenged. I got a bunch of people together and we put this show together, a bit haphazardly but we were learning along the way. Next thing you know the show exploded on us, we had over sixty artists. The place was packed, I never saw so many people in a space like that in my entire life, and I said, "Okay, I like this!" I decided I wanted to do more productions and become a producer.

MAHALIA VERNA: We worked together on *Que es Diva* in March 1996, and from there, when we reflected upon our collaboration we realized what was really cool is that we got a lot of young people together to put up a show, which was quite different from what was normally out there. *Que es Diva* was a combination of all sorts of different underground designers, mixed in with Jake Brown and Karen Stewart, and musical performers thrown in at the same time. So then we went into different avenues. We tried the fashion avenue, little fashion shows with a twist, and then we did the *Arte Moda* fashion / art show at Isart as well. We started using the space for those different things.

INOBE STANISLAUS: During the summer of 1996 Tanya Evanson used to perform at *YAWP!* a lot. I would go to *YAWP!* to support this and that, see Jake Brown, see everybody else, and one day Tanya

was sitting there and said, "Wait a minute, where are all the Black folks?" We saw it was an absence. It wasn't something I thought was done on purpose, I just saw a lack of colour there. Tanya Best said, "Let's do our own show." Clement said, "Yeah, do it."

MAHALIA VERNA: Tanya Best, who's part of the Inobe Productions crew, was attending a lot of spoken word shows also around the city. She came to us and said, "It would be really cool for us to sit down and actually put together a show at Isart." Because a lot of shows that were taking place were floating around town. They would take place in restaurants or cafés way deep in NDG or Montreal West or wherever people could find space to hold a show. Since the philosophy of Isart was to welcome anyone who needed a space to express something artistic, we figured, "Well we're already in here, we're already collaborating with them."

INOBE STANISLAUS: The first official *Coco Café* happened in November 1996. Thirty people, really small, really intimate, at Isart once again. We had a good time doing it, and then the audience was asking for more and more. They wanted us to do it every week, we said no, that's crazy. We started doing it once a month and it just grew.

Selena 'Buttaphly' Iles at the Coco Café
Photo by Juan Guardado from www.madgenta.com

[79] Atif Siddiqi hosted the performance cabaret show *Amethyst Tuesdays*, 1995-1996.

198

Tongue Tied / Langue Liée

Scott Duncan and Jasmine Châtelain had spent the fall of 1995 and spring of 1996 planning and organizing the Tongue Tied / Langue Liée *Word Festival. It was conceived as a bilingual festival, featuring both Montreal performers and guest performers from New York and the rest of Canada. It had four components:* Barauque, *at Cabaret Music Hall, showcased francophone performers;* M-8, *at Isart, was conceived as a rowdy spoken word event with a slam sensibility;* Pheromone, *at Bobards, presented female spoken word artists; and* Vues compressées *was a book art exhibit at articule gallery. It took place from May 3 to May 5, 1996. Although the event was well received by the media and the public, Duncan and Châtelain came into conflict with several established spoken word organizers, and became disillusioned.*

JASMINE CHÂTELAIN: Before *Tongue Tied*, I hadn't done that much producing. I did *Vox Hunt*, we did an erotic poetry event in the summer of 1995. And then I organized *Rough Trade*, a tribute to Ian Stephens in December.

SCOTT DUNCAN: Our understanding was it was the first bilingual literary festival in Canada.

IAN FERRIER: That was an interesting time, sitting down with Scott and Jasmine and Geneviève Letarte, and another *Québécois* poet... and we were asking each other who we knew in the English scene and who we knew in the French scene, and there was hardly any crossover at all.

GENEVIÈVE LETARTE: As individuals, we're a sampling of the population. So logically, if I start meeting anglophone artists and having exchanges with them, it automatically becomes the sign of a current social phenomenon. And in the last few years, with the bilingual events, among other things, you can sense there's something beginning to happen on this front.

HÉLÈNE MONETTE: I discovered the spoken word scene by talking with Geneviève Letarte, who knows it quite well, and also with *La Vache enragée* and then *Langue liée*, because these events put me in direct contact with anglophone performers. But in the eighties, it was still quite a nebulous area.

JASMINE CHÂTELAIN: I was really excited about what was going on in Montreal. I wanted to go with it, and push it, and see where it could go. That was the positive part of it. The negative motivation was feeling like there was so much creativity and energy and effort and commitment being put towards writing and performance in the city, and we weren't doing it justice. We were satisfied to have makeshift events in small venues for free, for audiences of thirty people. Which wasn't bad, that grassroots feeling, but we wanted to make it legit. What would happen if you did make it mainstream and went to a corporation and said, "Give us ten thousand dollars?" But the hard part of it was coming up against what felt like reverse snobbism, over and over again. People were really angry with us for doing something on a big scale. And people perceived it as arrogant, and as being controlling. There were incredible amounts of bitching and power-plays. Artists got really angry when they realized we didn't have hundreds of dollars to pay them.

Organizing that festival was the hardest thing I've ever done in my life. Partly because it's just a hell of a lot of organizing, and tedious amounts of time. Both Scott and I probably worked twelve hours a day for three months, at least. And then at the end, maybe got three or four hours of sleep a night for two or three weeks. I was incredibly discouraged many many times, but I'm really glad I did it. My motivation for wanting to do *Tongue Tied* was — how big can we make this for each other?.... I came away asking is it better to have a *YAWP!*, that is wonderful in its democracy, an open mic type of feeling? I don't know what's better.

SCOTT DUNCAN: When I moved to Montreal, I wanted to become an artist, and started to become involved in a literary scene. One of the exciting things about being an artist is that you're envisioning a different kind of world. And in my eternal optimism, I figured that that meant a better world. And I'd say by the end of the festival that I had a major disenchantment. I think in a lot of ways we — I'm not disclaiming my own contributions to this — created something that was almost dystopian. So much energy was put in places other than the creation of good events, or the creation of good art.

IAN FERRIER: I think that's what burned them out, is how much energy it takes.... They were totally obsessed at the time, I guess that's the only way you're going to do an event like that. But each time you do that... it establishes the possibility of doing another thing like that. It makes it easier.

"Nothing is being recorded here"

Two spoken word recordings were launched in the summer of 1996. Atif Siddiqi had received grants from the Canada Council's Explorations program, and from Heritage Canada for the creation of a live multi-disciplinary performance. It premiered at the Maison de la Culture Frontenac in October 1995.

ATIF SIDDIQI: The production of *Amethyst's Universe* for the stage and the idea of doing sound recordings for cassette and for CD all happened at the same time. The performances were developed first, and then once we'd honed the live versions, we went into the studio just a few days after. This was in October 1995. We put down all the tracks for the CD, and then put the CD out in the summer of 1996. It was the first time I'd ever done an application for funding. I had just come here the year before that, so it all worked out really well.

By this time Catherine Kidd had become interested in writing performative texts. She worked with Ouma Seeks Ouzo, and then began to present long, memorized stories. She incorporated theatrical elements and props, and her collaborative partner Jack Beets created complimentary soundscapes. In June 1996, she launched a cassette of her stories produced by Jack Beets, and Andy Brown's conundrum press published the accompanying book.

CATHERINE KIDD: Jack Beets and I had been doing these live things, and then Andy suggested the book. It was like, "Well, why not a book and tape?" Andy went off with the manuscripts and made the book. We had chosen a lot of

Aatif Y.S / Urania Records
Present a live multi-disciplinary performance

" projette le public avec grandiloquence et concupiscence dans le royaume délirant d'une hermaphrodite sirupeuse. "
Le Devoir
Maison de la Culture Frontenac
2550 Rue Ontario est
Metro Frontenac
18 et 19 Octobre 1995 (20h)
12$ à l'avance, 15$ à la porte

the images together but he made the book pretty well by himself.

ANDY BROWN: I was room-mates with Catherine and wanted to get into publishing, so I thought, "Wow, here's a great opportunity." The writing stands by itself, that's why I wanted to do it. I got thrown to the wolves with Catherine's book, because it was a *serious* undertaking. It was *extremely* labour-intensive.

CATHERINE KIDD: Consistent with the idea of performance pieces being first spoken, I was much more involved with the making of the tape. One of the lines in the 'I-Socket' piece is, "Nothing is being recorded here." Here I am saying this into a microphone. It was kind of strange. It was frankly a big hassle to start to think about how we would record these, because it hadn't been our intention initially. We had to reconstruct what we had done live. We ran around and collected these sound samples from all over the place.

ANDY BROWN: They spent an *enormous* amount of time in the studio, and I just twiddled away doing the book. A friend of Lee Gotham's came to the launch.[80] He took a couple of books back to Toronto, and two days later this guy from Somerville House calls to offer Catherine a book deal.

The Death of *index*, The Birth of *Agent* and *Fish Piss*

In its new incarnation index *magazine had been published monthly from April 1995 to July 1996. By then, many members of the original publishing collective had dispersed, and the surviving members found it increasingly difficult to find the advertising revenue to keep the*

Catherine Kidd, September 1999 at Concordia University

magazine afloat. It's entire publishing run had been designed and edited by volunteer staff, and distributed for free.

ANDY BROWN: At the end it was Tracy Bohan and myself, mostly, and Taien Ng-Chan partly, trying to carry *index* on. It was basically taking up two weeks solid out of every month for both of us, and that was time we weren't getting paid for. It was only sixteen pages, but it would take two weeks just to figure out how to lay it out and even then it would look bad because somebody would do one page, the font was wrong, everything was off and the leading was totally fucked.

I think Corey Frost did a lot better at getting ads than we did. We started paying out of our own pocket. So we would hit the pavement trying to get advertising, and I think that's what really killed it. It would be just so frustrating. Bistro 4 would take out an ad one month, and then not the next. That would pay for half the print run, so all you needed was a couple of big ads, but the people that

[80] At the Mea Culpa Space, 10 Ontario W., July 12, 1996.

Andy Brown, 1997

Fish Piss #2
cover art by Rick Trembles

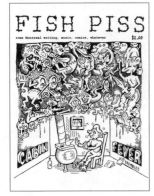

want to advertise in these places are all people who don't have any money, like independent bookstores.... We had these benefits, but a benefit would pay for one print run. Over the course of three months we got in debt fifteen hundred dollars, had a benefit, and we'd only pay off a third of that. It was always this panic to get it done at any cost, whether it looked like crap or something was missing.

I remember Golda Fried and Lydia Eugene came to one of our *index* meetings. All we talked about was money. We were in the hole a thousand dollars, where was this gonna come from? "What did we get for submissions? We have this, this, this. Does anyone like it?" "No." "Okay, we don't have anything we like, there's no advertising." Golda and Lydia were thinking, "Oh, literature, zines, this is fun!" but it wasn't at all fun! It was totally brutal and nasty. We weren't nasty to each other, but it was tense. We decided we would not pay anymore out of our own pockets and it died.

That summer, the first issue of Agent *was launched. Edited by Dan Mitchell of* Vox Hunt, *it featured poetry by Montreal slam champions Julie Crysler, David Jaeger and Sabrina Mandell, YAWP! regulars Elaine O'Connor and Emily S. Downing, and 'names' like Lee Gotham, Ian Ferrier, Todd Swift and Catherine Kidd. It also included editorial content by Jake Brown and Todd Swift, and a top ten guide to the Montreal spoken word scene.*

ANDY BROWN: There's a direct connection between grassroots publishing and the spoken word scene. Look at Dan Mitchell and *Agent*, which was basically a book about the show that happens for the launch. He whipped that off at work, hit the photocopy place on the day of the launch, and there it was. And the writing in there was extremely good, I'm quite impressed with everything he published.

At precisely the same time, a new zine was being put together by Louis Rastelli. Fish Piss differed significantly from index *and* Agent. *It was published irregularly, and its focus was on Montreal culture in general, rather than on literature and spoken word. The first issue appeared in September, 1996, with cover art by Billy Mavreas, and included poetry and prose by Jonathan Goldstein, Heather O'Neill, Golda Fried and Rastelli himself.* Agent *ceased to exist by 1997. Fish Piss continues to appear on an irregular basis.*

LOUIS RASTELLI: When I started I felt a gap, because for one thing there used to

Louis Rastelli with copies of Fish Piss

be *Flaming Poutine*.[81] It was similar, in that a lot of people were involved, maybe thirty per issue. It was very open, it was born out of the general party / drinking scene in the Plateau. *Flaming Poutine* stopped for a year, and people kept telling me I should keep it going, but I wanted to change the format a bit, play with it. Then I got *Fish Piss* going. It just had a snowball effect. Once one issue is out, it's a lot easier to get stuff for the second because all these people say, "Oh, now I see what it's like." It also really helped to try, out of choice, not to make something too fancy out of it, but to keep a lot of stuff that might be considered semi-mediocre. It actually encourages people to send stuff in.

HEATHER O'NEILL: Someone I met who was in Creative Writing at Concordia said, "We were in a class, and we were discussing your piece from *Fish Piss*." That's great, it's getting in there. People are taking it seriously because it's strong, and writers who are writing aren't actually going away. The names are staying.

Girlspit

In the fall of 1996, Zoë Whittall organized a regular series for women performers. Although not specifically a spoken word open mic, it provided a comfortable setting for new artists, like Alexis O'Hara, Anna-Louise Crago and Dayna McLeod. The series ran until the spring of 1997. It was part of a resurgence of grassroots feminist activity in the anglophone scene. Between 1995 and 1998, the organizers of the Bunch of Fucking Feminists *cabaret and the* Girlfriend Action Coalition *issued compilation cassettes featuring musicians and spoken word artists, and the* Women of Colour Collective *published the* Pen.umbra *anthology*.[82]

ZOË WHITTALL: I went to San Francisco, and got to see this amazing show out there called *SisterSpit*. It was a really supportive thing. I just showed up with my guitar and I did a song really quick; open mics only work if they're really short sets. So if you suck, you only suck for five minutes.

At the end of the summer, I was at the Concordia Women's Center and a lot of women were coming in saying, "I just want to play and I don't want to do the *YAWP!* thing," and, "I'm intimidated by that." I felt that there was a real need for a space where it wasn't competitive and it was very open to people who are inexperienced, just to give the opportunity that I got.

ANNA-LOUISE CRAGO: I think the first *Girlspit* show was the first time that I performed in public, reading something, and it was also the first time that [musician] Annabelle Chvostek performed in Montreal.... In Annabelle's case, she's gone on to become such a performing gal. Particularly at the beginning, the series was really important in my personal evolution.

DAYNA MCLEOD: I did a performance, 'The Maxi-Pad Princess', for the Concordia Fine Arts Graduate Students Open House. As a seamstress, I made this thing, and I thought, "You know what? If you can make a goddamn dress out of maxi-pads... you can sew anything." I went and spent about 120 dollars at Zellers, buying every feminine hygiene product they had, just to find shape and colour and size. In terms of presenting the work and presenting the text, it really went hand-in-hand. But in art school you're in such a bubble. It's

[81] *Flaming Poutine*, 1993 - 1995. A collectively-published cultural zine.

[82] Various artists. *Bunch Of Fuckin' Feminists vol. 1* cassette. Stanton, Megan & Whittall, Zoë Emily, producers. Montreal: independent, 1995; Various artists. *Girlfriend Action Coalition – ain't she a beautiful sight?* cassette. Grant, Maureen & Semper, Sam, producers. Montreal: independent, 1997; Various authors. *Pen.umbra*. The Women of Colour Collective, ed. Montreal: The Women of Colour Collective / QPIRG McGill, 1998.

83 Jailhouse Rock, a popular venue for Montreal bands, also welcomed spoken word events. Located on Mont-Royal Avenue near St. Laurent Boulevard.

84 Bloodsisters is a women's organization devoted to issues of menstruation and women's health. They organized the *Pussy Power* parties.

like, "OK, I made this great thing, and I have this performance, which exist as two separate things. What do I do with them?"

I was working with Zoë at that time, and she'd told me about *Girlspit*, and asked me if I would host it. What I wanted to develop, what I wanted to work on personally was one of these in-between personas. To be able to work off the top of my head, and see if I could do it. *Girlspit* was a really good thing for me, in the beginning. And also a really good thing for the community, in the beginning.

ZOË WHITTALL: I didn't realize how many people were interested and how many people needed a space like that. And I certainly didn't expect to have to leave Bistro 4, that was really shocking. At the second show it was like we were on a crowded bus! Moving *Girlspit* to Jailhouse[83] changed in that there was better sound. More band people felt they could go more electric. Somehow,

the café environment fosters this really quiet, serious thing, and I think it got a lot more fun, more loose, louder and gutsier.

DAYNA MCLEOD: With the development of the *Girlspit*, it was a really good opportunity for me to dress up in my fancy drag queen outfit, get to know people, talk to them. Seeing the patronizing introductions from the MCs at these other shows, and the sardonic sarcastic tone basically levelling the performers; it was really disheartening. Doing *Girlspit*, I just always tried to be the big warm hug, without going, "You know, I'm hosting it, and now I'm going to break into song here."

ZOË WHITTALL: I found that a real community came out of this entire year, with the Girlfriend Action Coalition and Megan Stanton doing the *Bunch Of Fucking Feminists* cabarets. *Girl-o-rama*, *Pussy Power* parties and Blood Sisters,[84] there was a lot of grassroots stuff going on.

Unusual Suspects and Volume

Other venues offering an alternative to YAWP! *and* Vox Hunt *sprang up in the fall of 1996, and the spring of 1997. Isart hosted two such series.* Volume *had a multicultural mandate, and* Unusual Suspects *featured an issues-oriented agenda, which offered longer sets within a cabaret setting to spoken word artists, musicians, dancers and political activists.*

VICTORIA STANTON: By the end of 1996 Vince Tinguely and I had been asked through Isart if we wanted to organize an event there. So our first cabaret, performance evening was in the beginning of 1997. Through doing *Unusual*

Dayna McLeod
as The Maxi-Pad Princess
Photo by Jennifer Crane

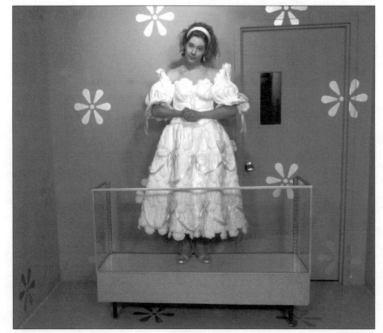

Suspects, we got to meet some more people working in performance, whose work and whose ideas we were interested in. We billed it as an event concerned with social and political issues. We wanted people there who had something to say, as opposed to just being filler onstage. The audiences weren't massive, but we had a good response, and very importantly, I think the performers who were involved felt really good about being there. Some people who had participated in *Unusual Suspects*, like Annabelle Chvostek, Alex Boutros and Kaarla Sundström, went on to organize their own series. They might have done this anyway, but the timing was such that *Unusual Suspects* was a catalyst, in a way.

ALEX BOUTROS: I worked a couple of times with *Volume*.[85] I had wanted to start my own show, but was a little bit daunted in the sense that there are so many shows in Montreal. When I chose to do *Volume* I had to step back and think about what I would bring to producing it that would be different from any of the other shows. So I looked at space and climate. *Volume* at least implicitly made itself known as a multicultural event. I thought that if I put certain combinations of artists together on a bill, that you get an audience that is willing to consume something that might be different. I really enjoyed the final outcome of seeing what does get created. It's really kind of a surprise when you get there on the night to see how the energy moves, and how — in my show anyway — things that didn't match were often put together.

National Slam

Montreal hadn't sent a team to the Portland, Oregon National Slam in the summer of 1996, but Vox Hunt *had set its sights on the 1997 Nationals in Connecticut. The members of the Montreal team were Edward Fuller, David Jaeger, Alexis O'Hara and Heather O'Neill.*

ALEXIS O'HARA: I moved to Montreal in February 1997.... I had this one piece I needed to exorcise, and I showed up at a *YAWP!* on a Saturday night. It was at Bistro 4, and I didn't like the vibe of it. It was a little too high school, it just

Alexis O'Hara as Miss Anthropy
Photo courtesy of the artist

wasn't very welcoming. I think I got there too late anyway, they were already full up. I knew that the *Vox Hunt* was the next day. I didn't know what this slam thing was, but I just showed up and did well! That was kind of an accident, but from that point on everything just kind of snowballed. I was getting asked to do shows all the time.

HEATHER O'NEILL: The first time I went and I did the *Vox Hunt* slam, it was a really fun experience. Probably because I won that night. If I didn't win, then I

[85] *Volume* was a multicultural cabaret series produced by Abacus Entertainment. It ran at Isart from 1996 - 1997.

would've said, "This sucks!" It was also the time I *had* memorized the poems, so I felt good about it that night. Also because you go up three times. When you're in the final round, there's all this anticipation. It was this nice, rounded-off performance piece, and at the end the marks are really close. It was like a television show (laughs), when in life do you get that sort of gratification?

Heather O'Neill, July 19, 1997

EDWARD FULLER: We went to Middletown, Connecticut, and that's where I performed as part of the Montreal slam team. The national spoken word championships is very competitive.

ALEXIS O'HARA: I did a piece that was really well received and I did really well and I didn't screw up and there was a lot of people in the audience that were cheering, and then I got the shittiest scores imaginable. I was supposed to be the ringer for our team that year, and I got the lowest score out of all four of us. If I had gotten even a halfway decent score, we would've won the bout. I was validated by the fact that a lot of people booed the judges, and that Marc Smith, the father of slam poetry, stood up and screamed at one of the judges. But still, it was a horrible experience. It was kind of weird too, because then you had all kinds of people coming up to you going, "You were robbed, man!" Which doesn't really make you feel much better. What I learned there is that no matter how good I am, there will always be people who will be offended by me. Here we are in very conservative New England, and I'm up onstage wearing kind of tight clothes with my voluptuous form, being really sassy and out there and sexual, and these three-quarter-male judge people — they just didn't groove on me.

HEATHER O'NEILL: I wasn't that crazy about the national slam. You assume just because a team is from New York that somehow they'll have some edge, but then they really don't (laughs). No, you just realize how it doesn't matter where you're from, or who's going to turn up with a really beautiful poem. It has nothing to do with anything. It was in a little city, a little college town. I think I found the audience in

206

Connecticut was just not very cool. I did a couple of other slams when I went to New York. At the Fez, which is this Mouth Almighty thing, it's a venue right near NYU, and I did something in Prospect Park. I actually liked them a lot more than the Connecticut ones. The one I did in Montreal, and the ones in New York similarly, I could really feel the vibe that they were picking up on things. If I had a good line, I had this sense that the audience knew, whereas Connecticut was like reading in a subway station (laughs), it might as well have been going right by.

EDWARD FULLER: When we went down there, we could see that the other people were working on another level. Our individual work was good, on par with the other teams, but the other teams were very cohesive — they had performed a lot together, I think, and had worked on developing, critiquing and refining their pieces. They had a strategy and a disciplined approach towards competing and performing in each round. Many seemed to have established a supportive environment in which to work, a way of working together that made them more than worthy adversaries, poetically speaking. They had prepared a number of group pieces that were very elaborate and professional. The term 'performance art' comes to mind — with the respect that is due any accomplished work of art. Our team wasn't as cohesive — we hadn't performed together as a team at all — and we had no group pieces. I'm not sure we knew we had that as an option.... That was just the way it was at that event — I'm sure it went better for Alexis and the team she formed just from having been through the *Vox Hunt* Middletown experience.

Officious Little Students

Victoria Stanton and Vincent Tinguely began performing together as a duo, Officious Little Students, in the fall of 1996. They were partly motivated by a desire to create longer pieces. They self-produced a cassette, Officious Little Students — Wooga Wooga!, *and did a half-hour performance in Toronto in October 1996.*

VICTORIA STANTON: Officious Little Students did a couple of shows; first, at a place called the Rustic Cosmo Café in Toronto. During that same visit we performed at *Canzine*, at the Imperial Pub and Tavern. Which was kind of a mess, because it was supposed to be on a separate stage, but it ended up being in the main area where the tables were, so that was engaging! We were just there looking at people who were sitting right next to us (laughs), at their tables.

VINCE TINGUELY: Literally, it was like standing in the middle of a food court in a crowded mall. Everyone was milling around looking at books. But that must've stuck in Hal Niedzviecki's mind — the guy from *Canzine* and editor of *Broken Pencil* — because the next year they asked us to write 'Reinventing the Word',[86] this article about the Montreal spoken word scene.

Officious Little Students also performed the half-hour performance at the first-year anniversary of the zine Perfect Waste of Time, *and at Forest City Gallery's 12th Annual Open Performance Festival in London, Ontario. The duo appeared several times at La Vache enragée, including a raucous appearance on Michel Garneau's nationally-broadcast* Les décrocheurs... d'étoiles *on CBF radio.*

Officious Little Students *at the Rustic Cosmo Cafe, Toronto October 1996*
Photo courtesy of Vince Tinguley

86 Stanton, Victoria & Tinguely, Vincent. 'Reinventing The Word: The Montreal Poetry Scene Speaks For Itself', *Broken Pencil # 6*, Toronto, October 1997.

207

Immaculate Misconceptions

Three women who had built a strong presence in the Montreal spoken word scene, Catherine Kidd, Julie Crysler and Buffy Childerhose, joined forces in June 1997 to present a full-length spoken word show at the Montreal Fringe Festival.

CATHERINE KIDD: Working with Julie and Buffy was remarkable, because Julie was living in Toronto, Buffy was very busy at the *Hour*, I was doing my novel ... we didn't see each other much, at all. We had spoken a little bit over the phone about the kind of things we wanted to write about, but it really wasn't until a week before the show that we got together with our pieces and tried to make a cohesive show out of it. God damn, we figured we were witches, or something, because the same images and the same themes kept coming up from piece to piece. There were just all these points of contact or points of identity that were completely unplanned.

JULIE CRYSLER: We wrote the monologues for that play separately, and we had only generally talked about the idea of what the play was about. When we came back together we found there were all these freaky connections (laughs) we hadn't discussed at all. I think probably just from knowing each other from over the years, we influenced each other. Catherine's work I really admire, because I don't know anyone who can take apart and put the language back together as smoothly and as deftly. I don't think I know anyone who thinks as easily in metaphor as Catherine.

CATHERINE KIDD: I think that all three of us were influenced by different things,

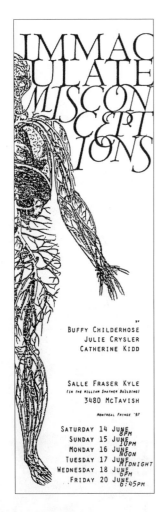

BUFFY CHILDERHOSE
JULIE CRYSLER
CATHERINE KIDD

SALLE FRASER KYLE
(IN THE WILLIAM SHATNER BUILDING)
3480 McTAVISH

MONTREAL FRINGE '97

SATURDAY 14 JUNE 8PM
SUNDAY 15 JUNE 10PM
MONDAY 16 JUNE NOON
TUESDAY 17 JUNE MIDNIGHT
WEDNESDAY 18 JUNE 6PM
FRIDAY 20 JUNE 6:45PM

208

depending on what the hunger or need in our own work was. My work tends not to be very funny, and Buffy and Julie are both funny and so, watching them do that, I could still talk about the same morbid things that I talk about, but be able to do it with a humourous looseness that doesn't usually occur to me when I'm writing.

One thing that discouraged me is that there were very few people from the spoken word community who came to the show. Maybe I can turn it into a good thing, there were completely new audiences there. And I loved the fact we had the stage. I work in movements and funky props, but I don't consider using the space much — and so to have a stage there, it was like the lines of those pieces became even less artificial. I almost felt I could say them in a more naturalistic tone than in performance because there was just more space to use, so you could sit down and say the next line like it was just occurring to you then.

Mainlines and The Devil's Voice

Summer in Montreal is generally seen as a lull time for spoken word shows; the university and CEGEP students who make up a significant part of both the audience and the performers have all either left town, or taken on jobs. But in the summer of 1997, two new series started up on The Main. Mainlines *marked a return to the traditional format of writers reading their poetry and prose to an appreciative audience. By virtue of it's off-campus orientation,* Mainlines *soon began to embrace work that fell decidedly outside of the parameters of academic literature.* The Devil's Voice *had a much less academic air, featuring spoken word artists and poets who often jammed with an invited band. One aspect the two series shared was to offer longer sets to the performers.*

MARTA COOPER: Dean Irvine and I started *Mainlines* because we wanted a place for people to go who didn't do spoken word. *Mainlines* started June 1997 at City Pub. It was successful because of the writing community at McGill. We didn't have an audience that wasn't from McGill until probably August of the first summer. We did a show every two weeks, which was insane. Once that started, I had this barrage of spoken word people who wanted to perform at *Mainlines*. I must've met a hundred people in the first two months of doing *Mainlines*, and I was completely baffled. "Where did all these people come from?"

THOTH HARRIS: I met Iz back in February 1997, and we ran into each other now and then. She saw a copy of my book, and we ended up being featured performers at the same *YAWP!*. That was kind of an impetus. We wanted to do something slightly different from *YAWP!*.

IZ COX: We seemed to have the same energy. We seemed to see eye-to-eye and we related to each other as human beings, even though we had completely different backgrounds. When Thoth started his show, *The Devil's Voice*, in August 1997, I realized that I had a lot more experience in performance. He did his first show, and then I got involved. I guess he and I made this *Devil's Voice* poetry show, because Thoth could get the people, and I could animate it. I had an idea that the performers get paid, because I was upset at the fact that after a certain amount of time, I'd never been paid. That kind of upset me, and what also had upset me

was that I did not relate to a lot of what was going on at the time in the poetry scene. I wanted to see a subculture too, I wanted to see something more hardcore, I guess. Just because of my background, and being tough and being street smart. So our idea was to get a different type of band every time, and see if we could do poetry with them.

Legba

Changes in both venues and organizers took place at a sometimes bewildering speed, but the overall effect was a wide availability of places to perform, from open mics to fully-realized stage productions. One important addition was Legba*, organized by Alex Boutros and Kaarla Sundström. The* Legba *series was first presented at Graffiti Tango, November 1997. The last* Legba *was at the Lion D'Or in January 2000.*

Iz Cox, June 6, 1999

ALEX BOUTROS: Our motivation for starting was to create a space where we felt comfortable performing, and where we could give that to other performers. We had had a couple of shows where we just felt on top of the world, onstage. We really wanted to try and create that, that goal always remained part of *Legba*. It was also about circulating information and knowledge about different things that were going on in the city. *Legba* was often a place for other shows to come and promote themselves.

KAARLA SUNDSTRÖM: We really liked to have dancers on, we thought that it wasn't a very well-attended art form. The mixing of all the disciplines was good exposure for everyone involved.

ALEX BOUTROS: We liked to get a diversity of artists onstage, so that each artist brought in that certain type of audience, and then that audience got to see a whole bunch of other artists that they'd hopefully never seen before. We brought in people sometimes from Toronto because that's the only city we could afford to bring people in from (laughs).

KAARLA SUNDSTRÖM: We really did have missions about the show, but it wasn't all self-sacrificing of our time for other people. Certainly putting ourselves on the best spot (laughs) — a stage we liked and we were comfortable on, with a big crowd — was something that we definitely liked to do!

"Getting so much food from their words"

The next two years were characterized by an intermittent, yet insistent increase in and focusing of activity. Part of this ferment came from a strong spoken word movement among young Black university students, for the first time since the days of the Diasporic African Poets.

Debbie Young
Photo courtesy of na ee lah

AKIN ALAGA: The Neudorfer brothers brought the spoken word scene to me, more-or-less.... It was around February or March 1998 when I started performing. It was *The YAWP! of Love,*[87] (laughs). I was bringing out some of my more personal secrets, problems, and my friend said to me, "Akin, don't — are you going to do that in front of people? I think you should keep some of that stuff for yourself." But I performed that, and after, I was sweating and I was extremely nervous, and I felt like I wanted to go cry somewhere. I felt at the end I had made a mistake. In fact, I decided, "I don't think I'm going to perform ever again."

87 Cabaret Music Hall, February 1998.

DEBBIE YOUNG: In February 1998, I had one of my poems at CKUT, just to do it for some show. I left it lying around and Karen Stewart saw it, and she asked me if I would do a show for Black History Month. I told her that I didn't have anything really new, but I could write something.

NAH EE LAH: In Montreal, I completely cut myself off from poetry, performance poetry, spoken word. I completely cut myself off from it when I left Toronto. Then I went to a Chapters book reading during Black History Month. Karen Stewart was organizing it.

DEBBIE YOUNG: I did that show, and it was so amazing. Oh my God, that show was so beautiful. So I was like, "OK, maybe I'll do this for a little bit." That show was at the end of February 1998.

NAH EE LAH: I saw Tanya Brown, and Karen Stewart perform. I saw Debbie perform, and I missed it. I was just getting so much food from their words.... I remembered what it is to be writing and not just have thoughts up in your head, but to actually be able to get them out of your head through writing. I started talking to Debbie and realized that she knew all the people in Toronto that I knew. We performed with the same people, but just never performed together.

AKIN ALAGA: Some of my poems evolved into a play that I collaborated on with Debbie. The first time I did 'The Drummers', a one-act play, was when there was a series of events called *The Gala Night* at McGill, put on by the African Students Society in March 1998. Debbie and I performed the play together. And then after, I did it one more time by myself. That summer, I put together another play by myself that came out of my poems.

NAH EE LAH: The first show that I did in Montreal was *Phenomenal Women,*[88] that Karen Stewart organized at Isart.

KAREN STEWART: The first *Phenomenal Women...* I was surprised because it was packed. I was like, "Oh my God!" I didn't even have my program all scheduled, I was just shocked. But then I had radio, and print, I'd used a lot of outlets that were able to reach people.

In the fall of 1998, Black spoken word artists performed regularly at the wildly-popular Chalice *series at Isart. The series brought in performers from the New York, Toronto and Ottawa hip-hop poetry scenes. Isart was already facing eviction at the time, because of the planned expansion of the neighbouring Palais des Congrès.* Chalice *was abruptly cut short when Isart's heating was cut off in January 1999, and the pipes burst.*

KAIE KELLOUGH: I first got involved in spoken word right when I got here from Calgary. I started going to open microphones around the area, just to meet people. Then there was a *Chalice* show at Isart, and I met some people and got a little further involved. It was the one with Sarah Jones,[89] that was a cool show. Debbie Young organized and produced that one.

NAH EE LAH: In October 1998, there was a show at Isart where they had, I think three or four poets from Montreal, and some poets from New York, and poets from Toronto. That was a huge show for me, because that was the first show in months where I was performing new material. And it was doing new materi-

al in front of people who I had performed with in Toronto, who knew the style that I had been in then.

JASON SELMAN: Some New York poets came up. That was amazing! And it was like, "Well, I have work to do!" I wished everyone who cares anything about poetry was at that *Chalice* show because that was what the level was; that was what I wanted people to see.

In addition to working on the Chalice *series, Debbie Young co-organized shows through Concordia University, and created a spoken word play with nah ee lah.* yagayah *was first performed in Young's loft on Avenue des Pins in May 1999.*

DEBBIE YOUNG: A part of the genre of dub poetry dictates that you use what is available to you. Which is why *yagayah* was done in my loft. Which is why we did the flyers on our own, business cards on the computer. Because I got to a point where I said, "OK, I'm feeling myself losing resources. And fuck it, that does not mean I'm not producing." I'm coming from the Jamaican ghetto, where there's nothing, nothing! Performances used to happen anyways. They were much better because people would use their bodies, use the tools that were available to them.

NAH EE LAH: The play *yagayah* was the first time, really writing something and working on it, from postering to writing to practicing to designing the program. It wasn't like where you just show up at 8 o'clock, you do your set and that's done.

Karen Stewart, 1999

88 In celebration of International Women's Day, March 1998.

89 A New York City-based poet performer.

9. THE MILLENNIUM GENERATION

The most recent phase of the Montreal spoken word scene marks a maturation both of the performances, and of the ability to create and distribute products. As the millennium approached, there was also another 'changing of the guard' of those who most influenced the spoken word scene.

The New Montreal Slam

The three main series, YAWP!, Vox Hunt and La Vache enragée, would all cease to exist by the summer of 2000. Vox Hunt went first, when Todd Swift moved to Hungary in 1998, but the Montreal slam continued, organized by Alexis O'Hara until the spring of 2000. The 1998 Montreal slam team competed at the National Slam in Austin, Texas.

DAYNA MCLEOD: Alexis O'Hara and I had performed together on the same bill at a *Sense Art* show.[90] She told me about this slam that she was organizing. I was very nervous and very apprehensive

about it at first, because for me, hiding behind some kind of costume-façade was a security that also gave me confidence as a performer. It took me a while to get into, and I still offer some resistance to it, just because of all of the rules.

ALEXIS O'HARA: The first slam poetry show I organized was in March 1998. I wouldn't have taken over the slam if it wasn't for Todd Swift and I having this big feud where he told me that I'll never perform again in Montreal.

DEBBIE YOUNG: I tried out for the slam and got in. On the Montreal team itself you had Alexis O'Hara, Dayna McLeod, Johnny Cheesecake and myself. And among us, our poetry is so different. But we came in first, in Boston. We came in first! We all got high scores, they appreciated our work across the board. And I think that, going into the Slam Nationals in Austin, Texas, really boosted our egos.

ALEXIS O'HARA: Atlanta was really good, we performed in a rock club. That was totally not a poetry scene at all, and they just went crazy for us, everybody was buying us drinks. Austin, Texas wasn't quite as good as I thought it was going to be. But the problem was that it was during the National Poetry Slam, so the audiences were spread thin because there were eight events going on at once.

DEBBIE YOUNG: The Nationals were about people coming from all over the place. Some people were more hip-hoppish. Some people were more typical reading-the-book-type-thing. Some

Johnny Cheesecake at the Impure benefit, November, 2000
Photo by Juan Guardado from www.madgenta.com

90 A multidisciplinary art exhibition, 372 Ste-Catherine, October 1997.

212

people were more theatrical. In Austin, Texas, we didn't do well at all. On one night, I did horribly, *horribly*, with the same work that I did in New York and in Boston. So it just goes to show that it's all up to people's preferences. Because from venue to venue, you did well depending on how many beers people drank that night, whether or not they were clued-in to social issues or they thought you were going to start playing on white guilt, a whole host of things that go into the make-up of the human being.

The 1999 Montreal slam team was Alexis O'Hara, Dayna McLeod, Johnny Cheesecake and Skidmore. They went to the tenth anniversary Slam Nationals in Chicago, an event that was featured on 60 Minutes; Alexis O'Hara placed ninth overall. Members of the team also creat-ed Wreck Election, *a collaborative performance which ran at the 1999 Montreal Fringe Festival.*

"Language is written and spoken and alive"

Mainlines *ran for over a year, first in various venues on or near St. Laurent Boulevard, then at Fauche le Vent, a restaurant on St. Urbain Street. It became two different series,* Rhizome *and* Figurehead, *in the Fall of 1998. Exposure to the freewheeling literary scene in Montreal had gradually changed Marta Cooper's opinion about spoken word as an art form.*

MARTA COOPER: Anne Stone and I became room-mates. She said, "Well, I find it really frustrating that people who write 'poetry' think that 'spoken word' is bad!" She started taking me to a lot more shows than I was going to on my own. I felt that I should understand it,

seeing as I had all of these people approaching me. Anne had a big influ-ence on me starting to be open to it, and also to realize that, OK, there are novices, but there are also some really incredible artists in this city.

August 1998 was the last *Mainlines*. Dean Irvine started the *Rhizome* read-ing series with Adeena Spivak that September, and I started *Figurehead* with Helen Polychronakos, Heather Bean and Kathleen Frederickson that October. One of the big differences between Dean and I was that Dean's measure, his standard of 'acceptable', was increasingly becoming, "This per-son is published." And I was saying, "But this isn't a magazine, this is a read-ing series." I wanted to have a sense of how the person is onstage. Our logo for *Figurehead* was 'language is written and spoken and alive'. And what we decided to try to focus on was bringing in artists who worked with language and who were aware of language being both oral and written. The other big thing is that we wanted to sponsor read-ings for people who, say, the Atwater library just wouldn't bring in. We had a lot of queer writers, we had writers of colour, and a lot of women.

November 1998 — four launches

The documentation of the scene pro-gressed from grassroots publishing and recording ventures to more and more polished work. In November of 1998, Wired on Words launched Millennium Cabaret, *a CD anthology of Montreal spoken word artists, at Bistro 4. Drawn largely from the anglophone communi-ty, its roster covered a wide swath of spoken word history in Montreal.*

IAN FERRIER: The *Millennium Cabaret* CD told a lot of people that they were all

Marta Cooper, 1999

213

in the same kind of community, which maybe they didn't know before. There's a lot for anybody who's interested in the different directions spoken word can go. With Fluffy Pagan Echoes it's about how voices go together, or there's the starkness of a solitary narrative in something that Ian Stephens does or Heather O'Neill does. And then what Jack Beets and Cat Kidd do, which is poetry and music and how they go together. I don't know quite what holds it together. I think that's what I like about performance literature in general, is that we haven't said yet what it's supposed to be. We're still exploring.

In the same month, La Vache enragée's *second anthology was published by Planète rebelle with an accompanying CD. Following Mitsiko Miller's mandate, the collection featured both English- and French-speaking performers. Ironically, the launch at Le Cheval Blanc marked the end of the series, which had run monthly for three seasons, from 1995 to 1998.*

Mitsiko Miller: The reason I stopped is I was completely burned out. The difficulty with the literary community here in Quebec, it's not like in the States, where you sell a book and you make twenty thousand dollars or thirty-five thousand dollars off the book. Demographically, geographically, you can't sell that much. So there's a lot of people who feel hurt, who need attention, who feel in competition towards one another. I guess it's the same anywhere, but I think Quebec is a microcosm of the rest of the world. It was really hard for me because you're promoting artists who basically just want to promote themselves. I really believe in a community, I really believe in community art, I truly believe we are

capable of building a vision or a group of people. I know maybe it's very emotional on my part, but I was completely disillusioned, and that's one of the reasons I stopped. I just couldn't deal with it, and I didn't have time to take care of my own projects....

D. Kimm: It's unfortunate that *La Vache enragée* ended but I understand Mitsiko Miller getting fed up at some point. Producing is hard and can get discouraging. Sometimes you get the feeling you're working for nothing, sometimes artists don't realize all the work that goes into making it possible for them to be in a show. Then the mic is bad and they're upset! A collective could be a good thing. A collective would ensure a certain regularity and, especially, the same person wouldn't always end up doing all the work. Organizers also have personal projects, remember, and there comes a point when they need time for this.

In October 1998, Zéro de conduite *and its performance series,* Mots-dits mercredis, *came to an end. The void was filled by the activities of André Lemelin, who had started his publishing career in 1985 with the literary magazine* Stop. *After publishing the first* La Vache enragée *anthology through* Stop, *he founded Planète rebelle, a publishing house with an emphasis on* l'oralité. *When he was still working with Mitsiko Miller in organizing* La Vache enragée *in its last year, he became involved in another series,* Les Dimanches du conte.

André Lemelin: I founded Les éditions Planète rebelle in September 1997. Since then I've become interested in orality, in storytelling, and with Jean-Marc Massie, in early 1998, I inaugurated *Les*

214

Dimanches du conte, which are held at the Sergent recruteur every Sunday except during the summer. We started these evenings together and at first, we both hosted the events. But Planète rebelle was taking up more and more of my time, so Jean-Marc Massie ended up being the solo MC. During these evenings you get young storytellers and more experienced ones. Slowly but surely, Les Dimanches du conte are gaining a reputation in the milieu. For example, the Festival interculturel du conte du Québec made room for our Dimanches du conte, and the city of Trois-Pistoles, which holds a similar festival, also invited us. I believe Les Dimanches du conte were and continue to be important because they get things moving, they're both a school and a laboratory for storytelling and its revival.

November 1998 also saw a showcase at Isart for Wordlife, a spoken word CD anthology on Anthony Bansfield's Revword label. Officially released in the spring of 1999, it featured Black spoken word and dub poets, including several Montreal performers. It must be noted that only by listening to all three CD anthologies — Millennium Cabaret, La Vache enragée and Wordlife — can one arrive at a clear sense of the full range of spoken word practice in Montreal.

ANTHONY BANSFIELD: I started recording the Wordlife CD in June or July 1998. I'd done this little chapbook anthology, The N'X Step,[91] and the CD was an extension of that. Just as a fan or a spectator, I always love going to these poetry readings, the people that I see and how they relate to the crowd, the whole environment. I thought it was important to get some of these pieces down from people that were regulars in a Black spoken word poetry scene, and

Les Dimanches du conte

In August 1998, writer-storytellers Jean-Marc Massie and André Lemelin founded the Productions du Diable vert. The aim of Diable vert is to promote storytelling and upcoming storytellers, notably by producing Les Dimanches du conte at Sergent recruteur microbrasserie, in Montreal, where emphasis is on traditional as well as contemporary storytelling. Diable vert's mission is to allow a flow between tradition and modernism by allowing a continual to-and-fro between the village made of logs and the village made of concrete.

For over three years now, Jean-Marc Massie has been hosting Les Dimanches du conte, where upcoming storytellers (and guest professional storytellers) come to tell their tales.

This initiative resulted directly from an evening of storytelling organized as part of the Festival interculturel du conte du Québec, where numerous storytellers expressed their desire to appear onstage on a regular basis in an appropriate venue; their desire is obviously shared by the public, which regularly attends Les Dimanches du conte in great numbers.

In 1998, thanks to the success of these evenings, Les Dimanches du conte adopted a weekly rather than monthly schedule by creating distinct evenings: first and third Sundays of the month remained collective storytelling evenings; second and fourth Sundays offered solos or duos by one or two storytellers; and the fifth Sunday (when there was one) offered storytelling workshops (improv, story canvas, relay stories, etc.). Les Dimanches du conte have in fact become so popular that the regular storytellers are now known as 'les conteurs du Sergent recruteur.'

— Jean-Marc Massie

91 Various authors. The N'X Step — A collection of writings by a Montreal-based black writers group, Bansfield, Anthony, ed., Montreal: RevWord Publishing, 1995.

also in a larger hip-hop scene.... Jill Battson took on a really big task, putting together that *Word Up!* CD. That was a real inspiration for me too, just to see that kind of thing done.

Véhicule Press launched a print anthology in November 1998 at Blizzarts; edited by Todd Swift and Regie Cabico, Poetry Nation gathered texts by anglophone spoken word performers from Montreal, as well as the rest of Canada and the United States.

TODD SWIFT: The book was my idea, and with Regie Cabico on board as co-editor, it wasn't too difficult to convince Simon Dardick to publish it. My only regret is that we weren't given enough pages to really include all the resonant voices. The book was a summing up to that point of where I stood on the state of poetry, with the added input of Cabico. My thesis, which Cabico shared, is that the best spoken word is the best poetry, period. Hence we introduced a new critical term into the debate at the end of the century: fusion poetry.

Putting Out The Word

Norman Nawrocki's new book heralded a flood of spoken word publications when AK Press released Rebel Moon — @narchist Rants & Poems in 1997. The same year saw its French version, Chasseur de tornades, published by Les Pages Noires / EDAM; and Planète rebelle launched Cinq couleurs et autres histoires by André Lemelin. DC Books started a new writers series in 1998, which included Anne Stone's first book, jacks — a gothic gospel, and Heather O'Neill's two eyes are you sleeping. Gutter Press published darkness then a blown kiss by Golda Fried in the same year. In 1999 the trickle became a tor-

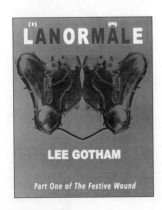

rent: Planète rebelle published books by André Lemelin, Christine Germain, Jean-Marc Massie and Mitsiko Miller; Lemelin's and Germain's books had accompanying CDs. Insomniac Press published Anne Stone's second book, Hush; *Lee Gotham's novella L'Anormale was published by éditions Nonplus; and DC Books launched Todd Swift's poetry book,* Budavox *at Blizzarts in October 1999.*

Anglophone spoken word artists also continued to self-publish in chapbooks and zines. The Devil's Voice launched Poopdeck, *a literary zine, in July 1998. Officious Little Students, Alexis O'Hara, Jonathan Goldstein, Ran Elfassy, Elaine O'Connor and Corey Frost all self-published their work between 1997 and 2000. conundrum press' continuing association with the Montreal spoken word scene included single-story chapbooks by Golda Fried and Catherine Kidd, and a book of posters by Billy Mavreas.*

Spoken word CDs by individual artists began to appear more frequently after the release of three CD anthologies in 1998. In July 1999, Fortner Anderson's Sometimes I Think *was released by Wired on Words, and Les Abdigradationnistes launched their first CD.[92] In the same year, Planète rebelle released two CD / books, Todd Swift and Tom Walsh produced The Budapest Tapes, a demo, and Mitsiko Miller appeared on DJ Ram's first album, and on the collaborative compilation album* Hybride, *produced by Sylvie Chenard.*

MITSIKO MILLER: Sylvie Chenard has a very spontaneous approach. She creates a lot of atmospheres, but she likes dynamics, so she likes to work with people to inspire herself. She came out with

216

La Chartre des Droits des Personnes, and said, "Look you guys, choose an article that really talks to you, write a piece about it, and we'll just jam together." Basically, I wrote a piece about hating the way work is, these days. I was quitting my job at the time, I felt like I was some McDonald's employee. It's a big rant. I thought it was fun, because I'm not usually very political. I was very perfectionist about it, although the project was very spontaneous.

At the beginning of 2000, Planète rebelle and Wired on Words co-published Ian Ferrier's book and CD, Exploding Head Man. *On the CD, Ferrier performed poetry backed by The Exploding Head Band. The CD was launched at Jailhouse Rock on February 18.*

IAN FERRIER: I started off working with Sam Shalabi and André Asselin as the Brio Trio. We added people as it went on.... We tried to work out a form where we could do poetry and music such that you could listen to music and hear the poetry, and one wouldn't be subordinate to the other. Sam had done that kind of work before with Clifford Duffy, I think that was called *The Invention of God*. I liked his music, and he was pretty interested too. We're lucky in this city that there's a bunch of really good musicians who seem to be interested in literature too, Alexandre Saint-Onge is another one. The CD / book covers about seven years of my own work, and then about three years of work with the band. We did lots of recording which didn't go onto the CD, but this project

started in June of 1999. Wired on Words thought we were gonna put it out ourselves, but since it was my work, and I was also editing it, I was looking in the back of my mind for a press to put it out. I ran into André Lemelin, he'd already worked out the format for a series of CD books with nice black covers with the CD tucked in the back. When he approached me and offered to put it out, I went, "Wow! Yeah! Sure, absolutely, that's great!"

92 Les Abdigradationnistes. *Vierges, mais expérimentées* CD. Montreal: L'Empire Kerozen, 1999.

CKUT 90.3 FM
YAWP! presents
Ian Ferrier
Exploding Head Man
a CD book launch
CBC radio ONE
88.5 NEWS AND MORE

a performance extravaganza with

Planète rebelle

Ian Ferrier
The Exploding Head Band
Fortner Anderson
Jake Brown
Corey Frost
Catherine Kidd with jack beets
Alexis O'Hara

Wired on Words

Friday February 18th
at Jailhouse Rock 30 Mt. Royal W.
$5
($12 gets you admission and the CD book)

"*YAWP!*'s winding down"

The YAWP! *machine continued producing shows that combined spoken word with musical acts at Bistro 4, Le Cirque, Cabaret Music Hall, Jailhouse Rock and Artishow until the summer of 2000. Jake Brown brought in playwright Richard Vaughn, sound poet John Sobol with AWOL Love Vibe, Kinnie Starr, and Mecca Normal. He also began performing more on his own, and encouraged* YAWP! *alumni like Thoth Harris, Iz Cox and Larissa Andrusyshyn to organize their own spoken word shows.*

JAKE BROWN: *YAWP!*'s winding down, and I think that I've been shifting myself out of the organizing chair to a point now where I'm not getting the calls from people touring with spoken word projects. Over the last year we haven't brought anybody in. What I've been doing is shifting from an organizer to someone who's wanting to concentrate on my own performances and writing, and I exported myself instead of my show to Toronto this time. I've been three times since September 1999, most recently at Lee's Palace, opening for a rock and roll band, which I love doing. I want to put the time I would've spent on organizing on that, because I want to make a product. I'd like to apply for funding from the government, this time not as an organizer, but as a spoken word artist.

You've got spoken word shows that are the kids from CEGEPs. Dawson's particularly active right now. Larissa Andrusyshyn and Paula Belina, they did an event at Jailhouse. It was full of Dawson kids and they talked over every single act, but they all seemed to have a great time. Larissa did an open mic series at Ciné Express[93] until the owner

of the place kicked her out.[94] She would bring all kinds of business in there that he'd never had, and all he could do was complain about it. But she got people to go see spoken word in an area of town where people don't go to see spoken word. She didn't just quit when she lost her venue, she went into Jailhouse, and they did one at L'X,[95] too. Their events are good because they have the kids at them, and the kids want to be bohemian kids. It's the next generation.

"It's germinating, but we just can't see it"

By the summer of 2000, the Montreal spoken word scene had moved into a new phase. The interest of publishers and film-makers, and a new Canada Council grant program, encouraged spoken word artists to concentrate on producing longer, more polished performances. Live spoken word series are few and far between, but live shows tied to CD, magazine and book launches have filled the gap.

HEATHER O'NEILL: I haven't left the house in the past year because I've been so busy. Everybody who was very involved in the scene is so busy writing books right now, and putting together what they've developed in the spoken word scene in the past few years. Everyone was testing stuff, and now it seems like a lot of people are putting it down on the page or recording.

IAN FERRIER: About a year ago, people had begun to reach the point where they'd played here a lot of times, and they were wanting to get their work out to other places, or get it down and put it on CD. So there was a lull where people were consolidating, trying to figure out what they were going to do next. If we

Streeteaters zine #5
Edited by Paula Belina
co-editors: Dave Levine and
Larissa Andrusyshyn

93 *A café / restaurant on Saint-Catherine Street West.*

94 *Open Mic*, 1999 - 2000. Andrusyshyn hosted the *Wednesday's Child* open mic at Yesterday's, on Bishop Street, 2000 - present. Belina published *Streeteaters*, a monthly literary zine, with its own series of performative launches, 2000 - present.

95 *An anarchist performance space on Saint-Catherine Street East.*

were a richer place, people might've been recording this stuff a year ago or two years ago. I think you're gonna hear about it more in the rest of North America now, what we've been doing.

HEATHER O'NEILL: It might also be me, because I'm more reclusive, but a couple of years ago I'd get a call at least every second week, "Do you want to read here?" All the time, constantly. Now nobody calls (laughs).

ATIF SIDDIQI: One thing I felt is that the spoken word scene here, especially in Montreal, was like a trend. It had a wave, and that wave went from 1995, peaked at around 1996, 1997, and then after 1998 is going down. I think the spoken word scene really had a prominence in that phase, and now it's on its way out. With the majority of people it lost its luster, in a sense. Almost like lounges or raves or whatever other trend has gone through in the nineties.

MITSIKO MILLER: I think it's much more of a cycle. There's a cycle where you need to be out there, and you have to respect that cycle. That cycle has passed, the 'out there'. Now, the cycle is hibernating ideas, creating them, and focusing on your work. And then it'll come back in a couple of years, where people will want to present stuff. I would never be fatalistic. I don't believe that it's *over* and it's *done*, it's dead. You have to respect the way nature works. It's germinating, but we just can't see it. It's absorbing contemporary art, multidisciplinarity, but it'll never die. Never. And in my opinion, it'll gather strength over time.

ANDY BROWN: The Montreal spoken word scene's obviously vibrant. There's certain people that I always go see, and I think these are the seriously talented people. I see these events advertised all the time, and I just can't go to all of them. I remember when *index* was going, everyone was saying, "This is the Renaissance of spoken word in Montreal, and everything's happening right now." Then Corey Frost got back from Japan, and he was saying that it had all ended. But I don't think it has. It's just who is willing to participate, who's involved.

CATHERINE KIDD: In some ways I have less of a sense of a 'scene', and in some ways I have more. There does appear to be a Renaissance phenomenon and a bandwagon in work of this type, in this city, but my stronger sense is that the people whose work I really admire and the people that I connect most with are there on that bandwagon for pretty individual reasons. It seems to be much more about a scene that didn't know it was one, until we started to meet and talk to each other.

Jonathan Goldstein and Andy Brown at Naked Launch *for Golda Fried's chapbook* Hartley's Stories *March 15, 1997 at Bar Sous L'Escalier*
Photo courtesy of Golda Fried

THE FUTURE

VIII

WHAT IS THE FUTURE OF
SPOKEN WORD IN
MONTREAL? WILL IT
SUSTAIN ITSELF? WHAT
POSSIBILITIES EXIST THAT
CAN BE EXPLORED? WHAT
CAN BE IMPROVED ON?
WHAT NEEDS TO HAPPEN TO
BRING THE PRACTICE OF
SPOKEN WORD TO A WIDER
AUDIENCE?

SUBSEQUENT SECTIONS
ADDRESS THE ELEMENTS
NECESSARY FOR THE CONTIN-
UATION OF THE PRACTICE:
ORGANIZERS TO PROVIDE THE
OPPORTUNITIES TO
PERFORM; POSSIBLE
SOURCES OF INCOME FOR
ARTISTS; AND THE MEANS OF
DISTRIBUTING CDS, VIDEOS,
AND BOOKS RELATED TO
SPOKEN WORD.

1. The Shape of Things to Come: "It's going to intensify"

In general terms, there's a lot of opti-mism for spoken word as an art form. This optimism arises from its continued popularity at street level, in the bars and clubs, and from the sense that it has begun to be recognized by the wider cul-tural community, including the initia-tion of the Spoken and Electronic Words Program by the Canada Council.

JAKE BROWN: Different people are going to try different experiments, and keep trying new things and bringing in new people.... We all love what's happening. We're all participating in it, putting our work into it, getting stuff back from it. We have a place to perform, we get asked to perform at other shows, we can create shows, it's wide open.

TODD SWIFT: The 'scene' has to try to work together more, recognize its touchstone history, which includes my pioneering work, with, perhaps, a dozen other figures at best; use those pioneers to build a myth of itself, sell itself as a legend in its own time, as Ginsberg did with the Beats; be less dismissive or snarky, and do what it does best: be sexy, funky, quirky, nerdy, weird, kick-ass, retro and Montrealian.

ENDRE FARKAS: My one observation is that when the Vehicle Poets were doing it, we weren't sure what we were doing. It was more experimental, I think. We knew it happened in the twenties and thirties, but we didn't consciously think of that when we were doing it. It was just poking in the dark. Now, there's already a lot of history, and people are refining it, as opposed to inventing it. But I'm sure there's always invention going on.... I *think* it's building on what's already there. Not the foundation but the structures. I don't know what floor you're on now, but that's my take. I'm sure somebody will come along and either blow it away for a while, or build a different wing to it.

RAN ELFASSY: I think there is more tech-nology and perhaps more people now. But I don't think what's being done these days is any different than what was being done three years ago, and what we were doing wasn't that different from what was being done, say, in the seventies. There is definitely a history to it. Certainly my kind of writing or my kind of performance isn't something that comes out of nothing. I've heard things and I'll somewhat emulate them. I imagine that in thirty years from now — although there'll be certain toys and certain things that are different, maybe the venue will change, maybe it won't be a small café, maybe it'll be a big thing — but I don't think the performances themselves will radically change.

PETER BRAWLEY: It would be great if it kept up, and kept up its diversity and its changing-ness. It's good that it's con-troversial, because it also weeds people out a bit.... The stronger people stay in the scene if it keeps on being as diverse as it is.

THOTH HARRIS: It's kind of urgent that we bring back that kind of experimental mode of thinking that started the scene. I want to be around people who are enthusiastic and who are inspiring.

220

That really turns my crank, to be around other living beings, not just people who are involved in some sort of trip for nothing. But not just within a scene. I mean, a scene has to communicate with other scenes, and other forms. Maybe even corporations. We can actually deal with corporations which are trying to do something useful, that aren't just trying to spend money to make more money, but actually trying to use it for something that is active and that's for people, not for death.

JAKE BROWN: My perception of it is that more, not less, is happening, and that the individual groups doing the events talk less to each other than before. I think it was a smaller number of people going to English spoken word events back in the day, five years ago, but they were more consistent and loyal to different events, so that made it natural that the producers would all be talking to each other, dealing with the same people. But the audience base is I think quite a bit larger now than it was before.... I think I lost significant portions of my audience recently to drum and bass and that style of event. The kids will tolerate nothing except funk and hip-hop. You used to be able to get fair numbers of kids out to see a band, but not now. The tolerance they show for spoken word, even the interest, is lower. What's happened is the CEGEP kids have organized *themselves* into doing smaller spoken word events, and it's split. The other CEGEP kids don't go to those events. They're making a bohemian event of their own with a new bohemian audience. They even dress the right way, to signify that they're not into mainstream culture. They're another generation of people marking themselves off as caring about reading and writing and speaking. Their events are always raucous and crazily organized and they have an energy that reminds me of shows back in the day.

TODD SWIFT: I think it will continue to fragment, to be guided by driven, talented poets and promoters, and suffer the same experiences as any movement based on a niche-mentality. For spoken word to survive and expand as a scene it has to win converts from the mainstream, which is difficult to do. Poetry is a commodity and an entertainment, but it's a damn demanding one in that it doesn't easily allow for the dream or trance to take hold, unlike music or film. Strong poetry constantly calls for attention, which in large doses becomes repetitive or threatening to most audiences — read: boring.

KAARLA SUNDSTRÖM: I'm an idealist, so given the interest in more content-oriented works that I see in popular culture, I think that spoken word could etch itself its own niche. It could be more and more accessible to an audience that doesn't really classify themselves as marginal. Just the sheer fact that the Canada Council's started giving grants for it is an indication that it might become something independent, on its own.

JOHN GIORNO: In my mind it's a golden age of poetry that never ever existed in history of the world. The content in the poetry for the last fifty years exists for a huge, vast audience, which is extraordinary. In terms of everything. In terms of women's consciousness — not only feminist, but women's consciousness, which is deeper, far more profound than feminism — and gay consciousness, which is complicated also; or political awareness; or just awareness of the nature of one's mind.

ENDRE FARKAS: Part of me hopes the spoken word scene keeps going. I've seen it move towards the theatrical. I always liked the idea of cabaret, but part of me over the years has also seen enough performances to say that some of it is really shallow, because it's entertainment on the cheapest level sometimes. But I still feel irreverent enough to want to see performance and spoken word, because I think all art needs a kick in the pants at various times. It needs that kind of energy to revitalize everything. I think that rap poetry has done a lot to re-energize rhyme, meter, rhythms in traditional stuff as well.

NAH EE LAH: Montreal affords you a chance to be very creative. What we are essentially doing is we're returning to the original ways. We're returning to people orally recording the histories of the day. That is the root of our culture. All cultures stem from that, the first people in Africa, and though there are several cultures within the continent, that is a common thread. The beauty of it is that there's a return to that within Black communities, but there is a return to that within other communities as well, because people respond to other people's voices. That's what it is. People can grasp clearly other people's voices, and not just their voices but their energies. It's the sharing of energy, it's intonation, it's how you express it, how you perform it. People are drawn to that. We're all returning to the original ways of communication and of art, and it's very very very oral.... It feels right, and so it will move forward, because it's the start. And that's revolution, it's completing the circle.

DEE SMITH: There is a definite place for this 'form' in Montreal and elsewhere. If I was to compare my limited travel

experiences, Montreal by far out-shines other cities. Some Torontonians most definitely will agree. Like anything else in life, everything goes through its up swing and its down swing.

MARTA COOPER: There's a lot of momentum building. I do have a little bit of a fear that a lot of the time when momentum builds, it reaches a breaking point and goes (exploding sound — laughs) and disperses. But when you get to those plateaus, then you need to have something that comes and injects the community with something that really excites them and gives them something to go with.

GENEVIÈVE LETARTE: I have a feeling that spoken word's popularity is going to intensify. For better or for worse. Who knows? Just because a phenomenon increases in intensity doesn't mean it necessarily improves the quality.

ATIF SIDDIQI: It can die out tomorrow, if people decide not to do anything and not present anything, or bring that to a public space. It's not for me to say what I could predict for it. I would hope that the community will keep it alive and continue to do things. And find new ways, and new audiences to reach, and diversify in some way. Or even keep it small and intimate in some cases. But yeah, keep it alive.

One cautionary note for the Montreal spoken word scene is that it should avoid the insularity that exists in other art communities. Several strategies are outlined by various artists. A more rigourous, disciplined practice is seen as one means to broaden the appeal of spoken word performance. At the same time, accessibility for new artists will ensure that the scene won't stagnate.

GENEVIÈVE LETARTE: La popularité du spoken word, j'ai l'impression que ça va s'intensifier. Pour le meilleur ou pour le pire. *Who knows?* Car ce n'est pas parce qu'un phénomène s'intensifie en terme d'activité qu'il gagne forcément en qualité.

Geneviève Letarte, 1996
Photo by Raymonde April

The cabaret form of multiple disciplines sharing the same stage is another way for spoken word artists to gain inspiration and energy from the larger community.

NORMAN NAWROCKI: I would love to see more artists, more writers, more performers go into the poorer neighbourhoods in this city and do their shows there. Make an effort to reach other people and not read for themselves and their friends and the same crowd of appreciative people all the time. That's one thing I'd like to see change. I think it would be beneficial both to the artists, to the writers, as well as to the public. But that's one thing I try to encourage all the time, is for artists to break out of the ghetto.

LEAH VINEBERG: I feel that the spoken word scene should be supported, but in order for it to be supported it has to have standards. Right now I see it as an amateur form with a lot of really talented people, who are working in a professional way in an amateur venue or an amateur show. I think it's really important to take the next step, because it's important, and I think it has merit. It needs to go to another level, in terms of audience. If you talk about audience, it's becoming very incestuous. It's important to take your work into a totally different audience and see how it fares there.... It's ready to shift. I feel that there are so many people having to stay at the same level, just because the shows stay the same. You can even check it out, with all these international slams, everything's staying at the same level. Everyone's getting really good at the same thing, in a weird way.

ANDRÉ LEMELIN: Personally, I believe the key lies in cultural cabarets. Otherwise,

we're going to keep having these small closed evenings where the same people read their texts among themselves. The cabaret concept makes it more possible to present bilingual events, like Mitsiko Miller succeeded in doing with *La Vache enragée*. Cabaret allows for a greater opening because you can get ten or twelve people from diverse cultures, influences and disciplines performing. You can experience things you wouldn't have seen elsewhere, all kinds of performances and, as performers, you can pick up some influences from it.

JASON SELMAN: I think it's important to measure myself, especially in terms of the Montreal scene. I think it's really small, and I don't know how it stacks up against Toronto and New York. I'd just like it to get to a level where people who are new, when they start, can aspire to something. It's good to have openings, open mics where anyone can go up so you can get a start. But without some type of standard I don't think things'll really get anywhere.

IAN FERRIER: We need to attract more people to what we do. There's a bunch of good performers now in Montreal that everybody knows, and who do all the shows on a rotating turntable. Probably because there's so many people doing good stuff that grew up around Wired on Words, conundrum press and ga press, that they fill up a lot of the slots. The more people who know what this medium can be, and the more they're attracted by it, the more chance that somebody coming along will say, "I want to do that, but the way they're doing it *sucks*! I want to do it *this* way!" I remember when Alexis O'Hara started performing around here, and being exactly like that. She came up to me and said, "I really don't understand what

ANDRÉ LEMELIN: Personnellement, je crois que la clef réside dans les cabarets culturels. Sinon, on va demeurer avec des petites soirées fermées, où les mêmes gens vont systématiquement lire leurs textes entre eux. D'abord, le concept du cabaret permet peut-être plus facilement de présenter des soirées bilingues, comme Mitsiko Miller a réussi à le faire avec *La Vache enragée*. Je crois que le cabaret représente une ouverture plus large, une plus grande richesse, parce qu'on peut y voir performer 10 ou 12 personnes de cultures, d'influences et de disciplines différentes. On peut y prendre connaissance de choses qu'on n'aurait pas vues ailleurs, des performances de toutes sortes, et en tant que performeurs, on peut en retirer une influence.

Leah Vineberg
Photo courtesy of the artist

the hell you're doing! But I think it should be *this*." That kind of spirit.

KAIE KELLOUGH: In order to really establish any kind of good spoken word scene — and what I mean by establish is perform it better at very good venues, get well-paid for it, of course, and also be able to play longer sets and reach a broader audience — spoken word artists have to be proficient in one of the art forms that informs spoken word, either theatre, music or literature. And I think if you have people who do consider themselves serious writers and who have the discipline to create a steady output of good work, and who are trying to establish themselves as writers as well, then the link will be established.

ANNE STONE: The most important thing that could happen would be a generous acceptance of the multiplicity of forms that you see happening at the best cabarets in Montreal. Just to see that happening in a lot of different areas, that openness, and that willingness to lean up and frict against other forms and places and ways, and take something away from that.... The more interesting, talented people that you're around, that you can go out and see or read, the better you are for it.

A particular aspect of Montreal culture is a diversity quite unique in North America. Divisions of race are further complicated by the division between French-speaking and English-speaking communities. Part of the excitement generated by the spoken word scene is its ability to occasionally transcend these boundaries.

JEREMIAH WALL: Let's face it, to have one point of view is always bad because it's homogeneity and it's monoculture and that's a problem in agriculture or culture and it's terrible.

HUGH HAZELTON: When I first started reading here — English over here, and the French scene — especially when I was translating and working on a couple of anthologies, I used to get invited to different events. I went to *le prix Émile-Nelligan*, at *Bibliothèque nationale*. There wasn't one anglophone. There were seventy-five, eighty people, there wasn't one anglophone. Now, that's breaking down, and the more that breaks down, the better.

SYLVAIN FORTIER: My wish is for the francophone and anglophone scenes to intermix more, and so it'll broaden out and result in bilingual shows.... I'd like more and more openness.

HUGH HAZELTON: I like the idea of blending different languages and linguistic groups together in the same reading. Actually there's a Chilean, Luis Martínez, who had readings at a place on Ontario and Amherst. You could read in whatever language you wanted. It was kind of expected that if you read in some third language, that you would also maybe read the same piece or some other piece in either English or French. There was an Algerian guy who read in Arabic, and you hear the rhythms of his Arabic poetry (gives sound example). Then he reads the same thing in French and the images — "I thirst for you," all these desert images. There were people from all different cultures. So I like the idea of multi-language readings.

DEBBIE YOUNG: I would like it if, even within recognizing that we all talk to different people, that there's a bit more flexibility, a bit more openness towards crossing certain boundaries and doing

SYLVAIN FORTIER: Je souhaite que les scènes francophone et anglophone se mélangent. Que ça s'élargisse et qu'on présente des spectacles bilingues... C'est ce que j'aimerais... que ça s'ouvre de plus en plus.

Sylvain Fortier at Club Soda, 1998
Photo by Guy Caron

shows together. People who are considered very apart. There's a very distinct English-language poetry scene north of Avenue des Pins on St. Laurent. There's a very specific scene there. And then there was a scene at Isart, that area. That was a very specific scene. And then there's a scene in parts of NDG, which is predominantly Black. And there's not a lot of inter-performing, not that I've seen.

ALEXIS O'HARA: I think that it's important to try to have some kind of cross-cultural stuff happening. I know Karen Stewart has tried that, I know Debbie Young is very active. I've talked about this with Alex Boutros, she feels concerned about being part of this tokenism in a sense, to always be the one brown girl on the bill. There is a dearth of communication between different cultural scenes. We'll see what happens. I would hope that it would just grow and grow, and that there would be more bilingual events, and maybe somebody will start up a bilingual slam.

The Montreal spoken word scene has always had to adapt to the shifting availability and different demands of venues. Francophone spoken word artists lament a general lack of places to perform their work, while anglophone performers debate the pros and cons of bars, cafés, clubs and art galleries.

D. KIMM: On the francophone side there's a pool of artists who do performance, but presently there aren't really any venues associated with it. This is something that's missing because francophone performance is actually a rather lively reality and would benefit from having a place — maybe a bilingual place — to ensure a certain regularity in the presentation of shows. This is an unfortunate situation because it's always important to leave room for the younger ones, the next generation, and when a place gets established, when there's a tradition, new voices can become integrated into the place by coming to see the others. You need to see what other people are doing before you commit. I also think that a stable place would help improve the quality of performances. When you go to the same place every week for three months, you get a sense of what goes on and which continuity — or non-continuity — you see yourself in.

PASCAL FIORAMORE: I'd like to open a bar to present shows in. I'd like us to determine at least one venue where you'd know that when you go there, you can see a show. The problem in Montreal is that when there are events, that's just it, they're *events* — it's not a regular thing. Ever since Mitsiko Miller stopped organizing *La Vache enragée* cabaret evenings, there's nothing else like it. There are some things but not as many as before. I think the current problem is the lack of structure. On the francophone side, anyway. In the sixties, with the Western music trend and people like Claude Blanchard, there were cabarets, evenings where people told stories, jokes, there was music too and all this took place in taverns. Taverns easily become warm places because they're small, simple and unpretentious. I think we should bring back and reuse these places instead of just waiting for something to happen.

TORREY PASS: What I find now is you'll have more events and you'll have shows, whereas the casual venues have drifted out. It used to be people would amass on a weekly basis. I'd like to see

D. KIMM: Du côté francophone, il y a un bassin d'artistes qui donnent des performances, mais en ce moment, il n'existe pas vraiment de lieux qui soient associés à ce mouvement. Et je trouve que ça manque, car la performance francophone est quand même une réalité qui est très vivante, mais qui gagnerait s'il y avait un endroit — bilingue, peut-être — qui assurerait une certaine régularité dans les spectacles. Je trouve ça dommage car c'est toujours important de laisser de la place aux jeunes, à la relève, et quand un lieu s'installe, quand il y a une tradition, des nouvelles voix peuvent s'intégrer au milieu en venant voir les autres. Il faut que tu vois ce que les autres font avant de te commettre toi-même. Aussi, je crois que s'il y avait un lieu stable pour donner des spectacles, ça aiderait à améliorer la qualité des performances. Quand ça fait trois mois que tu y vas à toutes les semaines, tu vois un peu ce qui se fait et dans quelle continuité — ou non continuité — tu peux te situer.

PASCAL FIORAMORE: Moi, je voudrais ouvrir un bar dans le but d'y présenter des spectacles. J'aimerais qu'on puisse réussir à cerner au moins un endroit où l'on saurait qu'en s'y rendant, on pourrait toujours y voir un spectacle. Parce que le problème, à Montréal, c'est que lorsqu'il y a des événements, c'est des *événements*, justement. Ce n'est pas régulier. Depuis que Mitsiko Miller n'organise plus les soirées cabaret de *La Vache enragée* au Cheval Blanc, il n'y a plus vraiment de soirées du même type. Il y en a encore, mais pas autant qu'avant. Je crois donc que présentement, le problème est qu'il n'y a pas de structure. En tout cas, du côté francophone. Dans les années 60, avec la vague western et des gens comme Claude Blanchard, il y avait souvent des cabarets, des soirées où des gens allaient raconter des histoires, des blagues, et où il y avait aussi de la musique, et ça se passait dans les tavernes. Les tavernes sont des endroits qui deviennent rapidement chaleureux, parce que c'est petit et simple, sans prétention. Et je pense qu'on devrait réinvestir, réutiliser ces endroits-là, au lieu d'attendre bêtement que quelque chose se passe.

Louise Dubreuil

Louise Dubreuil from 'Mindfull Compositions', Play Group, 2000
Photo by Lou Nelson

spoken word shows in my neighbourhood. I'd like to see it become less of a Cabaret Music Hall event. Something where you don't necessarily pay six bucks to see, and it's going to be a big night and seem so much like people on a stage. I'd like to see it go back to being in restaurants, or in cafés or in bars.

VICTORIA STANTON: I hope that there'll continue to be audiences for these smaller scale performance evenings or cabarets. I'd also like to see it become more incorporated into the programming of artist-run centres, so that we'll see text-based performances happening at galleries, or being organized through galleries. They have money to do that, they get an operating grant, and that in part goes to pay artists to exhibit or perform.

LOUISE DUBREUIL: I'd like to see it become a little less tucked away in the galleries, for performance anyway. That's one of the things that I find appealing in the spoken word [scene] — it seems to be in bars, and just kind of out there, in little venues. I'd like something between, a hybrid, a kind of sticking different things together, so it's a public place, it's more on the street. It's like a café and it's artsy, but it's not a downright bar. That kind of in-between space. And small spaces. I think Montreal is a really good place for those kinds of small, small events. Not small in terms of their importance, but in terms of how many people can be there.

ENDRE FARKAS: The thing that we discovered — it's an old Marxist saying — is you've gotta control the means of production. And you've gotta control the means of your space. With Véhicule gallery, we were on the board, and our mandate was the word. I've read at Bistro 4 and it was a fine café space, but

it wasn't a place where you could go and hang out, where other artists came and did things... that's what we did have. We had that space, so people were still more involved in the place, going in there, sweeping up, hanging out, having coffee, beer in the fridge. You stuck around for a show, but you also went out after to the local cheap bar. We used to discuss, "What's the vision?" And part of the vision was the luck of having the gallery space, of having your own space.

The increasingly high standard of performance in spoken word demands larger audiences; this brings up the possibilities of larger venues, and of spoken word tours travelling from city to city.

VINCE TINGUELY: Spoken word could end up in these off-Broadway circuits, or it could end up in the alternative music clubs. It's a very flexible form. The question is, will there be spoken word venues opening? Will there be a touring circuit of spoken word venues? That's quite possible because of the slam circuits. That could open up. I think that maybe the next phase coming up will be people doing longer sets; people who've done the five, ten minute circuit for a few years and have a bunch of material. And then probably touring, because touring is more possible. You can get a grant to tour. You can only do so much before you saturate the scene in one city, so touring seems like the next step, for some people anyway.

ALEXIS O'HARA: The travel opportunities of the slam poetry network are really interesting. If I wanted to I could organize a tour that would go into forty cities in the United States, and I would be guaranteed audiences. I think a lot of people in Montreal don't recognize that potential.

CATHERINE KIDD: It would be really great if there were enough of us who could get together and make a spoken word festival. Maybe one that travelled. Maybe get a grant for it. That would be my most optimistic vision. If spoken word is now sort of getting tacked on the end of larger festivals that concern some other medium, then maybe it's not unreasonable to hope that there could be a travelling circus of spoken word artists, that got good coverage, and that got funding, and where the artists were paid well for it.

IAN FERRIER: One thing we'd like to do is a video of some of the performance people, and try and export that. "This is what we do in Montreal, if you want us to put a show on in Vancouver, say, or in Toronto or in San Francisco, here's something we can show you that says what we do." In Montreal we have this idea of cabarets, where writers, musicians and performers put on one show. I think that's a really beautiful idea. It's fun and various and interesting, and the crowds like it. I think that's something we can export to other places.

VICTORIA STANTON: It would be really nice to bring artists from other cities here, like what Scott Duncan and Jasmine Châtelain did with the *Tongue Tied* festival, in the context of some kind of event, a performance poetry or spoken word festival. Get some people from cities across the country to come to Montreal and show us their stuff. And then set up the performance for Montreal performers too. That requires money, so I'd like to see spoken word continue to get funding.

GENEVIÈVE LETARTE: Lots of Montréal artists — myself included — are very productive but don't necessarily travel around the world much.... It's probably because such trips are very complicated to organize, you have to have the means, find contacts abroad, etc. Also, we can get art grants here, and it's easy to fall into a rut and constantly be creating new shows. So it can be a double-edged sword. I mean that this is why our scene is so dynamic but at the same time, it's interesting to present shows elsewhere, it helps them mature in different ways.

KAREN STEWART: There's a huge female-oriented talented market out there. And I know that we have phenomenal talent here. I think a lot of people think they need to go to the U.S. to really be something. But I think if you have the product and you're willing to move it, and you have the resources to help you move it, then really you can.

ANTHONY BANSFIELD: I think the expansion, the networking and becoming involved in exposing our stuff to a broader audience is what would interest me. Not so much what is happening in Montreal locally, but how will we become part of a global network of cultural workers of similar intent and similar ideas. It comes down to doing this for a real love of it. That noncommercial element has always been pretty strong. It's what tied the scene together with the punk scene or even the hip-hop scene. I think the exposure thing is good, we can build these artist networks, and use it to at least reach a broader audience and maybe expand our horizons as people and artists. And maybe renumerate us a bit, at least cover our costs. That's another movement, where people are finding out how

GENEVIÈVE LETARTE: Ce que je constate, c'est que plusieurs artistes de Montréal – dont moi, d'ailleurs – sont très productifs, mais ne circulent pas nécessairement beaucoup dans le monde... C'est probablement dû au fait que c'est très compliqué de s'organiser pour le faire, il faut avoir les moyens, trouver des contacts à l'étranger, etc. Aussi, vu qu'ici on peut bénéficier de subventions pour nous aider à créer, il est facile de tomber dans un engrenage et de monter continuellement de nouveaux spectacles. Donc ça peut devenir une lame à deux tranchants. C'est-à-dire que c'est ça qui fait que notre scène est vivante, mais en même temps, je pense qu'il est intéressant de présenter nos spectacles ailleurs, car ça les fait mûrir d'une autre façon.

Ian Ferrier at the benefit for the Anarchist Bookfair, May 2000
Photo by Vince Tinguely

they can get access to some resources. I hope the links between New York and Toronto and England, those links continue. England is a move that *we* would like to make.

Within such a wide range of speculation, there is a sense that the public awareness of spoken word performance has reached a level sufficient to ensure that it won't disappear. It's an art form with the potential to appeal to a broad demographic, without necessarily becoming simplistic or empty of meaning. Ideally, it holds out the possibility of countering the homogenizing effects of mass popular culture.

JOHN GIORNO: Just to think back thirty-five years ago or even forty years ago, who would have thought all these things would happen? Once you open a door it can never be closed. Because it's not about anything real, everything is empty and illusory, so poetry can't be retarded unless the world comes to an end. You'll never stop poets from performing the way we've seen them performing, going back these many decades.

MICHEL GARNEAU: I think the spoken word phenomenon is going to go the way of other movements I've seen evolve. The artists are going to exaggerate, do too much, go too far, and everybody will get tired of it. Spoken word will go through a certain decadence, but some things will remain. For example, at a certain time, in Quebec, there must have been a thousand *boîtes à chansons* [folk clubs / coffee houses]. They were everywhere, everybody had one, until people lost the urge to go because they were all the same, always the same artists doing the circuit. Some singer-songwriters earned a good living during

those ten years because they were playing in a *boîte* every night.... Except that they killed the phenomenon.... Currently, spoken word is becoming a trend, so in a way it's dangerous. It doesn't worry me though. I'm just old enough to have seen a number of things come and go. These movements always transform themselves into something else. When a movement like this one reaches its climax, it ends up making the territory bigger. Such is the human adventure.

SIMON DARDICK: Regardless of what any of us say, it is going to change, and it is going to evolve. The exciting thing is prognosticating and trying to figure out what it's going to be, what it's going to morph into. But I don't think we know.

2. Organizing and Promoting: "We all gonna go down to the hole-in-the-wall"

The organization of spoken word events is as necessary as the performers themselves. Often, events and series are organized by performers, both to give themselves a place to play, and to offer others a chance to reach an audience. While performers might complain about this series or that organizer, there is a consensus in the spoken word scene that organizing and promoting events is one of the hardest jobs to take on, and it can sometimes be a thankless task.

ALEXIS O'HARA: It was cool to go to Chicago and see in *The Reader* there that they have a page basically devoted to spoken word events in a week. Any day of the week, you'd be able to find something. There's no reason why that couldn't happen here.

MICHEL GARNEAU: À mon avis, le phénomène du spoken word va connaître le même destin que d'autres mouvements que j'ai vus évoluer. Les artistes vont exagérer, en faire trop, et tout le monde va se lasser. Je pense que le spoken word va subir une certaine décadence, mais qu'il va quand même rester de tout ça un certain nombre de choses. Par exemple, à une certaine époque, au Québec, il devait exister mille boîtes à chansons. Il y en avait partout, tout le monde en ouvrait, jusqu'à ce que les gens n'aient plus du tout le goût de s'y rendre, parce qu'elles se ressemblaient toutes. C'étaient toujours les mêmes artistes qui faisaient le circuit des boîtes à chansons. Des chansonniers ont très bien vécu pendant une dizaine d'années parce que tous les soirs, ils donnaient un spectacle dans une boîte à chansons. Sauf qu'ils ont tué le phénomène... Alors ce que je pense, c'est que présentement le spoken word est en train de devenir une mode, puis à un certain niveau, c'est dangereux. Par contre, ça ne m'inquiète pas. Je suis juste assez vieux pour avoir vu un certain nombre de choses, et je crois que tous ces mouvements finissent par se transformer en quelque chose d'autre. Chaque fois qu'un mouvement comme ça atteint son paroxysme, il finit par élargir le territoire. C'est l'aventure humaine.

JUSTIN MCGRAIL: You don't have to know what you're doing to organize a poetry reading. This also lends itself to the actual poetry. In a lot of ways this is what worked for Fluffy Pagan Echoes and worked for a lot of people in Montreal. There wasn't a question of, "I don't know what I'm doing, so I'm not ready yet." Maybe that's the inevitable thing, is that all of a sudden all these people were doing it. They just crossed that line. And we fed on that, however you identified with it, punk rock or whatever. When I talk to poets in Vancouver, they ask me, "How do I get a reading series?" I answer, "Well, start one."

KAREN STEWART: I love promoting. And I know that there are people who are talented at different things, while they're not so talented in other ways. So if we all get together as a gang and say, "OK, somebody's really good at doing TV interviews, and somebody else is really good at handing out flyers, and writing up press releases," and so in that kind of cup you can make a nice little brew, all of us together doing stuff.

JOSEPH NEUDORFER: You need the organizers. Those putting up posters, spreading the word on a very grassroots level, who aren't necessarily performers themselves. The case in Montreal is that most of the performers are their own promoters. But you definitely need that promotion and those people who know how to spread the word, which is an art form in itself.

The motivations behind organizing vary as much as the personalities of the organizers. Some are interested in bringing artists together to celebrate their talents; others are concerned with controlling the way in which their own performance work is presented to the public.

MITSIKO MILLER: You need somebody that truly believes in a community, and that won't get disillusioned, and that won't be emotional like me. I'm too sensitive to play the mama thing, which you really need. Like an aficionado, someone who is absolutely selfless and that truly believes in everybody. If you don't have that, each one is going to do their own thing, especially when you're talking about a kind of medium where you can't make much money.

TODD SWIFT: I model myself after Richard Nixon. He was a hero of mine, in everything but his politics. He used to say, "The best way to confound your enemies is to get up in the morning." And I think this is something that you've really gotta do, is just constantly reinvent yourself. He had this need to become president. I have a need to be an Ezra Pound figure. I've always loved Ezra Pound. It's always scary to think that you might not be able to write 'The Wasteland', but there's no reason to think that you can't discover someone else who could. It's easier. So, I'm very much driven — psychologically and fanatically — to do this, in a way that Jake is as well. When Jake and I talk about this, we have real psychological needs to promote poetry and do shows. Which anyone who does anything in entertainment feels. It's an over-determined need, and I'm not gonna hide that. But luckily, I identify with a very benevolent cause.

Justin McGrail
Vancouver, February 1999

229

Mitsiko Miller at La Vache
enragée, *March 1998*
Photo by André Lemelin

JAKE BROWN: I used to throw parties. When I was teaching at McGill I'd invite my students and colleagues to a party, have a nice mix of people, and it would be wonderful. The first show that I did, I had more fun than I ever had at a party. And I love parties, I love hosting. I always did, and then this was like hosting times ten! There's performances, and people are brought together in a way that you wouldn't otherwise see. That became instantly addictive. Not so much as an organizer, but as a host. Wanting to host and put on a party, as opposed to organize and produce a show. Then I was so enthusiastic about wanting to perform that I thought the best way to have chances to perform was to organize events myself. And then, accidentally, lots and lots of young people came both as audience members, and to get help.

DEBBIE YOUNG: I'm moving into more producing for two reasons. I want to explore my own work and explore my own constructed limits, but also because — the whole ten minutes of performing — people go home, they forget. It doesn't really touch them. Perform for fifteen minutes, so you get somewhat of a name, and what is the point of that? So what. If my objective is to actually talk to a community, then they need to come and listen for two hours. Ten minutes won't do it. That's partly too why I'm moving into that, and also because I don't want the art to depend on who gives me gigs. I refuse to have people have that type of control over me, like I'm a puppet. I don't have a lot of resources, but really, if you're trying to do something different then you don't need a lot of resources. We need to get back to old school word-of-mouth, you tell your friend, your friend tells her friend, her friend tells another

friend, and we all gonna go down to the hole-in-the-wall and listen to some shit. And that's cool, that's cool.

The most important aspect of organizing a spoken word series is the facilitation of community-building. By creating a space where the artists can gather on a regular basis, the series sets a learning and networking process in motion.

MITSIKO MILLER: *La Vache enragée* was about community art. Definition of community art? Sharing. Sharing with artists, sharing with people, sharing artistic views, *ton matériel*, and the same with my artistic process. It's my curiosity that I wanted to share with other people.

MARTA COOPER: Whether written or spoken, we have a very vibrant writing scene in Montreal. Part of that vibrancy is that people get excited about other people's work. So part of my role as a producer is to provide a forum for an audience. To give an audience to those writers. Montreal is becoming known in other places in North America as having this amazing writing scene, for starters. And we're getting the influence from other places on the continent. The members of the *No Fixed Address* reading series really respected *Figurehead* as a series. Through them, people approached us from out-of-town, so we were able to bring people in. I think when you get that infusion maybe it creates interest in something that we didn't know about before.

ALEXIS O'HARA: Every time there is a slam, new people that I've never seen before will come up and read. And they're not all great, but I think that a big portion of people that come up and

230

slam have potential. I think that it's an interesting environment. It's a medium that will give you immediate feedback, and will send you back home to your desk to get back to work. Whereas an open mic, everybody's just going to be like (polite applause), "That was great." People don't really know. Was it great, or was it not great? Of course it's entirely subjective, those five judges picked from the audience. That's why I try to be the big guidance councillor, afterwards, go talk to people. Especially because there's a lot of young people that are coming in there. That's my community service, in a way, to go to these people afterward and say, "You know, this was good, but this is where you need work." It's not like I'm some expert or anything, but I have a lot of experience and I know what works and what doesn't work.

MARTA COOPER: One of the things that's nice about a series, definitely with *Mainlines*, is that we sought to bridge gaps. I wanted to bridge the gap between McGill and Concordia, and I wanted to bridge the gap between off-campus and on-campus. I think to a certain extent we succeeded in doing that. I don't know how far we got with that, but we laid some groundwork.

Most organizers of spoken word events are also practicing artists. Here, they discuss the difficulties that arise from wearing more than one hat in the spoken word scene.

TODD SWIFT: If there's one thing I want on record, it is that, except for once in all of the shows that I've done, I have never read my own poetry at my own show. I'm always considered an ego-maniac, but I felt that the idea was that I was hosting, and giving other people

an opportunity for their voices to be heard. I get in enough joke-y banter anyway, in between. Somewhere along the line, people forgot that I was a poet, which I am first and foremost. I'm not simply a comedian, or an organizer.

MARTA COOPER: I consider myself to be a writer and a producer. There are things that I would like to do with my writing, with music. If I weren't producing, I could probably get into memorizing my pieces a lot more. But I just don't have the time. First off, you can learn just from being the producer. But also to have the series there; if I'm not there being one of the motivating forces, then a) there might not be somebody else to do it, or b) they might do something that I'm not interested in (laughs). So some of these other ideas have been put on hold because of the producing, because there's only so much that I can get done, and earn a living at the same time.

PASCAL FIORAMORE: I'm currently going through a contradiction. Organizing the *Rodrigol* evenings is very interesting, you invite plenty of people and present a show together, but financially these events bring nothing in, and most of all, they require a huge amount of energy to organize. Sometimes I feel I'd rather concentrate this energy on the *Abdig-radationnistes*, on our texts, our musical side, maybe make music videos, anything that touches our personal projects.

JAKE BROWN: I've been doing less organizing, and I'm gonna be doing even less of it. My enthusiasm for the party aspect of it, and suddenly having a role where I'm being asked to help people, put me in a position where I was having to ask myself questions about it. Is this the most effective way for me to use my mind and resources in the service of

Mitsiko Miller at La Vache enragée, *March 1998*
Photo by André Lemelin

PASCAL FIORAMORE: Présentement, je vis une contradiction. C'est bien intéressant d'organiser les soirées *Rodrigol*, d'inviter plein de monde puis de présenter un spectacle ensemble, mais financièrement, ces soirées ne nous rapportent rien, et surtout, ça demande énormément d'énergie pour les organiser. Parfois je me dis que j'aimerais mieux concentrer cette énergie sur les Abdigradationnistes, sur nos textes, sur le côté musical, peut-être pour faire des vidéoclips, en fait sur n'importe quoi qui touche nos projets personnels.

grassroots culture, or not? Because I don't have a mandate. I don't have any funding or mandate, I applied a few times. I had a sponsorship for a while, that was good for a year and then they pulled out. Without a financial mandate, the amount of time and effort I have to put in to get an audience out to a grassroots cabaret is prohibitive now, compared to before, and I've been scaling back a bit.

3. Making a Living: "I want to eat my art"

The greatest challenge facing the spoken word artist in Montreal is making a living. Currently, there are no spoken word artists who live solely off the money they earn for their work onstage. They supplement their income with odd jobs, they teach in schools, CEGEPs and universities, they practice other, more lucrative forms of art such as writing or acting, or they have 'real' jobs and fit in their spoken word practice where they can.

Kaarla Sundström and Alex Boutros, 1999

JOHN GIORNO: A friend of mine said that in the Hindu tradition, the goddess of poetry is Sarasvati. And Sarasvati has a sister, her name is Laksmi, which is the goddess of wealth. The Hindus say every time Sarasvati gets a bit successful with her poetry, and people love her and appreciate her poetry, Laksmi gets very jealous and takes all the money away so she's poor, so she's penniless. So they say if you're a Hindu poet and you venerate Sarasvati, you must also do one of the wealth deities, Laksmi or another one. If you are doing a Sarasvati practice, you *must* do a wealth deity practice. Because otherwise you're in trouble (laughs) with your money! In the basic nature of it all, being a poet in this world, there's a money problem.

Traditionally, if you're a painter or a sculptor, if you don't sell, you're broke. So you're dependent on the patronage. Poetry's not dependent on any of it, so actually it's a great benefit.

LEAH VINEBERG: Sometimes I've been very afraid to go through my life as an artist, and be recognized after my death. That really bothers me, that notion, because I believe that we need art, and I know that art stands to make a really big difference. I'm sure every single artist since the beginning of time has gone through these pains. But by the same token, I wouldn't want it any other way. We need to be extra-sensitive to the world because that's what we need to reflect back through art. So we're not going to fit in, and I don't mind. You need to respect that you are an artist and this is what you have to do, and so you have to make money in order to be able to do art, and ultimately make money doing art. To find a way to make a living either off of the art, or teaching the art.

KAARLA SUNDSTRÖM: I want the ability to do what I'm doing, for a living. It's not that I want to be rich, I would just love to be able to do this for a living. I don't want to be teaching, working odd jobs, and then being an artist on the side. I don't want art to be something that I fit in between survival. I want to eat my art (laughs)!

ANNE STONE: Some of the reasons that this city has produced so many incredible, talented performers, is because it is a little harsh, it is a little poor, and it is very sophisticated. And the people who get up there and go onstage get good very quickly, because they work their goddamn asses off. Montreal is a sort of an artists' colony because there's such a high vacancy rate and no one has any jobs, and so we can afford to live here as artists. And that's really great, but I would like to see money and support and interest to sustain the community, to have lateral movement that would allow the breakdown of regionalism, and to have people come in and out of this community.

CATHERINE KIDD: It's not easy work. It's kinda funny that if something can be called a song instead of a spoken word piece, it automatically has a sort of legitimacy that what we do doesn't have yet. And why is that? I'm not knocking music, but what I'm saying is, what we do is also work. It's fucking work. You write the thing, you memorize the thing, you rehearse the thing. It's like doing a play. I'm absolutely determined to find a way of trying to make a living, doing what I do.

For many spoken word performers, the idea of supporting themselves on their art is simply out of the question. Here, they discuss the alternatives; the kinds of jobs which might complement their work, the utility of taking shelter in academia, versus the instability of depending on part-time work to get by.

ANDRÉ LEMELIN: My creative projects allow me to get certain grants but I survive mostly by freelancing. It doesn't bother me because I don't create to survive. This may be contradictory but, the day I start making a living from my creative work is the day I've turned professional, and I fear that day; I don't want to find myself in that situation. As a storyteller, interesting opportunities sometimes come up and it's happened a couple of times that I've been confronted with the fact that I could turn pro. I wondered if I should accept certain

offers, but in the end I turned them down. I want to continue creating and performing when I want to, without being restricted by criteria — financial ones for example. I want to be free to take part in an evening where everybody will get paid, as well as to attend a fundraiser for a community organization and not get paid. I just want to be able to do what I'm doing mostly for the pleasure of it, and I want to keep my creative process separate from the commercial process. If I commercialize myself, if I become a professional storyteller who performs every day, I think I'll get bored, I'll be sad.

MITSIKO MILLER: When I finished my Masters, my parents asked me, "You've been offered a job in this huge corporation, $45 000 to start, and now you've refused? Why did you refuse this, are you crazy?" I said, "Well, I need to do something where I feel comfortable." No matter what I do, if it's to put bread on my table, it has to be something where I can be creative. Journalism, for me, or work as a publicist was the best way to stay creative. These were ways for me to be creative, to keep on writing, and to grow as well. I write not only for the pleasure of writing, but also I love to observe things and make *un bilan* of either values, *des mœurs, des valeurs, ou des patterns que des gens ont.* So I'm able to do that *and* make a living. I don't see it as something that disenables me to be creative, it just pushed me deeper into what I want to do.

GOLDA FRIED: I want an income, I've always wanted to be an independent girl. I'm sure it's a lifelong thing, to figure out how to get by. I still don't know (laughs), I'm still working on that. At this point my parents are telling their

ANDRÉ LEMELIN: À l'occasion, mes projets de création me permettent de recevoir des bourses, mais c'est surtout grâce à des contrats de pigiste que je peux survivre. Or, ça ne me dérange pas, car je ne crée pas pour susbsister. C'est peut-être contradictoire, mais le jour où je vivrai de ma création, c'est que je serai devenu professionnel, et j'ai peur de cette journée; je n'ai pas envie de me retrouver dans cette situation. En tant que conteur, on rencontre parfois des opportunités assez intéressantes, et une ou deux fois j'ai été confronté au fait où je pourrais éventuellement devenir professionnel. Je me suis demandé si je devais accepter certaines propositions, puis j'ai finalement décidé que non. Je veux pouvoir continuer de créer et de performer quand ça me tente, sans être contraint par des critères monétaires, par exemple. Je veux être libre de choisir de participer à une soirée où tout le monde sera payé, autant que d'aller dans une soirée de financement pour un organisme communautaire et de ne pas être rémunéré. En fait, je désire simplement continuer à faire ce que je fais pour le plaisir avant tout, et je veux que mon processus de création reste en dehors du processus commercial. Si je devenais un conteur professionnel qui se produisait à tous les jours, je pense que je me blaserais, je serais triste.

233

Fortner Anderson performs at Concordia Univerity, September 1999
Photos by Owen Egan

friends that I'm a writer, but with me they're always like, "Why don't you teach?" I always think that when you're teaching, it's not that you can't be an artist, but it definitely works the other side of the brain. It's not the same thing. If you're still going to be an artist, you have to make time for that. I'm always scared if I teach, then that's it, it'll be over. But at the same time, so far — my waitressing job and my clerical job — I haven't been able to write either, because I'm totally burnt out.

FORTNER ANDERSON: One of the problems with work, of course, is that it takes up so much time. It takes up physical, emotional and intellectual energies. It's hard to put aside enough of those energies to continue to create after work, as well.

JONATHAN GOLDSTEIN: I went back to school. I actually just finished the course work and I gotta get my thesis in. I had been working really crappy jobs for at least the past ten years, since I moved out of my parent's home. Being in school made me realize that I was kind of in a rut. You end up doing a crappy job in order to be able to do other things that you want to do, but at a certain point I realized once I got out of that, that the job had me more than I realized. I dealt with it with a high degree of irony, but I think it was kind of depressing in ways that I didn't even realize. You lose a lot of years. There's not always a way around it, but you could kind of short-change yourself in that way too. So getting out of that for a while was, I think, a really good thing. In school, I taught for the first time. I was teaching a composition class last semester, and that opened new doors. I realized I like it. It beats having to sell *The Gazette* on the telephone, or teaching magic in elementary

schools. I wasn't a good magician. My hands would always sweat, I would always drop things.

Money is available for spoken word artists from various levels of arts council funding. Although crucial, there is rarely enough money from these sources to sustain a career over the years. This is a situation not likely to change in the near future given the current political climate, which questions government funding for anything but business and industry.

ANNE STONE: I had dropped out of law school after three weeks, because I was horrified. I didn't like it, and I didn't like the people. I didn't like anything about it. I was writing stories and poetry all the time when I came home from law school, and so I quit to live in a basement and write. But I wasn't a writer. This was just what I wanted to do instead of law school (laughs). Eventually I packed up all my things and I came to Montreal. It was when I came to Montreal that I started to write seriously, and I applied for a grant and got it. And that moment where I actually got money to write, that was pretty... unbelievable, for me, at the time.

FORTNER ANDERSON: Certainly one of the things about the Canada Council and these others, good work does get supported. But most of the work that's supported by the Canada Council is mainstream. If I'm not mistaken, the majority of the funds go to symphonies, ballets, major art galleries and museums that service another stream of expression than the one I'm particularly interested in.

ALEX BOUTROS: I think that that's really important for all artists, the grants are hugely necessary and hugely important. But I fear — and maybe it's just my thing — those aren't always going to be a viable option for artists in the future. I really believe that government funding is going to disappear. I think for artists, that's in the back of their mind. A grant isn't a salary.

JOHN GIORNO: When in the United States the National Endowment for the Arts vanished (laughs)... when the money vanished, it didn't affect poetry. A lot of it had to do with various elements of a university academic milieu. If it ever trickled down to us, it trickled down as a few small books that got published or you got a little fee for performing. But never any real money to live on, for instance. When they start cutting back, suddenly you're no longer getting your small salary, if you're a poetry administrator, but it doesn't affect the poetry. Poets, they go ahead and do it in a church. Poetry, as we know, is as strong as it ever was in the eighties. It just shifts. For instance, for doing all those Giorno Poetry Systems albums, I used to get grants from the National Endowment and from the New York State Council, separately. Ten thousand dollars a year from each, which was in the seventies a lot of money. The last album I applied to the National Endowment for was *A Diamond Hidden In The Mouth Of A Corpse,*[96] which is a compilation, it had the Keith Haring cover. And the usual, when you finish the album, you send in the album and a fiscal report. So I got a letter back from the National Endowment, from a woman called Mary McCarthy. And then four months later I got back *another* letter from her saying, "We have re-evaluated your final fiscal report, and we consider that you have not satisfied the guidelines from your grant because there is not enough 'literary content' on this album to justify fulfillment of —" or whatever it was. Then a second paragraph explaining it in more detail, and then a third paragraph that said, "Because there is not enough literary content on this album, you are not eligible to apply next year for a grant from the small presses category." I knew her slightly. I thought, "Why didn't she call me and tell me?" I was sitting here, I was saying, "I could almost frame this letter, it's so extraordinary!" But this was Ronald Reagan. One of the pieces on the album was William Burroughs' piece called 'The President', who's on longevity drugs in the White House. And then on and on, the cocaine in the Pentagon and the heroin in the State department. William was so brilliant. They must have listened to it and said, "What if somebody in *Congress* listened, and sees it was funded by the National Endowment for the Arts?" So they pre-empted it by sending out this letter. When I got that letter, it didn't occur to me for a second to challenge it. It's not my problem. I was working on a million other projects, I had already gone on. But the point is, that did not inhibit poetry in the least. The point is... this doesn't depend on your lousy money! That's one of the great joys of poetry, that it's not dependent. It's wisdom, it's not dependent on economics, really.

FORTNER ANDERSON: I think grants can be a trap for artists, in that as they become dependent upon the grant structure for their livelihood, their work will tend towards an orthodoxy. It will no longer push the boundaries of expression, but will tend more towards work that will be acceptable by their peers. That's one problem. Another problem is that like counterfeit money,

96 Various artists. *A Diamond Hidden In The Mouth Of A Corpse*. New York: Giorno Poetry Systems, 1985.

235

bad art, heavily funded by the state, will push to the margins other expression which doesn't have those same resources. The scene in the late sixties, with Louis Dudek and Irving Layton — their work would be published on mimeographed sheets of paper, and distributed. It would nonetheless have an effect, people would read it even though the resources used to create it were minimal. Now, artists must have a certain amount of resources behind them to make the object presentable to the public. I think that's a problem, artists who don't receive grants become even further marginalized. And personally, I find it very disturbing to think that my creative process will be determined by someone else. That if I decide to go forward on a project, its realization is dependent on the faceless bureaucracy of the Canada Council. Even though of course it's a smaller bureaucracy, and it tries to fulfill a role which it deems to be important in the society, it's still nonetheless, as a control over my particular work... an anathema.

The popularization of spoken word holds out the possibility of earning a living from the practice, without depending on government grants. Given the known parameters of popular culture, however, what will such a broadening of spoken word's appeal do to its integrity as an art form?

KAARLA SUNDSTRÖM: There's so many things you have to weigh. A grant doesn't pay your rent, so you have to find some sort of job. But you have to start negotiating the viability of what it is that you're doing. It's hard, because in our culture there's this aura of authenticity around being a starving

Vince Tinguely at La Vache enragée, *March 1998*
Photo by André Lemelin

artist, you get a lot of support from the people you're generally around. You start to make that an economically viable thing and people are like, "You sold out. I'm gonna go find the other artist who hasn't made it yet, and support them." So you always have to constantly make choices. "Should I make my work more accessible? Does that mean I won't have the audience that I have now? Will that mean I'll have a different audience, and who is it I want to talk to anyway?" The people who generally are in the audiences are there supporting you because they believe in the things that you say. Who are you challenging?

VICTORIA STANTON: The positive side in popularizing spoken word is, it could mean that if an artist is using this form as their primary means or creative form of expression, they could actually live on it. They could make a living off of being a spoken word performer (laughs). On the other hand, if it gets co-opted by the mainstream, then maybe it won't be spoken word any more.

VINCE TINGUELY: Everything gets co-opted by the mainstream. We're in late capitalism, and not everybody, but every form will be co-opted by the mainstream if it can be. That's how it works. When you talk about the entertainment industry, there's this sense of, "What's going to sell to a larger audience?" You can talk all you want about censorship in the arts, but what I find is the least talked about is the kind of censorship or self-censorship that artists go through in order to reach a larger audience. Where you have to drop all kinds of stuff in order to appeal to Mom and Pop in the suburbs.

4. Distribution: "The word can travel"

In a sense, 'the Montreal spoken word scene' is an intellectual construct, created for the purposes of this book. While live performances are a central part of the scene, the activities of these artists extend beyond the stage into various grassroots means of distributing their work. Production includes publishing in the form of zines and chapbooks, recordings of spoken word performances on cassettes and CDs, and even video and film documents. The distribution of the work of spoken word artists is a steadily-expanding phenomenon in Montreal.

TETSURO SHIGEMATSU: The most successful theatre run will reach a maximum of a few thousand people. And I guess that's part of the sadness, and also part of the appeal of live performance and theatre and spoken word, is that it's so evanescent, it's so ephemeral, it's here and it's gone. But in regards to wanting to fulfill the objective of reaching a larger number of people, you have to consider other mediums for the sake of dissemination, distribution. Even if I want someone else to be familiar with my work, I give them a videotape. So I have no idea what medium, be it radio, film or whatever. But I would like to guide this particular project into seeing how it played in other mediums. I think my first love will always be live performance, and everything else in a sense will be a trade-off and will inevitably pale in comparison, for my sake. But maybe that's a selfish interest.

JOSEPH NEUDORFER: Performance is very immediate, which has its own offerings. Except that at the end of the night I'd like to be able to digest, to be able to

appreciate what's out there, or analyze it even more. So that's where the written material comes in, or recordings. The performance is very immediate and very quick, and it's difficult to appreciate. If there are literary devices used, alliteration or rhyming, it's often difficult as an audience member to pick up the intricacies of the performance.

IAN FERRIER: I'd just like to see us broadcasting spoken word, getting it out to other parts of the country, other parts of North America and Europe. The first time we taped this stuff and put it out, in 1993, till now, it hasn't died off, and people are getting better all the time. Which means the quality of what people are doing is international.

Publishing texts has become increasingly easier to do in the last twenty years, with the advent of desktop computer publishing programs, and the relative cheapness of photocopying compared to traditional printing costs. In the nineties, 'zine' culture exploded in North America, spawning literally thousands of publications. With relatively low print runs and largely local distribution, such publications can have a real cultural impact. More recently, digital publishing technology and the world wide web offer new means of distribution to the artist.

ANDY BROWN: I look back at all the projects I've done, and it's all very documentary-oriented. I think I'm a frustrated documentary film-maker who doesn't make films, so I'm putting it all into books. I've done single-story fiction. I'm going to be doing a poetry book. I've done a poster book, a performance book, comic books, and in *Matrix* I wrote an article on the Montreal *bandes dessinées* community.[97] It's all

Tetsuro Shigematsu

97 Brown, Andy. 'Comix en Ville', *Matrix* # 56, April 2000.

documenting a time and a place. I think it's valuable, I think it's worth documenting, but it's not like Montreal's the greatest place in the world! I think other people should be doing it in other places as well, but I feel that conundrum press has some sort of role in documenting a very specific, talented group within Montreal. I think somebody should do it, and I'm constantly amazed at how few people do.

HEATHER O'NEILL: I think when I started, there weren't a lot of places to put poetry, as far as publications in Montreal. A lot of the presses aren't very interested. There needs to be a growth in presses here too.

IZ COX: I'd like to see more publishers, and I'd like to see more of a commitment to spoken word. Somebody who's really in the interest of getting spoken word out there, or poetry out there. 'Cause you go to New York and you go to Toronto and you see hundreds of publications and people helping writers get along. Rich eccentrics who give their money.

THOTH HARRIS: I think we need a vibrant publishing scene, which is really not happening. It's all been eaten up and swallowed by presumptions of what people like or think. For instance, Grove Press back in the sixties, they were open to any manuscripts from all over, and you could just take it in personally. You can't do that anymore.

ANDY BROWN: I've been thinking about this mutually beneficial relationship I'm developing with people, essentially my friends. Catherine Kidd's book came out, a week later she has a book deal. Dana Bath's book comes out, she gets all these great reviews, she wins a few awards and has book deals and various

things. I think people are starting to come to me with the knowledge that if I publish their book, perhaps they can go on to bigger things. It benefits me in that they do quality work, I like to think I'm doing quality work, and my logo is attached to their quality work, so I look good too.

JOSEPH NEUDORFER: What the Rhythmic Missionaries have gotten out of what Montreal has to offer, is self-publication. Being able to see your writing in print... slim volumes, chapbooks. You organize everything on your computer, you just need a very basic program, then you go to a copy shop and make fifty copies, a hundred copies. The more copies you make, the cheaper it is per copy. There's so much freedom, possibility, from the artwork of the cover to the display of the poems to photographs to compliment the poetry. The amount of books you want to publish is dependent on how much money you're willing to invest. My brother and I sell our books at shows, and to friends. We basically cover our costs. There's no real money — at least in my own experience — in making these chapbooks.

ANDY BROWN: I see publishing chapbooks as a political act, in a way. Who the hell can afford books any more, and who can afford to publish them? So, sell a book for a dollar. Make it cheaper than a dollar to make, sell it for a dollar. As long as it's good, keep doing that sort of thing. But ultimately there's such a small group that really cares, and it's always the same group. Which is fine, but it's frustrating.

IZ COX: I have people who want to publish me, but I did this art book instead. All hand-made, spoken word in an art book, three poems and a tape. So

Thoth Harris, 1999

I guess I'm starting my own little publication company with a tape and a book.

COREY FROST: It's becoming so much easier to publish a book, in terms of designing it and printing it. Especially now that there's digital printing. Robert Majzels and Erin Mouré and I have been talking about putting together a publishing collective, where it would be a democratic choice as to what was published, and it would be published digitally. So that you could publish one copy at a time with the same price as a major printer. It's kind of exciting, because it's more along the lines of artist-run centres.

JONATHAN GOLDSTEIN: I think the whole do-it-yourself thing — we take it for granted. I just read this posthumous collection of Bukowski's letters. The letters begin in the late sixties, I think, and his first chapbook is supposed to be coming out. You really realize it was different then, because everyone didn't have access to a Xerox machine, and everyone didn't have access to printers. Now we can just do it, and it's no problem. But you realize what a precious thing it was at the time. He describes getting the box of his first chapbook, which was called *Flower, Fist and Bestial Wail*. Drinking beer and poring over it, looking over each page all night and feeling like you've just given birth or something.

VINCE TINGUELY: We found that we're often more satisfied with what we do ourselves, with our zines, than what gets published somewhere, because we make the choice ourselves to put it in our zine and put it out there. As opposed to sending something off to a publisher when you're in one mood, and then it gets published when you've changed your mind.

JAKE BROWN: A one-off book you just do as a project in time – I liked that idea, because it meant that you didn't really need an apparatus for culture, and it can never be killed then, ever. Your mental gesture becomes something that's concrete, and yet ephemeral. Yes, it's gone, but the very fact that it came and went means that you can come and go again. There's a kind of organic quality to a one-off. But if your whole artistic career is a one-off, then it's at risk of subsiding into history.

ANDRÉ LEMELIN: I've always had a certain sense of urgency. I write now, not tomorrow, not in a month, and I want to get my work out there now, not in a month or a year. This is what led me to self-producing. And my self-producing activities have allowed me to provide an audience for friends or performers who were doing things I found interesting. *Planète rebelle* was born from this drive, just like the magazine *Stop* and *Les Dimanches du conte*.

SIMON DARDICK: Spoken word can be published in book form, or it can be published on the Web. *Gopoetry.com*[98] out of New York is another way of publishing. It has a huge archive of performances. Here I am, basically a print publisher — although we've had occasional forays — but I see publishing as being in the broadest sense. Publishing in different media.

Unlike print distribution, film and video production has only just begun to document or distribute spoken word performance from the Montreal anglophone spoken word scene. Lessons can be learned from the francophone scene, which is the subject of an NFB film,[99]

ANDRÉ LEMELIN: J'ai toujours eu une espèce d'urgence. J'écris maintenant, pas demain, ni dans un mois, et puis je veux diffuser mes œuvres maintenant, pas dans un mois, ni dans un an. C'est ce qui m'a amené à m'autoproduire. Et dans cette activité d'autoproduction, j'ai donné la possibilité à des amis ou des performeurs qui faisaient des choses qui m'intéressaient d'être diffusées. Planète rebelle est née de cet élan, comme ça a été le cas pour la revue *Stop* et *Les Dimanches du conte*.

[98] A website devoted to poetry.

[99] *Les mots-dits*. Dir: Marie Brodeur. ONF et Publivision, 1998.

and which is frequently showcased on Quebec television.

PETER BRAWLEY: The spoken word scene would make an interesting documentary film.

JEAN-PAUL DAOUST: In 1998, there was *Les mots-dits*, an hour-long film about poetry where we tried to do a very fast-paced edit, like a music video. I thought this was a good idea.

ATIF SIDDIQI: For sure film is a medium that can be explored. I think one of the reasons why *M: Mom, Madonna, The Millennium and Me* went into a video / film direction, for me personally, is because the text had more than one character. It wasn't just a solo about me. It's all about the different anecdotes and stories of these last fifteen years, all coming together around themes of crosscultural context and migrations and crossing boundaries. So it just seemed like a film and a video would be much more appropriate, and an easier medium for me to work in than to put this piece onstage. I want to reach more people, rather than just the

JEAN-PAUL DAOUST: En 1998, il y a eu *Les mots-dits*, un film sur la poésie d'une durée d'une heure, où on a essayé de faire un montage très nerveux, à la manière d'un vidéoclip. Et ça, j'ai trouvé que c'était une très bonne idée.

Performance sketch by Atif Siddiqi

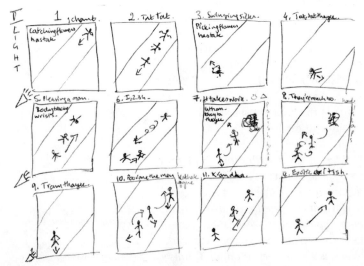

people I can reach here. In a medium such as a film or a video, the word can travel. Like 'Erotic, Exotic', when I ended up making a video of that piece in 1998, I was able to get distribution for it through V-Tape in Toronto. Since then it's gone to Europe, and it's played in different cities in Canada. So I can really reach more people through this medium. I feel like images are very poetic. The quality of spoken word or written word can go in there, movement can go in there, costume can go in there, and just everything. It can take everything that a text can only take as words. So it suits me, it feels natural to really go in that direction of video / film.

JAKE BROWN: Unless you have enough money to make the film production or video production value at a level where people will accept it, it won't work. People of all ages are very used to an extremely high quality of video documentation, in terms of the lighting and the sound and the montage and the editing. I could show you. We're videotaping, it looks like a grade five talent show. There's not enough light, nobody knows how to use the camera. Even if it just sits there it's very static and staged and it looks like it's a thousand years old. We looked into it, and the lowest price is eight thousand dollars. You need three cameras, and eight thousand dollars to pay for it professionally.

VINCE TINGUELY: Given the way that the scene has come up from nothing — the whole idea being you could put on a show for nothing — there's probably ways to get at the technology that you need without forking over all that money. That would be one option, because people are doing this stuff now on computers.

240

JOHN GIORNO: Kids just seeing an MTV video could say, "I can do better than that." And then they go into their high school media workshop with a million dollars worth of equipment that I never had. And they're poets. They're not trying to be rock and rollers. Or they're poets who are rock and rollers, it doesn't matter. They go into the high school media shop or the college media shop and they do a poetry video. We didn't have that back forty years ago. So MTV alone is enough of an inspiration. There are lots of directions it may go into, like the advent of CD-ROM which then goes into DVD. It hasn't even begun yet because scarcely anybody's worked with it, even the video part of the CD-ROM on the computers is still so primitive. But the point is, that's just the beginning. Lord knows where that will take it, because the quality of DVD, which is perfect live performance video, is so fabulous. Since it hasn't even begun, one doesn't know what it can become.

JEAN-PAUL DAOUST: I did a poetry segment on *Cent Titres*, which started airing on *Télé-Québec* in the fall of 1998. Once a month I'd get about five minutes to talk about poetry — everything from Acadian poetry to an author like Denis Vanier. In terms of the visuals, there was a whole montage around the content; you couldn't see me on screen while I was talking, but you'd see images of books or of the city, if I was talking about an urban poet, for example. I think presenting montages like these in a show about books would have been unthinkable ten years ago, but things have evolved in this sense.

BENOÎT PAIEMENT: We appeared on a few commercial TV shows, such as *Fax*, the *MusiquePlus* show, in the summer of 1994; *Les Choix de Sophie*, on *Télé-Québec*, in January 1999, and we were on *Bien branché*, on Cable 9, twice. Our work comes through well on TV because we adapt it for the medium, we frame it differently. Instead of playing on a twenty-five foot wide stage, we're playing in a very reduced space. Obviously, we keep the absurdity of the texts, except that there's less room for movement, so we concentrate more on the gaze. Our director has a camera, we've experimented with video, and I think this has helped us present our work on the small screen.

Spoken word lends itself well to audio recording and, by extension, radio. Even before chapbooks and zines began to appear in the nineties, Fortner Anderson and Ian Ferrier were recording and broadcasting local performers for their Wired on Words label. Audio recordings have the advantage of capturing the nuances of spoken word that print cannot hope to do, while being a far more affordable and accessible medium than film and video.

JOHN GIORNO: 1965 was the pivotal year for me, because that's where I really began Giorno Poetry Systems.[100] It was the idea of the venue, that poetry wasn't just books and magazines that nobody wanted to publish you in. What any venue means is anything you do in your everyday life, like listen to phonograph records, or listen to the radio, or talk on the telephone. One by one, those became projects.

JEAN-PAUL DAOUST: J'ai fait une chronique de poésie pour l'émission "Cent titres", qui a commencé à être diffusée à Télé-Québec à l'automne 1998. Une fois par mois, on m'allouait environ cinq minutes pour parler de poésie – je pouvais tout aussi bien parler de poésie acadienne que d'un auteur comme Denis Vanier. Au niveau de la forme, il y avait tout un montage qui était réalisé autour de ça; on ne me voyait pas à l'écran pendant que je parlais, mais on montrait plutôt des images de livres, ou bien des images évoquant la ville – si je parlais d'un poète urbain, par exemple. Il y a dix ans, c'était impensable, je crois, de présenter de tels montages dans une émission traitant de livres, mais je crois qu'il y a eu une évolution en ce sens-là.

BENOÎT PAIEMENT: On a fait des apparitions à la télé commerciale à quelques reprises, notamment à *Fax*, l'émission de MusiquePlus, à l'été 1994, puis aux *Choix de Sophie*, à Télé-Québec, en janvier 1999, et deux fois à l'émission *Bien branché*, au câble 9. Et notre travail passe très bien à l'écran, dans la mesure où on l'adapte en conséquence, où on le cadre différemment. C'est-à-dire que plutôt que de jouer sur 25 pieds de large, on joue dans un espace réduit. À ce moment, évidemment, on conserve toute l'absurdité des textes, sauf qu'il n'y a plus autant de place pour les mouvements, alors on doit davantage concentrer notre jeu sur les regards. Mais comme notre metteur en scène possède une caméra, on s'est souvent filmés, on a expérimenté des choses avec la vidéo, et je crois que ça nous a aidés pour présenter notre travail à la télévision.

[100] Giorno Poetry Systems is a record label devoted to documenting the spoken word.

MICHEL GARNEAU: J'ai commencé à dire mes textes à la radio, et j'aimais beaucoup profiter de ce média pour expérimenter diverses formes poétiques. Par exemple, en 1961, j'animais une émission dans laquelle je lisais des lettres que j'écrivais à des personnes imaginaires... Entre autres, j'avais écrit une lettre d'amour à la dame de la rue Panet, parce que je me faisais toujours dire: "Tes textes sont bons, mais penses-tu qu'ils vont intéresser la dame de la rue Panet?" Alors j'avais écrit cette lettre, et deux personnes m'avaient répondu, deux dames qui habitaient sur la rue Panet, d'ailleurs (rires). C'était extraordinaire. Aussi, j'avais écrit à l'espionne Gerda Munsinger, une Allemande qui vivait à Montréal et qui couchait avec un ministre nommé Pierre Sévigny. Et à un certain moment, l'entourage du ministre s'était aperçu que Gerda était une agente soviétique, et Pierre Sévigny avait été soupçonné de lui avoir transmis des renseignements secrets. Toute une histoire... Parmi d'autres formes poétiques que j'ai expérimentées à la radio, ces lettres constituaient une certaine forme d'étude.

MICHEL GARNEAU: Un jour, en ondes, on a lu un recueil d'une auteure qui écrit encore aujourd'hui, mais qui en était alors à sa première publication. J'avais demandé à Diane Lebeau, qui est une actrice très subtile, de faire la lecture, et à Maryse Poulin, qui est tout aussi extraordinaire, de créer une musique d'accompagnement. Le résultat fut magnifique, et il stimula incroyablement l'auteure du recueil. Par la suite, elle m'avait dit: "Moi, je suis quelqu'un qui écrit peu, et lentement. Mais après avoir entendu ça, je me suis mise à écrire." Donc évidemment, d'entendre ainsi lire ses textes à la radio lui avait donné de la confiance, mais ça avait aussi eu l'effet d'élargir ses horizons. Alors si une émission de radio peut à la fois présenter de la création et être utile à celle-ci, pour moi, c'est merveilleux.

MICHEL GARNEAU: I started saying my texts on the radio, and I enjoyed making the most of this medium to experiment with various poetic forms. In 1961 for example, I was hosting a show in which I'd read letters I'd written to imaginary people.... Among others, I'd written a love letter to The Lady of Panet Street, because people were always saying to me: "Your texts are good but do you really think The Lady of Panet Street will care?" So I wrote that letter and two people responded, two ladies who lived on Panet Street, as a matter of fact (laughs). It was extraordinary. Also, I'd written to Gerda Munsinger, the German spy who was living in Montreal and sleeping with a Quebec minister named Pierre Sévigny. At one point the minister's entourage realized that Gerda was a Soviet spy, and Pierre Sévigny was suspected of having transmitted secret information to her. Quite a story.... So among other poetry forms I experimented with on radio, these letters constituted a kind of investigation.

ANNA-LOUISE CRAGO: French CBC is very pretentious and pompous, and full of crap, but there's this show that I've been on, *Les décrocheurs... d'étoiles.* They always have these political commentators on for the first little while. It's actually an arts and poetry show run by this fabulous guy who's this old poet, Michel Garneau. I love him to bits, because he reads all these dirty poems, but they have all these great ornate words in them, so you don't realize how they're all about debauchery (laughs) and the pleasures of life! He himself is a most fabulous storyteller, I think. I went on this show to prepare a political commentary on the Coalition for the Rights of Sex Workers, and they loved it! It totally turned me on to how much

I love radio... in terms of activism and sometimes in terms of spoken word, when I'm dealing with sex work. If you're dealing with issues that are so sensationalized generally, and particularly sensationalized with visuals, then you're really in this confusing game of images all the time. You have to outsmart the images, and by the time you've figured out how to outsmart the images you're way behind trying to figure out how to outsmart the sound byte. I think radio is so much more interesting, the conversations can go on longer.

MICHEL GARNEAU: One day, on the air, I read a book of poetry by a woman who's still writing today, but it was her first publication. I'd asked Diane Lebeau, a very subtle actress, to do the reading, and Maryse Poulin, who is just as extraordinary, to create music to accompany the reading. The result was magnificent, and it was an incredible stimulant for the author. Afterwards she said to me: "I write very little, and slowly. But after hearing that, I started writing." Hearing her texts on the radio boosted her self-confidence, but it also had the effect of broadening her horizons. If a radio show can present creative work and be of use to create the work too, then in my mind this is marvelous.

JOHN GIORNO: Brion Gysin had used electronics in his poetry, and William Burroughs had worked with tape recorders, separately. Brion really introduced me to the possibilities, in those years, of using electronics in your poetry. We did a bunch of collaborations, my poems with him helping me. He did the sound composition part of it, using my voice. Things that sound really simple now, doing these complicated loop compositions, multileveled loops. We did one thing called 'Subway Sound' that was then sent to Paris. It was in the *Biennale de Paris* and it was in the *Musée d'Art Moderne* in Paris in 1965. Suddenly I was part of that group, the *Poésie Sonore* movement in France. The LP record with 'Pornographic Poem', the first one that came out in 1967, had some early tape experiments, the very early ones of Bob Moog.

IAN FERRIER: There's something deeply haunting about spoken word. It's so much a part of the personality of a person. In March of 1997 we did a memorial for Ian Stephens, people reading his stuff, and part of it was a tape of him reading. Whatever it is about a person is contained so much in their voice, and we experience it so much through their voice that it's really very close to what we are as humans.

CATHERINE KIDD: A couple of people who bought *everything I know about love I learned from taxidermy* said, "I gotta admit, I read the book right away." But the tape, they didn't listen to it for the longest time. They thought, "A tape with somebody talking, I don't know, do I really want to listen to that?" Three or four people said this. And then somebody said, "It's the perfect thing to put in the tape deck when you're driving, because you're driving and listening to somebody tell you a story," and I thought, "Well that's great!" Here's a medium that's a driving cassette, it's perfect. I think that people like to listen to stories.

ANTHONY BANSFIELD: I had to posit an audience for a CD, as a product. I saw that it was a meeting place of a lot of different demographics. The people who listen to alternative radio. The people who listen to hip-hop, the people who listen to reggae. The people who

just listen to something on the radio in their car on their way to work, and they like to hear somebody in an interview, they'll listen to a spoken word piece. Even there, you see that you can touch a lot of different audiences with the kind of stuff we're doing. Buttah Babies[101] — Ziplocks and Manchilde — had an interesting demo CD they put out. You've got some stuff that is rap, some is spoken word stuff, and some is a capella and some has beats. I think if it takes a musical context, there's always going to be an attraction to it. So the fact that the audience can be open to different forms of what qualifies for spoken word is good. Because it means that maybe some of us can find something of a commercial market, or at least a broader market, because of the musical context of a CD.

IAN FERRIER: I'm really knocked out by the quality of the stuff on the *Millennium Cabaret* CD. When we were starting to record spoken word, we'd be lucky if one piece in ten was good. But now, it's surprising if I *can't* find a really good piece that a performer does.

FORTNER ANDERSON: I'm very happy that we've done this, we've archived a body of work, a snapshot. I think it's a very important time, certainly for us personally (laughs), and we'll see what kind of importance it has in the world at large.... I think some of the work on that CD is very strong, and will continue to be heard and touch people for years and years to come. For my own work,[102] I've been similarly very happy to have archived it and put it out into the world. For me, it captured a group of poems and performances that I've been working on for some time.

Catherine Kidd
Photo by Vince Tinguely

[101] Buttah Babies is the Montreal-based spoken word / hip-hop duo Ziplocks and Manchilde.

[102] Anderson, Fortner. *Sometimes I Think* CD. Montreal: Wired on Words, 1999.

While the technologies for the recording of spoken word on the page, on video and on audio discs has become more accessible, the distribution of the products remains problematic. Whether in print or other forms, producers complain that there is no way to make money, or even to simply break even, because the distribution of spoken word material is almost nonexistent.

FORTNER ANDERSON: It was such an immense labour to get the Wired on Words compilation CD out. We funded it with the Standard Broadcast Award in part, but everything else has come out of our own pockets. We've never seen a return on Wired on Words' recording projects, it's all a total loss.

ANDY BROWN: In Toronto or Vancouver people have heard of conundrum press. But I've never had a single order for a book. I made hundreds of catalogues and a little order form, and I've never received one in the mail. The only thing I receive in the mail are other people's zines saying, "Will you distribute me?" I write back saying, "I'm not a distributor." There is a network, but it's a network based on networking, and not based on selling books. It's like, "Can I come and launch my book at your show? Can I get a review?" That's fine, reviews, media stuff, but someone actually ordering a book and reading it? Outside of a certain group it doesn't really happen, and I think a lot of it has to do with the perceptions that the general public have toward books a lot of the time. Most people would be very dismissive of anything that wasn't the standard Canada Council book: perfect-bound, forty-eight page, printed, blah-dee-blah.

VINCE TINGUELY: I see parallels with where the underground music scene in Canada was in the late seventies, early eighties, where there was no distribution.

ANDY BROWN: It's hard, because the bookstores don't make money, it's basically an act of charity for these places to carry chapbooks. Or an act of them having some sort of street credential. Most places won't carry them. The more independent bookstores get canned, the more you have to produce a book that the big chains will carry, and the big chains will only carry very standard books with bar codes and the whole bit. There's no one who would distribute *psittacine flute* by Catherine Kidd, a single-story chapbook that's nicely produced. I think there's a limited amount of people who *would* buy it; if you could get it into all those people's hands, it would be great. It doesn't go beyond that limited amount of people, but the fact is, you can't even get it to that limited amount of people as it stands. It's the same in distribution, they can only distribute what they can sell. It's really a small market. What should happen, I think, is there needs to be one person that says, "I will distribute these things." Then they have a monopoly on it, and in that way, perhaps, be able to survive. Or have some way of getting government funding so that they can operate. The problem is, there's tons of distributors. It's ridiculous. And they all take a percentage. A book store takes forty percent and the distributor takes a fair percentage, so you have very little to pay your printing costs, your authors, your designers, editors. What the hell is that?

VINCE TINGUELY: It's also an economy of scale. If you're putting out five thousand books, and you get your percentage, it probably works out, as opposed to putting out a hundred.

ANDY BROWN: I'm very conscious of when someone walks in and sees the price on the book, and what they're willing to pay. It's different everywhere. It's different in Toronto than in Montreal. I think it's different in Vancouver and Saskatoon. But then you go to a chain like Chapters and every single book is twenty dollars. You can't buy a book for less than twenty dollars. The reason they're twenty dollars is because a large percentage of that twenty dollars is going to the chain and the distributor. It costs the publisher three dollars to make that book, they *have* to sell it for twenty dollars to get it distributed and sold. That's the problem. If you could do it all yourself you could charge five.

JOHN GIORNO: I've never let it become a problem for a second. I've always realized that you just have to do it. One of the secrets of my success is never depending on anybody or anything. Just doing it with brute strength, making it happen. With *Dial-A-Poem*, I just wanted to do it, and made it happen, and it was hugely successful. If you wait for Warner Brothers to do a CD, forget about it. That shouldn't stop anyone. I've done forty albums and they've all been successful, they've all sold well. You just do it. If they don't sell, you do it anyway. It's not about money or even getting back the cost. It's doing it for the joy of doing it. And it isn't about supporting yourself. I've never let the money thing become an obstacle.

ANTHONY BANSFIELD: In the States, they have such a hustler entrepreneurial mindset. They're putting stuff out without the benefit of much money at all, if any, and selling their stuff to their audiences. Some of their stuff isn't as well produced as some of the stuff up here, that I've heard. But look at the size of the market they're dealing with, and the amount of clubs they have where people go to check out this sort of thing. Promoting a CD is a touring and promotion project. Which involves more than just the CD, it involves doing some shows, and networking people is one of the key things underneath all that for me. It's nice that I hooked up with you all in Montreal. In the same way, I've been able to set up something in New York where some of the people from Toronto, Montreal and Ottawa could come down. That's been our little circuit so far, and not beyond that. Through the internet now, too, I'm meeting people from all over.

ANDRÉ LEMELIN: At first, Planète rebelle was a small-scale publishing house filling publication needs on an ad hoc basis. I wanted it to stay this way instead of creating expectations I wouldn't be able to meet. We held small launches for a target group of readers or friends. But since 1999, I've had more funds and the situation is very different. I publish literature which is quite distinctive — not underground but almost. In any case, it's not commercial in the sense that it's not mainstream literature. But I want these works to be accessible to as many readers as possible. I've sort of created two worlds with Planète rebelle. First I choose the work and I don't wonder whether it's going to sell or not. What's important to me is that it's high quality, original, and especially that it corresponds to Planète rebelle, meaning that it's close to orality, to dailiness, if you like. Then, once the work is printed in book form, I start thinking about marketing. At this stage

ANDRÉ LEMELIN: Au début, Planète rebelle était une maison d'édition à petite échelle, pour combler des besoins de diffusion ponctuels. Et je préférais que ça reste ainsi plutôt que de créer une attente à laquelle je n'aurais pas pu répondre. On faisait des petits lancements, pour un groupe de lecteurs ou d'amis bien ciblés. Mais depuis 1999, j'ai davantage de moyens, et la situation est très différente. Ce que je publie, c'est une littérature très particulière. Pas underground, mais presque. En tout cas, ce n'est pas commercial, dans le sens que ce n'est pas de la littérature pour grand public. Mais moi, je veux que ces œuvres puissent quand même être accessibles au plus grand nombre de lecteurs possible. Ma façon de travailler avec Planète rebelle est la suivante: dans un premier temps, je choisis une œuvre, sans me demander si elle va se vendre ou non. L'important, c'est que l'œuvre soit de qualité, qu'elle soit originale, et surtout qu'elle corresponde à Planète rebelle, c'est-à-dire qu'elle se rapproche de l'oralité, ou du quotidien, si l'on veut. Ensuite, une fois que l'œuvre est imprimée, sous forme de bouquin, je me pose alors la question de la mise en marché. À ce stade, j'entre dans un tout autre processus et je dois me mettre dans un état d'esprit totalement différent afin d'élaborer une batterie d'arguments commerciaux pour que le livre se retrouve en librairie. Mon distributeur a des représentants qui sont payés, et il faut que je convainque le libraire que le livre va se vendre, sinon il le mettra de côté. C'est dire que moi, en tant qu'éditeur, dans un deuxième temps, je deviens diffuseur, j'essaie de faire en sorte que l'œuvre soit diffusée le maximum possible. J'ignore à quel point elle va se vendre, mais au moins, je la rends accessible.

I enter into a whole different process and I have to put myself into a totally different mind set to develop a battery of commercial arguments so that the book can find its place in bookstores. My distributor has payed reps, and I have to convince the bookstore owner that the book will sell, otherwise he'll overlook it. So this means that as a publisher, in step two I become a distributor, I try to get the book circulating as widely as possible. I don't know how much it'll sell, but at least I'm making it available.

LOUIS RASTELLI: Partly why I put *Fish Piss* together is that I can hardly buy any magazines that are out there. The mainstream is getting more and more ephemeral and glossy and I don't know what, it just doesn't click for me any

LOCAL MAGAZINE MADNESS VARIETÉ

Launch #5 Lancement
Wednesday · Mercredi Jan. 6 1999
7 p.m. – 1 a.m.   Free · Gratuit
Cheval Blanc 809 Ontario E.

Art by Siris

more. I think that's a very general feeling out there, so there's a lot of room and a lot of promise for things like this. And obviously it's taking off on its own right now. It's a good sign. We've got to take advantage of this mainstream being so clued out. Before they catch on and start getting hip and hiring, cruising through town and picking up key players. The big catchword now is 'content', in this on-line business thing. They're saying, "OK, we've pushed all the CD-ROMS and formats for so many years, and now we need *content* because people have bought these things and they're not reading anything on them."

ANDY BROWN: The positive view of this would be that these chain stores take over so much that there's this backlash. And you see it, I think that's partly why people give a damn about what I'm doing. Everything else is Hollywood or Oprah or whatever you want to equate it with, Celine Dion. That's all that's being presented, and then you see over here there's this other thing that has a different feel. It's more grassroots, it's more careful. You take your twenty dollars, instead of buying your book at Chapters you buy that. That's the mentality that has to happen with people. I think that will happen more and more as this independent stuff is being crushed. People will go, "Where is it? Where is it?" and look for it. They'll miss it. I see it as a period you have to wait out, and then ride a backlash (laughs). Ride the backlash! Surf the backlash! Ultimately it's something you do for the same reason you paint a painting. The same reason you doodle while you're on the phone. You're not doing it to become rich and famous, obviously.

POSTSCRIPT

During the gestation of Impure: Reinventing the Word, *we've discovered that there's no way to get a handle on everything that ever happened and is happening in our spoken word scene(s). The more we dig, the more there is to explore. No tidy summing-up is remotely conceivable, given the breadth of activities we've touched on, and their ever-evolving nature. Even in the two-and-a-half years that we've been working on this book, much has changed. Perhaps most significant is the growth in popularity of the francophone* oralité *phenomenon. As media interest in spoken word was waning in the anglophone community, public interest was beginning to peak on the francophone side.*

According to our chronology, there has been some form of spoken word activity taking place in Montreal since at least the 1960s. But it seems to us that a communal awareness of this art comes and goes. Ultimately, it's the 'scene' that really matters; the performance and practice among artists of l'oralité' *or of 'spoken word'. Individuals stumble upon the notion in any number of ways — they might have attended the first* Nuit de la poésie *in 1970; witnessed one of the* Poetry Marathons *at* Véhicule Gallery *in the mid-seventies; seen the* Four Horsemen *at the* Festival D'In(ter)ventions 2 *in Quebec City in 1984; heard Allen Ginsberg read at the* Jack Kerouac Symposium *in Quebec City in 1987; or seen Saul Williams do slam poetry at the* Tongue Tied *festival in 1996. But there isn't a scene until spoken word artists are able to come together and develop their work in relation to a community of fellow practitioners.*

Specific events and venues allowed this coming-together to happen again and again, over the decades. The awareness was there in the sixties at the Poèmes et chansons de la résistance *events, galvanized by the* Québécois *nationalist movement. It was there in the alternative galleries that came into being in the seventies. It was there in the mid-eighties at* Foufounes Électriques *and other rock venues. And it was there in 1994 when the* Lollapalooza *auditions brought a new generation of spoken word artists, performance poets and others together at the* Phoenix Café.

We don't know if the current spoken word revival will continue to grow, or if it will fall into obscurity like previous movements. Part of the impetus for writing this book was the desire to preserve something of this most recent upsurge of interest in spoken word, and to pass on some of the lessons we've learned to the next wave of Montreal artists. Regardless of the outcome, the practice of spoken word itself — the author reciting, performing, animating her text onstage for an audience — will continue to become an ever more popular form. There is something in us today, as we become more urbanized, technologized and globalized, that hungers for the intimacy of a small space, the company of fellow humans, a voice raised to remind us again of our own secret thoughts and dreams.

RELATED TEXTS AND RECORDINGS

1. Fiction and Poetry Publications

Arbour, Marie-Christine. *Deux et deux*. Montreal: Planète rebelle, 2000.

Bath, Dana. *what might have been rain*. Montreal: conundrum press, 1998.

Bath, Dana. *Plenty of Harm in God*. Montreal: DC Books, 2001.

Bell, Chris. *Tales of the Lost Cheebah-Ha*. Montreal: ga press, 1995.

Blomgren, Lance. *Walkups*. Montreal: conundrum press, 2000.

Brown, Andy. *Booked into the Wartime*. Montreal: conundrum press, 1997.

Brown, Andy. *Machines that speak of distance*. Montreal: conundrum press, 2000.

Brown, Andy. *Intruders*. Montreal: conundrum press, 2001.

Bruck, Julie. *The Woman Downstairs*. Toronto: Brick Books, 1993.

Crysler, Julie. *Vision Songs*. Montreal: self-published in co-operation with Egg Sandwich Press, 1995.

Crysler, Julie. *All Consuming*. Toronto: self-published, 1996.

Dandurand, Anne. *Les porteuses d'ombre*. Montreal: Planète rebelle, 1999.

Daniels, Dan. *The Curse of Gutenberg – Storytelling with Dan Daniels*. Fredericton: Broken Jaw Press, 2000.

Daoust, Jean-Paul. *Oui, cher, recit*. Montreal: Editions Cul-Q, 1976.

Daoust, Jean-Paul. *Chaises longues*, livre-objet. Montreal: Editions Cul-Q, 1977.

Daoust, Jean-Paul. *Black Diva* (Selected Poems 1982-1986). Montreal: Guernica, 1991. Translation by Daniel Sloate.

Daoust, Jean-Paul. *Blue Ashes* (Selected Poems 1982-1998). Toronto: Guernica, 1999. Translation by Daniel Sloate.

Daoust, Jean-Paul. *Le Desert rose*, roman. Montreal: Stanke, 2000.

Daoust, Jean-Paul. *Le poeme deshabille*, collectif, poesie. Les Editions L'Interligne, 2000.

Daoust, Jean-Paul. *Les versets amoureux*, poesie. Trois Rivières: Ecrits des Forges, 2001.

Doyon, Denis-F. *Sale temps pour être jeune*. Montreal: Planète rebelle, 1999.

Duffy, Clifford. *Blue Dog Plus*. Montreal: Dromos Editions, 1984.

Dumas, Michel. *Cut-ups*. Montreal: Planète rebelle, 2000.

Edgar, Stephen. *Truth, Memory and Lies*. Montreal: ga press, 1994.

Elfassy, Ran. *wild segments*. Montreal: self-published, 1994.

Elfassy, Ran. *Spaetzle*. Montreal: self-published, 1994.

Elfassy, Ran. *$ell Portraits*. Montreal: self-published in cooperation with Egg Sandwich Press, 1996.

Elfassy, Ran. *M FAS IS – A Book of Love*. Montreal: self-published, 1997.

Elfassy, Ran. *W-hole-here lies-titles*. Montreal: self-published, 1998.

Engels, Stacey. *Camel Light Years*. Montreal: second edition, Archaeopteryx House, 1994.

Evanson, Tanya. *blood in, blood out — a universal preparation*. Montreal: Bluestone House, 1996.

Farkas, Andre. *Szerbusz*. Davinci Press, 1974.

Farkas, Andre. *Murders in the Welcome Café*. Montreal: Véhicule Press, 1977.

Farkas, Endre. *Face-Off*. Montreal: Muses' Company, 1980.

Farkas, Endre. *From Here to Here*. Montreal: Muses' Company, 1982.

Ferrier, Ian. *From Yr Lover Like An Orchestra*. Montreal: Davinci Press, Eldorado Editions, 1974.

Ferrier, Ian. *Exploding Head Man — jazz poems and a story*. Montreal: self-published, 1997.

Ferrier, Ian. *Exploding Head Man — jazz poems*. CD / book. Montreal: Planète rebelle / Wired on Words, 2000.

Fluffy Pagan Echoes (Scott Duncan, Ran Elfassy, Justin McGrail, Victoria Stanton and Vincent Tinguely). *Episode One — A Word Circus*. Montreal: Egg Sandwich Press, 1994.

Fried, Golda. *check the floor*. Montreal: a wrapped in rags inside my head thing, 1996.

Fried, Golda. *a small trail of voice poems*. Montreal: self-published, May 1997.

Fried, Golda. *Hartley's stories*. Montreal: conundrum press, 1997.

Fried, Golda. *Darkness then a blown kiss*. Toronto: Gutter Press, 1998.

Fried, Golda. *as if from the mountains*. Montreal: conundrum press, 2001.

Frost, Corey. *Tonight you'll have a filthy dream — Backwards Versions 2*. Montreal: self-published, 1999.

Frost, Corey. *Three odd numbers — Backwards Versions 1*. Montreal: self-published, 1999.

Frost, Corey. *I feel perfectly fine — Backwards Versions 3*. Montreal: self-published, 2000.

Garneau, Michel. *Small Horses & Intimate Beasts*. McGee, Robert, trans. Montreal: Véhicule Press, 1985.

Gélinas, Yannick B. *Mordre suivi de Parenthèse* CD-ROM / livre. Montreal: Planète rebelle, 2000.

Germain, Christine. *Textes de la soif* CD / livre. Montreal: Planète rebelle, 1999.

Gold, Artie. *cityflowers*. Montreal: Delta Can, 1974.

Gold, Artie. *Even Yr Photograph Looks Afraid of Me*. Vancouver: Talonbooks, 1975.

Gold, Artie & Young, Geoff. *Mixed Doubles*. Berkeley: The Figures, 1976.

Gold, Artie. *5 Jockey Poems*. Montreal: The Word, 1977.

Gold, Artie. *Some of the Cat Poems*. Montreal: CrossCountry Press, 1978.

Gold, Artie. *Before Romantic Words*. Montreal: Véhicule Press, 1979.

Goldstein, Jonathan. *Blow Hard Pomes*. Montreal: self-published, 1994.

Goldstein, Jonathan. *Head On The Table*. Montreal: Pop Mo Press, 1996.

Goldstein, Jonathan. *a carwash the size of a peach*. Montreal: Pop Mo Press, 1997.

Goldstein, Jonathan. *Lenny Bruce Is Dead*. Toronto: Coach House Press, 2001.

Gotham, Lee. *L'Anormâle*. Montreal: éditions Nonplus, 1999.

Harris, Thoth. *Blank*. Montreal: self-published, 1997.

Hazelton, Hugh. *Sunwords*. Montreal: Red Giant Editions, 1982.

Hazelton, Hugh. *Crossing the Chaco*. Montreal: White Dwarf Editions, 1982.

Hazelton, Hugh. *Ojo de papel*, a collection of poems in Spanish. Montreal: Editorial El Palomar, 1988.

Jeppesen, Sandra. *People Like Us*. Montreal: self-published, no date.

Kalynchuk, Valerie Joy. *All Day Breakfast*. Montreal: conundrum press, 2001.

Keightley, Liane. *Ten Cent Packs*. Montreal: conundrum press, 1998.

Kellough, Kaie. *Fire Escapes*, with images by Stefan Christoff. Montreal: Tongue Between The Teeth Press, 2001.

Kenny, William. *1st Book of Poems*. Montreal: self-published, 1996.

Kidd, Catherine. *everything I know about love I learned from taxidermy*. Montreal: conundrum press, 1996.

Kidd, Catherine. *psittacine flute*. Montreal: conundrum press, 2000.

Konyves, Tom. *Love Poems*. Montreal: Asylum Press, 1974.

Konyves, Tom & Norris, Ken. *Proverbsi*. Montreal: Asylum Press, 1977.

Konyves, Tom. *No Parking*. Montreal: Véhicule Press, 1978.

Konyves, Tom. *Write care of ....* Montreal: Asylum, 1978.

Kroker, Arthur and Gibson, Steve. *Spasm: Virtual Reality, Android Music, Electric Flesh* CD / book. Montreal: New World Perspectives, 1993.

Kroker, Arthur and Marilouise. *Hacking The Future: Stories For The Flesh Eating Nineties* CD / book. Montreal: New World Perspectives, 1995.

Laberge, Marc. *Ma chasse-galerie* CD / book. Montreal: Planète rebelle, 2000.

Lack, Stephen & Vitale, Frank. *Hitchhike*. Montreal: Véhicule Press, 1973.

Lamontagne, Patricia. *Les Faits Saillants*. Montreal: Paje Editeur, 1989.

Lamontagne, Patricia. *Rush papier ciseau suivi de Allumette*. Montreal: L'Hexagone, 1992.

Lamontagne, Patricia. *Somnolences*. Montreal: les éditions Triptyque, 2001.

Lapp, Claudia. *Honey*. Montreal: Véhicule Press, 1973.

Lapp, Claudia. *Dakini*. Montreal: Davinci Press, Eldorado Editions, 1974.

Lapp, Claudia. *Horses*. Montreal: privately printed, 1977.

Larocque, Ronald. *Sept mémoires*. Montreal: Planète rebelle, 1999.

Lavoie, Yves. *Octave Grognard, détective* CD / book. Montreal: Planète rebelle, 2000.

Lemelin, André. *Cinq couleurs et autres histoires*. Montreal: Planète rebelle, 1997.

Lemelin, André et Zéro de conduite. *Hold-up! Contes du Centre-Sud* CD / book. Montreal: Planète rebelle, 1999.

LeMesurier, Glen. Series of poems displayed in his front-door window on St. Laurent Boulevard, Montreal, 1989 - present.

Letarte, Geneviève. *Station Transit*. Montreal: Éditions La pleine lune, 1983.

Letarte, Geneviève. *Soleil Rauque*. Montreal: Éditions La pleine lune, 1986.

Letarte, Geneviève. *Les Vertiges Molino*. Montreal: Éditions Leméac, 1996.

Lord, Alan. *Etats Limites*. Montreal: Les Éditions Dromologiques, 1986.

Lord, Alan. *Limit States* (translation of *États Limites*). Montreal: Dromos Editions, no date.

Marchand, Amanda. *June Makes A Friend*. Montreal: conundrum press, 1996.

Massie, Jean-Marc. *La dernière tentation du Lys*. Montreal: Planète rebelle, 1999.

Mavreas, Billy. *Mutations*. Montreal: conundrum press, 1997.

Mavreas, Billy. *The Overlords of Glee*. Montreal: conundrum press / Crunchy Comics, 2001.

McAuley, John. *Nothing Ever Happens in Pointe Claire*. Montreal: Hy Jack Press, 1973.

McAuley, John. *The Chocolate Monograph*. Montreal: Hy Jack Press, 1973.

McAuley, John. *Nothing Ever Happens in Pointe Claire* (expanded and revised). Montreal: Véhicule Press, 1977.

McAuley, John. *Hazardous Renaissance*. Montreal: CrossCountry Press, 1978.

McAuley, John. *Mattress Testing*. Montreal: CrossCountry Press, 1978.

McAuley, John. *What Henry Hudson Found*. Montreal: Véhicule Press, 1979.

McGrail, Justin. *Of Fire and Sword*. Montreal: published in conjunction with the Duodance Company performance, 1995.

McGrail, Justin. *Deus Fax Machina*. Vancouver / Montreal: self-published in cooperation with Egg Sandwich Press / Éditions Sandwich aux Ouefs, 2000.

Miller, Mitsiko. *Trajectoire*. Montreal: self-published, September 1995.

Miller, Mitsiko. *Back to Basics*. Montreal: compte d'auteur, 1996.

Miller, Mitsiko. *Carnages*, Photoroman virtuel with Eva Quintas. Agence Topo (agencetopo.qc.ca), 1999.

Miller, Mitsiko. *Le coeur en orbite*. Montreal: Planète rebelle, 1999.

Monette, Hélène. *Montréal Brûle-t-elle?*. Montreal: Éditions Boréale, 1987.

Monette, Hélène. *Unless*. Montreal: Éditions Boréale, 1995.

Monette, Hélène. *Le Goudron et les Plumes*. Montreal: Éditions XYZ, 1995.

Monette, Hélène. *Plaisirs et Paysages kitsch*. Montreal: Éditions Boréale, 1997.

Monette, Hélène. *Le Blanc des yeux*. Montreal: Éditions Boréale, 1999.

Monette, Hélène. *Crimes et Chatouillements*. Montreal: Éditions Boréale Compact, 2000.

Monette, Hélène. *Un jardin dans la nuit*. Montreal: Éditions Boréale, 2001.

Montreal Slam Team (1998 — Johnny Cheesecake, Dayna McLeod, Alexis O'Hara, Debbie Young). *How You Like Me Now*. Montreal: self-published, summer 1998.

Montreal Slam Team (1999 — Johnny Cheesecake, Dayna McLeod, Alexis O'Hara, Skidmore). *Puzzles, Poems and Personality Tests*. Montreal: self-published, summer 1999.

Morrissey, Stephen. *Poems of a Period*. Montreal: privately printed, 1971.

Morrissey, Stephen. *the insecurity of art*. Montreal: what is, 1976.

Morrissey, Stephen. *divisions*. Dewittville, Quebec: Sunken Forum Press, 1977.

Morrissey, Stephen. *The Trees of Unknowing*. Montreal: Véhicule Press, 1978.

nah-ee-lah. *time to let go*. Montreal: yah ga yah productions, 2001.

Nawrocki, Norman. *Rebel Moon — @narchist Rants & Poems*. San Francisco: AK Press, 1997.

Nawrocki, Norman. *Chasseur de tornades*. Montreal: Les Pages Noire / EDAM, 1997.

Nawrocki, Norman. *No Masters! No Gods! Dare to dream*. Vancouver: Smarten Up! / Get To The Point Publishing, 2000.

Neudorfer, David. *Homegrown Poems of Urban Intimacy*. Montreal: self-published, 1997.

Neudorfer, David. *Rough Earth*. Montreal: New Villager Press, 2001.

Neudorfer, Joseph. *And Poet I Hero Be*. Montreal: self-published, 1997.

Norris, Ken & Smith, Jill. *Vegetables*. Montreal: Véhicule Press, 1975.

Norris, Ken. *Under The Skin*. Montreal: CrossCountry Press, 1976.

Norris, Ken. *Report on the Second Half of the Twentieth Century*. Montreal: CrossCountry Press, 1978.

Norris, Ken. *The Perfect Accident*. Montreal: Véhicule Press, 1978.

Norris, Ken. *The Book of Fall*. Montreal: Maker Press, 1979.

Norris, Ken. *Autokinesis*. Montreal: CrossCountry Press, 1980.

Norris, Ken. *To Sleep, To Love*. Montreal: Guernica Editions, 1982.

Norris, Ken. *Eight Odes*. Montreal: Muses' Company, 1982.

O'Connor, Elaine. *Somatophobia*. Montreal: self-published, 1997.

O'Hara, Alexis. *Bitte! Crotchless Verse*. Montreal: Arts & Crafts / I Hate Poetry, December 1997.

O'Hara, Alexis. *Filthy Lies vol. 1*. Montreal: self-published, July 1999.

O'Hara, Alexis. *Filthy Lies vol. 1.3.1 the big tease*. Montreal: self-published, Jan 2001.

O'Neill, Heather. *two eyes are you sleeping*. Montreal: DC Books, 1998.

Péan, Stanley. *La nuit démasque*. Montreal: Planète rebelle, 2000.

Rastelli, Louis. *Book Day*. Montreal: self-published, no date.

Rastelli, Louis. *Five Stories (Montreal)*. Montreal: self-published 1997.

Renaud, Alix. *Ovation*. Montreal: Planète rebelle, 1999.

Robitaille, Renée. *Conte coquins pour oreilles folichonnes* CD / livre. Montreal: Planète rebelle, 2000.

Selman, Jason. *Grasshopper*. Montreal: self-published, 1998.

Shikatani, Gerry. *Aqueduct — 1979 - 1987 — Poems and Texts from Europe*. Toronto: The Mercury Press / Underwhich Editions / Wolsak & Wynn Publishers, 1996.

Stanton, Victoria & Tinguely, Vincent. *Drop Names*, edition of 100. Montreal: Egg Sandwich Press, 1995.

Stanton, Victoria & Tinguely, Vincent. *Officious Little Students*. Montreal: Egg Sandwich Press, 1997.

Stephens, Ian. *The 1st Morning I called For Daphne To Come Home*. Montreal: Sidewalk Press, no date.

Stephens, Ian. *Bad Reputation*. Montreal: Sidewalk Press, no date.

Stephens, Ian. *La Flèche*. Montreal: Sidewalk Press, 1987.

Stephens, Ian. *Diary of a Trademark*. Montreal: The Muses' Company, 1994.

Stone, Anne. *Sweet Dick All*. Montreal: self-published, 1997.

Stone, Anne. *jacks — a gothic gospel*. Montreal: DC Books, 1998.

Stone, Anne. *Hush*. Toronto: Insomniac Press, 1999.

Stone, Anne & mcLennan, rob. *Inflections of desire / bridge of sighs*. Vancouver: Is Been Books, 1999.

Swift, Todd & Dougherty, James. *Suburban Sublunar*. Montreal: Map-Maker's Press, 1994.

Swift, Todd. *American Standard*. Montreal: Vox Hunt, 1996.

Swift, Todd. *Budavox*. Montreal: DC Books, 1999.

Tinguely, Vincent. *Art = ('=', '+', '@', '&', '-', . . .)*. Montreal: Egg Sandwich Press, 1995.

Tinguely, Vincent. *Shit Jobs*. Montreal: Egg Sandwich Press, 1998.

Tinguely, Vincent. *de[con]struction*. Montreal: Egg Sandwich Press, 2001.

Turenne, Joujou. *Ti pinge* CD / book. Montreal: Planète rebelle, 2000.

Vehicule Poets, The (Endre Farkas, Artie Gold, Tom Konyves, Claudia Lapp, John McAuley, Stephen Morrissey, Ken Norris). *The Vehicule Poets*. Montreal: Maker Press, 1979.

Vézina, Christian. *Doux comme dans fauve* CD / livre. Montreal: Planète rebelle, 2000.

Whittall, Zoë. *Love ~~Sometimes~~ Sucks*. Montreal: self-published, no date.

Various authors. *The Concrete Island: Montreal Poems 1967-71*. Bowering, George, ed. Montreal: Véhicule Press, 1976.

Various authors. *Montreal English Poetry of the Seventies*. Farkas, Andre & Norris, Ken, ed. Montreal: Véhicule Press, 1977.

Various authors. *Cross/cut: Contemporary English Quebec Poetry*. Norris, Ken & Van Toorn, Peter, ed. Montreal: Véhicule Press, 1982.

Various authors. *Schizotexte*. Montreal: Dromos Editions, 1986.

Various authors. *Compañeros, an Anthology of Writings About Latin America*. Geddes, Gary & Hazelton, Hugh, ed. Dunvegan: Cormorant Books, 1990.

Various authors. *HENCE An Anthology of New Poetry*. Power, Michelle, ed. Montreal: Render Press, 1993.

Various authors. *For Example*. Montreal: ga press, 1994.

Various authors. *HENCE An Anthology of New Poetry*. Power, Michelle, ed. Montreal: Render Press / ga press, 1994.

Various authors. *Oralpalooza '94 Montreal*. Montreal: ga press, 1994.

Various authors. *Eat My Words — Poetry and Prose from the Moveable Feast Writer's Workshop*. Montreal: Editions Errant Publications, September 1994.

Various authors. *The Sentence That Thought Life Was Simple*. Montreal: ga press, October 13, 1994.

Various authors. *Wired on Words series 1* cassette / booklet. Anderson, Fortner & Ferrier, Ian, ed. Montreal: ga press / Wired on Words, 1994.

Various authors. *The N'X Step — A collection of writings by a Montreal-based black writers group*, Bansfield, Anthony, ed. Montreal: RevWord Publishing, 1995.

Various authors. *Word Up — Spoken Word Poetry in Print*. Battson, Jill & Norris, Ken, ed. Toronto: Key Porter Books, 1995.

Various authors. *Dollar Stories — An Anthology of Montreal Poetry*. Kaslik, Ibi, ed. Montreal: A Queen's Production, 1995.

Various authors. *Revival: Spoken Word from Lollapalooza '94* anthology. Torrez, Juliette; Belile, Liz; Baron, Mud & Joseph, Jennifer, ed. San Francisco: Manic D. Press, 1996.

Various authors. *Prose Poems & Sudden Fictions — Moosehead Anthology # 6*. Allen, R.E.N & Loewen, Grant, ed. Montreal: DC Books, 1997.

Various authors. *La Vache enragée — anthologie 1996-97*. Miller, Mitsiko, ed. Montreal: Revue Stop, 1997.

Various authors. *The Point Of Impact — An Accidental Anthology*. Bishop-Stall, Shaughnessy, ed. Montreal: Velocity Planet Press, 1998.

Various authors. *Pen.umbra*. The Women of Colour Collective, ed. Montreal: The Women of Colour Collective / QPIRG McGill, 1998.

Various authors. *La Vache enragée — anthologie 2* CD / livre. Miller, Mitsiko, ed. Montreal: Planète rebelle, 1998.

Various authors. *Concrete Forest* anthology. Niedzviecki, Hal, ed. Toronto: McClelland & Stewart, 1998.

Various authors. *Poetry Nation*. Cabico, Regie & Swift, Todd, ed. Montreal: Véhicule Press, 1998.

Various authors. *La grande nuite du conte* CD / book. Montreal: Planète rebelle, 2000.

Various authors. *Running with Scissors*. Brown, Andy & Sircom, Meg, ed. Montreal: Cumulus Press, 2001.

Various authors. *You & Your Bright Ideas: New Montreal Writing*. Brown, Andy & mclennan, rob, ed. Montreal: Véhicule Press, 2001.

Various authors. *Ribsauce*. Ng-Chan, Taien, ed. Montreal: Véhicule Press, 2001.

2. Critical Publications

Dudek, Louis & The Vehicle Poets. *A Real Good Goosin' — Talking Poetics*. Montreal: Maker Press, 1980.

Konyves, Tom. *Poetry in Performance*. Montreal: The Muses' Company, 1982.

Massie, Jean-Marc. *Petit manifeste à l'usage du conteur contemporain*. Montreal: Planète rebelle, 2001.

Nadel, Ira B. *Various Positions: A life of Leonard Cohen*. Toronto: Random House of Canada, 1996.

Various authors. *The Insecurity of Art: Essays on Poetics*. Norris, Ken & Van Toorn, Peter, ed. Montreal: Véhicule Press, 1982.

Various authors. *Montreal Story Tellers*. Struthers, J.R., ed. Montreal: Véhicule Press, 1985.

Various authors. *Oralités — Polyphonix 16: 'La pensée se fait dans la bouche'*. Sous la direction de Chamberland, Roger & Martel, Richard. Québec: Les Éditions Intervention, Octobre 1992.

Various authors. *Vehicle Days — An Unorthodox History of Montreal's Vehicle Poets*. Norris, Ken, ed. Montreal: Nuage Editions, 1993.

Various authors. *Slam: The Competitive Art of Performance Poetry*. Glazner, Gary Mex, ed. San Francisco: Manic D. Press, 2000.

Various authors. *ART ACTION 1958-1998*. Richard Martel, ed. Quebec City: Les Éditions Intervention, 2001.

Various authors. *Writing Aloud: The Sonics of Language* CD / book. LaBelle, Brandon & Migone, Christof, ed. Errant Bodies Press, forthcoming.

3. Radio Programming

Anderson, Fortner. *Dromostexte*, weekly spoken word program. CKUT FM
Montreal. 1987 - present.

Luc Desnoyer. *Zigzags Bohemes* weekly program, featuring excerpts from *Soirée
des contes*. CIBL FM Montreal.

Garneau, Michel & Germain, Christine. *Décrocheurs... des étoiles!* CBF 100.7 FM,
Montreal.

Miller, Mitsiko. Live in-studio broadcast of *La Vache enragée* on *Décrocheurs...
des étoiles!* CBF 100.7 FM, Montreal. August 29, 1997.

Opolco, Frank.*Word Wide Web* spoken word program, featured as part of
ArtsTalk, hosted by Mitsiko Miller. CBC AM Montreal. January - April 1998.

Opolco, Frank. *Word Wide Web* feature broadcast of five spoken word perfor-
mances, from Ian Ferrier's *Exploding Head Man* CD launch. CBC-1 Montreal.
March 4, 2000.

Rosen, Estelle. *Upstage*, weekly theatre program, CKUT FM Montreal.

Stanton, Victoria & Tinguely, Vincent, co-organizers. 'Street Speech', live remote
spoken-word broadcast, Doc Love / Mont Royal Street Fair. CKUT FM
Montreal. August 25, 1995 .

Stanton, Victoria & Tinguely, Vincent, co-organizers. *Reading In The Stacks*, live
remote poetry broadcast, McGill Bookstore Café. CKUT FM Montreal.
September 17, 18, 20, 1998.

Weintrager, Richard. *Literature Montreal* weekly program. CKUT FM Montreal.
1993 - 1996.

4. Audio Recordings

Les Abdigradationnistes. *Vierges, mais expérimentées* CD. Montreal: L'Empire
Kerozen, 1999.

Amethyst's Universe (Siddiqi, Atif). *Alive* cassette / CD. Montreal: Urania
Records, 1996.

Anderson, Fortner & Wiernik, Neil. *BROKENSPOKEN* cassette. Montreal: Wired
Words, 1994.

Anderson, Fortner. *Sometimes I Think* CD. Montreal: Wired on Words, 1999.

Dawson, Ted (includes 'Close-Up', a collaboration with Endre Farkas). *CAPAC
Musical Portraits — Portrait 8* 7" EP. Toronto: CAPAC, 1980.

Derome, Nathalie. *Les 4 ronds sont allumés*. Montreal: Les Ambiences
Magnetiques, 2000.

Disappointed A Few People (Stephens, Ian). *Fuck With Christ* 7" single.
Montreal: Les Disques Noir, 1984.

Disappointed A Few People (Stephens, Ian). *Dead In Love* LP. Montreal: Psyche
Industry Records, 1985.

Doucette, Derek & Tinguely, Vincent. 'Smokey & The Paper Tiger', *Broad Casting
For Reels* cassette. Halifax: Center For Art Tapes and CKDU FM, March 1996.

Ferrier, Ian. *Exploding Head Man — jazz poems* CD/book. Montreal: Planète
rebelle / Wired on Words, 2000.

Fluffy Pagan Echoes (Scott Duncan, Ran Elfassy, Justin McGrail, Victoria Stanton & Vincent Tinguely). *Pseudo Studio Recordings,* limited edition cassette. Montreal: independent, 1996.

Gélinas, Yannick B. *Mordre suivi de Parenthèse* CD-ROM / book. Montreal: Planète rebelle, 2000.

Germain, Christine. *Textes de la soif* CD / book. Montreal: Planète rebelle, 1999.

L'Infonie. *Vol. 3.* Montreal: Polydor, 1969; re-issued by Mucho Gusto, 2001.

The Invention of God. *Links Between Day and Desire* cassette. Montreal: Rhizome Records, 1995.

Jimmy Brain (O'Hara, Alexis & Stephens, Rob). Demo. Montreal: independent, 2000.

Kidd, Catherine & Beets, Jack. *everything I know about love I learned from taxidermy* cassette. Montreal: The Swamp / conundrum press, 1996.

Kroker, Arthur and Gibson, Steve. *Spasm: Virtual Reality, Android Music, Electric Flesh* CD / book. Montreal: New World Perspectives, 1993.

Kroker, Arthur and Marilouise. *Hacking The Future: Stories For The Flesh Eating Nineties* CD / book. Montreal: New World Perspectives, 1995.

Laberge, Marc. *Ma chasse-galerie* CD / book. Montreal: Planète rebelle, 2000.

Lavoie, Yves. *Octave Grognard, détective* CD / book. Montreal: Planète rebelle, 2000.

L'Ecuyer, John. *Use Once And Destroy* CD. Toronto: Rabid Dog Records, 1997.

Lemelin, André et Zéro de conduite. *Hold-up! Contes du Centre-Sud* CD / book. Montreal: Planète rebelle, 1999.

Letarte, Geneviève. *Vouse Seriez Un Ange* CD. Montreal: Les Ambiences Magnetiques, 1990.

Letarte, Geneviève. *Chansons d'un jour* CD. Montreal: Les Ambiences Magnetiques, 2000.

Manchilde. *Baby Mother / Science,* 12" single. Montreal: Bandit Records / Butta Babees, 2000.

Nawrocki, Norman. *"I Don't Understand Women!"* cassette. Montreal: Les Pages Noire, 1994.

Nawrocki, Norman. Included on *Less Rock, More Talk* CD anthology. San Francisco: AK Press Audio, 1997.

nth digri, the (Bansfield, Anthony). *Return Of The Rappoet* cassette. Toronto: Revword Co., 1997.

Officious Little Students (Victoria Stanton & Vincent Tinguely). *Officious Little Students:Wooga Wooga!* cassette. Montreal: independent, September 1996.

Pintard, Michael. *Multiple Comings* cassette. Toronto: Verse to Vinyl, 1991.

Ramasutra (includes collaborations with Mitsiko Miller). *The East Infection.* Montreal: TOX Records, 1999.

Red Shift (Stephens, Ian). Included on *Primitive Air, Montreal '84* LP anthology. Montreal: Psyche Industry Records, 1984.

Red Shift (Stephens, Ian). Included on *PanicPanic* LP anthology. Montreal: Psyche Industry Records, 1985.

Red Shift SubUnit (Stephens, Ian). Included on *Cadavres Exquis* LP anthology. Chimik Comm., 1985.

Red Shift SubUnit (Stephens, Ian). Included on *Voices End Abruptly* LP
   anthology. Chimik Comm., 1985.

Rhythm Activism. *Live*. Montreal: Dial-A-Poem Cassettes / Les Pages Noire,
   1987.

Rhythm Activism. *Resist Much — Obey Little* cassette. Montreal: Les Pages
   Noire, 1987.

Rhythm Activism. *Louis Riel in China* cassette. Montreal: Les Pages Noire, 1988.

Rhythm Activism. *Perogys, Pasta & Liberty*, cassette. Montreal: Les Pages Noire,
   1990.

Rhythm Activism. *"Un logement pour une chanson"* cassette. Montreal: Les
   Pages Noire, 1990.

Rhythm Activism. *OKA* cassette. Montreal: Les Pages Noire, 1990.

Rhythm Activism. *Fight The Hike* cassette. Montreal: Les Pages Noire, 1990.

Rhythm Activism. *Tumbleweed* cassette. Montreal: Les Pages Noire, 1993.

Rhythm Activism. *Blood & Mud* CD. Montreal: Les Pages Noire, 1994.

Rhythm Activism. *More Kick! — Live in Europe* CD. Montreal: Les Pages Noire,
   1995.

Rhythm Activism. *Jesus Was Gay* CD. Winnipeg: G-7 Welcoming Committee
   Records, 1998.

Robitaille, Renée. *Conte coquins pour oreilles folichonnes* CD / book. Montreal:
   Planète rebelle, 2000.

Snitches, The (includes collaborations with Andrea Clark). *A Day at the A.*
   Montreal: independent, 1995.

Stephens, Ian. *Wining, Dining, Drilling* CD. Montreal: EnGuard Records, 1993 .

Stephens, Ian. *Diary of a Trademark* cassette. Montreal: Wired on Words, 1995.

Swifty Lazarus (Swift, Todd & Walsh, Tom). *The Budapest Tapes* demo CD.
   Budapest: independent, June 1999.

Turenne, Joujou. *Ti pinge* CD / book. Montreal: Planète rebelle, 2000.

Vézina, Christian. *Doux comme dans fauve* CD / book. Montreal: Planète rebelle,
   2000.

von Baeyer, Matthew & Gossage, David. *Melopoiesis* CD. Montreal: independent,
   1998.

Wall, Jeremiah. *Kerouac Hill* cassette. Montreal: Earthshake Records, 1993.

Wall, Jeremiah. 'Down in the Valley', on split 7" with Eugene Vincent. Montreal:
   Earthshake Records, no date.

Wining, Dining, Drilling (Stephens, Ian). Included on *Two Solitudes* CD
   anthology. Montreal: EnGuard Records, 1992.

Wining, Dining, Drilling (Stephens, Ian). Included on CD anthology. Toronto:
   Raw Energy / A&M, 1993.

Young, Debbie. *When The Love Is Not Enough* CD. Montreal: Spirit of 3, 2000.

Ze Zinjanthropes Brachycéphales Ft'gh! (Stéphane Despaties). *Musiques Qui
   Empechent L'Erection!* Montreal: Brachycéphales Communications, 1994.

Ze Zinjanthropes Brachycéphales Ft'gh! (Stéphane Despaties). *Je Ne Peux Plus
   M'Retiendre!* Montreal: FT'GH, 1995.

Various artists. *Six Montreal Poets*. Gesser, Sam, producer. Folkways Records,
   1957.

Various artists. *Canadian Poets 1*, 2xLP. Canadian Broadcasting Corporation, 1966.

Various artists. *poêmes et chants de la résistance 2*, 2xLP. Dufresne, Yvan, producer. Montreal: Trans-World, 1971.

Various artists. *Sounds Like — sound poetry by eight Montreal poets* LP. Farkas, Endre & Norris, Ken, producers. Montreal: Véhicule Press, 1980.

Various artists. *Festival D'In(ter)ventions 2 — In Memoriam Georges Maciunas* 2xLP. Martel, Richard & Rochette, Daniel, producers. Quebec City: Les Éditions Intervention, 1985.

Various artists. *Ultimatum — The Montreal Urban Poetry Festival, 1 - 5 May 1985* LP. Lord, Alan & Jo, producers. Montreal: Psyche Industry Records, 1985.

Various artists. *Wired on Words* series — poems recorded for broadcast. Anderson, Fortner & Ferrier, Ian, producers. Montreal: CKUT FM, 1993 - 1996.

Various artists. *Wired on Words 1* cassette. Anderson, Fortner & Ferrier, Ian, producers. Montreal: Wired on Words / ga press, 1994.

Various artists. *Word Up* CD. Battson, Jill & Kulawick, Geoff, producers. Toronto: Virgin Music Canada, 1995.

Various artists. *Sex FM — a day of anticensorship programming*, poems recorded for broadcast. Ferrier, Ian, producer. Montreal: CKUT FM, November 16, 1995.

Various artists. *Bunch Of Fuckin' Feminists vol. 1* cassette. Stanton, Megan & Whittall, Zoë Emily, producers. Montreal: independent, 1995.

Various artists. *Girlfriend Action Coalition — ain't she a beautiful sight?* cassette. Grant, Maureen & Semper, Sam, producers. Montreal: independent, 1997.

Various artists. *Poetry in Motion* series — poems recorded for broadcast. Hazel, Cheryl, producer. Montreal: CKUT FM, 1998.

Various artists. *Millennium Cabaret* CD. Anderson, Fortner & Ferrier, Ian, producers. Montreal: Wired on Words, 1998.

Various artists. *La Vache enragée anthologie 2* CD / book. Miller, Mitsiko, producer. Montreal: Planète rebelle, 1998.

Various artists. *Word Life: Tales of the Underground Griots* CD. Bansfield, Anthony, producer. Toronto: Revword, 1998.

Various artists. *All Points In* CD. Ottawa: Sweet Chin Music, 1999.

Various artists. *Hybride — 11 Duos Solidaires, inspirés des droites du monde* CD. Chenard, Sylvie, producer. Montreal: Projet de la Baleine, 1999.

Various Artists. *Unheard of* CD. Pilgrim, Derek, producer. Toronto: Tupperware Sandpiper Spoken Words, April 2000.

Various authors. *La grande nuite du conte* CD / book. Montreal: Planète rebelle, 2000.

Various authors. *Soul Shack* promo cassette. Stewart, Karen, producer. Montreal: independent, May 2001.

Various authors. *Ribsauce* CD. Boutros, Alex & Sundström, Kaarla, producers. Montreal: Wired on Words, 2001.

5. Zines

Agent. Published by Vox Hunt Press, 1996 - 1997.

Brazen Orality (aka *Blazin' Auralities, Brazen Auralities, Brazen Oralities...*), a review of spoken word recordings. Also available as an e-zine at: {http://www.infobahnos.com/~brazen/}. Produced by Fortner Anderson, 1993 - present.

Da Vinci. Published by Allan Bealy. 1973 - unknown.

Draecena. Published and edited by Jeremiah Wall.

Fish Piss. Produced by Louis Rastelli, 1996 - present.

Gap-Toothed Bitch. Produced by Buffy Bonanza, 1996.

Gaz Moutarde. Founder: Jean-Sebastien Huot, 1989.

The Independent Voice For The Sick and Wrong. Produced by Zoë Whittall, 1995 - 1996.

index. Volume One published by Stephanie Blanshay, March 1994 - March 1995. Volume Two published by Stephanie Blanshay (Apr - Jun 95) and the editorial collective, April 1995 - July / Aug 1996.

It's A Bunny! e-zine, 1996.

Kerozen. Produced by Pat K., Gilberte Blate et al, 1997 to present.

Los. Founded by David Skyrie, Dr. Patrick Holland & Ian Ferrier, 1975.

Perfect Waste Of Time: the monthly broadsheet. Produced by Victoria Stanton and Vincent Tinguely, December 1995 to November 1998. 36 issues.

Perfect Waste Of Time volume 2. Produced by Victoria Stanton and Vincent Tinguely, October 1999 - present.

Poop Deck. Produced by Thoth Harris et al, July 1998 - present.

Raw Verse. Published by Jésus Cardozo, Les Editions Blue Midnight. Circa 1984.

Red Alert. Produced by Blood Sisters, 1997 - present.

Rhythm Activism — Les Pages Noire. Produced by Rhythm Activism to publicize their latest works.

Speakeasy. Webzine and cyber-cabaret produced by Patti Sonntag and Taien Ng Chan, February 2000 - present. Attached to *Wired on Words* website.

Steak Haché. Produced by Richard Gingras, A.-A. Painchaud, Robert Tanguay and others, 1998 to present.

Streeteaters. Edited by Paula Belina with co-editors Dave Levine and Larissa Andrusyshyn, 2000 - present.

Wired on Words. Website produced by Ian Ferrier and Fortner Anderson, 1998 to present. www.wiredonwords.com

Xero. Literary zine co-edited by Ian Stephens, collectively published in 1984.

Zéro de Conduite, Fondateurs: Yves Lavoie et Daniel-Paul Bourdages; le comité de rédaction: Yves Lavoie et Sonia Ritter. 1994-1998.

6. Video & Film

Ladies and Gentlemen... Mr. Leonard Cohen. Dir: Donald Brittain & Don Owen. Montreal: NFB, 1965.

Nuit de la Poésie. Dir: Jean-Claude Labrecque & Jean-Pierre Masse. Montreal, 1970.

Poetry on Tape (compilation). Dir: Tom Konyves. Montreal, 1977.

See / Saw (document). Dir: Tom Konyves. Montreal, 1977.

Sympathies of War. Dir: Tom Konyves. Montreal, 1978.

Mummypoem: Sympathies of War, a Postscript. Dir: Tom Konyves. Montreal, 1978.

Ubu's Blues, The First Voyage of the Vehicle R. Dir: Tom Konyves. Montreal, 1979.

Yellow Light Blues. Dir: Tom Konyves. Montreal, 1980.

Nuit de la Poésie 1980. Dir: Jean-Claude Labrecque & Jean-Pierre Masse. Montreal, 1980.

Poetry in Motion. Dir: Ron Mann. Canada, 1982.

Black Wine by Disappointed a Few People. Dir: Claude Grégoire. Montreal, 1986.

Nuit de la poésie 1990. Dir: Pierre Bastien. Montreal, 1990.

Nuit de la Poésie 1991. Dir: Jean-Claude Labrecque & Jean-Pierre Masse. Montreal, 1991.

She's Not Crazy by Wining Dining Drilling. Dir: Melanie Johnson & Carol Guidry. Montreal, 1993.

Rows of Photos (Montreal's Most Wanted) by nth digri. Producer: Jill Battson, MuchMusic *Word Up* Video Poetry Series. Toronto, 1994.

Diary of a Trademark by Ian Stephens. Producer: Jill Battson, MuchMusic *Word Up* Video Poetry Series. Toronto, 1994.

Les mots-dits. Dir: Marie Brodeur. Quebec: ONF et Publivision, 1998.

Erotic, Exotic. Dir: Atif Siddiqi. Montreal, 1998.

Rainin' Threes / Trocar Lados. Dir: Scott Duncan. Toronto, 2000.

How to Fake an Orgasm (Whether You Need To or Not). Dir. Dayna McLeod. Montreal, 1998.

Saint Jude (screenplay by Heather O'Neill). Dir: John L'Ecuyer. Toronto, 2000.

Letters From The Ice Age by Ian Ferrier. Dir: Marc Gagnon. Montreal, 2000.

SPLIT: the second half by Victoria Stanton. Dir: Victoria Stanton & Laurent Soussana. Montreal, 2000.

I Am The One by Ian Ferrier. Dir: Blair Ewing. Baltimore MD., 2001.

Courtship by Ian Ferrier. Dir: Blair Ewing. Baltimore MD., 2001.

INTERVIEWS

All interviews conducted in English (except where indicated) by Vincent Tinguely and Victoria Stanton, except ‡ conducted by Scott Duncan, * conducted by Corey Frost, and ° conducted by Vincent Tinguely.

XI

Akin Alaga
May 7, 1999

Fortner Anderson
July 30, 1997
April 4, 2000

Anthony Bansfield
September 4, 1999

Alex Boutros
July 18, 1997
November 18, 1999

Peter Brawley
November 10, 1999

Andy Brown
July 17, 1997
April 19, 2000

Jake Brown
July 19, 1997
April 12, 2000

Jasmine Châtelain
July 24, 1997

Buffy Childerhose
October 5, 1999

Marta Cooper
May 29, 1999

Iz Cox
June 6, 1999

Anna-Louise Crago
May 17, 1999

Julie Crysler
October 5, 1999

Jean-Paul Daoust (F)
May 27, 1999

Simon Dardick
June 30, 1999

Nathalie Derome (E & F)
June 25, 1999

Pascal Desjardins (F)
November 3, 1999

Louise Dubreuil (E & F)
May 13, 1999

Scott Duncan
July 24, 1997
January 5, 2000 (e-mail)

Ran Elfassy
March 29, 1999
December 28, 1999 (e-mail)

Endre Farkas
June 4, 1999

Ian Ferrier
July 16, 1997
February 15, 2000 (on CKUT FM)
April 3, 2000

Pascal Fioramore
November 3, 1999

Sylvain Fortier (F)
May 12, 1999

Golda Fried
September 27, 1999

Corey Frost
May 31, 1999

Edward Fuller
May 14, 1999

Michel Garneau (F)
October 15, 1999

John Giorno
June 10, 1999

Jonathan Goldstein
May 7, 1999

David Gossage
April 20, 2000

Lee Gotham
August 3, 1997

Thoth Harris
May 10, 1999

Hugh Hazelton
May 12, 1999

Kaie Kellough
March 24, 1999

Catherine Kidd
July 19, 1997
March 27, 2000

D.Kimm (F)
August 25, 1999

Tom Konyves
September 1, 1999 (e-mail)

Nancy Labonté (F)
June 24, 1999

Patricia Lamontagne (F)
June 2, 1999

André Lemelin (F)
September 17, 1999

Geneviève Letarte (F)
June 4, 1999

Billy Mavreas
May 28, 1999

Justin McGrail
February 12, 1999

Dayna McLeod
August 22, 1999

Mitsiko Miller (E & F)
July 17, 1997
March 28, 2000

Hélène Monette (F)
June 28, 1999

nah ee lah
April 23, 1999

Norman Nawrocki
May 27, 1999

David Neudorfer
March 28, 1999

Joseph Neudorfer
March 28, 1999

Ken Norris
July 29, 1999 (e-mail)

Alexis O'Hara
April 5, 1999

Heather O'Neill
July 19, 1997
April 21, 2000

Benoît Paiement
June 8, 1995 (CKUT FM) ‡
July 15, 1997 (E & F)
April 6, 2000 (F)

Torrey Pass
August 12, 1999

Louis Rastelli
July 17, 1997

Félixe Ross (F)
April 6, 2000

Trish Salah
October 6, 1999

Jason Selman
April 26, 1999

Tetsuro Shigematsu
April 19, 1999

Atif Siddiqi
August 17, 1999

Dee Smith
January 3 & 7, 2000 (e-mail)

Inobe Stanislaus
February 10, 2001 °

Victoria Stanton
August 20, 1999 *

Karen Stewart
April 16, 1999

Anne Stone
May 28, 1999

Lynn Suderman
December 29, 1999 (e-mail)

Kaarla Sundström
November 18, 1999

Todd Swift
July 30, 1997
August 18, 1999 (e-mail)

Vince Tinguely
August 20, 1999 *

Mahalia Verna
February 10, 2001 °

Leah Vineberg
August 4, 1999

Jeremiah Wall
July 14, 1997

Zoë Whittall
July 26, 1997
October 6, 1999

Debbie Young
May 5, 1999